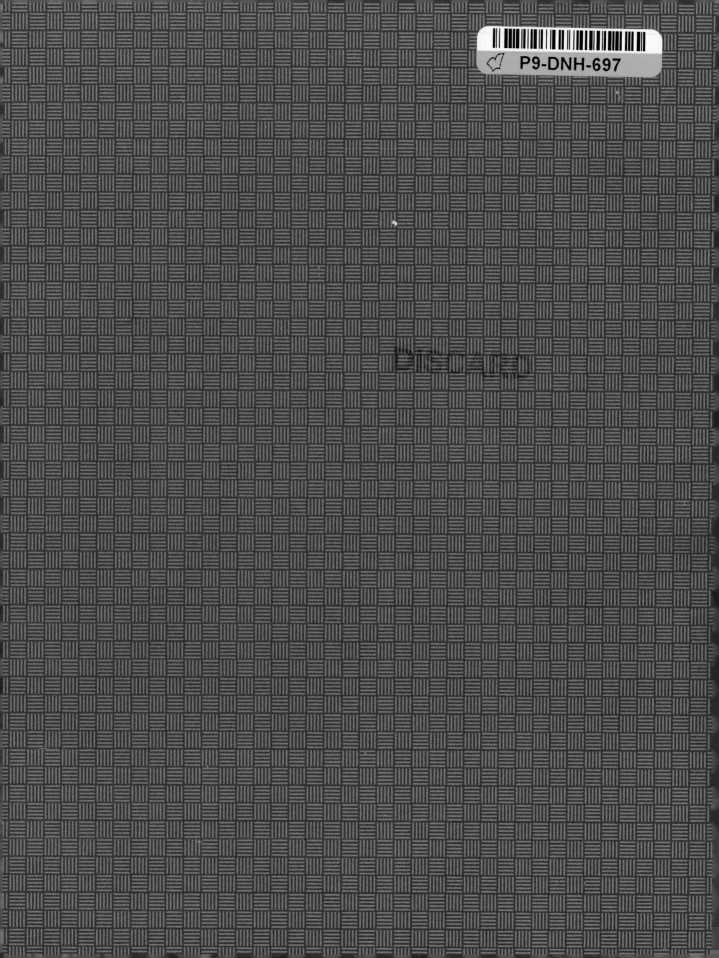
P9-DNH-697

The GERSHWINS

· AND ME ·

MELCHER
MEDIA

ALSO BY MICHAEL FEINSTEIN

Nice Work If You Can Get It: My Life in Rhythm and Rhyme

The
GERSHWINS
• AND ME •

A Personal History in Twelve Songs

MICHAEL FEINSTEIN

WITH Ian Jackman

Cabarrus County Public Library
www.cabarruscounty.us/library

SIMON & SCHUSTER

New York • London • Toronto • Sydney • New Delhi

Produced by Melcher Media

Simon & Schuster
1230 Avenue of the Americas
New York, NY 10020

124 West 13th Street
New York, NY 10011
www.melcher.com

Copyright © 2012 by Terwilliker

All rights reserved, including the right to reproduce this book or portions thereof in any form whatsoever.
For information, address Simon & Schuster Subsidiary Rights Department,
1230 Avenue of the Americas, New York, NY 10020.

First Simon & Schuster hardcover edition October 2012

SIMON & SCHUSTER and colophon are registered trademarks of Simon & Schuster, Inc.

Pages 350–351 constitute an extension of the copyright page.

For information about special discounts for bulk purchases,
please contact Simon & Schuster Special Sales at
1-866-506-1949 or business@simonandschuster.com.

The Simon & Schuster Speakers Bureau can bring authors
to your live event. For more information or to book an event,
contact the Simon & Schuster Speakers Bureau at
1-866-248-3049 or visit our website at www.simonspeakers.com.

Designed by Paul Kepple and Ralph Geroni @ Headcase Design

Printed in China

1   3   5   7   9   10   8   6   4   2

Library of Congress Cataloging-in-Publication Data
Feinstein, Michael.
The Gershwins and me : a personal history in twelve songs / by Michael Feinstein with Ian Jackman.
p. cm.
1. Gershwin, George, 1898–1937. 2. Gershwin, Ira, 1896–1983. 3. Feinstein, Michael. 4. Popular music—Writing and publishing—United States.
I. Jackman, Ian. II. Title.
ML385.F337 2012
782.42164092'2—dc23   2012006833

ISBN 978-1-4516-4530-9
ISBN 978-1-4516-4533-0 (ebook)
ISBN 978-1-4516-4532-3 (special)
ISBN 978-1-4516-9653-0 (library)

· FOR IRA. ·

CONTENTS

INTRODUCTION

AT THE AGE OF TWENTY, I met one of the legends of American popular music, Ira Gershwin. It was the most exciting moment of my life and I recall it in vivid detail. I worshipped what he had created with his brother George and had never dreamed I'd meet him. As he spoke about his lifetime of work I knew everything he was referring to, even though it had all taken place decades before I was born. When he eventually realized that I knew all his stories at least as well as he did, he suddenly stopped and stared at me, taking in my twenty-year-old countenance as if for the first time. In a perplexed voice he said, "How many more of you are there?"

So there it was, the moment I had been unconsciously waiting for my whole life, and a course-altering moment it was. It was the culmination of years of obsession, which I'd spent as a kid finding everything I could on the Gershwins, and now here I was at the feet of the master. These many years later, I'm still at his feet, still feeling the pull of the Gershwin mystique and still telling stories and putting their work out there as best I can. Lord knows I need them more than they need me. And yet, after devoting myself to the learning and love of their work over all these years, I feel we've developed an unexpected symbiosis, and now it is time to share the joy and excitement of my experience.

This book is a celebration. It's my attempt to capture and preserve the essence of an era of song-writing and creativity that is nearly impossible to fathom today; it was a time when the names George and Ira Gershwin were synonymous with everything that was fresh, exciting, and vital about the creative arts. It was a time when songs and songwriting were an essential part of the fabric of our culture and helped shape attitudes, morals, and beliefs through their inherent power and ability to reach the hearts of the nation, a time when the craft of creation was supreme, existing on a very high level and flowing as freely as air so it was usually taken for granted.

As the world continues to move and change at lightning speed, many things have gotten lost along the way. Arts and culture are ever evolving and reflect our dissonant times, yet the link to the classic era still exists (however oblique it may seem) and can be traced from any contemporary work back to George's first hit, "Swanee." Nothing could exist today without whatever came before it, and with the Web's infinite resources, new generations are discovering this classic music and embracing it.

The Gershwin legacy remains a mighty force that can catch a new initiate off guard through the power it still yields. Its sound was once the voice of the Jazz Age and the Depression, but it has stayed contemporary through the intervening decades, proving that musically too, history can repeat itself. Music always mirrors the time in which it is created and its survival depends on whether it will resonate across the generations.

Gershwin songs still resonate. They are part of the fabric of our society. Many years ago, the legendary writers Carl Reiner and Mel Brooks were working on a television program together when Carl announced he had to visit a doctor for an ailment. When Reiner returned, Mel asked about the diagnosis. "The doctor said I've got arrhythmia," said Carl. "Who could ask for anything more?" was Mel's instant rejoinder. See what I mean about being a part of the fabric of society? Even if such a reference feels more remote now, I am that odd duck whose fascination with musical history makes me feel a close kinship with past generations. There are many others like me—you know who you are.

The idea of preservation has always been very important to me, and I was involved with it long before I understood what it meant. At age five I was already curious about the old records and sheet music my parents and relatives owned, and I wanted to know more about those odd pieces of the past. My love for both older kinds of music and the vanished worlds that produced them has taken forms I had never imagined.

Through the years I have been blessed to meet and know many of the personalities involved with this music and I have always tried to remember and hold on to what I have learned from them. Their stories are rich and moving. Meeting so many and hearing their stories, watching their body language, and feeling a psychic sympathy with the times that shaped them have impelled me to preserve their legacy.

As I have grown older and in some ways wiser, the desire and need to share what I know about the Gershwin era have only increased. Now with this book, and the CD of songs that accompanies it, I can share some of what I have learned and gleaned. I have used each of the twelve songs to illuminate some aspect of the rich musical world I inhabit. We travel from the smoky, jazz-filled clubs and vibrant concert halls of the twenties through opera houses and piano bars to the present, chronicling the lives of the Gershwins and their extraordinary collective genius as songwriters and how that has intersected with my own experience, beginning with my life-changing friendship with Ira Gershwin. Though I'd rather engage with a song by performing and living it than analyzing it, I've tried to say what it is about these songs that fires my imagination, hoping you will share my enthusiasm.

Not too many years ago, there was a time when music played a much more important role in our society, and it was as essential to our lives and as comforting as eating Wheaties in the morning and making family outings to the park on Sunday. As a kid growing up in the sixties and seventies, I caught the tail end of that rose-colored time and am startled at the way the arts have been diminished, to the detriment of our society. The level of communal significance they once played is largely unfathomable to our contemporary world and I literally cry sometimes at what we have lost. Where are the songs that we can all sing together—not just some of us, but all of us?

But that old music has turned out to be longer-lasting and more important to our world than we realized.

All around there are young people whom I meet that love older music not of their time and have been captivated by its unique qualities; those who like me are different from the rest of their generation and respond to the excitement and passion found in the sound of Gershwin. They are discovering it fresh and cherishing it. The magic still works.

Over the last few years I created an organization for the purpose of preserving classic standards, the Michael Feinstein Great American Songbook Initiative. We are headquartered in a beautiful space in Carmel, Indiana, contiguous to Indianapolis, but with our significant Web presence we can be accessed by anyone, anywhere. Our greatest goal is to keep the music alive, through master classes, concerts, visits to schools, competitions, a research center filled with music, recordings, memorabilia, and a soon-to-be-built museum that will house the multitude of artifacts that I have collected and have been donated by so many others. Finally, there will be a physical place to celebrate this music, just as there are halls of fame and museums for rock and roll in Cleveland and country music in Nashville. It's a dream come true and it reflects the promise and potential we can still experience from the heritage of the Gershwins and their compatriots. Lives can still be transformed by these songs.

When I am no longer here I don't care if I am remembered; what the hell difference does it make anyway? Conversely, I deeply care about doing what I can to help keep the Gershwin name alive. Why? Because my life would be poorer without their legacy and it gives me immense pleasure to look at the face of someone discovering a Gershwin song for the first time. It's like witnessing a birth.

As long as people care about music, they'll care about Gershwin.

WOULDN'T THAT BE 'S WONDERFUL?

Michael Feinstein

"STRIKE UP THE BAND"

from *Strike Up the Band*, 1927

We fought in 1917,
Rum-ta-ta tum-tum-tum!
And drove the tyrant from the scene,
Rum-ta-ta tum-tum-tum!

We're in a bigger, better war
For your patriotic pastime.
We don't know what we're
fighting for—
But we didn't know the last time!

So load the cannon! Draw the blade!
Rum-ta-ta tum-tum-tum!
Come on, and join the Big Parade!
Rum-ta-ta tum-tum,
Rum-ta-ta tum-tum,
Rum-ta-ta tum-tum-tum!

REFRAIN 1

Let the drums roll out!
(Boom-boom-boom!)
Let the trumpet call!
(Ta-ta-ra-ta-ta-ta-ta!)
While the people shout—
(Hooray!)
Strike up the band!

Hear the cymbals ring!
(Tszing-tszing-tszing!)
Calling one and all
(Ta-ta-ra-ta-ta-ta-ta!)

To the martial swing,
(Left, right!)
Strike up the band!

There is work to be done,
to be done—
There's a war to be won, to be won—
Come, you son of a gun—
Take your stand!

Fall in line, yea bo—
Come along, let's go!
Hey, leader, strike up the band!

REFRAIN 2

(REPEAT REFRAIN 1, LINES 1–14)

Yankee doo doodle-oo doodle-oo,
We'll come through, doodle-oo doodle-oo,
For the red, white, and blue doodle-oo,
Lend a hand.

With our flag unfurled,
We can lick the world!
Hey, leader, strike up the band!

· CHAPTER 1 ·

GEORGE AND IRA—

The Music and the Words

AMONG THE MANY TREASURES Ira Gershwin preserved in his house on Roxbury Drive in Beverly Hills was a cache of his brother George's unpublished music. When I worked for Ira as a young man, I knew it was an extraordinary privilege and honor to be able to see and hear melodies by my favorite composer that had been unavailable for decades. Some of the music had lyric ideas provided by Ira while others had no lyrics. Some of the tunes had been assigned numbers: "unpublished melody number 27," and so on. Ira kept a floral binder that contained other scraps of George's music—some were notes jotted on a half-page of lined paper; others were just fragments.

Over the forty years since George's death, Ira had allowed a select few to examine these unheard gems. He considered these tunes as precious as the rarest of vintage wines, or blue-chip stocks that increase in value with each succeeding year. The burden of protecting that legacy was at times overwhelming for him, but he knew that it must be done, and no one else would or could do it.

I particularly loved prospecting through that floral binder, which contained the most fragmentary of fragments. It was here that I would find a melody, a small nugget, sometimes just a single line of music, scratched out on a piece of scrap paper. One day, when Kay Swift was visiting, I played her a fragmentary tune from that binder that had

George and Ira Gershwin.

George in 1919, during his Tin Pan Alley days.

touched my curiosity. Kay had been a longtime lover of George's and was a talented composer herself—she had a hit on Broadway with the musical *Fine and Dandy* in 1930, the first woman to achieve this feat. The whole story of Kay's relationship with George has finally, and beautifully, been written by her granddaughter Katharine Weber (*The Memory of All That*). It's a doozy of a story too.

Kay was married to a famous banking scion, James Warburg, and had three children with him, but that did not stop her from falling hard for George and divorcing her husband in the hope that George would marry her. He didn't. Upon

seeing them at a party one night, the legendary wit Oscar Levant is purported to have said, "There goes George Gershwin with the future Miss Kay Swift." (There are other attributions of this story, to Kitty Carlisle and Paula Lawrence, but it works well for our purposes here, don't you think?) Still, she remained an intimate friend until the day George died. I simply adored her for her everpositive attitude and simple ability to survive in a time that had outgrown her formidable talents.

Kay had an encyclopedic knowledge of the Gershwins' music and an almost perfect recall of it. Ira had no recollection of this particular tune but she recognized it at once: "Oh, yes," she said. "That was an early version of 'Strike Up the Band.'" "Strike Up the Band" appeared in the musical of the same name in 1927, but it seems there were multiple early attempts at the title song and this was one of them. It was only a melody line, just enough to jog George's memory when he went back to it. George must have played it for Kay, or perhaps she was around when he was working on this earlier version, and typical of her prodigious memory, she could recall it even when Ira couldn't. Since there were no harmonies to accompany the melody in Ira's floral binder, I wish that I had asked Kay to harmonize it, for if George had come up with some harmonies to go with the tune, Kay would have remembered them. Alas, she took any such knowledge with her when she died in 1993 at the age of ninety-five. In retrospect there are always questions we wish that we had asked, or words that should have been expressed.

THE FACT THAT JUST this fragment of the tune was recorded in that notebook doesn't mean George hadn't written more of the song. George wouldn't write out a fair copy (the song as written out to be played on the piano) until he had completed a song. He might not even have bothered to do a fuller copy until Ira had written a lyric, which would usually come later in the process. Once the two parts of the song had come together—the music and the words—George would write up the song and give it to a copyist. The song would then go to the orchestrator, who would create a full instrumental version, replete with extra dance choruses if it was being prepared for a theatrical production. Then it would again be given to the copyist, who

would now write out the individual parts for each instrument in the orchestra, and so a Gershwin song was sent on its journey into the world.

Since most people in those days didn't get to hear songs performed in their original theatrical incarnations but first learned them through sheet music, the theater orchestration of the song was of vital importance, and George would work closely with the orchestrator or arranger (the two terms are interchangeable) to ensure that the translation from piano to ensemble was appropriate and what he wanted it to be. The arranger can make or break a song and has the power to make it sound an infinite variety of ways. That the arrangers sometimes had contempt for the composers they served never seemed to diminish the quality of their results.

George and Kay Swift in the late 1920s.

An orchestration can clothe a song with rhythms and styles from rumba to rap, waltz to reggae, march to dirge, and everything in between. It can make a song sound happy, sad, urgent, lugubrious, weighty, ironic, pompous, insolent, autumnal, or celebratory. All this comes from the arsenal of instruments in an orchestra and the way they are combined. Arranging and orchestrating are the most important and underappreciated skills in music. Without the great arrangers, the work of Gershwin and other composers would never have been fully realized. Gershwin himself began occasionally orchestrating his own works as early as 1922, and by 1935 he was confident enough to completely orchestrate his opera, *Porgy and Bess.* The process took him nine months.

WHEN ONE LOOKS AT HIS ORCHESTRATION FOR *PORGY AND BESS* THE NOTATIONS ARE VERY SURE-HANDED.

There was a famous music editor named Albert Sirmay, a kind and gentle man who followed George when he switched music publishers from Harms to Chappell. Sirmay edited and prepared piano copies of songs for George and other greats like Richard Rodgers and Jerome Kern, along with all of the workmanlike songs he had to whip into shape when not working with a more illustrious talent. During production of a show he would sometimes help notate a piano score, but later his job was to simplify the songs to make them manageable for the average pianist. It wasn't his pleasure to do so, as he knew better, but it was his job.

Sometimes George's original score, when we have it to compare, is markedly different from the published version. Songwriter Milton Ager, who was a close friend of George's, looked at a printed copy of "The Man I Love" and wrote in the margin of the sheet music, "Not the way George played it." I discovered that incidental notation while paging through his former copy of a Gershwin songbook that I had inherited. It's amazing what bits of ephemera can later become so significant. On another piece of music, once in the possession of skillful pianist and composer Hal Borne, Gershwin's Beverly Hills phone number is noted in pencil, perhaps the only record of such.

George was also very facile at notating (writing) music himself. When one looks at his orchestration for *Porgy and Bess,* or a copy of any of his song manuscripts, the notations are very sure-handed, written very boldly and cleanly with very few corrections. He sometimes wrote in ink, and here and there are only a few notes crossed out and replaced. When I see a passage like that, I imagine George working quickly, grasping at some fleeting idea and making sure he gets it down on the page as the inspiration courses through him.

George was absolutely clear in what he wanted to notate and how he wanted to notate it. This is fascinating, because there are so many choices one can make. With a piano copy, which in the traditional sense is the Bible for a song, the writer has to decide what the accompaniment is, where the chords fall, how the music flows. There are many ways a song can be played on a piano, because playing the chord on the melody note, or a half-beat or even a beat later, changes the way something is notated. The person who is going to be playing the song also has to be taken into consideration. Can they read the music easily? Can they understand what you intended? For example, it might be too difficult to include a syncopated idea—to delay the playing of a chord—because then when the song is notated, it's much more difficult to read. And if somebody knows that the feel of it is to play a little bit off the beat, you write it on the beat with the understanding that in interpretation it can be varied a little bit.

Not everyone found the process of notating as easy as George did. It was a laborious task for Cole Porter, for example, and it shows in his manuscripts. You might see his hand early on and then Albert Sirmay takes over as if to say,

"Move over, let me finish it." A single sheet of paper can reveal so much.

Irving Berlin couldn't write music at all and only tried once, when asked by a collector to notate "God Bless America." Burton Lane, one of the great musical theater composers, had to learn how to make piano copies even though he was a formidable pianist and could play his songs brilliantly. He did learn and was very proud of his acquired skill. Harry Warren could not make piano copies—he played by ear and it took him many years to learn to read music, let alone make a piano copy. Again, the ability to create a song doesn't mean you can easily write it down or even play it on the piano. Inspiration does not always include technical ability. Conversely, when Tchaikovsky nervously showed the great German composer Brahms one of his newly completed works, Brahms perused it carefully and finally replied, "What beautiful manuscript paper you have," thus devastating Tchaikovsky, which was evidently the intended effect.

Vincent Youmans, one of the great theater songwriters, had a very limited output. He died young, at the age of forty-seven, and published fewer than one hundred songs. But almost all of them are spectacular. Fortunately, there are arduous recordings of him at work. Youmans worked laboriously, playing melodies over and over for hours, making one little variation here and another there until he had what he considered the perfect combination of the notes. His process—the incessant honing and editing—was what turned a melody in his head into a beautiful song. There were no shortcuts for Youmans. Listening to a song like "Tea for Two," it's hard to believe it took so much labor to achieve such a joyously carefree melody.

A portrait of George's hands.

George was the exception to all of these rules. He could do it all with an ease that was maddening to his contemporaries, and that was because his creation of music was more organic than many and he had the rare gift of musical assurance and knowing when something was right. The end result is the same to the listener but the process varies wildly from creator to creator. No wonder George was surrounded by such jealousy. From a distance he appeared wildly vain, yet from a more intimate perspective, he was adored by his songwriter friends for his frankness of expression, musically and otherwise.

GEORGE WROTE MUSIC so easily that not only did he work much faster than Ira wrote the words, but he usually nailed melodies on the first try and rarely had to rewrite them. More often than not, the way the song first came to him was the way it stayed. But not with "Strike Up the Band." The version we know now is at least the fifth. When it came to melody, George Gershwin had extremely high standards. Often he would play a tune to Ira, and Ira, who was no pushover, might say, "That's great, I'll write it up." But George wasn't satisfied till he, too, thought it was right and finally he could say, "This is the one." While he didn't often do major rewrites, sometimes finding the right tune was more elusive than on other occasions.

Ira rarely had to wait for George to finish a melody and was more often under the gun to turn in the lyric, thanks to his habit of being a proud procrastinator. In his later years he seemed to cultivate a sedentary nature as part of his persona. He even expected his cat, Tinkerbelle, to come and fawn over him, not wanting to exert the energy to pick her up. Ira really should have had a dog, but his wife was a cat fancier.

I own one of Gershwin's tune notebooks. Today these books are historical gold mines. Ira had told me that most of these extraordinary volumes had been accounted for, but one in particular was lost decades earlier. Who knew how important they would become? Years later one mysteriously turned up at auction, and I bought it. Paging through the book offers a rare glimpse into the creative process of the composer and his working methods. Music was constantly running through George's head, and he spent most of his time at the piano trying to turn that music into hit songs. He could compose away from the piano but frequently, while improvising at a party or just relaxing at his favorite pastime, he would hit upon another tune worth remembering. He carried a tiny notebook so that he could capture ideas while out and about. On some pages of his notebooks he'd write on the top, "G.T."—Good Tune. The tune would live in his notebook for any period of time until he'd find a use for it. If he came up with an idea when he wasn't carrying a notebook, any handy scrap of paper would do. Later on, he had special score paper prepared with his name printed on it.

The book I own was used by George between 1928 and 1930. Its ninety-nine pages contain among many others the germ of an idea that became "I Loves You, Porgy," an aria from *Porgy and Bess*, which was finished in 1935, so we now know that the concept for the song existed for at least five years before it was completed. In my notebook the seed of the song is just a few bars on a page that included other melodies. Here they would remain until they were plucked out of the book

(FOLLOWING PAGES) *Selected pages from the notebook that is in the author's collection. The ninth and tenth staves on the next spread, right, contain his original inspiration for the melody of "I Loves You, Porgy."*

FRAGMENTS
SKETCHES

(33 Riverside Dr.) BELONGING

to GEORGE GERSHWIN
316 W. 103 STREET NY

and written into a score, and in the case of this one melody, it became part of *Porgy and Bess*. No one knew this scrap was the genesis of the song until George's tune notebook turned up—another piece of the giant puzzle that is George's musical career. Still, we don't know what made him go back to that particular melody so many years later and use it as a pivotal aria in his great masterwork. Nothing else in the notebook had such a long gestation period as far as I can tell. I often wonder what the process might have been that led him back to that particular tune for *Porgy*. Did it just pop into his head one day, reminding him of its existence, or did he go searching generally through papers, looking through song scraps? We'll likely never know.

In the notebooks there are all kinds of bits and pieces that have never been heard—bars of music that George couldn't find a place for, complete tunes with no accompaniment, and melody lines without choruses, among other things. There are many unpublished songs, some of which I have recorded, but most of them—and the fragments—are destined for obscurity.

Melodies came so easily to George that he had far more than he could ever use. He once told the conductor Andre Kostelanetz, "I write thirteen songs a day to get the bad ones out of my system." Oscar Levant wrote, "He had such fluency at the piano and so steady a surge of ideas that any time he sat down just to amuse himself something came out of it." The irony of my owning this particular notebook is that I believe it's the very same volume that Ira once told me about, and he would have been flabbergasted at its reemergence. It disappeared while the brothers were working on a show out of town, and George didn't

realize it was gone until they were already driving back to New York. Even though they were about forty minutes away from the hotel where it was left behind, they made the trek back, to no avail. The book's disappearance was a disaster that would have crippled most other composers, but George was unperturbed—he was confident there would be plenty more where those melodies had come from. That self-confidence unnerved many of his colleagues. What were the chances that this precious notebook casually mentioned to me by Ira would one day come into my life?

IN THE NOTEBOOKS THERE ARE ALL KINDS OF BITS AND PIECES THAT HAVE NEVER BEEN HEARD.

George seems to have been born with that great self-assurance, as well as his talent. His parents, Morris Gershvin (born Moishe Gershovitz) and Rose Bruskin, were born in St. Petersburg, in Imperial Russia. They emigrated in the great wave of East European Jews coming to the United States from the 1880s through the start of the First World War. Morris and Rose knew each other in the old country and they married in the New World in 1895 and settled in New York City.

The couple had four children: Israel was born on December 6, 1896; then Jacob (September 26, 1898); Arthur (March 14, 1900); and Frances (December 6, 1906). As a child, Israel was called Izzy,

ARTHUR, GEORGE, AND IRA WITH THEIR MOTHER, ROSE, AND THE MAID IN PROSPECT PARK, BROOKLYN, IN 1901.

and then Ira. He thought his given name was Isidore and only discovered the truth when he was thirty and applied for a passport. (When I asked him why he changed his name from Isidore to Ira, he said it was because there were too many Isidores in his class!) The family name changed, too—Morris took on "Gershvin" sometime after arriving in the States.

Jacob was called "George" in the family, and as a teenager George started experimenting with other spellings for his surname. He used "Gershwin" when Ira was still Gershvin, but around the time George's first song was published in 1916, the whole family followed him in adopting the more fully Americanized version of their name. And vy not?

(CLOCKWISE FROM TOP LEFT) *Ira in 1908 • George, Arthur, and Ira with their cousin, Rose Lagowitz, in 1912*
Morris and Rose Gershwin on their wedding day, 1895 • George in 1916 • Ira at his uncle's photo studio.

Morris Gershwin pursued his American dream, frequently moving from job to job. When Ira was born, he designed "uppers" for ladies' shoes. With modest success, Morris managed all manner of businesses: bathhouses, bakeries, restaurants, stores, and every time he changed occupation, he moved his family so he could be near his place of work. Ira was born when the Gershwins lived on Hester and Eldridge streets on Manhattan's Lower East Side and George when they were at 242 Snediker Avenue in Brooklyn. Ira and George once spent the better part of a day trying to recall all the places they had lived as children and figured they had moved two dozen times or more.

(CLOCKWISE FROM TOP LEFT) *George at age 17* • *Arthur and George* • *Frances* • *George, in "drag,"*
with Jacob Arnold at a Catskills camp • *George, Arthur, and Ira with their parents.*

George's birthplace was torn down in the late seventies, a victim of failed urban renewal. Neither Ira nor his sister, Frances (known as Frankie), seemed to care that the house was being razed. I appeared on a radio show with Frankie and people called in complaining about the destruction of the Gershwin house, but Frankie had no attachment to the house or interest in its preservation. Author Ed Jablonski said the monument to the Gershwins was not in a house but in their songs. Still, there was surprisingly little outcry at the news that George's birthplace was to be demolished; today I think it would be different.

Recently I received a letter from descendants of a family who shared the house at 242 Snediker Avenue with the Gershwins. It turns out that the Gershwins rented the second floor, and the occupants of the first helped Rose Gershwin in many ways. The lady of the house acted as a wet nurse for Ira, feeding him because Mother Rose wouldn't or couldn't oblige. Knowing all that I've been told about her, my tendency would be to believe that Rose chose not to breast-feed. If this is the case, it might help to explain Ira's distant relationship with his mother.

I have a copy from the *Daily News* of a column published on January 27, 1932, called "Tintypes," written by Sidney Skolsky. It's packed with eclectic Ira-related information (he's five feet six and 152 pounds; he smokes ten to fifteen cigars a day; he once used a seven-syllable word—"incompatibility"—in a lyric in the song "I Don't Think I'll Fall in Love Today," from *Treasure Girl*). Included is the information that up to age five, Ira had long curls and wore starched dresses. "His mother wanted him to be a schoolteacher," the

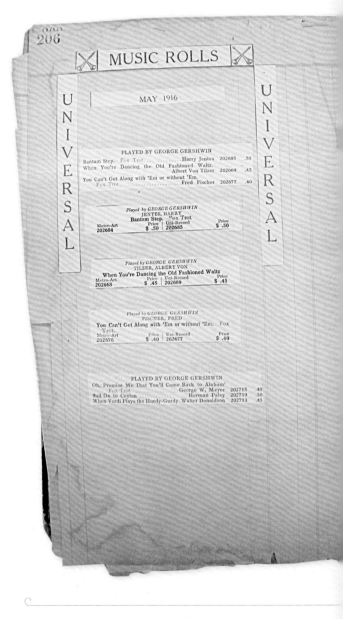

THAT GEORGE COULD LEAVE SCH[...]
A DEMONSTRATION ᴏꜰ HIS CL[...]

Ledger book for George's music rolls.

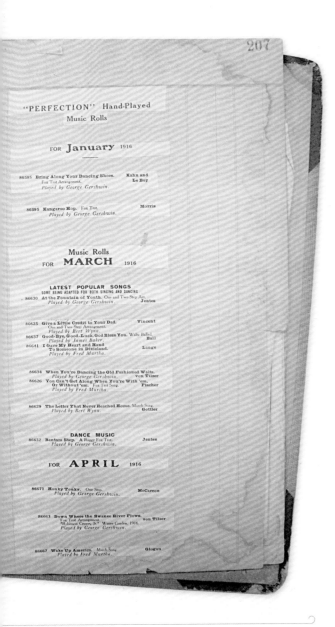

> "PERFECTION" Hand-Played
> Music Rolls
>
> FOR **January** 1916
>
> 86585 Bring Along Your Dancing Shoes.   Kahn and
>   Fox Trot Arrangement.   Le Boy
>   *Played by George Gershwin.*
>
> 86595 Kangaroo Hop. Fox Trot.   Morris
>   *Played by George Gershwin.*
>
>   Music Rolls
>   FOR **MARCH** 1916
>
>   LATEST POPULAR SONGS
>   SOME BEING ADAPTED FOR BOTH SINGING AND DANCING
> 86630 At the Fountain of Youth. One and Two Step Arr.
>   *Played by George Gershwin.*   Jentes
>
> 86625 Give a Little Credit to Your Dad.   Vincent
>   One and Two Step Arrangement.
>   *Played by Bert Wynn.*
> 86637 Good-Bye, Good-Luck, God Bless You. Waltz Ballad.
>   *Played by James Baker.*   Ball
> 86641 I Gave My Heart and Hand   Lange
>   To Someone in Dixieland.
>   *Played by Fred Murtha.*
>
> 86634 When You're Dancing the Old Fashioned Waltz.
>   *Played by George Gershwin.*   von Tilzer
> 86626 You Can't Get Along When You're With 'em,
>   Or Without 'em. Fox Trot Song   Fischer
>   *Played by Fred Murtha.*
>
> 86629 The Letter That Never Reached Home. March Song.
>   *Played by Bert Wynn.*   Gottler
>
>   DANCE MUSIC
> 86632 Bantam Step. A Raggy Fox Trot.   Jentes
>   *Played by George Gershwin.*
>
>   FOR **APRIL** 1916
>
> 86671 Honky Tonky. One Step.   McCarron
>   *Played by George Gershwin.*
>
> 86663 Down Where the Swanee River Flows.   von Tilzer
>   Fox Trot Arrangement.
>   *Winter Garden, 1916.*
>   *Played by George Gershwin.*
>
> 86667 Wake Up America. March Song.   Glogau
>   *Played by Fred Murtha.*

PURSUE A CAREER IN MUSIC WAS
W OF WHAT HE WANTED.

piece reveals. "She still does." Boy, that Rose; always supportive.

THE GERSHWIN PARENTS weren't religious—Ira was bar mitzvahed; George wasn't. (Near the end of his life Ira could still remember his Aunt Kate rescuing him when he forgot some words during the service.)

As kids, the brothers were quite different. Ira was bookish; George wasn't. When George got in trouble at school, Ira would be the family member delegated to go find out what the problem was because his English was better than that of his parents. Ira was shy and withdrawn while George was gregarious and strong-willed. The brothers were dissimilar physically as well—George lean and athletic; Ira shorter, stouter, and more sedentary. How had they come from the same family? George was always closer to their mother and Ira to their father, and each resembled his favored parent: George and Rose; Ira and Morris. Morris was sweet-natured and charming and had a great sense of humor, like Ira. Rose was hard and somewhat cold, which George wasn't, but he shared her strong-willed nature.

When I was working with Ira, he would sometimes tell me details about his upbringing. Despite the fact that Morris changed jobs as often as some people change their socks, the family managed to maintain the trappings of a middle-class lifestyle. The Gershwins always had a maid, for example. Ira remembered his tenth birthday quite vividly because it was the day his sister, Frances, was born. He recalled going to the barbershop and looking at the pulp novels they kept for customers to read. He said he read *A Study in Scarlet*—the first Sherlock Holmes story—around this time.

This was 1906, and Ira said the Gershwins were living in a building with an elevator, which impressed him because he didn't know many people who lived in buildings that had one.

Rose Gershwin was constantly concerned with what the neighbors would think. She liked the finer things and when George became successful she was quick to outfit herself with nice jewelry and furs. When George died, Ira was mortified that the throws and stoles, and especially the diamonds, came out right away for his mother to wear, and he asked her to show some restraint and wait a few more days before wearing them.

A piano was a symbol of middle-class success and when the Gershwins bought theirs in 1910, it was with studious Ira in mind. But it was George who sat down and showed he already knew how to play the hit songs of the day. Because he demonstrated a precocious and prodigious talent, George ultimately got the piano lessons, as Ira could only make it to page thirty-two in the Beyer exercise book. George had a number of piano teachers, the most important being Charles Hambitzer, from whom George received a thorough grounding in classical works right up to Hambitzer's death in 1918. From Edward Kilenyi, George first learned the art of composition and music theory. George continued to study music formally throughout his career. He also readily absorbed the music he heard around him: Yiddish songs, pop songs, the early jazz of James Reese Europe's band, the songs of Irving Berlin. George was both taught and self-taught, determined to gain as eclectic a musical education as possible.

George was enrolled in the High School of Commerce with a view to his becoming an accountant, but academics didn't come easily to him and he envisioned a future in music. Evidently the theory that musicians are good with math did not apply to George. Already by 1913, he was working the summer playing piano in Catskills resorts. (He must have had a lot of fun there, because I have a photo of him in very unattractive "drag," with the back of the picture autographed to a lady he had met during his stay. He sure didn't make a pretty-looking woman, and perhaps that was the point.) That same year, when he was fifteen, he left school to work for Jerome H. Remick & Co., a music publisher on Tin Pan Alley. George was a song plugger: His job was to play tunes for prospective buyers. Publishers made their money selling sheet music to the public and they needed performers to find their songs and turn them into hits that people would buy to play at home. That George

Sheet music cover and, on next page, contract for George's first published song,
"When You Want 'Em, You Can't Get 'Em, When You Got 'Em, You Don't Want 'Em."

26

could leave school to pursue a career in music was a demonstration of his clear view of what he wanted, as well as his parents' inability to persuade him to finish his education. It was there that he met many of the people with whom he would later cross paths, and he was often indelibly remembered from his song-plugging days.

"Tin Pan Alley" first referred to West 28th Street in Manhattan, where a number of music publishers were clustered (so much so that the noise of playing sounded like tin pans being banged together). The center of music publishing in New York changed often, and in 1912, Remick's moved to 219–221 West 46th Street. Other publishers moved uptown, too, nearer to Broadway, the last stop before many of them, including Remick's, were bought by movie companies. Just as "Broadway" meant theater, "Tin Pan Alley" came to refer collectively to the publishers, whatever their location.

Remick's, like all of the publishing houses of Tin Pan Alley, was a maelstrom of activity, and countless singers, dancers, producers, directors, and vaudevillians came calling, hoping to find the perfect song for their show, their act, their bit. George, with his dazzling play, could make anything sound better than it was. He also augmented his income by playing piano rolls, recording pieces on the paper scrolls used on self-playing pianolas. Ira recalled that George would go "across the river" to New Jersey and record piano rolls for $5 apiece, or six for $25. Years after George's death, about 125 of them were catalogued, an invaluable chronicle of his formative musical years. About two dozen of these rolls have been reissued on compact disc and the rest are scattered among private collections and a few archives. A few more

GEORGE AT THE PIANO IN 1925.

have turned up since the initial list was created, thus giving hope for even more unheard Gershwin performances to surface.

Soon, George was writing songs, and in May 1916, when he was seventeen, the first of them was published: "When You Want 'Em, You Can't Get 'Em, When You Got 'Em, You Don't Want 'Em." The lyric was by Murray Roth, with both making $5 for their efforts, while George also made a piano roll of his new composition. George and Murray wrote another song called "A Voice of Love" and though it was never published, a copy recently surfaced. Ira told me that Gershwin and Roth might have written more songs together, but one day they started playfully wrestling and it turned into a true struggle for dominance, leaving the two so shaken that their contact permanently ceased.

After his first song was published, George wanted more. Inspired by the music of Jerome Kern (in the form of tunes from *The Girl from Utah*) he heard at a relative's wedding, George wanted to be on Broadway itself, not Tin Pan Alley. He quit Remick's and took a job as a pianist at a vaudeville house playing for acts when the band was on break. He lasted one night, having been heckled by a comedian who used his inexperience and a few mishaps as fodder for his act. George fled in shame. His fortune changed when he worked as a rehearsal pianist for an actual Broadway show, which happened to be *Miss 1917*, the latest show by his idol Kern. A piano roll exists of George playing "Land Where the Good Songs Go," one of the songs from the score. When I played it once for Ira, he sang along, getting every word by lyricist P. G. Wodehouse perfect though he likely hadn't heard the song for fifty years.

While George moved quickly into the center of professional music making, Ira, after leaving City College and his own path to a desk job, made his way toward lyric writing more methodically. He read poetry—from the classics to the witty, urbane offerings in the numerous daily newspapers—and wrote it. Ira submitted light verse to local papers and journals and in 1917, his piece "The Shrine" was published in a magazine called *The Smart Set*. Ira received a dollar for his short submission. Meanwhile, George was taken on as a composer for T. B. Harms Company, making good money—$35 a week—at a time when Ira was handing out towels in the St. Nicholas Baths to make ends meet.

If it hadn't been for George's influence, Ira might never have written lyrics and might have stuck to poetry and short stories, though growing up he loved listening to musical selections on the family phonograph, especially Gilbert and Sullivan. Ira was also inspired by Jerome Kern's musicals—shows like *Leave It to Jane* and *Miss 1917*—but it was P. G. Wodehouse's lyrics for those shows that moved him more than the tunes. Ira started writing lyrics when he was working at the baths, and he showed one of his songs to George, who liked it and set it to music. But George's music didn't fit Ira's lyric, so after trying to make it work maybe twenty times, Ira started over. The song they came up with using George's new melody, "The Real American Folk Song (Is a Rag)," was added to singer Nora Bayes's 1918 show *Ladies First* but suffered a common fate for "interpolated" songs—songs written to order for an existing show to fill a perceived need: it was quickly dropped. But a pattern was set with that early collaboration: Ira came to prefer having a tune first when working on a song with George and was inspired by the variety and invention of what George played. They could also work the other way, but most of the time the music came first.

Ira's lyric for that first song showed he understood what George was trying to express in his music. George was creating a unique synthesis of American music, drawing on his deep familiarity with jazz: the original African-American music. In 1922, for example, George wrote a one-act opera featuring all black characters (played by whites in blackface) called *Blue Monday* that was orchestrated by Will Vodery, an African-American who was a major influence on Duke Ellington.

In "The Real American Folk Song," Ira wrote:

Each nation has a creative vein
Originating a native strain.

And later,

The real American folk song is a rag—
A mental jag—
A rhythmic tonic for the chronic blues…

The song wasn't published until after it was given its first recording by Ella Fitzgerald in 1959. Though he might have considered it juvenilia, Ira was sufficiently proud of his work to release it belatedly to the public. He even had a hand in assuring that Fitzgerald's premiere recording had the right feel, by suggesting they hire the ragtime pianist Lou Busch to supply the accompaniment after a first attempt was not quite successful.

George wasn't just doing his brother a favor by working with him. Although the two were close and still lived in the family home, George took on Ira as a lyricist only because he was good. The other two Gershwin siblings, Arthur and Frances, dabbled in different fields of entertainment, but they didn't share their brothers' talent. In 1936, a year before George's untimely death, George published a couple of younger brother Arthur's songs. None of them became successes, nor did Arthur possess his brother's distinctive sound. Ira described Arthur's writing style as sounding more like the operettas of Sigmund Romberg than Gershwin. After George's death, much to Ira's shock Arthur proposed to become Ira's new writing partner, but George's shoes were impossible for anyone to fill. Arthur's only song to achieve any kind of attention was "Invitation to the Blues," recorded in 1944 by Ella Mae Morse.

IRA CAME TO PREFER HAVING A TUNE FIRST AND WAS INSPIRED BY THE VARIETY AND INVENTION OF WHAT GEORGE PLAYED.

Ira continued to read and to learn, studying Gilbert and Sullivan, reveling in how they blended contemporary references in their songs, creating something weightier and more literary out of popular culture. Eventually, in his own way, Ira became as accomplished in his field as George was in his, although Ira never would have agreed with such a statement and never showed any jeal-

"Waiting for the Sun to Come Out," by George and Arthur Francis, aka Ira, their first published collaboration.

THE MERRY MUSICIAN

NO. I 19 — NEW YORK — 1st WEEK, OCTOBER — 14 VOL. I

THE MERRY MUSICIAN

EDITOR -- GEORGE
-- to -- GERSHWIN
CONTRIBUTOR -- INC.

OFFICE and PRINT-
ING ROOMS ------
91 SECOND AVE.

NEW YORK CITY

PUBLISHED ---
A COUP'LA TIMES
A YEAR

UNDER A LARGE EX-
PENCE AND ENERGY
WE FINALLY HAVE
SECURED THE SERVE-
ICES OF THE WELL
KNOWN ----

U. FATHEAD -

FOR A SERIES OF
LECTURES ON
MUSICIANS
HE IS THE BEST
AUTHORITY ON
MUSICIANS, BECAUSE
HIS BROTHER-IN-LAW
ACCOMPANIED MME.
BREEZY, THE NOTED
CONTRALO, FOR 5

MONTHS, LAST YEAR.
BELOW YOU SEE
MR. FATHEAD LEAD-
ING HIS ORCHESTRA
OF 6 PEICES, NAMELY
1 VIOLIN ---------
4 BASSES --------
1 DRUM ---------

THE FIRST MUS-
ICIAN TO BE LEC-
TURED UPON WILL
I.M. STOOPID,
THE FAMOUS COM-
POSER OF SWISS
CHEESE AND SE-
VERAL OTHER
VEGETABLES.
THE STORY CAN
BE FOUND ON P. R.

EXTRA !! NEW INVENTION
EAR-STOPS! 9 FOR 13¢
PUT ON YOUR EARS   25¢
WHEN YOU PRACTISE.
GUARENTEE TO SAVE
WRINKLES — ADVERTISE-

MR + MRS. ——
MADE A PARTY
IN HONOR OF THEIR
DAUGHTER ——,
AT THEIR HOME.

THEIR DAUGHTER
WAS GIVEN SEVERAL
BOUQUETS OF FLOWERS
+ ONE MEDAL.
THE AFFAIR WAS
MADE BECAUSE THEIR
DAUGHTER GREW
LARGE ENOUGH TO USE
THE PEDAL, + WAS
ABLE TO CROSS HER
HANDS IN "MOTHERS
PRAYER."
THE PARENTS
THINK THEIR DAUGHTER'S
GENIUS IN CROSS-
ING HER HANDS
IS AMPLE CAUSE FOR
THEM TO SEND HER
ABROAD (TO BROOKLYN)
TO STUDY.
I AGREE WITH
THEM (IN SENDING HER
TO BROOKLYN)

MR + MRS. FELIX OF THE
ABOVE ARTICAL AGREED
ME NOT TO MENTION THEIR
NAME IN THIS ARTICAL
BECAUSE THEY DON'T WANT
THEIR NAME IN PRINT

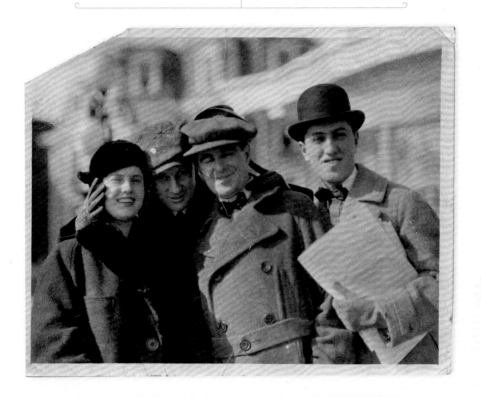

ousy or competitiveness with George. Ira never found the craft of lyric writing as easy as George seemed to find making music. (Initially George worked with other lyricists while Ira found his feet and searched for a songwriting job.) Frankie said Ira might struggle all night over one word in a song, but without that rigor there would not have been the perfection of the songs they wrote together.

Like most lyricists, Ira preferred to have a tune to work from because he had learned that a lyric could be ruined by the wrong musical setting. The key for any lyricist is to crystallize and bring forth the hidden essence locked in the music. W. S. Gilbert was one of the few artists who wrote the words before he had the melody. Most lyricists are worried the composer is going to ruin their work or will not capture the right accent or won't be able to create the tune that gives wings to their words. Having the tune allowed Ira to go on lyrical flights of fancy while he listened to the melody.

When much later he worked with composer Kurt Weill, Ira had to supply all lyrics first. It was not easy to engage in a collaboration like that, so Ira eventually started coming up with his own "dummy tunes" to finish the job. One of his

(ABOVE) *George with Al Jolson (second from the right) and friends.*
(OPPOSITE) *George's childhood comic* The Merry Musician, *1914.*

George in London in 1925.

dummies actually ended up in their show *Lady in the Dark*. It was called "Girl of the Moment."

Ira likened his work to that of a jeweler. He worked in a small "space," confined by what was allowed by George's notes. Ira had to write with a character in mind; the song could only be so long; and, almost without exception, the lines had to rhyme. When working on a song, he would often come up with the title first. (As he said in verse: "The title is vital; once you've it, prove it.") He might write the last line of the chorus first and track back from there. He talked enviously of Buddy DeSylva's being able to take a yellow pad, write a title and a final line, and fill in the rest in an hour, as if doing a crossword puzzle.

Ira had to hustle in the early days, something for which he was not characteristically suited, yet his March 17, 1920 letter to a successful writer for the *Ziegfeld Follies*, Gene Buck, reflects his eagerness to succeed in his hoped-for profession:

Dear Mr. Buck,

I am a brother of George Gershwin and have just placed some numbers with him in Dere Mabel *and* Sweetheart Shop. *I am sending you the first draft of a lyric which I know you and Mr. Stamper [composer Dave Stamper] could develop into a good* Follies *number. As George is doing the '20* George White Scandals, *I thought it might be interpolated there but George told me he couldn't work on it as the George White show is practically all set, and he suggested that I try you. If not for the* Follies, *how about making it a popular song? Whether favorably or not, hoping to hear from you soon, I am sincerely, Ira B. Gershwin.*

Even though George and Ira had been writing together sporadically for a few years, their first published song was "Waiting for the Sun to Come Out," for a show called *The Sweetheart Shop*, in 1920. The song was added while the show was previewing in Chicago. Before playing it for the producers, Ira decided to adopt a pseudonym to conceal his relationship to George. With characteristic modesty, Ira didn't want to trade on George's burgeoning success by using the family name. Using his other siblings' first names, he became Arthur Francis, a mask he wore until 1924. I own a piece of sheet music autographed by composer Vincent Youmans and Arthur Francis, the latter clearly written in Ira's instantly recognizable handwriting. In 1920, when asked who this Arthur Francis was, George said, "He's a clever college kid with lots of talent."

The Sweetheart Shop did well in Chicago but closed quickly on Broadway. Before the final curtain fell on the show, George made sure he got the $250 he had been promised for the song (he said the "college kid" needed the money) and gave Ira half. That year Ira made a healthy $723.40 from sheet music and $445.02 from phonograph sales. That was good money for him, but George was already in a much higher income bracket.

GEORGE WROTE HIS FIRST FULL BROADWAY SCORE IN 1919, WHEN HE WAS TWENTY-ONE.

George wrote his first full Broadway score in 1919, when he was twenty-one, thus making his soon-to-be-former mentor Jerome Kern jealous. *La La Lucille* marked the entry into the family business for Alex Aarons, son of established Broadway producer Alfred Aarons, who helped his son put together the musical with George writing the music and Buddy DeSylva the lyrics. The show's run of 104 performances at Henry Miller's Theatre (since demolished and rebuilt as the Sondheim) was cut short by an actor's strike, and although it produced no major hits, it did receive the attention of critics and the public, who heard a fresh musical sound.

George's first hit also came in 1919. The one-step was a popular form of song at the time.

IRA IN THE 1920s.

It was a fast and furious dance that caught on just before the introduction of the Charleston. Many of the most popular one-steps, with names like "Hindustan," were set in real or mock Asian locations. George and a lyricist named Irving Caesar had the idea of setting an American one-step in the South. The two men knocked out "Swanee" in half an hour in the Gershwins' apartment on 144th Street. (Or perhaps it was only a matter of minutes, depending on what source you believe. Caesar shortened the time it took to write the song every time he told the story through the decades, even taking credit for the music the last time he repeated the tale.) George's father, who was playing poker in the apartment as the song was being written, put down his cards long enough to play a kazoo-like accompaniment on a comb.

In October 1919, "Swanee" was added to the *Demi Tasse Revue* at the new Capitol Theatre, but it wasn't a hit. It would have remained that way except that it was heard by singer Al Jolson approximately six weeks later at a gathering he hosted in a whorehouse run by a madam named Bessie Bloodgood. George was among the guests, along with Buddy DeSylva, a songwriting contemporary of George's who had just had his first big break writing songs for Jolson on Broadway, discovered by Jolson on Catalina Island when DeSylva was a beach bum and, in the words of Ira, "the best ukulele player I ever heard." He eventually became a producer at Paramount Pictures and was a founder of Capitol Records. DeSylva was a facile lyricist and had an immensely likable personality. It is ironic in light of the setting of this story that DeSylva likely died from complications of syphilis.

It was DeSylva who generously asked the fledgling writer to play his new composition. When the song was over, Jolson told his conductor, Louis Silvers, that he wanted to add the song to his current show as soon as possible. Consequently Jolson sang "Swanee" in his roving revue, *Sinbad*, then playing in Brooklyn, and it gave George the biggest hit he would ever have.

George made $10,000 from sheet music and phonograph royalties in the first year "Swanee" was published, and he was soon writing with DeSylva for the popular annual revue the *George White Scandals*, a plum writing gig. It always dogged George that he never eclipsed the popularity of "Swanee" with his later, more sophisticated hits. Decades after the story of its creation had turned into legend, Caesar invented a charming story that after the success of their song, they made a pilgrimage down south to see the actual Swanee River. Upon finally reaching their destination to disappointedly observe a "muddy little stream," Caesar reported George as saying with impeccable timing, "If I had seen the river first, I never would have written the song."

Arthur Francis had by this time written lyrics for songs written by other composers. He worked with Vincent Youmans on a show called *Piccadilly to Broadway* in 1920 that played in Boston but never made it to Broadway, and again with Youmans the following year on *Two Little Girls in Blue*, producing a hit called "Oh Me, Oh My, Oh You." *Two Little Girls in Blue* ran for 135 performances on Broadway, and Ira was thrilled to have a hit show. That same year, George wrote the music and Arthur Francis the lyrics for *A Dangerous Maid*, another show that closed out of town.

(FOLLOWING PAGES) *Letter from George to Ira written in London in February 1923.*

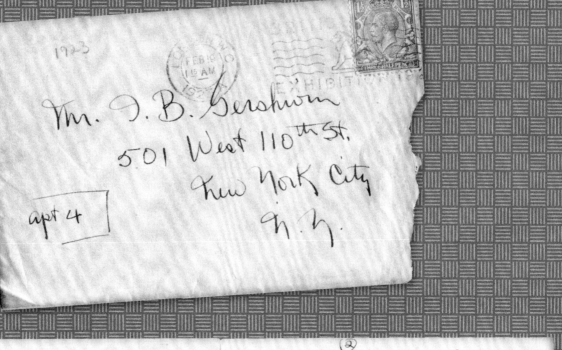

Envelope:

1923

Mr. I. B. Gershwin
501 West 110th St.
New York City
N. Y.

apt 4

Letter:

SAVOY HOTEL,
LONDON.
W.C.2

Sunday, noon.

Dear I,

Well, ol boy, here I am in London almost 24 hours, or rather only 24 hours & the rain is coming down in the manner we've heard about for years. It is not raining hard — but hard enough to keep one from going out. It will not however keep me from going to C. Grey's house in a few minutes to start on a show that begins music rehearsals Tuesday. Writing the Scandals in a month, will seem an eternity compared to the time alloted us to write what will probably be called "Silver Lining"

②

A funny thing happened yesterday which made me very joyful & for the moment very happy I came here. The boat was in dock at Southampton & everyone was in line with their passports & landing cards. When I handed my passport to one of the men at a table he read it, looked up & said, "George Gershwin writer of Swanee? It took me off my feet for a second. It was so unexpected, you know. Of course I agreed I was the composer & then he asked what I was writing now etc. etc. I couldn't ask for a more pleasant entrance into a country. When I reached the shore a woman reporter came up to me & asked for a few words. I felt like I was Kern or somebody.

3

Last night a man called me on the phone & said he was from the weekly Dispatch & would like to have an interview. I met him & spoke a while to him. He asked my opinion about the possibility of a rag-time Opera & when I thought it would come about. I told him my opinion & when it is published I'll send it along to you.

Last night we went to see Jean Bedini's "You'd be surprised" A Review. It's a fast show with many scenes from burlesque & music by Melville Morris. I wonder what he wrote as all I heard were popular American Songs. George Robey, a famous comedian is in the show & I think he is a fine artist. He puts over a lyric song

4

as good as anyone I've seen. The hit of the Show is an orchestra. The Savoy orchestra. And who do you suppose is the leader? Bert Ralton the Sax player who recorded my Mexican Dance with me. He's got a great band and is a riot over here.

From what I can see America is years ahead of England theatrically both in wealth of material & money. They're shy of ingenues, leading men composers etc. They have a half dozen good lyric writers however.

The English are the politest people I've yet met. Even the taxi drivers are polite. How different from the Yellow Cabs of New York.

I'm finding a little difficulty in understanding the money system here. They go by 12s instead of 10s. For instance a penny is equal to two cents. A six pence piece is, of course,

5

12 cents. A Shilling is 24. This is their par value. At present they are under par as you know. The cars drive on the left of the street which is also a bit befuddling.

I could go on & tell you more observations of my first few hours here but I must trot along to Greg's. Did you notice 'trot along'?

Give my love to Mom & Pop & Frances & Arthur & tell them to drop a line to their brother.

Am stopping at above Hotel but only for a few days. Until I can find a suitable apartment for Foster & myself Address my mail to Chappell mus. Pub 50 New Bond St London, until I find out where I shall definitely stay.

Give my regards to the 'boys' individually.

Write heaps & heaps.
(notice 'heaps & heaps?)

Your brother,

George.

By the time Arthur Francis became Ira Gershwin he was an experienced lyricist. He worked with George on several songs that were interpolated into shows, like "Tra-La-La" (1922), used in *For Goodness Sake* and again, much later, in 1951 (and with a different lyric supplied by Ira), in *An American in Paris*. Arthur/Ira worked with George and Buddy DeSylva on a song they finished in one evening for the 1922 *Scandals*: "(I'll Build a) Stairway to Paradise." Surprisingly to Ira, the musically complex and sophisticated song was a hit and his one-third share of the royalties—$3,500— kept him afloat for a year.

In 1923, Ira wrote the lyrics (and Joseph Meyer the music) for "Singing in the Rain." Not *that* "Singin' in the Rain," which was published a few years later with lyrics by Ira's friend Arthur Freed. I've had fun stumping people about Ira's "Singing in the Rain" when people are expecting "Singin' in the Rain" à la Gene Kelly.

Ira worked on the show *Be Yourself* which had music written by Lewis E. Gensler. Among Ira's collaborators was George S. Kaufman who surprisingly helped with the lyrics. He also worked on the musical *Primrose* with Desmond Carter as co-lyricist and his brother as the composer. *Primrose* was produced in England and was so musically endemic to those shores that it never came to the United States as a full musical production.

This was an extraordinarily fertile period for George. Late in 1923, he wrote the musical *Sweet Little Devil* (called *A Perfect Lady* in its out-of-town tryout) with DeSylva. Between the show's run in Boston and the opening in New York, George wrote *Rhapsody in Blue* in a matter of weeks. It premiered on February 12, 1924, and the reaction was instant history, but George was too busy at first to comprehend the ramifications of the *Rhapsody*. George also scored that year's version of the *George White Scandals* (his songs included the soon to be standard "Somebody Loves Me"). The first successful show George and Ira wrote together for Broadway was *Lady, Be Good!* The show was commissioned by the producers Alex Aarons and Vinton Freedley, who would work with George and Ira on a string of musicals.

Primrose had a healthy run (255 performances) at the Winter Garden in London. Clearly not everyone in London knew Ira, because one English reviewer now famously referred to him as George's sister. While in London George came up with the first eight bars of what would become "Fascinating Rhythm," one of the key songs of *Lady, Be Good!*

At this time, the traditional standard format for modern popular songs had evolved to a familiar and comfortable form that has remained the template for classic songs as we know them. Tin Pan Alley writers produced their songs in this thirty-two-bar format in which the chorus (or refrain) was made up of four eight-bar pieces, most often in AABA pattern, in which the A melody is broken up by B, a different "bridge." George followed this for most of the songs he wrote in this period but was already occasionally stretching the form and testing the limits of what he could get away with without upsetting his audience in the process.

It is songs like "Fascinating Rhythm" that show best how George could work within the conventions of the thirty-two-bar form without being constrained by them. The song was introduced (performed in public for the first time) in December 1924 by Fred and Adele Astaire, the first time these two sibling sets of American legends—the Astaires and the Gershwins—worked together. An earlier version of the song was called "Syncopated City" (a "dummy" title that was descriptive of the composer's musical architecture and the all-pervasive influence of his hometown), but when George came back to New York, Ira thought of the title "Fascinating Rhythm," which George liked. Ira worked on the rhyme scheme of the refrain for days before settling on ABAC—ABAC. George suggested that the C rhyme should consist of a two-

THERE WAS ALWAYS a good deal of give-and-take between the brothers as they strove to make the best possible song. Ira might ask George for another note at the end of a phrase, and George could insist on a particular length of word to fit his needs. Ira sometimes made helpful suggestions to George. Ira thought that a beautiful, broad theme in George's *Second Rhapsody* could be extended to good effect, and so it was. He also came up with the title for *Rhapsody in Blue* (suggested cavalierly at a party)—a perfect embodiment of a piece of music in words.

RHAPSODY IN BLUE PREMIERED ON FEBRUARY 12, 1924, AND THE REACTION WAS INSTANT HISTORY.

syllable word, instead of the one-syllable that Ira had used. George argued that a conductor would put the emphasis on the last-but-one beat in the fourth and eighth lines, and so the two-syllable word was necessary: "quiver," "flivver." Back and forth they went until Ira, as he put it, "capitulated."

Fascinating rhythm
You've got me on the go!
Fascinating rhythm
I'm all a-quiver

What a mess you're making!
The neighbors want to know
Why I'm always shaking
Just like a flivver.

Producer Edgar Selwyn was the man who put the "wyn" in the Goldwyn movie company (Samuel Goldfish provided the luster, and the bluster). In 1927, Selwyn had the idea of teaming writer George S. Kaufman, one of the giants of American musical theater, with the Gershwins, and they set about writing their operetta, an antiwar musical. Kaufman had worked with Ira on *Be Yourself* and with Morrie Ryskind would write three satirical musical comedies with George and Ira: *Strike Up the Band, Of Thee I Sing,* and *Let 'Em Eat Cake.*

The title song "Strike Up the Band" was written in an unusual way, affording us a glimpse into the way the brothers worked. Although George found melodies easy to come by, he might find something he liked but not be completely satisfied right away. He'd bounce an idea off Ira, but George knew in his musical heart when he had a tune and when he didn't. It might take a while to get there. In his book *Lyrics on Several Occasions*, Ira recounted the story of writing the title song for *Strike Up the Band*. In the spring of 1927, George and Ira were in Atlantic City to meet with Selwyn about *Strike Up the Band*. It was Saturday night and Ira got back to his hotel room late, carrying the Sunday papers. He checked his brother's adjoining room and there was no light showing under the door, so he assumed George was asleep. A short time later, however, George, in pajamas, came into Ira's room. He said he'd been lying in bed thinking about the march they'd been working on. He said he now had it right, and sat down at the piano and played the refrain, slightly altered from the previous version. George asked Ira if he liked it. Ira said he did, but wanted to be sure his brother wasn't going to change his mind once again.

sponded, "Yes, this is it." And Ira started working on the lyric. "Interestingly enough," said Ira, "the earlier four had been written at the piano; the fifth and final came to George while he was lying in bed."

"Strike Up the Band" is one of the few marches George composed. Most of his work, from orchestral pieces to ballads, used jazz-tinged chords and intervals that clearly mark them as works by George Gershwin. Even though "Strike Up the Band" is a typical march, a fast-paced style of music normally associated with a military band, it includes elements that on closer examination are distinctively Gershwin.

I've lost track of the fragment of "Strike Up the Band" that I played for Kay Swift, but I do remember that the title "strike up the band" came at the end of the phrase as it does in the final version of the song. However, I do recall that the statement was more deliberate in this earlier version, explicitly made by using notes on each beat.

EVEN THOUGH "STRIKE UP THE BAND" IS A TYPICAL MARCH, IT INCLUDES ELEMENTS THAT ON CLOSER EXAMINATION ARE DISTINCTIVELY GERSHWIN.

"The reason I wanted assurance was that over the weeks he had written four different marches and on each occasion I had responded with 'That's fine. Just right. O.K. I'll write it up.' And each time I received the same answer: 'Not bad, but not yet. Don't worry. I'll remember it: but it's for an important spot, and maybe I'll get something better.'"

Finally, with this fifth melody, George was satisfied. "Are you sure?" said Ira, and George re-

Now, we hear a jazzier, syncopated rendition here, which is unusual in a march. George retained the original military feel of the march in the first lines, but the added syncopation at the end of the phrase is what makes the song distinctive and gives it the delicious Gershwin sound.

It was typical for George Gershwin to take a traditional form like a march, that even in the thirties was a bit old-fashioned, and make it fresh and

vital. In an era when Richard Rodgers and Lorenz Hart were considered to be superior writers of sophisticated songs, here come George and Ira writing a song in march time. Its distinction is once again found in George's ability to find a nonclichéd tune, combined with its beautiful dressing in Ira's satirical syllables. There has never been a march like it before or since, and it remains a pleasing combination of patriotism, satire, cynicism, joy, and freshness.

Leave it to the Gershwins to stretch the boundaries of Broadway yet make it seem so natural, and in the process create a tune that later would help define a nation in times of war and peace. That was the genius of the Gershwins, and that energy still magically hovers around their work, a timeless creation yet a product of its time. It would have been hard for contemporary audiences to believe that a decade later Gershwin would be dead at age thirty-eight.

ALAS, AFTER TRYOUTS at theaters in Long Branch, New Jersey, and Philadelphia, the show didn't make it to Broadway. It's easy to say that *Strike Up the Band* was ahead of its time, because it was reworked and rereleased on Broadway in 1930 and became a big hit. Kaufman's original book was probably too acerbic. It was about a war, albeit one between the United States and Switzerland over cheese, and that didn't play well in the peacetime America of 1927.

The book was rewritten by Morrie Ryskind, who had attended Townsend Harris High School with Ira. The cheese was replaced by chocolate, but it's hard to imagine that made much of a difference, though Ira said that the sweeter confection mirrored a sweeter book. (The opening number from 1927, "Fletcher's American Cheese Choral Society," became "Fletcher's American Chocolate Choral Society" in the 1930 version.) The show still made its political points but not with a sledgehammer. The revised version moved from Boston through New Haven and arrived in New York in January 1930, where it ran for 191 performances at the Times Square Theatre.

There is some very rare newsreel footage of George playing "Strike Up the Band" in 1929, when the reworked show was trying out on its second run. George is playing the famous refrain as accompaniment while the chorus girls do a "buck dance," a kind of cross between a shuffle and a tap routine. He plays the march with dazzling precision and rapidity. Any footage of George playing is a gift and this piece is a particular treasure, as

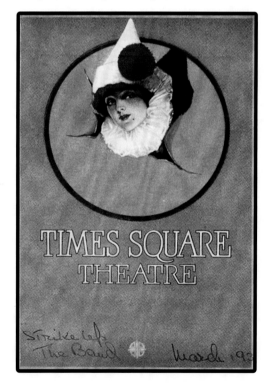

Original program cover for Strike Up the Band *at the Times Square Theater, 1930.*

you'll never hear anyone play "Strike Up the Band" the way its creator could. (Kay Swift recalled hearing George play it at a party one night in the very difficult key of F sharp, just for a lark. It was still letter-perfect.) George wrote a solo piano variation for his 1932 songbook, one of a number of versions of the song that we have. I like the original harmonies George wrote, and when they are missing, the song isn't always musically as interesting to me. It is thus with many Gershwin creations. They sound best as set by the composer.

"STRIKE UP THE BAND" (the song) enjoyed a number of reworkings. In the 1940 movie version, producer Arthur Freed took George and Ira's song and built a Busby Berkeley production number around it with Mickey Rooney and Judy Garland as the stars. The movie had nothing to do with war and included none of the other songs or any of the book from the stage show.

Ira rewrote the lyric a couple of times over the next fifteen years to bring the song up to date with what was going on in the world. In 1927, the original song went as noted on this chapter's opening spread. In 1940, with Europe under the Nazi cosh and the United States making up its mind about whether to join the war, Ira felt the "pastime / last time" rhyme in the verse might sound unpatriotic, so he changed the verse:

We hope there'll be no other war,
But if we are forced into one—
The flag that we'll be fighting for
Is the red and white and blue one!

In 1942, America was in the war full force and the conditional sense of that lyric was abandoned.

Again the Hun is at the gate
For his customary pastime;
Again he sings his Hymn of Hate—
But we'll make this time the last time!

There's not much satire in that.

Ira also adapted the song for another martial but slightly less lethal pursuit than war: football. In 1936, when George and Ira were in Hollywood working on the movie *Shall We Dance*, UCLA asked them to write a marching band song for their football team. The brothers adapted "Strike Up the Band" into "Strike Up the Band for UCLA." The 250-strong UCLA Bruins band still plays it.

We're Sons and Daughters of the Bear,
We're the California Bruins;
We fight the foe and do and dare,
And the foe is left in ruins!

For their trouble, George and Ira received season tickets for UCLA football games. Ira lived a long and fruitful life, so the song's "royalty" turned out to be a good deal: they were very good seats, which he used for a very long time—he would occasionally go to games or give the tickets to friends. When Ira died, the tickets stopped coming. Ira's widow, Leonore (who was usually known as Lee), had a fit and the tickets reappeared. She kept receiving them until she died.

THERE WAS ONE FURTHER rewrite of the lyric of "Strike Up the Band," which Ira did not undertake and did not like. I wrote about this episode at length in my autobiography, so I'll tell the story quickly here. In 1982, I agreed to represent Ira's interests on what started out to be a revival of George and Ira's *Funny Face*, which was later called *My One and Only*. It had Tommy Tune and Twiggy as stars, initially under the direction of Peter Sellars, who was fired after the opening night in Boston. There were a lot of problems with the production. Everything was supposed to sound like 1927, but in many places it didn't. "'S Wonderful," for example, was rearranged with a completely inauthentic ragtime countermelody that was wildly anachronistic and removed George's delightful ascending bass line, yet only seemed to bother me.

Then there was "Strike Up the Band," which was the finale for the first act. Ira didn't want the song in the show in the first place—it hadn't been in *Funny Face*, and if he allowed Gershwin songs to appear randomly in shows, he believed it might hurt the chances of reviving those other musicals in their original form. But the producers got what they wanted. The song was in. Then, for purposes of the plot, Tommy Tune changed the lyric. Originally it went:

> *Hear the cymbals ring!*
> *Calling one and all!*
> *To the martial swing*
> *Strike up the band!*

This show had nothing martial about it, so Tommy wanted to lose the martial swing and sing "Calling one and all" twice. When I told

Ira, he said, "Oh, my God, this is terrible. It ruins the rhyme scheme." So he wrote a new line, "Now's the time to swing." But Tommy didn't want to use Ira's line, and the last iteration of the song heard on Broadway was one that displeased the lyricist.

I tried to defend Ira's position until I came to be seen as a meddlesome presence around the production. For Ira, who spent hours, days, and years perfecting his art, such lyrical changes were a matter of pride, craft, and history. After I was on the wrong end of a tirade by Tommy Tune (who was also under tremendous pressure as co-director to create a hit), Ira's wife, Lee, said to me, "If you keep insisting on these things, they're going to lose their star and then they're going to be in big trouble. So we can't interfere with them; we have to give them what they want." Ira never knew that it was actually his wife who prevented some of his wishes from being reinforced, yet she always lived by a certain code and absolutely believed that she was doing what was right for the show, feeling that it was more important to have a hit than to deny anything the producers asked for when they were in trouble. I felt differently in that it seemed a compromise should have been possible, but it wasn't, without her support.

I kept trying to steer the show away from what I perceived to be a mauling of George and Ira's work, but when I tried to persuade them to take snippets of *Rhapsody in Blue* and the Concerto in F out of "Kickin' the Clouds Away," I got another earful. Finally the show's orchestrator colorfully told me, in the bar of the Copley Plaza, to get out of town. Eventually Ira threw up his hands and said, "Let them do their worst."

In fairness, I have to note that *My One and Only* was a big hit. I should also mention that Tommy Tune and I have become friends again. In retrospect, I can better understand both sides of the argument. Tommy, perhaps justifiably, felt that I was treading on his creativity, and I'm sure everyone was frustrated that I was creating an obstacle when they needed to focus on saving their show. My argument was, if the show was truly meant to be a celebration of Gershwin, then it was essential that it sounded authentic. The new version irritated Ira because it was unrepresentative of him, and certain participants kept invoking his name, especially for publicity purposes, while not respecting his work. My apologies to Irving Berlin, but not everything about show business is indeed "appealing."

Ira was not an absolutist about his songs—he would make a change—but it had to be well done. For the 1934 show *Life Begins at 8:40* that he co-wrote with E. Y. "Yip" Harburg to Harold Arlen's music, there's a song called "Let's Take a Walk Around the Block." The song includes a section that goes "And then in Caracas / On a jackass, / We'll sit and ride around the block." The rhyme of "Caracas" and "jackass" is inspired, but Bing Crosby wasn't allowed to sing it on the radio. So someone changed it to ". . . in Mexico / On a burro" with "Mexico" pronounced "Meh-ico." Ira was very upset by that because it didn't rhyme. And, of course, a jackass is a real animal—it's a male donkey—but I guess the radio censor, perhaps too closely resembling the animal in question, was a little too imaginative to allow that to pass.

Ira was always most comfortable and fulfilled when he was able to work with George, an inspired and inspiring collaborator. As the writing of "Strike Up the Band" demonstrates, George and Ira's was a full and equal partnership that challenged their creativity and brought out the brilliant best in both men.

MORE THAN FORTY YEARS after George's death, Ira was still protective of his brother and their work. They were closer to each other on an emotional level than they were to anyone else. The only thing they didn't talk about was George's love life. He had other friends to discuss that with, and Ira knew but didn't want to know about it.

THE NEW VERSION IRRITATED IRA BECAUSE IT WAS UNREPRESENTATIVE OF HIM.

The bond between the brothers was so strong that it even startled them at times. When working on a song they shared a musical shorthand that made them feel deeply connected in a mystical way. Ira talked of the creation of "A Foggy Day" and how, when he suggested an "Irish verse," George instantly played a strain on the piano that was perfection itself and felt like it was plucked from the inspiration that radiated from Ira's imagination. They would sometimes speak the same phrase at the same time and laugh at the shared moment. They were in so many ways, to quote Ira, "two halves of a whole."

Ira was the first to recognize what George had—he knew his brother was a genius from the moment George sat down at the new family piano and showed he already knew how to play. Ira saw beyond George's bravado and understood what made his brother tick. And although he considered George to be light-years ahead of him talent-wise, Ira wanted to work with him. From the time they started writing together, Ira protectively—and sometimes jealously—maintained his partnership with George, even after George was gone. In 1978, lyricist Yip Harburg ("Brother, Can You Spare a Dime"; "It's Only a Paper Moon"; *The Wizard of Oz*), who'd been friends with Ira since high school, wrote Ira a letter saying his dream had always been to write with George; he asked if Ira would allow him to take some of George's unpublished melodies and write lyrics for them. It was a beautifully constructed and eloquent plea. Ira was very upset by this request. He wasn't about to allow Yip to write with George. That was still Ira's domain and was the one thing that he owned unequivocally and uniquely. It simply would have been too painful to let Yip near George's music, and to add to it, Yip was still working creatively in his eighties, while Ira had given it up decades earlier.

George looked upon Ira as his equal even if Ira always insisted that George get the lion's share of the money they earned together. The customary split was 50:50 but Ira saw to it that George got more. Ira was content to stay in the background and even demanded it. Ira's focus was on glorifying George. He wanted other people to recognize the breadth of his genius in the same way he did. He truly felt George deserved more money. He was proud of his brother's rapid ascent, even when he

was still handing out towels in the St. Nicholas bathhouse and George had a show on Broadway. Their love for each other was complex and deep.

George gave Ira a significant gift on the opening night of their show *Girl Crazy*, which premiered on October 14, 1930. By this stage, George and Ira were commanding figures on Broadway, with a stream of hits to their names, and *Girl Crazy* featured some of the best work they did together, songs like "Embraceable You" and "I Got Rhythm." The gift was a silver cigarette lighter with an inscription that showed George considered his brother an equal partner in their labors and achievements. "To Ira, the Words," it read, "From George, the Music." •

Sheet music cover for Strike Up the Band *from 1927.*

"THE MAN I LOVE"

from *Lady, Be Good!*, 1924

VERSE

When the mellow moon begins to beam,
Ev'ry night I dream a little dream;
And of course Prince Charming is the theme:
The he
For me.
Although I realize as well as you
It is seldom that a dream comes true,
To me it's clear
That he'll appear.

REFRAIN

Some day he'll come along,
The man I love;
And he'll be big and strong,
The man I love;
And when he comes my way,
I'll do my best to make him stay.

He'll look at me and smile—
I'll understand;
And in a little while
He'll take my hand;
And though it seems absurd,
I know we both won't say a word.

Maybe I shall meet him Sunday,
Maybe Monday—maybe not;
Still I'm sure to meet him one day—
Maybe Tuesday
Will be my good news day.

He'll build a little home
Just meant for two;
From which I'll never roam—
Who would? Would you?
And so all else above,
I'm waiting for the man I love.

CHAPTER 2

THE MUSICAL THEATER

S A MUSICIAN, I tend to look at the dates of a particular creation as if they were made in a vacuum, but when one thinks of them in the broader context of history, their juxtaposition to world events can lend some insight. In 1924, the world was in the false calm between the two world wars. Lenin died and Stalin's rise to absolute power in the Soviet Union gained momentum. Hitler was in jail, writing *Mein Kampf* after leading the failed Beer Hall Putsch against the German government. Also in 1924, André Breton's first *Surrealist Manifesto* was published and Franz Kafka metamorphosed out of this life and into whatever awaited him beyond the grave. In the United

States, Thomas Watson renamed his company IBM, J. Edgar Hoover was appointed head of the FBI, and the uncharismatic incumbent Calvin Coolidge was victorious in the presidential election.

Nineteen twenty-four was a banner year in George Gershwin's career, during which he produced two landmark works: *Rhapsody in Blue* and the musical *Lady, Be Good!* Many people don't realize that most Gershwin songs they know originated in musicals like *Lady, Be Good!* and were not written as stand-alones. Of course a Broadway show was an excellent way to promote a song and had about it a certain highbrow cachet that was attractive to its audiences. Still, even if they're familiar with "Fascinating Rhythm" or "Embraceable

Fred Astaire, George, and Ira at the piano.

You" or "Someone to Watch over Me," most folks aren't aware of the provenance. And almost nobody knows that "Love Is Here to Stay" came from the movie *The Goldwyn Follies,* because it was a song barely given an airing in an unsuccessful film.

Any description of George and Ira's songs must take account of the context for which most of them were written, the musical theater.

Lady, Be Good! was in fact a landmark in both George and Ira's careers, being the first full-book Broadway musical with songs by George for which Ira wrote the lyrics. Before *Lady, Be Good!,* George had worked with other lyricists, most notably Irving Caesar and Buddy DeSylva, and while Ira had written lyrics for George ("(I'll Build a) Stairway to Paradise") and for other songwriters, he'd done so as Arthur Francis. In 1924, for the musical *Be Yourself,* when Ira teamed with George S. Kaufman and Marc Connelly he did so publicly as Ira. No longer concerned that he would be perceived as exploiting the family name, Ira took ownership of his craft by collaborating openly with his brother on *Lady, Be Good!*

This was also the first in the impressive string of successful musicals produced by Alex Aarons and Vinton Freedley that were George and Ira's bread and butter for a number of years. It was their first show with the writers Guy Bolton and Fred Thompson, and the same creative and producing teams would go on to work together on *Oh, Kay!* in 1926. *Lady, Be Good!* was also the first time the brothers collaborated with Fred and Adele Astaire.

George met the Astaires when he was a song plugger at Remick's on Tin Pan Alley. Fred and Adele had been child performers in a traveling vaudeville show and eventually they came around to Tin Pan Alley looking for new material. George and the Astaires were a similar age—as Fred would later say, they were kids together basically. At Remick's, George would occasionally sneak in one of his own tunes when he was supposed to be playing songs by other people, something he could have been fired for. Confident in his own material, George once said to Fred and Adele, "Wouldn't it be great if we did a show together?" and now, with *Lady, Be Good!,* it came to pass.

> ANY DESCRIPTION OF GEORGE *and* IRA'S SONGS MUST TAKE ACCOUNT OF THE CONTEXT *for* WHICH THEY WERE WRITTEN.

Years later, when asked if he recognized that he was working with a genius, Astaire laughed and said, "No, we were trying to get our blasted dance steps right and George was trying to get the blasted tunes right."

The show produced major hits like "Fascinating Rhythm" and "Oh, Lady, Be Good!" Both have been recorded many times. "Oh, Lady, Be Good!" was a hit record for Ella Fitzgerald in 1947, showcasing her signature ability to scat and further establishing her fame as a unique singing talent. "Fascinating Rhythm" remains one of the best known of all Gershwin songs.

Another great song written for the show was "The Man I Love," one of George's personal favorites. In May 1928, Richard Simon (of Simon & Schuster, and Carly's father) wrote his brother Alfred, who coauthored a Gershwin biography, "By the way, you'll be interested to know that G.G. likes 'The Man I Love' best of all the tunes he has written." Despite that, the song was dropped during the show's tryout in Philadelphia. When it was first heard, there was no inkling that this simple tune would become one of the most recognizable of all George's creations, and a decade later would become the theme song of his radio series. Its strange fate sheds light on the sometimes mysterious ways of musical theater in its heyday.

This is how musicals were usually put together back then. The producer signed the stars he wanted and booked a theater for a period of time beginning a few months hence. He then hired writers for the book (the story told in the narrative between the songs) and a composer and lyricist for the songs themselves, along with a director, a choreographer, and stage and costume designers.

Once he had a script he liked, the producer mapped out what kind of songs were needed—a ballad here, a dance number there. George and Ira would sometimes joke about how the producers would ask for a "hit" in a particular spot, as if they had the automatic ability to write an instant standard. The songs were then written with the plot in mind, following certain conventions writers had to adhere to, like including an opening chorus. A composer like George Gershwin always overwrote so the producer could switch out songs from the pool of prepared material. It was possible that a new song or songs would be commissioned right up to the last minute before opening night. In a rush toward the end, the show came together in what was often a haphazard fashion. The shows were wonderfully entertaining, but they included elements of a topical revue that had a short shelf life. With plots so wafer-thin, it was easy to play musical chairs with the songs and the score.

Take the plot of *Lady, Be Good!* Having fallen behind on their rent, brother and sister Dick and Susie Trevor (Fred and Adele Astaire) are kicked out of their house. "Trouble may hound us, / Shadow surround us," they sing in the opener, "Hang On to Me." "If you hang on to me / While I hang on to you, / We'll dance into the sunshine, / out of the rain." It's a little maudlin, a little uplifting. The down-on-their-luck Trevors then head to a garden party held by wealthy Josephine Vanderwater and there's "flirting and romancing

George with producer Alex Aarons on Vinton Freedley's Connecticut farm in 1926.

THE PLAY

PICTORIAL

With which are incorporated
"THE PLAY" "THE PLAY SOUVENIR," "THE STAGE SOUVENIR"

"LADY, BE GOOD"

NO. 291

VOL. XLVIII.

FRED ASTAIRE

ADÉLE ASTAIRE

1 S. NET

MONTHLY

so sublime" ("End of a String"). Things don't look so bad for Dick and Susie but the romancing—Dick's with Shirley and Susie's with a hobo (actually someone called Jack Robinson, who has just returned from Mexico)—is thwarted by their newly indigent status. Dick decides to settle for someone who can bail them out—Jo, the party's hostess. (It turns out that Jo had Dick and Susie evicted for the express purpose of landing Dick.)

At the party, Dick and Susie, together with a singer named Jeff White, perform "Fascinating Rhythm" for the guests. Despite the presence of the very suitable Jeff, Susie finds she's still taken with Jack, the hobo. In 1924, a hobo was a slightly romanticized figure, a migrant worker who rode the rails and definitely higher in status than a tramp or a bum. Susie was happy to call Jack "my hobo," and Jack called Susie "hoboess."

Down in Mexico, Jack Robinson has inherited a large fortune, but he is believed to be dead. He was apparently married in Mexico, so he left an heiress. A lawyer, Watty Watkins, enlists Susie's help in a scheme to impersonate Juanita, Jack's Mexican bride, to secure the millions of dollars of inheritance money. (Watty sings "Oh, Lady, Be Good" to Susie. Susie is unaware that her Jack—the hobo—and this Jack are the same person.) Dick reluctantly proposes to Jo Vanderwater, believing he can't have the woman he loves, Shirley. "Ting-a-ling, the wedding bells will jing-a-ling-a-ling," the ensemble sings at the end of Act One.

In Act Two, at a hotel in Connecticut, downcast Dick sings "The Half of It, Dearie Blues" to Shirley: "I've got the You-Don't-Know-the-Half-of-It-Dearie Blues. / It may be my heart isn't broken, but there's a bruise." Susie is serenaded in "Juanita"—"Tell us senorita, do they grow / Any more like you / Down in Mexico?" We also learn that Jack Robinson was never really married—the alleged wife's brother is simply trying to extort a payoff from Watty. Nor is he dead. Watty, who has been arrested for fraud, is freed.

No longer disguised, Susie and Jack—whom we now recognize as Susie's hobo—are reunited. Everyone proclaims their love—Dick and Shirley and Jack and Susie, even Jo and Watty, and yet another couple, Bertie and Daisy. At the end, all four couples are engaged to be married. In other words, it's a lot of silly fun, or was in those days.

With mistaken identities, fake Mexican brides, and hobos who are secretly rich, *Lady, Be Good!* is more *Days of Our Lives* than *Caucasian Chalk Circle*. And that's by no means a criticism. The book serves to provide pretexts for songs, including parties for up-tempo numbers with well-choreographed dances. The plot allows the cast to display the talents the audience has come to see: Fred and Adele's dancing, Fred's singing, the comedy of actors Walter Catlett (Watty) and Gerald Oliver Smith (Bertie). The popular entertainer Cliff "Ukelele Ike" Edwards (Jeff White) performed "Fascinating Rhythm" at the party and "Little Jazz Bird" at the hotel. Edwards had a significant role in the show and in a block in Act Two, after "Little Jazz Bird," he interpolated his own non-Gershwin songs: "Insufficient Sweetie" (by Edwards and Gilbert Wells), "Who Takes Care of the Caretaker's Daughter" (by Chick Endor and Paul Specht), and "It's All the Same to Me" (by Chick Endor). Edwards would have brought his own fans to the box office, and so would the dual pianists Phil Ohman and Victor Arden, who became longtime Gershwin performers.

(OPPOSITE) The Play *magazine featuring* Lady, Be Good! *starring Fred and Adele Astaire in 1926.*

Recently a fragment of Edwards singing "Little Jazz Bird" turned up in an obscure short film, thus adding an exciting, albeit brief, contribution to Gershwin original cast renderings. Cliff Edwards is now primarily remembered as being the voice of Jiminy Cricket for Walt Disney's 1940 animated feature film *Pinocchio*, but he remains one of the pioneers of jazz singing.

In its original form, "The Man I Love" was sung by Adele Astaire (Susie) early in the show. Adele and Fred have been evicted and are standing in the street with their belongings when the guy Adele is sweet on walks by. Cue the song. At least that was the original intention. When the show was in tryouts in Philadelphia, the song failed to elicit a good response from the audience. First it was moved within the show, but by the end of the first week it was cut altogether.

HE'D DO WHATEVER IT TOOK TO MAKE THE SHOW WORK, EVEN IF IT MEANT SACRIFICING A GREAT SONG.

Perhaps the song was removed because the audience found it too dramatically weighty in the context of this somewhat frothy and lighthearted musical. In this case, the song was too good for its own benefit because it (literally) stopped the show. George was above all else a man of the theater and he'd do whatever it took to make the show

work, even if it meant sacrificing a great song, the fate of which was not his immediate concern. However, it would take more than this setback to keep "The Man I Love" from the world.

PRODUCER ALEX AARONS had played a significant part in George's rise to prominence when he gave the composer his big Broadway break with *La La Lucille* in 1919. Aarons worked with enormous success with Fred and Adele Astaire on *For Goodness Sake* (called *Stop Flirting* in London) and now, partnered with Vinton Freedley (a former performer), he hired the Astaires again for a show that originally had the working title *Black-Eyed Susan*.

Once Aarons and Freedley had Fred and Adele Astaire in hand, they signed up George and Ira. But there was another project they wanted George's help with first, so he went to London to score the musical *Primrose*. George and Ira wrote the score of their Broadway musical debut while they were in London in the summer of 1924. When *Primrose* premiered at the Winter Garden on September 11, 1924, it was immediately hailed a success. The score is markedly different from that of *Lady, Be Good!* and sounds very "British," thus proving that George could write with ease in more than one particular style. It ran until April 1925, when it was replaced by another of George's musicals, *Tell Me More*. That show had a longer run in London—264 performances—than it had on Broadway, where it closed after one hundred.

After *Primrose* was under way, George returned to New York to work on what would become *Lady, Be Good!* Once they were commissioned, songwriters and lyricists would only have a couple of months to come up with a complete musical, but George never had trouble finding enough tunes. Ira felt the pressure of deadlines more than George because of his more laborious way of working. A musical's plot may have been somewhat weightless, but Ira worked diligently to integrate plotlines into his lyrics.

Some musicals were created very quickly—anything produced by Florenz Ziegfeld (*Rosalie* in 1928, *Show Girl* in 1929) was hastily thrown together. The real Ziegfeld bore no resemblance to the legendary figure repeatedly depicted in classic films. Ziegfeld was a master at knowing what the audience wanted, but Ira said he was difficult to work with because he treated songwriters badly and had poor musical taste. He would demand that songs be produced in short order, even shorter than was the case with other musicals. Because Ziegfeld was so capricious in his song selection, songwriters had to overwrite more than usual, which is why George and Ira had help on the shows they did for him: Sigmund Romberg and P. G. Wodehouse on *Rosalie* and Gus Kahn on *Show Girl*. This was also why there was a lot of "trunk music"—recycled songs—in those shows.

Often a song had to be added when the show was in tryouts on its way to Broadway. Many great Broadway songs were written out of town under considerable pressure, songs like Irving Berlin's "There's No Business Like Show Business" and "You're Just in Love" and Jerry Herman's "Before the Parade Passes By"—the Act One closer from *Hello, Dolly!* The producer might say, "There's a lull in the second act, so we need something up-tempo." Or the star of the show would complain, "I haven't been onstage much the last half hour; I need another big song here." In the Gershwins'

Strike Up the Band, one of the producers had a girlfriend he wanted to feature, so the Gershwins wrote a charming waltz called "I Want to Be a War Bride" to accommodate him and her. Unfortunately (or perhaps not), the lady in question left the show before it opened on Broadway, so the song was cut.

When they heard George and Ira's song "Oh, Lady, Be Good!" Guy Bolton and Fred Thompson suggested dropping the show title *Black-Eyed Susan* and using *Lady, Be Good!* The show had its pre-Broadway tryout at the Forrest Theatre in Philadelphia on November 17 and it was worked on furiously up to that point, and even more so between then and the first night on Broadway on December 1. In Ira's opinion, the show that went on in Philadelphia ran about an hour too long.

Portrait of Fred and Adele Astaire.

George and Ira had written more songs than were needed—more than twenty in total—and changes were made to the lineup and the songs.

The key for the producers and songwriters was to get the right balance of songs. When a show was performed for an audience, more changes would be made based on the house's reaction. "The Man I Love" was one of eight songs dropped at some point, further evidence that how good a song was often had nothing to do with whether it stayed in the show. The wealthy banker and patron Otto Kahn had liked "The Man I Love" so much when he first heard it (by some accounts George played it for him on the boat trip back from London after *Primrose*) that he put $10,000 into the show.

HOW GOOD A SONG WAS OFTEN HAD NOTHING TO DO WITH WHETHER IT STAYED IN THE SHOW.

For *Lady, Be Good!* songs came and went at a dizzying pace. "A Wonderful Party" was added in Philadelphia, "So Am I" replaced a song called "Will You Remember Me?" in rehearsal, and "Linger in the Lobby" replaced "Weatherman" and "Rainy-Afternoon Girls" soon after the opening. The songs "Seeing Dickie Home" and "The Bad, Bad Men" were introduced in Philadelphia but dropped before the opening. A song written for Fred's paramour Shirley called "Evening Star" wasn't used (but was later recycled for a British production), and "Singin' Pete" (the reason for dancin' feet), a song written for the entertainer Jeff White, was mercifully dropped in rehearsal.

After opening on Broadway, the tinkering with the show continued—"Little Jazz Bird" didn't make it to London. One song, "Leave It to Love," was a favorite of Ira's and decades after George's death had partially disappeared, causing Ira to constantly lament that he was never able to find a copy of the lyric to match the surviving music, and that he had seen it somewhere in the house only recently. It wasn't just songs that got the boot: the performers who played Daisy and Shirley were also replaced.

In a letter to Lou and Emily Paley from Philadelphia on November 26 (written at the Hotel Sylvania in the wee small hours), Ira brought his friends up to date on the progress of *Lady, Be Good!* four days before the show was due to open on Broadway. Ira wrote that it looked "pretty good" but still needed "lots of fixing," with the first half-hour being very slow. Ira wasn't confident the show could be repaired in time.

Ira's letter helps us appreciate how many projects the brothers—particularly George—were involved in at this time. After performing *Rhapsody in Blue* at the Aeolian Hall concert in February, George made the first recording of the piece with bandleader Paul Whiteman in June. Ira's letter mentions reviews of a Carnegie Hall Whiteman concert George had participated in, and says he was looking forward to a performance in Philadelphia the next day (Thanksgiving). (George was also scheduled to play in Boston on December 4, after *Lady, Be Good!*'s opening.) Meanwhile, Ira

noted the 1924 edition of the *Scandals* was about to close after running since late June at the Apollo. Ira's *Be Yourself* had just gone on the road; *Primrose* was going well in London; *Sweet Little Devil* less so back home. George was in New York working on orchestrations for *Lady, Be Good!* and while British producers wanted him in London after the opening, George was going to take a rest. Ira wrote he was busy rewriting songs. He was looking forward to the forthcoming holiday take for *Lady, Be Good!*: $9,000, of which his share, he was happy to relate, would be a healthy $90.

Despite Ira's concerns, *Lady, Be Good!* ran for 330 performances on Broadway. The *New York Times* review praised the performance of Adele Astaire, always a graceful dancer but now adding comedy to her repertoire. (Adele was the real star of the Astaire duo—Fred was considered talented support for his sister.) The *Times* review pronounced George's score excellent, saying "a number of the tunes the unmusical and serious-minded will find hard to get rid of." And sounding like a teacher's report card, the paper judged Ira's lyrics as "capable throughout and at moments excellent."

Ira between Leonore (left) and her sister, Emily, in 1926.

"THE MAN I LOVE" and "Fascinating Rhythm," which have endured as Gershwin classics, are songs that just happened to be featured first in *Lady, Be Good!* When putting together a musical, a composer like George Gershwin didn't think of a single song; he thought of the show as a whole and tried to integrate the scores musically to compensate for the deficiencies of the book. Once the show was set, individual songs could be given more focus. Usually only a few songs became popular from any given score. The fashion of the time was for the publisher and the composer to pick on average six songs from a show to publish in sheet music form. Sometimes more than six were printed, especially when the show was in its tryout phase, but that number would be quickly winnowed to the standard handful-and-one. In the

time before record players replaced most parlor pianos, sheet music was still a major source of income. People watching the show could purchase the music in the theater lobby, or later from their local music dealer.

"The Man I Love" and "Fascinating Rhythm" were both innovative creations that helped signal the emergence of the distinctive Gershwin sound. "Fascinating Rhythm" represented a style of music that hadn't been heard coming out of Tin Pan Alley before. Two elements make the song stand out: the accent changes on the notes for rhythmic effect and the shift of the accompaniment. It has a restless energy about it that quickens the pulse, with a juxtaposition of the jagged phrases of the music competing with a lyric that must simultaneously anchor the song while pointing up the carefree abandon of its syncopation. When people first heard the song they recognized it as something new, and it was an instant success.

When George played the tune for Ira for the first time the provisional title he was still using was "Syncopated City." George was drawing inspiration from the sounds of New York that he'd been soaking up his whole life, from the subway, buses, streetcars, and all the insistent, percussive machinery of the modern New York. In 1982, when I was working for Ira, I was sent to examine the contents of the Warner Brothers warehouse in Secaucus, New Jersey, where a vast trove of musical material had turned up, including many Gershwin manuscripts. Ira was doubtful that anything of value would turn up in Secaucus, and it was Leonore who persuaded him to let me travel east and search the facility. There, I found a manuscript for "Fascinating Rhythm," written when it was still called

The
DUO-ART
M O N T H L Y

GEORGE GERSHWIN

MAY, 1925

George on the cover of The Duo-Art Monthly *in 1925 publicizing his piano roll of* Rhapsody in Blue.

"Syncopated City." I also found an early version of "The Man I Love" in the same cache. That was an exciting, almost surreal day, and I can still remember with clarity looking at the burst of creation boldly notated on the yellowed paper I was holding in my hands. In those moments, one feels very close to the music's creator.

"The Man I Love" as we know it today is not the song's first incarnation. In the earlier version, the music for the chorus ("Some day he'll come along . . .") was the music for the verse. (This was before there were any lyrics.) But the verse music was so good that George made it the chorus. It's something like realizing that the appetizer you planned for a dinner is better than the main course, and switching your menu around. The story of the verse becoming the chorus was well documented, but the tangible proof containing the discarded music did not turn up until I found the manuscript in Secaucus in 1982. It was clear that George was spot-on in his assessment to give his delicate verse an upgrade.

Today, we can see that "The Man I Love" is characteristically Gershwin, but in its time it was considered somewhat revolutionary. It's a torch song, but not like any torch song a contemporary audience had heard. The song uses the distinctive Gershwin device of the blue note—a flatted note. On the scale it's a seventh that is flatted a half-step (a semitone). I can imagine Gershwin noodling at the piano as the blue note is sounded over and over again in the first line of "The Man I Love": "Some day he'll come along . . . and he'll be big and strong." These notes are repeated with a descending chord in the left hand, making it interesting and unusual. That repeated blue note is part of the wonder of the song. The 1928 Irving Berlin song "How About Me" uses the same descending chromatic chord effects and reminds me of the Oscar Levant quip "Imitation is the sincerest form of plagiarism."

Gershwin used this device many ways, so it's remarkable that his songs don't sound more alike. But George was an alchemist, able to transmute something like that simple blue note into countless permutations and come up, more often than not, with pure gold. Yet it is the manipulation of those simple elements that makes his sound so special. Sometimes it is the change of just a few notes that causes the heavens to open in celebration of originality; thus the mysterious nature of such minute changes continues to beguile and confound those who try to figure out the source of such inspiration.

> GEORGE WAS ABLE TO TRANSMUTE SOMETHING LIKE THAT SIMPLE BLUE NOTE INTO COUNTLESS PERMUTATIONS.

In the previous chapter we talked about the brilliant synergy between George's music and Ira's lyrics in "Fascinating Rhythm." While "The Man I Love" was one of George's best songs, it's not Ira's most immortal lyric, I think, and Ira would have been the first to admit that, but it was written at a particular moment in history. As times have changed, one looks at these lyrics, written to

(FOLLOWING PAGES) *George's handwritten score for "Fascinating Rhythm," when it was named "Syncopated City."*

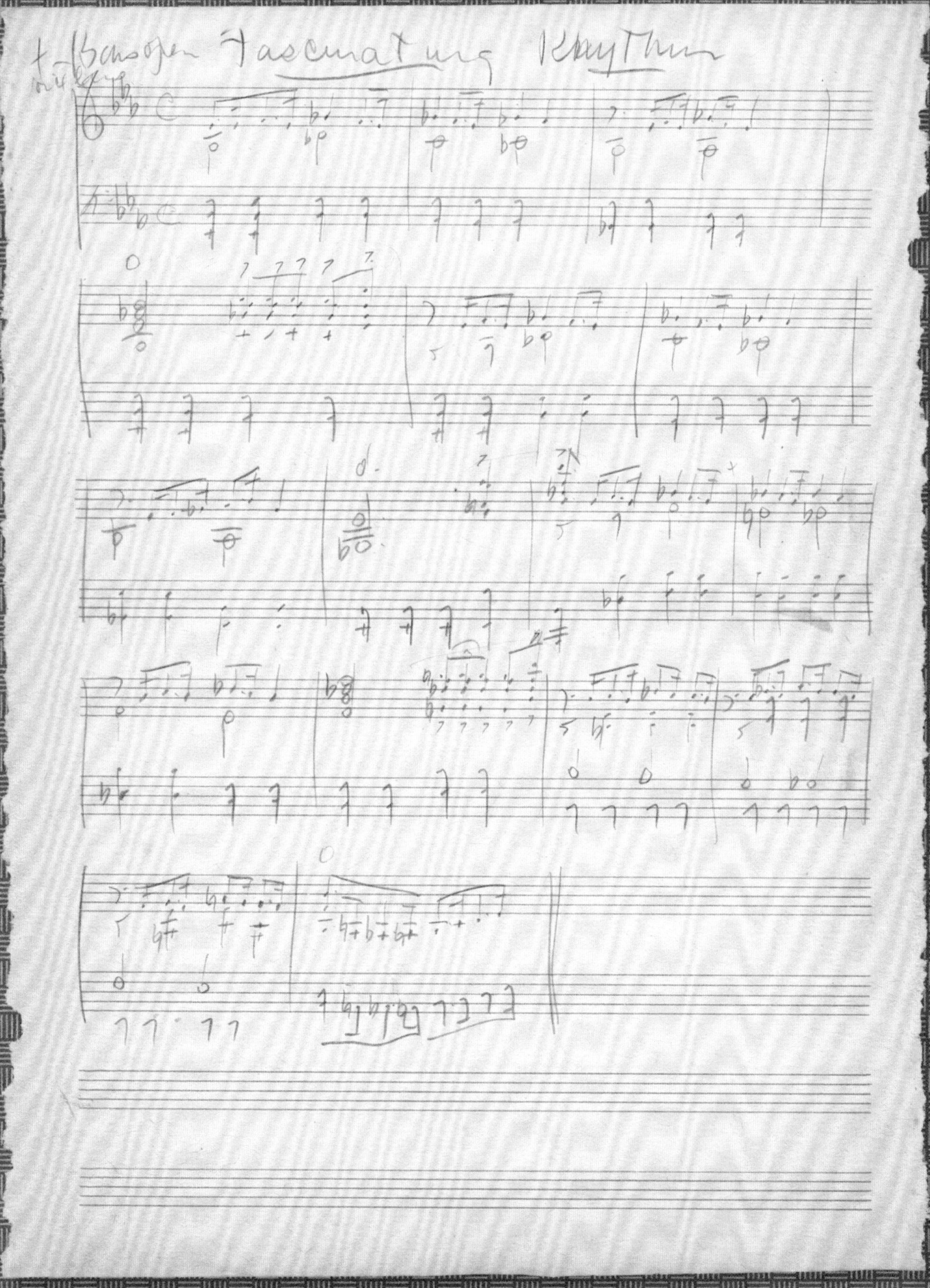
Fascinating Rhythm

be sung by a young single woman, differently. "He'll build a little home / Just meant for two / From which I'll never roam / Who would? Would you?" These are the words of a young Ira—in later years he would have written a more worldly lyric, though aside from the point of view, the turn of phrase is in itself cleverly expressed. The fact that his words are a product of his times must be taken into account, as well as the specific expression engendered by the requirements of the plot.

One day, while working for Ira, I was looking through his file for the show *Strike Up the Band* and found a copy of the 1927 lyric for "The Girl I Love," a version of "The Man I Love" Ira wrote to be sung by a man, and Ira instantly tore it up. I asked him why he'd done that and he said the song was so popular as "The Man I Love" that he didn't want anyone singing it any other way. To Ira, changing the gender of the song amounted to sacrilege. It was painful for me to witness this destruction, but fate had other plans for this lost lyric.

The libretto for *Strike Up the Band* had gone missing after the show had closed in 1927, but it was found in a library many years later and I got hold of a copy and excitedly showed it to Ira. This was a couple of years after Ira had destroyed the lyric of "The Girl I Love" and, lo and behold, the lyric for "The Girl I Love" was contained in the recently recovered script. I knew it could no longer be permanently lost, regardless of Ira's feelings, so I showed it to him. This time he said, "Oh, that's not bad," and I sang it for him and he liked it.

Ira gave me permission to sing this version of the song in the piano bars where I was making extra money at night. Patrons of the bar were startled to hear me announce this unknown lyric

by Ira Gershwin they were hearing "with permission of the author." (Playing it in a gay bar at the time probably made it all the more startling.) In 1985, I made the first recording of "The Girl I Love" from *Strike Up the Band* on my all-Gershwin debut album. Previously I had offered it to Tony Bennett, who mysteriously chose instead to change the original lyric himself and sing it in third person as "The Man She Loves," a clumsy and self-conscious choice, I thought.

A question we ask of these ninety-year-old songs is whether the lyric holds up. The original "The Man I Love" lyric has been criticized by some feminists. The singer's life is clearly incomplete without a man who will come along and save her. For "The Girl I Love," the refrain is different: the girl's not "big and strong" and she's not expected to build a little home:

Some day she'll come along,
The girl I love;
Her smile will be a song,
The girl I love;
And when she comes my way,
I'll do my best to make her stay.

And:

For her I'll do and dare
As n'er before;
Our hopes and fears we'll share—
For evermore;
And so, all else above
I'm waiting for the girl I love.

Little Theatre

Catlett & Girls [2]

Leading lady, I have an improvement
On the W. K. little theatre movement
Where I know we never will be baffled
When we find the house is only half-filled.
I mean a theatre so small
That there will be no audience at all.

We'll build a little theatre of our own   *highly moral tone*
So small that we will ~~never~~ *always* be alone.
Where I will be your Barrymore
The finest (handsomest) of mimes   (histrionic crimes)
And you'll be Frances Larrimore
          Because it rhymes.
I'll write a play with oh! so many charms.
Where ~~you'll be alway~~ you'll be nestling in my arms
I've a suspicion
There'll be no inter ... mission   *no mammy songs*
In that little theatre of our own

THINK THE LYRICS to "The Girl I Love" have stood up much better than those for "The Man I Love." It talks about sharing hopes and fears. This is a much more enlightened, if less exciting, view of a relationship than waiting winsomely for a man on a steed to come rescue you. When I sing a song I don't think of the protagonists in terms of gender; I think of them as characters expressing emotion in the context of the song. Other people like to read more into a lyric than is there. It has been claimed that Ira's lyric in "Love Is Sweeping the Country"—"All the sexes / From Maine to Texas / Have never known such love before"—was his nod to other possible types of relationship. Yeah? So what was he thinking when he wrote a song called "Bronco Busters" in *Girl Crazy*: "On Western prairies, we shoot the fairies / Or send them back to the East"?

Some in the gay community have wanted me to sing these songs male-to-male, but I usually sing them the way they were written because I feel that the important point is that love knows no gender. While I well understand that some like to hear a palpable expression of that too often unexpressed point of view, I usually, but not always, leave such choices to one's own imagination. However, I will admit to having sometimes changed the words to accommodate an audience that mostly preferred to hear them sung that way—doing so has engendered a tremendously positive response that was

Ira's handwritten lyrics to "Little Theater," an unused song for Lady, Be Good!.

PHOTO WITH INSCRIPTION FROM
MARILYN MILLER TO GEORGE.

moving in its power and catharsis and simply made me feel good as well.

In musical moments, the question for me sometimes is, "What would Ira do?" and perhaps that is not as relevant as it once was with the world changing so fundamentally in attitudes and morals. Ira worked with gay people and was very comfortable with them, but he never thought his songs might be sung by one man to another. One day I played Ira a recording of "The Man I Love" performed by the San Francisco Gay Men's Chorus and I knew by his reaction he'd never considered the possibility. It's an extremely full-bodied rendition—"Some day he'll come along . . ."—and Ira was squirming all the way through it. I laughed about it afterward but I could see it upset him. (Ironically, after relating the story in the liner notes of my first recording, I later received a letter unique in its point of view: accusing me of homophobia, the writer having missed the point of my reason for sharing the story.)

I HAVE THE ORIGINAL PROGRAM from the Philadelphia tryout of *Lady, Be Good!* that includes among the song listings "The Man I Love." The program is so very rare that even Ira didn't have a copy and I know of only one other person who has one, who has it because I gave it to them. Almost as rare is the first-edition sheet music of "The Man I Love" with a *Lady, Be Good!* cover. Even rarer is the version that includes the misprint "The Man I Loved," of which there are only two in existence. One, which was in Ira's collection, is now in the Library of Congress, and the other is in the Morgan Library in New York City courtesy of its former owner, Mr. James Fuld, an

enthusiastic Gershwin aficionado and late lamented friend.

The Gershwins knew "The Man I Love" was a good song, so they kept it in reserve. In 1927 they were writing *Strike Up the Band* and the song was inserted in the score along with the aforementioned male lyric ("The Girl I Love") for Morton Downey, Sr., to sing. But the show closed out of town, so the song wasn't heard by many audiences. The song was reprinted, and one of the more common editions of "The Man I Love" notes that it is "from *Strike Up the Band*." This *Strike Up the Band* version was kept in print despite the fact that it still hadn't been recorded much and was unknown to all but the intimates of the Gershwin circle.

In 1928, when George and Ira hurriedly cowrote their Ziegfeld musical *Rosalie* with Sigmund Romberg and P. G. Wodehouse, "The Man I Love" was included in the show, this time sung by the

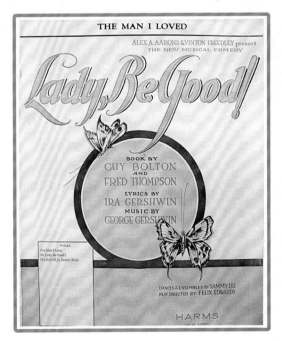

(ABOVE) *Sheet music cover of "The Man I Love," with misprint, from* Lady, Be Good!
(FOLLOWING PAGES) *Opening night program for* Lady, Be Good! *in Philadelphia.*

BOLES & WESTWOOD

Members Phila. Stock Exchange

INVESTMENT SECURITIES

Land Title Bldg., Philadelphia

PHONE: LOCUST 4721

Miss L. C. Bell

La Belle

·IMPORTER·

Millinery Shop

1833 CHESTNUT STREET

Bell Phone

Forrest Theatre

Thos. M. Love, General Manager

BEGINNING MONDAY, NOVEMBER 17, 1924

2—WEEKS ONLY—2

Nights at 8.15; Mats.: Wed and Sat. at 2.15

Alex A. Aarons and Vinton Freedley

Present

"LADY, BE GOOD!"

The New Musical Comedy
Book by Guy Bolton and Fred Thompson
Music by George Gershwin
Lyrics by Ira Gershwin
Book Staged by Felix Edwardes
Dances and Ensembles staged by Sammy Lee
The settings designed by and executed under
the direction of Norman Bel-Geddes

Red Lights Denote Exits

Derham car painting is painting de luxe.

Sheet Music of Musical Selection 35c a Copy—3
for $1.00—AT WEYMANN'S, 1108 Chestnut St.

Forrest Theatre

Box Office Open 9 A. M. to 10 P. M.

Orders for seats may be sent by mail or telegraph.

Ladies' Parlor on the left of the Main Foyer.

Gentlemen's Smoking Room on the right of the Main Foyer.

Physicians or persons expecting a call during the performance should notify the Head Usher.

All articles found in the Theatre should be handed in at the Box Office.

Inquiries regarding lost articles should be made to the Treasurer.

Hats, Wraps, Umbrellas, etc., may be checked in the Ladies' Parlor or Gentlemen's Cloak Room free of charge.

PAGE & SHAW CANDIES

FRESH DAILY

One Sale in Rear of Foyer

OUR FAMILY WASH SERVICE

Ironed at Washwoman's Prices

COMPLETE FAMILY SERVICE

means Flat Work such as Bed and Table Linen and all wearing apparel, completely finished ready to wear or use.

METHOD OF CHARGING

Total weight of bundle @ 10c. per lb., plus additional charge for Ironing the Wearing Apparel 35c lb.

Minimum Charge on this Bundle $2.00

LOCUST LAUNDRY

236-242 S. 9th St.

Phone, Walnut 4011

Forrest Theatre

THE CAST
(Characters as they appear)

News Girl ....Edna Farrell
Milk Boy ....Dorothy Hollis
Housemaid ....Janearl Johnson
Errand Girl ....Dorothy Donovan
Policeman ....Don Rowan
Dick Trevor ....Fred Astaire
Jeff ....Cliff Edwards
Susan Trevor ....Adele Astaire
Jack Robinson ....Alan Edwards
Shirley Vernon ....Brenda Bond
Bertie Bassett.......Gerald Oliver Smith
Daisy Parke ....Cecil Bruner
J. Watterson Watkins...........Walter Catlett
Josephine Vanderwater ....Jayne Auburn
Ruth ....Paulette Winston
Flunkey ....Edward Jephson
Manuel Estrada ....Bryan Lycan
Victor Arden ....Victor Arden
Phil Ohman ....Phil Ohman
Rufus Parke ....William Wadsworth

Ladies of the Ensemble

Mary Hutchinson, Lillian Michell, Esther Morris, Tony Otto, Peggy Hart, Dorothy Hollis, Paulette Winston, Sylvia Shawn, Gertrude Livingstone, Janearl Johnson, Jessie Payne, Edna Farrell, Dorothy Hughes, Madeline Janis, Mildred Stevens, Dorothy Donovan, Frances Lindell, Peggy Pitou, Doris Waldron, Peggy Quinn, Louise Wright, Elmira Lane, Irene Wiley, Grace Jones and Maxine Henry.

Gentlemen of the Ensemble

Dan Sparks, Richard Devonshire, Alfred Hale, Jack Fraley, Harry Howell, Charles Bannister, Lionel Maclyn, Richard Renaud, Hal Crusins, Ward Arnold, Francis Murphy and Charles LaValle.

ACT I.

Scene 1. Sidewalk in front of the old Trevor Homestead, Beacon Hill, R. I.
Scene 2. Entrance of the Vanderwater estate.
Scene 3. The Vanderwater Garden Party.
(Three days elapse between Acts I and II.)

ACT II.

Scene 1. The Anchorage Hotel, Eastern Harbor, Conn.
Scene 2. A suite in the hotel.
Scene 3. Garden of the hotel.
Scene 4. The Eastern Harbor Yacht Club.

MUSICAL NUMBERS

Orchestra under the direction of Paul J. Lannin

ACT I.

1. Opening—Seeing Dickie Home........Boys
2. Numberette—The Man I Love.......Susie
3. Hang On to Me...........Dick and Susie
4. End of a String.................Ensemble
5. We're Here Because..........Daisy, Bertie and Guests.
6. Fascinating Rhythm..Susie, Dick and Jeff
7. So Am I..................Jack and Susie
8. Oh, Lady, Be Good........Watty and Girls
   (Piano Specialty—Victor Arden and Phil Ohman)
9. Finale .... Ensemble

NOW PLAYING

A musical event of more than ordinary interest is promised at the Forrest Theater, on Monday evening, November 17, in the presentation of "Lady, Be Good," a brand-new musical comedy in which the Astaires, Fred—Adele, and Walter Catlett are the chief luminaries. The engagement is just for two weeks.

Incidentally, the piece marks the return to the American stage of the Astaires, who recently returned to this country after scoring a tremendous success in London, in a musical play entitled "Stop Flirting." The pieces opened at the Shaftesbury Theater on May 20, 1923. The Astaires appeared in the production for exactly 18 months and during this engagement they never missed a single performance. They simply danced their way into the hearts of every one in the British capital. The Mountbattens rarely let a week pass by since the opening of "Stop Flirting" without seeing them; the Princess Royal, an inveterate theatergoer, who generously chooses plays of a more intellectual kind, witnessed the piece five times; and the Duke and Duchess of York, the Prince of Wales, and the other two princes attended the show on numerous occasions. The Astaires dined publicly with royalty, and have been the guests at the houses of some of the most exclusive English society. They could have remained another season in London had it not been for a contract they entered into last summer calling for their appearance in America in "Lady, Be Good."

"Lady, Be Good," by the way, is the latest production to be sponsored by Alex A. Aarons and Vinton Freedley, who have been confining most of their activities to the London stage. Incidentally, Mr. Freedley was born and bred in Philadelphia and, tho a lawyer by profession, he gave up his law practice so that he could devote his entire time to the theater.

The principal comedy role in "Lady, Be Good" is in the capable hands of Walter Catlett. who is said to have a role that fits him like the proverbial glove.

Cliff Edwards. known in vaudeville and on the recording discs as "Ukulele Ike." is another player of note in the piece.

Alan Edwards portrays the juvenile role: Miss Brenda Bond is the ingenue: Victor Arden and Phil Ohman, two ivory incinerators. make their stage debut in "Lady, Be Good." They have been confining their efforts heretofore to phonograph recording: Gerald Oliver Smith has also been cast for an important role: and last, but not least, the piece also boasts of a fascinating chorus.

great Marilyn Miller, and again it was cut before the show reached Broadway. Three strikes, but the song wasn't dead yet.

Then English socialite Lady Edwina Mountbatten heard the song—maybe she caught George playing it at a party in New York. She took a copy back home and it was arranged for the Berkeley Square Orchestra. Bands in England started playing the song and it became a hit. Helen Morgan, a well-known torch singer, sang it in her nightclub act, and by 1929 "The Man I Love" was a very familiar Gershwin number, having received

ship with him. Knowing what I do about the two of them, my guess is that the gregarious and canny Adele pursued George with a vengeance but he, for various and perhaps complex reasons, was not ultimately interested. A signed photo given to Adele from him around the time of *Lady, Be Good!* is poignantly inscribed with several bars of music from "The Man I Love."

Following Helen Morgan's there came many great renditions of "The Man I Love," from Sophie Tucker's to Art Tatum's to Billie Holiday's to Eydie Gorme's, though Ira always preferred a

> GREGARIOUS AND CANNY ADELE PURSUED GEORGE WITH A VENGEANCE, BUT HE WAS NOT INTERESTED.

several recordings the previous year. In 1934 on his radio show, George credited Morgan for much of the song's success. Despite being famous for performing the song, Helen Morgan never recorded it. She would have sung it with depth, resonance, and pathos as a woman wronged. (When Gershwin appeared on Rudy Vallee's radio show, the accompanying rendition of the song was performed by Kitty Carlisle. According to songwriter Hugh Martin, Morgan supposedly did once sing it on Vallee's show herself, but that rendition, perhaps the only chance we have of ever hearing it, has never surfaced.)

By contrast to Helen Morgan, Adele Astaire was a flapper with a chirpy voice that had fewer nuances than Morgan's, yet in an ironic twist, in life she was quite nuanced enough to have a crush on George and desired to have a deeper relation-

relatively straight, nonhistrionic rendering that was not jazzy. It's very moving to hear Gershwin's own recording of the work, thankfully preserved on a scratchy 1934 radio broadcast of *Music by Gershwin*, a series from which only three episodes still exist. George mentions Helen Morgan and then plays a virtuoso piano version with a woman singing the song in Morgan's style. Even in dim low fidelity, the song shines through. George's rendition of the deceptively simple theme was captured before decades of reinterpretations embellished the song until it became a slick emotional opus. Because it's for radio, the rendition seems a little rushed. There's a piano variation in George's 1932 songbook emotively arranged for that solo instrument, and the song is quite languid and beautiful there. This is the version—so plaintive and honest—I like best.

It's impossible for me to hear the instrumental rendering of a song without the lyric popping into my head. Even though there is a naïveté about Ira's lyric, its sincerity is evocative of a point of view that has since disappeared. As a chronicler of historical music, I love to be transported to another era, and that happens the instant I hear the first bars of "The Man I Love."

I've played "The Man I Love" many times and in many different ways. Women singers have asked me to accompany them and I always say a prayer that all will turn out right. The overwrought interpretation is the style today, and singers think they have to stomp on a song. I'd rather these singers tried some sort of primal scream therapy, out of public view. Restraint is required to capture the emotion of this song. The delicacy of the lyric requires a very specific emotional point of view to justify the purveyor's behavior and thus engender empathy, not a standing ovation.

I frequently get requests for "The Man I Love." There's still something so damned insistent about the melody. You hear it once and you must hear it again. It's like eating potato chips—only more satisfying and heart-healthy to boot.

LADY, BE GOOD! was a huge success. Its long run established the brother-and-sister team of Fred and Adele Astaire as Broadway stars. It established the Gershwin brothers as a hot Broadway writing team and helped them buy their new house on West 103rd Street in Manhattan. It established Alex Aarons and Vinton Freedley as a successful producing team and was part of the reason they could build the Alvin Theatre (named for ALex Aarons and VINton Freedley), which opened in 1927 at 52nd and Broadway and is now called the Neil Simon Theatre. The Astaires worked with George again in 1927 with *Funny Face*, and Aarons and Freedley continued to produce Gershwin shows until the Depression caused their finances—along with those of millions of others—to fall apart.

George and Ira's musicals played in many other of the same theaters we have today. *Oh, Kay!* was staged at the Imperial Theatre, built in 1923. It was home in the thirties to the Gershwins' *Of Thee I Sing* and *Let 'Em Eat Cake* and, in the decades since, to *Oliver!*, *Cabaret*, *Les Miserables*, and more recently *Billy Elliot*. The Imperial seats more than 1,400 people and if the audiences who go to the theater have changed, so surely has the way they listen to the show. People are now so accustomed

Photo and message from George inscribed to Adele Astaire with a quotation from "The Man I Love."

George performing at the opening of the Manhattan Theatre in 1931.

to amplified sound that they take it for granted. Back then, the audience had to listen closely if they wanted to hear everything. I think the concentration that seeing a show required made the experience that much more intense. I also believe this is why sopranos were so popular then, because a higher voice carried very well in the theater. A high tenor or a baritone also worked well because those are loud, full-bodied voices. Crooning and any singing into your beard had less chance of being heard. Even the pit orchestras had to play relatively quietly so they didn't drown out the singers.

THE BROTHERS' NEXT SHOW after *Lady, Be Good!* was *Tell Me More*, which opened at the Gaiety Theatre in April 1925, just four and a half months after the opening of *Lady, Be Good!*, which was still running. Part of the writing team for that show was reassembled: the book was by Fred Thompson and William K. Wells, George wrote the music, and Ira the lyrics, with Buddy DeSylva. The *Times* review lauded the songs "Tell Me More," "Kickin' the Clouds Away," and "My Fair Lady." The reviewer looked forward to being annoyed hearing them for the thousandth time, "on the country's radios and in the country's road-houses" over the summer. The book, the reviewer said, would just about do, and he noted that there were skilled comedians (Lou Holtz and Andrew Tombes) to entertain between songs.

The last paragraph of the review could be used as a summary of what worked with all of these musical comedies when they were successful: "There is, then, a first-class Gershwin score, adequate comedy, intelligent lyrics, an appealing young heroine [in this case, Phyllis Cleveland] and fast and furious dancing by a personal chorus to *Tell Me More*. It seems to be enough."

Notable Gershwin musicals of the twenties include: *Lady, Be Good!* (1924), *Tell Me More* (1925), *Tip-Toes* (1925), *Oh, Kay!* (1926), *Funny Face* (1927), *Rosalie* (1928), *Show Girl* (1929), and, ushering in the new decade, *Strike Up the Band* (1930). So many of the greatest Gershwin songs originated in these shows. The songs are still standards but the lightweight shows from whence they came are rarely performed, explaining why *My One and Only* and the 1992 all-Gershwin show *Crazy for You* have supplanted them for contemporary theater audiences.

This is not to criticize George and Ira for not being involved in more "serious" musical theater. George's desire to do weightier work would soon come to fruition, as he was about to conceive the idea to write *Porgy and Bess*, and most of Ira's lyrics were as sophisticated as they came. But there are reasons we remember the songs rather than the shows. The musical comedy itself was evolving. These eight shows of George and Ira's are the apogee of one particular style, but another was coming into vogue. In the mid-

twenties the Broadway musical was moving toward the integration of the songs with the book to produce a fuller theatrical experience. There was a yearning for more, and a few brave souls were part of the vanguard of change.

TWO SHOWS ABOVE ALL others are seminal in the history of musical theater. The first is *Show Boat*, which premiered in 1927. Ira and George were working on *Funny Face*, which played out of town at the same time *Show Boat* had tryouts in Washington, D.C., Pittsburgh, Cleveland, and Philadelphia, before opening in New York on December 27. (Think about how much theater was available on Broadway back then: eleven productions opened the previous night.) *Show Boat* ran until May 1929. Ira said there was no talk at the time that it was a groundbreaking musical as it previewed out of town during the same time they were feverishly working on *Funny Face*. For *Show Boat*, Jerome Kern and Oscar Hammerstein adapted Edna Ferber's 1926 novel of the same name. Set in part on the *Cotton Blossom*, a Mississippi riverboat, from the 1880s on, the play deals with miscegenation—two of the characters, Julie and Steve, are barred from performing because Julie is black and Steve is partly white. Marriages break up; people drink. The music is teamed with the sharply drawn characters and the plot is advanced by the songs. And Kern and Hammerstein wrote wonderful songs—"Ol' Man River" and "Can't Help Lovin' Dat Man"—but they were fully integrated into the plot. This was a serious play with music, rather than a standard musical with a book that mainly served to set up the songs. The show was all the more surprising because it was produced by

Florenz Ziegfeld, the last producer one would imagine caring about a solid book for a show; he was all about pretty girls and glamour.

Show Boat didn't change musical theater overnight, or even over a decade. Through the rest of the twenties and into the thirties, stars were still the paramount consideration, followed by the songs. Still, the books for shows in the thirties were generally stronger than those of the previous decade, and choreography started to become slightly more integrated to story.

Early in the thirties, reviews and operettas were very still much in vogue. Operettas were something of a throwback to an earlier style of

(CLOCKWISE FROM TOP) *Gertrude McDonald and Fred Astaire in* Funny Face • *Lawrence at the time of* Oh, Kay! • *Ginger Rogers in* Girl Crazy *in 1930* • *Gertrude Lawrence and the cast of* Oh, Kay!

music. While there is a lot of overlap, an operetta is lighter and less formal than an opera, but it has more conventions than a musical. There might be sung recitative as in an opera, for example. Operettas are Old World and European-style, and are often about royalty, as opposed to musicals with American settings and more snap and swagger.

Things started to change with the death of composing giant Victor Herbert in 1924, but Sigmund Romberg, Rudolf Friml, and many others continued to thrive with the last great wave of gorgeous unfettered melody in operetta form, though Romberg (later a next-door neighbor to Ira) was a well-rounded composer who easily

(CLOCKWISE FROM TOP) *Oscar Shaw and Gertrude Lawrence in* Oh, Kay! • *Lou Clayton, Eddie Jackson, Ruby Keeler, and Jimmy Durante in* Show Girl • *Ginger Rogers and The Foursome in* Girl Crazy.

adapted with changing musical styles. A younger group of songwriters and composers—like Rodgers and Hart, and Howard Dietz and Arthur Schwartz—was writing a more modern type of musical that advanced the form, integrating the book and the songs into more of an artistic whole. *The Band Wagon* (1931) was a big success, one of the best of all the revues. (Fred and Adele Astaire danced together in it for the last time.) George S. Kaufman wrote the book and Dietz was an exceedingly clever lyricist and a great satirist who deserves his own biography. He wrote songs that reflected the morals and feelings of the time, like "Confession":

> *I've never kissed a man before /*
> *Before I knew his name.*

PERHAPS LYRICISTS ON BROADWAY were able to get away with more than writers in other media. Cole Porter's "Love for Sale," from *The New Yorkers* of 1930, was banned from the radio. In the show, the song was taken away from a white character and given to an African-American because it was considered unseemly for a white woman to be a prostitute. Oy. Porter and Rodgers and Hart were ushering in a new kind of sensibility in their songs, and the plots inevitably had to follow suit.

While there were other interesting experiments over the years, the second generally accepted groundbreaking show was Rodgers and Hammerstein's first collaboration, *Oklahoma!*, which opened on Broadway in March 1943 and ran for over five years—more than 2,200 performances. It seemed an unlikely show to change the world. It was based on a moderately successful 1931 play, *Green Grow the Lilacs*, by Lynn Riggs. Rodgers and Hammerstein's musical seemed to lack all the elements that were de rigueur at the time. The show was still called *Away We Go* when producer Mike Todd saw it in tryouts in New Haven. He was overheard in the lobby of the theater expressing his displeasure. Gossip columnist Walter Winchell anonymously quoted him uttering the now famous line: "No jokes, no legs, no chance" (and substituted "legs" for "tits," which is what Todd actually uttered).

It's true that there were no chorus girls, no comedians, and no traditional "eleven o'clock number"—the roof raiser at the end of the evening. If the plot, the story of the romance of cowboy Curly McLain and Laurey Williams and of Jud, the farmhand who stands between them, wasn't revolutionary; what *Oklahoma!* did have was a stirring ballet, a dance that was tied into the story. This was the point. All the elements were closely integrated to create a modern musical play. And there were so many great songs: "Oh, What a Beautiful Morning," "The Surrey with the Fringe on Top," "People Will Say We're in Love," and, of course, "Oklahoma!" The dramatic strength of the show combined with the great music are what made *Oklahoma!* popular for revivals. The same is true of *Show Boat*. They will play as long as there are theaters and people willing to spend money to visit them.

The most lasting shows are the ones with books that are equal in power to the score and have become universally recognized as the greatest examples of musical theater: *My Fair Lady, Gypsy, Guys and Dolls, West Side Story, The Music*

Man—all of these have survived because they possess a timeless quality that appeals to each succeeding generation.

The influence of *Show Boat* and *Oklahoma!* on American musical theater is incalculable. Change came slowly but the public's expectations shifted, and eventually it wasn't enough just to have a good score. Years later when I worked for him, Ira realized in retrospect that he and George had been left behind. How could their shows ever have a chance of being revived? Who could have predicted that people would even care about their work fifty years later?

HAD GEORGE LIVED HE WOULD HAVE WRITTEN MORE MUSICALS WITH IRA, AND THEY'D HAVE THRIVED UNDER THE NEW RULES.

Ira blamed the Gershwins' principal producers, Aarons and Freedley, for making shows with a limited shelf life. He thought that Aarons and Freedley cared less about plots than did other producers of the twenties and thirties and believed that the Gershwin shows would have had stronger books and more potential for revival if they had been produced by Laurence Schwab and Frank Mandel.

I'm not sure that Ira's argument stands up. Schwab and Mandel were indeed very prominent producers—George worked with them in 1923–24 on *Sweet Little Devil* (Schwab and Mandel wrote the book and George and Buddy DeSylva the songs). They also produced the Sigmund Romberg–Oscar Hammerstein shows *The Desert Song* (1926) and *The New Moon* (1928) and the DeSylva-Brown-Henderson musicals *Good News!* (1927) and *Follow Thru* (1929). (Buddy DeSylva, lyricist Lew Brown, and composer Ray Henderson teamed up to write a string of hit musicals between 1925 and 1930.) Perhaps the plots of these shows are a little more cohesive than the standard fare of the time, but I don't think they hold up any better than other shows of the period, and they certainly aren't of the *Show Boat* caliber. It's clear to me, however, that had George lived he would have written more musicals with Ira, and they'd have thrived under the new rules.

WHILE THE AIM OF THE GAME on Broadway today is the same as it has always been (to fill the house!), the rules have changed completely. In George's day, the producer would start with the stars and proceed from there; now you have to make sure every element—the producer, the money, the stars, the show, the theater—is in place before you make the leap into commitment. It takes a lot more money, relatively speaking, to stage a musical than it did in 1924, and there are fewer theaters to stage them in. The book also needs to be more sophisticated than it was then, although that's not the case on every occasion. It's the other elements that interest people, like the staging and choreography, or spectacular production values or the charisma of a star, and they can be enough to make a show successful. For a show to succeed in spite of a mediocre or bad musical

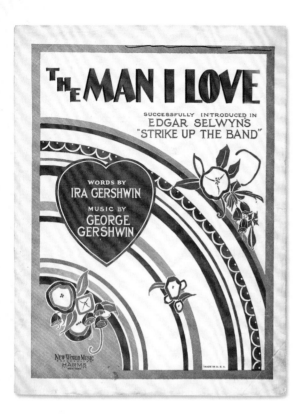

score was unthinkable in the Gershwin era, and it's not necessarily that people were more sophisticated; they just knew the difference.

Andrew Lloyd Webber has brought about a return to some of my least favorite characteristics of the operetta form. At the same time as George and Ira were working, Sigmund Romberg and Rudolf Friml were writing operettas with long recitatives, sometimes syrupy melodies, and music that could go on far too long because it usually wasn't supported by lyrics of quality and contemporary significance. Yet the craft of such masters made the shows acceptable, as their music was often inspired and heartrending. Emotion was expressed in the music and that seemed to be enough to

satisfy an audience when plot was often not present in any situation. The great Oscar Hammerstein worked with Romberg on some of those operettas, yet while his lyrics contain some fine work, many of them are light-years away in sensibility from what he was to create a short time later.

By the forties, the modernizers, especially Rodgers and Hammerstein, came along and eventually found a way to integrate plot and story. They were talented and sophisticated enough to also give us the classic theater songs that cleverly and concisely expressed the human condition on a level that resonated with the audience and sounded the death knell for the long-winded operetta form with all its artifice.

Sheet music covers and, second from right, an ad for "The Man I Love."

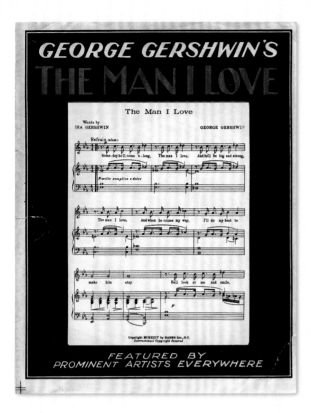

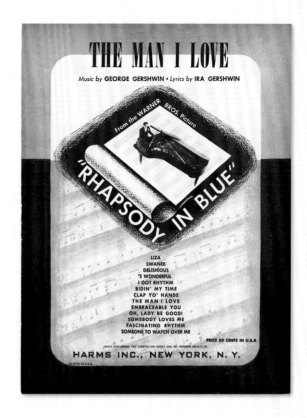

Similarly, the past few decades' return to the premodern conventions of operetta has provoked a counterreaction of its own: we have shows with scores of rock and pop amalgams, intended to better express contemporary life. If they work, it's healthy for Broadway, but most of these, too, I've found limited in what they express, not because of the form itself, but because of the way these particular shows are written. The goal of musical theater is to say through songs what cannot be expressed in any other way, and in the process move the audience a quantum leap forward by the end of the song. In *Gypsy*, when the character of Mama Rose sings "Everything's Coming Up Roses," we truly understand the depth of the deter-mination and drive of the character in a way that was not palpable hitherto. It's a defining moment in the show. How many songs in shows today produce such searing and defining experiences?

My hope for today's musical theater is a return to the kind of song that leaves an audience breathless with excitement and fervor for the portrayal of humanity with all its flourishes and flaws. The hope of musical theater is first and foremost in its music, and I resolutely carry hope that the many talented writers who are working today can put the focus back on that aspect. It's not about going back to the old days; it's about finding the new voices that can evolve the form and remain pertinent. We already have the great music of the past and it will never go away, and we can learn a lot from its staying power, but not always when those songs are recycled into a new musical.

Other current shows succeed because they take existing songs and weave a book around them. *Jersey Boys*, which tells the story of the 4 Seasons pop group utilizing many of its songs, is brilliantly conceived. The book by Marshall Brickman and Rick Elice puts the songs into a theatrical context that amplifies them. For me it works dazzlingly well.

The number of musicals that have wings and last has vastly diminished over the years. Real longevity comes from going on the road, from a recording, and perhaps eventually a movie. While a show might be a great success on Broadway, there are many factors that might inhibit its chances of having a long, healthy life, the first being the financial consideration. It's like hitting the lottery to have a hit, and when a show hits, it hits big. A musical's success can also depend on how well it will travel to schools, colleges, and community theaters.

One of the shows that has been a huge success and will certainly become one of the most produced musicals of its generation is *Hairspray*. *Wicked*, in spite of tepid reviews, will likely become a classic because of its appeal to a younger generation and its producibility for regional theaters, whenever it becomes available for smaller theaters. The producers have cannily held back amateur rights until they feel it has run its course on Broadway.

Chicago has become an unexpected classic. While it originally had a respectable run on Broadway, its revival spawned a renewed appreciation, and turned a show that was dimly remembered into a blockbuster. Sondheim's shows, particularly *A Little Night Music* and *Sweeney Todd*, are regularly revived and will always be timeless in their appeal. *Follies*, which was recently revived at the Kennedy Center and on Broadway, is one of my favorite scores and yet the book of the show has never totally satisfied me. I always wish that there had been one more song written for the four main characters at the very end, thus giving the audience the final musical-emotional moment it craves. Still, there's a lot I love about that show.

I truly don't know if anyone will care about *Spring Awakening* in fifty years, nor do I suspect that *The Book of Mormon* has the resonance to appeal to future generations in the way it affects us now, but your opinion is as valid as mine. It's all a crapshoot!

The classic shows will continue to be revived at the demands of other theatergoers, but we're getting further and further away from doing anything that's even slightly obscure. People now want to see revivals of *Gypsy* and *Guys and Dolls*. *Finian's Rainbow*, a show with an incredible score and a once socially significant book, finally came back to Broadway in 2009. It had a great cast—Kate Baldwin, Cheyenne Jackson, Jim Norton—and it got good-to-great reviews but ran fewer than a hundred performances. I liked the inventive way that *South Pacific* was gently massaged and reworked to give the impression that people were seeing the original production faithfully remounted when it secretly had an expert face lift of the libretto for a modern sensibility, but, boy, that "Honey Bun" number still made me cringe.

Today there are very few producers who will stage a show for the art alone. The producer Jeffrey Richards has produced many kinds of theater, and staged some significant and successful musicals, but he produces at least one straight play a season that he simply considers culturally important and hopes the audience will agree. He knows there is a chance it's not going to make money, but he insists on putting on a classic play because he feels it's his responsibility. There are very few people who will do that.

IT'S ESSENTIAL to TRY and MAKE ALL KINDS of ENTERTAINMENT AVAILABLE to EVERYBODY and NOT a SELECT FEW.

It's also much more difficult to succeed in the musical theater now because the cost of seeing live entertainment has gone up dramatically and so has the cost of staging it. Ira told me that it was relatively inexpensive to produce a lavish show like *Of Thee I Sing,* and he even uncharacteristically invested in it. By the sixties the cost of putting on a show had skyrocketed. P. G. Wodehouse wrote a letter to Ira after reading that a million dollars was spent to produce a show, then considered an astronomical amount. In conclusion, his letter said, "Ira, we are well out of it."

My club, Feinstein's at the Loews Regency, is housed in a union-run hotel, and the staff are wonderful, dedicated people with whom I love to work. To earn the appellation of a five-star hotel we are required by the union to hire a minimum number of employees. So even to open the doors,

it costs a set amount. Yet we always have a number of lower-priced seats for every show, without the expected minimum food or beverage charge, and for one reason: it's essential to try and make all kinds of entertainment available to everybody and not a select few. That's what helps keep the place alive. It's never been easy to make money in the nightclub business; it truly is a labor of love. The old joke goes: How do you own a nightclub and have a million dollars? Easy, start with two million!

Certain kinds of rules and regulations have led to problems of perception of the musician's union when it comes to Broadway. Producers are using smaller bands and in many cases synthesizers and recorded music to deal with the economics of such situations. There's a fine line between protecting the interests of the musicians and sabotaging them by asking for too much. It's a tough call, and yet I can't stand to see a classic show like *Gypsy* revived with a smaller orchestra. In my head I can always hear the voice of composer Jule Styne screaming from the grave about what they're doing to his score. And, boy, could he scream when he wasn't happy! (One time in a recording session with Jule, we finished a take of a song and the recording engineer asked for another because he didn't quite capture the first one. When eighty-six-year-old Jule started screaming, the engineer said, "Take it easy, Mr. Styne, or you'll have a heart attack." Jule screamed back, "I'll cause a heart attack but I won't have one!")

Another factor in the relative marginalization of Broadway is the lack of any kind of musical education in schools and the ensuing fragmentation of musical taste. When I was growing up it wasn't only gay people who had original cast recordings in their homes. Everyone had *My Fair Lady*, *The Music Man*, *Gypsy*, *West Side Story*. Now if someone has these CDs in their home, a certain assumption is made. I'm half kidding, but a lot of people do jump to a conclusion.

Today, we consume Broadway in show-sized portions, when in the twenties music lovers were more likely to go song by song. Songs like "The Man I Love" could be set adrift on the river, get caught in eddies and whirlpools, yet emerge in the bay in one glorious piece. There were so many shows opening and closing on Broadway and they existed primarily as vehicles for the songs. When a new show does get produced on Broadway and it turns out not to be a success, there might be certain songs that are gold nuggets in the river, but it's harder for those songs to survive. Usually they're lost with the production.

And songwriters are creating great songs, but their shows aren't being seen as widely. There are the Ricky Ian Gordons and John Bucchinos; Adam Guettel, Marcy Heisler, and Zina Goldrich; and a formidable number of others. But they aren't getting produced on Broadway in today's climate that ensures producers want to play it safe. The craft of the composer and lyricist, while still appreciated and loved by knowledgeable fans, is reduced in importance. To George and Ira, today's Broadway would look a lot like their Hollywood—the bottom line is the bottom line and art be damned. The financial stakes are so high that producers will go with an apparently safe bet like *The Addams Family* or *Spider-Man* because they are familiar brand names that are more likely to bring in an audience than an original work, which while far superior in quality will not resonate with the masses.

So where does it all leave us? To quote another George and Ira song, "Who Cares?" Who cares for the songs and the musical theater? Who is able to nurture their soul in song when most of the world is more concerned with finding a cloud to keep their music on? In short, where does "The Man I Love" fit in today?

It saddens me to see the reduced emphasis on music in today's culture. Perhaps the confused and hurried nature of our era, coupled with our emphasis on technology and immediate gratification, has erased the ability to appreciate a more subtle craft. But as we move through these volatile times, I continue to hope that music will take back the role it once played in society, bringing back a calmer and more communal spirit. The shared bond of music is one that can erase the chasm between red state and blue state. Bringing people together is what, for example, the Gershwin songs have always done.

One friend of mine observed that people no longer whistle. After pondering that thought I went out to roam the streets to see if it was true. The thought alarmed me, because my father always whistled and that sound was of seminal comfort. So I spent what seemed like an eternity wandering around, strolling the streets in search of any whistler, anywhere. Exhausted and disheartened by the sea of silent iPods, I was ready to surrender and head home. Then I thought I heard the faint, ghostly sound of a trill in the air coming from somewhere. But where? I rounded the next corner to find the sound emanating from a man blissfully whistling to no one in particular. Then I recognized the familiar melody.

"The Man I Love." ·

(OPPOSITE) *Humorous lyrics for "The Man I Love" in Ira's handwriting.*

I knew I'd come along
the man I love
My mirror can't be ~~wrong~~ strong
song

And when I came my way

I'm building me a home
~~For~~ ~~August~~ meant for one
From which I'll never roam

And so all else above
I'm lucky I'm the man I love

"'S WONDERFUL"

— from *Funny Face*, 1927 —

VERSE 1
PETER:

Life has just begun:
Jack has found his Jill.
Don't know what you've done,
But I'm all a-thrill.
How can words express
Your divine appeal?
You could never guess
All the love I feel.
From now on, lady, I insist,
For me no other girls exist.

REFRAIN 1

'S wonderful! 'S marvelous—
You should care for me!
'S awful nice! 'S Paradise—
'S what I love to see!
You've made my life so glamorous,
You can't blame me for feeling amorous.
Oh, 's wonderful! 'S marvelous—
That you should care for me!

VERSE 2
FRANKIE:

Don't mind telling you
In my humble fash
That you thrill me through
With a tender pash.

When you said you care,
'Magine my emosh;
I swore, then and there,
Permanent devosh.
You made all other boys seem blah;
Just you alone filled me with AAH!

REFRAIN 2

'S wonderful! 'S marvelous—
You should care for me!
'S awful nice! 'S Paradise—
'S what I love to see!
My dear, it's four-leaf clover time;
From now on my heart's
working overtime.
Oh, 's wonderful! 'S marvelous—
That you should care for me!

CHAPTER 3

IRA AND ME

'VE ALWAYS LOVED OLD THINGS, any object that had history attached to it. For as long as I can remember, I'd go out of my way to find curios from the past, in my home or a relative's or, later, at an antiques shop or Goodwill store. Even the most insignificant piece of bric-a-brac tells a story. I'd pick up an old plate or a newspaper or a pocket watch and long to experience the times in which the object I was holding first existed. An old magazine or book can provide a fascinating glimpse into the past, but for me, nothing is more evocative than music. If you put an old record on a turntable and close your eyes, you're transported back to, say, 1924 and that precise moment in time comes alive. (What, you don't have a turntable? What era are you living in? Oops, I forgot.)

I have always connected with music on a deep emotional level, and to old music much more than the contemporary stuff I was hearing on the radio. Why, I don't know. Perhaps I was reincarnated and "remembered" the older music from another life. Or perhaps the pull of the beautiful harmonies and peerless melodies was a balm for a delicate soul left cold by the music of my own era. People should give youngsters more credit when it comes to musical taste. (If I had been exposed to *Barney* when I was a child, I might have grown up to be an axe murderer in protest.)

Ira and Michael Feinstein.

In my earliest memories there was always music in my house, and I was about five when I started collecting records. My family and I lived in Columbus, Ohio, and I'd constantly ask my parents to take me to thrift shops or junk stores to look for 78s (referring to 78 rpm, the speed of old-style singles). Why 78s? Because I was always fascinated by things that were old. When I was old enough to travel on my own, I'd pay fifty cents to take the bus downtown so that I could hunt for treasure. I'd trawl through used bookstores and record stores and anywhere else where something might turn up. It wasn't easy for me to find old records in those days (it's a snap now with the Internet) yet I still managed to amass a respectable collection.

It was a solitary pursuit and a secret one. None of my friends was interested in music, especially the kind of music I liked. Collecting 78s was an unusual passion for a kid. My family knew about my obsession, of course. My father built shelves out of cement blocks and boards to hold all the 78s I unearthed. He painted the cement white and the boards black, and I remember my mother commenting that the cinder blocks soaked up a lot of paint. Mom had a penchant for the black-and-white decor, so the shelves fit in with her grand aesthetic plan.

Once I came into a windfall from someone in the family. My uncle and aunt had hundreds of 78s in their basement and, before they moved to Florida, my uncle Henry gave me the whole collection. Every time he saw me after that, Uncle Henry would remind me how much the records he'd given me might have fetched if he'd sold them instead, until I was ready to give them back just to get him to cease and desist. Later I got some more records from my aunt Sylvia, with one of the songs being "Whispering," played by Art Hickman's orchestra, which was the oldest record I had ever encountered. It was from 1920 and had a tinny acoustic sound that fascinated me as I played it over and over. It brought a pang to my heart as I imagined all of the musicians making music in earnest, now all long gone, and here I was listening to those three minutes, captured forever. Other relatives would tell me how they'd thrown out all their old 78s—a painful story that's familiar to many people. I just wish that they wouldn't tell those stories with such sadistic glee as they describe the destruction process.

I started playing the piano at the age of five and it came naturally to me. I simply sat down and started to bang out a tune with both hands. I always found the piano quite a natural thing, so much so that I once assumed that I might be

The author, left, in costume in 1961.

able to play other instruments with equal facility. (I was wrong, of course.) The first thing I played on the piano was "Do-Re-Mi" from *The Sound of Music*, and from then on I'd try and play whatever I heard. Later, as I learned more formally, I taught myself about the history of music. I was most interested in pianists but I discovered singers like Bing Crosby and Al Jolson along the way.

I was listening and learning all the time. I'd ask relatives about a song and they'd tell me what they remembered. Eventually I started to recognize composers and songwriters and their shows. I'd also pick up sheet music every now and then. Once I bought a box of old promotional sheet music that had belonged to a theater organist named Ora Shore. (I know that because her name was written on many of the song sheets, a habit that greatly devalues a vintage sheet.) Thus I instantly had a collection of prime twenties tunes, but without the decorative covers that appeal to most collectors.

Before long, I preferred the kind of music reproduced exclusively on 78s, a period that began in the 1870s and ended in the fifties. At first I was mainly interested in the twenties and thirties, but I soon branched out into the forties and fifties and eventually included some theater music from the sixties and seventies in my library. Along the way I also discovered wire recordings (a precursor to the tape recorder in which the sound was stored on a very thin wire) and old reel-to-reel tapes, and occasionally would find large (sixteen-inch!) radio transcription discs that I was unable to play until I found an old, oversized turntable that had been abandoned at my high school.

Around 1973–74, my last years in high school, a number of Gershwin recordings were

released to celebrate the seventy-fifth anniversary of George's birth. I couldn't get enough of them. Several related books came out then, notably the coffee table book *The Gershwins*, by Robert Kimball and Alfred Simon, and an updated version of Ed Jablonski and Lawrence Stewart's *The Gershwin Years*. The former had a discography detailing every major original Gershwin cast recording, and the latter listed all the songs that could be found on LPs. This gave me a catalogue of all things Gershwin to search for. My birthday was in September, the same month as Gershwin's, so I was lucky enough to receive an infusion of the Gershwiniana that was issued in that month. The Kimball and Simon book alone was $25 and I couldn't have afforded it on my own.

A young Michael performing onstage.

Living in Columbus, I didn't have the collectors' outlets that once existed in other cities, but I still managed to find a good number of Gershwin recordings, including a few rarities. I was very happy to pick up the first original cast recording of a Gershwin work, a disc called *The Songs of Long Ago* on the Brunswick label. It was performed by Lester O'Keefe and featured in the *George White Scandals* of 1920. This record and all the 78s I've collected over the years have followed me from home to home and are now with me in California. It's not easy to transport 78s from place to place, because they are heavy and fragile. I play my 78s often because the sound has a special quality. Once you hear it, you understand. I don't have a problem listening to CDs, unlike some music professionals, who know that the sound on a CD is just an approximation of the music reassembled in digital bits. A 78, however, is a true acoustic reproduction of the original performance. While all music evokes a time and place, with a 78 I feel like I am just one step removed from being in the room with George Gershwin as he sits at the piano.

I T WAS THROUGH HIS RECORDING of Gershwin's *Rhapsody in Blue* that I became aware of the concert pianist Oscar Levant (he was many things, but a pianist first and foremost). Aside from Gershwin himself, Levant was the first pianist to record *Rhapsody in Blue*. He produced a book in 1940 called *A Smattering of Ignorance* (ghostwritten by music writer Irving Kolodin, to whom Oscar dedicated the book). The chapter on George is one of the best pieces of writing about him anywhere. Even Leonore Gershwin lauded it as the best, a high compliment. Composer Johnny Green said that of all of the acolytes surrounding Gershwin, Levant was the closest. At the recommendation of a teacher in my junior high school, I read Levant's other two books, *The Unimportance of Being Oscar* and *Memoirs of an Amnesiac*. When I found a paperback copy of *The Unimportance of Being Oscar* downtown in Columbus, I had just enough money to buy it for ninety-five cents and still pay the bus fare to get home. Levant was still alive at this time and I toyed with the idea of sending him a fan letter. Knowing what I do now about his struggles with drug addiction and mental illness during that time, it is doubtful that he

Gershwin's own recordings of the songs from Funny Face.

Oscar Levant, Jesse Lasky, Ira, Leonore, and Robert Alda during the filming of the George Gershwin biopic, Rhapsody in Blue, *released in 1945.*

would have been able to respond. Little did I dream that just a few years later his widow would become my close friend, and my first mentor.

I also knew of Oscar Levant from the all-but-fictitious Gershwin film biography *Rhapsody in Blue*, in which Levant played himself. (This film should be taken with a large pinch of salt: Levant himself described it as "preposterous.") I became fascinated, almost obsessed, with Levant because I thought he was so unusual, so talented, and so funny, plus I felt a resonance with his morbidity. I was an outcast at school and saw that Levant managed to achieve distinction for his nonconformity. Of course, I didn't take into account that he was also a genius. He was addicted to prescription drugs, including sleeping pills and Demerol, and spent time in and out of mental hospitals in the years before he died in 1972, but his remarkable wit always shone through in his books and on his syndicated television show, which ran from 1958 to 1960. My interest was also fueled by the fact that he had been very close to the Gershwins.

In 1976, when I was twenty, I moved to California. I'd wanted to live in Los Angeles for as long as I could remember. I knew I wanted to perform show music, so it would probably have made more sense for me to move to New York City, where there were more opportunities for someone with my specific interest in classic American popular songs and an audience to appreciate them, but it was Los Angeles or bust for me.

One of the first things I did when I got to L.A. was to visit a used record store in Hollywood to look for a copy of Oscar Levant's last album, issued in 1961. At one time Levant had been the best-selling classical artist for Columbia Records, but his career had waned by the time this disc was released, and it became the hardest of his recordings to find. Levant had retired from active concert performing in 1958 and was better known for his wicked wit than his music, a fact that pained him. Yet how can one forget his brilliant observations? For example, when singer Eddie Fisher left Debbie Reynolds for Elizabeth Taylor, Levant's comment

was "How high could anyone stoop?" He said Zsa Zsa Gabor discovered the secret of perpetual middle age. And he asked George, "If you had your life to live over, would you fall in love with yourself all over again?"

THIS WAS BY FAR THE MOST EXCITING TROVE I'D EVER SEEN AND I WANTED EVERYTHING.

The store I went to, the Record Collector, didn't have the desired album, but, to my great delight, the guy behind the counter said he had some of Levant's personal record collection for sale, which he had bought at an estate sale. My heart pounded as I discovered they were acetates, movie studio discs, and private recordings going back to 1934, and they included marvelous radio performances of Levant playing Gershwin, including renderings of George's pop songs he'd never recorded commercially. This was by far the most exciting trove I'd ever seen and, needless to say, I wanted everything. The price was $200. I put down fifty bucks and borrowed the rest from my parents. Just like that, the recordings were mine, though at the time it was for me a tremendous amount of money, and if my parents hadn't loaned me the dough, I probably would have robbed a bank to get it.

I settled down in Los Angeles working two jobs. At night I played in piano bars and by day I sold pianos at a store called Finnegan's Pianos in the

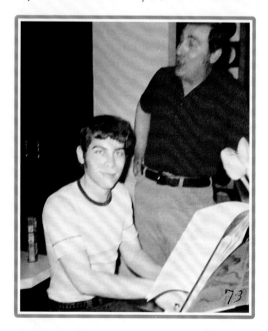

A teenage Michael at the piano with his father, Ed.

San Fernando Valley. I was a terrible salesman. I hated to see people spend so much money on a piano when I knew exactly how much Bill Finnegan, the store's owner, was marking them up. Finnegan would do anything to make a sale. He had a Steinway built in the 1870s in the store, and he'd tell customers that Richard Wagner had written *Lohengrin* on it. He also had exclusive marketing rights on a little ceramic shelled peanut warmer that he called "Liberace's Hot Nuts," which was emblazoned with the pianist's signature and a keyboard. For some reason nobody wanted Liberace's nuts, and Finnegan was stuck with a warehouse full of them.

I happened to mention my Levant recordings to a woman who worked with me at the piano store, and she said I should get in touch with

Levant's widow, June. This woman had a friend who worked at the William Morris agency and, a short time later, I was given a slip of paper with June Levant's home number and address. June lived in the Sierra Towers, the iconic high rise in Los Angeles that sits on the border of Beverly Hills and West Hollywood.

So I called June Levant from the piano store one day and introduced myself. When I told her I'd just bought some records that had belonged to her husband, she said that wasn't possible, since she had all of her husband's records. Then I told her that I'd found a letter addressed to Oscar tucked into the sleeve of one of the records. She recognized the name of the author of the letter—"Oh, that's Schuyler Chapin, who worked at Columbia Records," she said, but then got off the phone abruptly, telling me to try back in a couple of hours.

When I called back, she told me to come over and to bring the records. I didn't want to have to give the recordings back, so I said that they were very fragile and I didn't want to move them. It was true that some of them had been cut on a glass core and really were quite delicate, but, in reality, I didn't want to risk losing them.

When I went over the next day, June answered the door and was surprised to see this twenty-year-old kid standing before her. There was an older man there whom she introduced as Sam Marx, her attorney. I learned later that the two of them were dating, and June had him there for protection. Sam, I also discovered, was an old friend of the Gershwins' and had been present at the first performance of *Rhapsody in Blue* in 1924, and had saved the printed program. She asked me why I was so interested in her husband and I told her

The author, in the late nineteen seventies, doing what he loves.

that I loved his music. She said, "*His music*? What do you mean 'his music'?" Levant had written a number of songs, about eighty in all, but he felt so inferior to Gershwin as a songwriter that in 1942 he stopped composing. He also wrote a number of orchestral works, including a piano concerto, which was his last major work. I told June that I was referring to Oscar's songs and she said, "You know his songs?"

So I sat down at the upright piano in her living room and noticed that on top of it was an autographed photo of Horowitz inscribed to June with the apt inscription "To June Levant from HIS sincere admirer, Vladimir Horowitz." Then I played some Levant tunes. His only well-known song by that time was "Blame It on My Youth," but I played a bunch of the more obscure ones. June instantly warmed up and told me stories about her husband, but I already knew them all because I'd read his books. I had also audiotaped a television show in 1973 called *Jack Paar Tonight*, in which June had appeared a few months after Oscar died. (In the late fifties, Oscar had cemented his unique reputation via his frequent, and frequently memorable, appearances on Jack Paar's shows.) The 1973 show was a tribute to Levant that consisted of clips of his previous appearances, with June telling charming anecdotes throughout. Every time June started a story, I'd finish it. At one point, she started a story, then stopped to ask me, "Do you know this one?" When I said yes, she said, "Point killer."

June and I quickly became friends and she was very sweet to me. I'd go over to her apartment for lunch, and she'd take me to parties—one at the studio of Tony Duquette, a famous Hollywood designer, who worked with Oscar on the 1953 Cyd Charisse and Fred Astaire movie *The Band Wagon*. I went to Sam Goldwyn, Jr.'s house with June and played the same piano that George Gershwin had once played for Mr. Goldwyn, Sr., when previewing the score of *The Goldwyn Follies*, shortly before his death.

June finally figured out how her husband's records had turned up in that Hollywood record store. When she had moved from the home she had shared with Oscar on Roxbury Drive to her condo, she had designated which possessions should be sold. The records weren't supposed to be part of the consignment, but somehow about half of them ended in the estate auction. She had some of the discs, but I had the rest. There was no real rhyme or reason to what had been sold—I had parts one and two of Oscar's appearance on the *Bing Crosby Show*, for example, and she had parts three and four. June told me I could keep the

I WENT TO SAM GOLDWYN, JR.'S HOUSE WITH JUNE AND PLAYED THE SAME PIANO THAT GEORGE GERSHWIN HAD ONCE PLAYED FOR MR. GOLDWYN, SR.

records when she realized that I had no desire to make money from them.

June sometimes talked about the Gershwins, how sweet Ira was, and about how "unsweet" Ira's wife, Lee, could be. Lee's older sister, Emily Paley, was an old friend of George's, and was beloved by all. (George had once said to Emily, "A warm day in June could take lessons from you.") Emily came out to California to visit her sister each year and they'd have lunch with June. I told June I'd love to meet Ira, and she said she'd see what she could do when she next saw Lee.

A short time later, June told me that Ira's long-time friend and later secretary Eddie Carter was dying of cancer; she asked if I'd be interested in the job. I didn't have any secretarial skills but I told June, "Of course!" But before I got to meet Leonore, Eddie died and was replaced by Walter Reilly, who had worked for the Theatre Guild in New York. Well, that's that, I thought. But over lunch, June told Lee that I'd helped put her records in order and make a discography, and Lee asked to meet me. June told me to call Lee and be very polite. "And be sure to call her Mrs. Gershwin. She's very tough." I said, "June, of course I will," realizing I'd called June "June" from the very first.

So I called. Lee was the kind of woman who either loved you or hated you immediately. On the phone she said in her faux English accent, "June says you're an absolute treasure and I can't wait to meet you. When are you available?" We set the meeting, and I drove over at the appointed hour in my '73 Datsun compact. As I stopped in front of her house, a 1964 Rolls-Royce Silver Cloud silently pulled into the driveway with Lee at the wheel. I called out to her and she turned and greeted me.

As she opened her front door, I could see Ira sitting at a small table in the back of the house. I was nervous. He was older than he'd looked in the pictures I'd seen, but he was still unmistakably a Gershwin. Lee's sister Emily was sitting with him. When I extended my hand, Ira said, "Pardon me for not getting up." The experience was heady and exciting. Was this all really happening?

Ira was autographing copies of the Houston Grand Opera recording of *Porgy and Bess* that had just been issued. I told him that I preferred this to the one made by Lorin Maazel and the Cleveland Orchestra that had also come out recently, and he said he agreed. He then signed an album called *Ira Gershwin Loves to Rhyme*, which was a two-LP compilation of home recordings and demos of Ira singing. When I said that I had a copy of the record he said, "You bought this?" I said yes, and he said, "Why?" I explained that I liked his work and he

Lee Gershwin with Michael, in 1977.

said, "Really?" He told me I was the first person he'd met who owned that record who wasn't a friend or relative. I told him that I had a very old 78 of Gershwin songs—gems from *La La Lucille*, back in 1919—and he said it probably included the two most popular songs, "Tee-Oodle-Um-Bum-Bo" and "Nobody but You," and I said, "That's right." Lee turned to her sister and said, "Isn't that cute? He's telling Ira, 'That's right.'"

LEE TOOK ME TO A WALL AND OPENED A CONCEALED DOOR TO REVEAL A LARGE WALK-IN CLOSET.

Lee took me to what appeared to be a wall and opened a concealed door to reveal a large walk-in closet. It was packed from floor to ceiling with records and all sorts of other media, some labeled "home recordings." She said they needed somebody to organize the records and then described her travails in trying to keep the house in good order. Ira wasn't well and Walter Reilly, whom they had just hired, was too busy with secretarial matters. When Lee decided to focus on something, it immediately became a crisis. Suddenly, it was absolutely urgent that these records be catalogued.

So I was hired. I'd been in L.A. less than a year and I was working for Ira Gershwin. At first I was overwhelmed. I'd worked with the Levant collection a few months earlier, but this was even more exciting. I wondered just what I was going to find. One thing I noticed in a corner of the closet was Ira's personal phone directory from many years earlier. I picked it up and saw the names and numbers of a lot of deceased people whom I would have loved to have called. Lee asked me how long I thought it would take to organize the closet, and I naively said, "Oh, a month; a couple of months." When she asked me how much money I wanted, I said that I'd like to ask my father for advice on that, which she thought was a great idea. Then I asked her if she thought the material should be organized chronologically, or by song title, or by composer—there were many different ways it could be done. "Let's ask Ira," she said. So I asked him, "Mr. Gershwin, how would you like the records organized?" He answered, "Every way," which I soon learned was a typical response of Ira's. If you asked him what he wanted on his pizza he'd say, "Everything."

I started the next day and asked Lee if Mr. Gershwin would sign some things for me. She said to bring just three items—she didn't want me to wear him out. As for the money, my father suggested I ask for $1,000 for the whole job, so I did, and Lee wrote me a check right away. I soon realized that this job was going to take more like a year than the month or two I'd predicted. Remember, this was before computers and the work involved arduous research. After I'd been at it for a while, Lee announced, "This is ridiculous; we have to put you on a salary." She mentioned a figure that was fine with me, and I was put on Ira and Lee Gershwin's payroll.

The closet was a seemingly bottomless treasure trove. In addition to a huge number of 78s, there were incredible rarities like test pressings,

IRA WITH HIS EVER-PRESENT CIGAR.

production discs, aluminum air checks from the early thirties for radio shows, sixteen-inch transcription discs, and reel-to-reel tapes—extraordinary material from a lifetime of music. Air checks are especially precious: if an artist was appearing on the radio and wanted to preserve a recording, he would call up a recording service that would produce a live air check. The earliest air checks were recorded on twelve-inch aluminum or, later, on black lacquer discs, and a label might read, "Expressly recorded for George Gershwin," along with the name of the service. One disc would have sides one and three, another two and four, because the operator had to use two turntables in order to be able to immediately start the second disc once

got so mad that he grabbed me by the shoulders as if he was going to attack me. Then he said something I heard for the first time, but not the last: "I'll see to it that you never work in this town again." You haven't really arrived in Los Angeles until you hear that line. I filed a complaint with the Labor Board and got my money.

I KNEW I HAD BEEN LUCKY to find Ira. It was a strange set of circumstances that brought us together, and our meeting felt almost preordained. By the time I met him, he was quite ill and his focus was on his health. He saw hardly anyone. He was embarrassed because he had trouble walking and didn't want people to see him in his diminished

ONE TIME HE DESCRIBED HIMSELF AS BEING A "RHAPSODY IN BRUISE." HIS DELICIOUS SENSE OF HUMOR WAS A GREAT DIVIDEND, AND IN TURN HE LOVED TO BE ENTERTAINED IN SPITE OF HIS AILMENTS.

the first side had run out. Then he'd flip the first disc over and use that for the third side. Unless a second engineer made the same recording, an air check is a unique document. This was the kind of find that really got my blood flowing.

I still had a gig playing in the lounge of a restaurant in the Valley. I quit my day job as a piano salesman, but Bill Finnegan refused to pay me the commission I'd earned on a few pianos I'd sold. The money involved was about $200, no small amount at the time, and I got into it with him. He insisted he didn't owe me any money and

state. One time he described himself as being a "Rhapsody in Bruise." His delicious sense of humor was a great dividend, and in turn he loved to be entertained by me in spite of his ailments.

In the Gershwins' house, the closet was off what Lee called the music room—evidently called that "for tax purposes." (I later learned this was significant because Ira liked taking the deduction and hated paying taxes, in comical contrast to Irving Caesar, who wrote a propaganda song for children about the joys of paying taxes.) It was a sitting room that had four white leather chairs that swiveled and a coffee table loaded with books. He was an avid reader, though that ability would wane in the following years. Every day Ira would come down and have a very late breakfast at the table where I'd first seen him. A nurse would help him to his chair, and he'd read the *New York Times*. I would sit at a little card table behind him and write down details of the records. Sometimes I'd play one. One day, I absentmindedly whistled an obscure piece that he and George had written and Ira stopped reading. He slowly used his feet to swivel the chair around so he was facing me. "Mike, that's a verse of 'Beginner's Luck.' I wrote that with George in 1936 for *Shall We Dance*." I said, "I know."

Ira was delighted to discover how much I knew about his work. He asked me to play the piano, and I played "I Got Rhythm" in the style of different composers: Beethoven, Rachmaninoff, and Strauss. He loved that, and I think it was then that we really bonded. This was about a month after I had started working for him. We'd debate about some song and he'd say, "That was 1931," and I'd say, "No, that was 1930." He'd say no, he remembered because of such and such and I'd prove I was right by getting out a book. "Well, you're right again," he'd say, "but you have an advantage over me." "What's that?" I said, and he answered, "I've only lived my life. You've thoroughly researched it."

I was lucky to find Ira, but perhaps he was lucky to find me, too. One thing was clear: the time we spent together was a mutual tonic. It was the most electric and exciting time of my life. Ira talked about his brother a great deal. George would inevitably come up in conversation, or else I'd ask him something about him. I was always pulling out books or pieces of ephemera that reminded Ira of something that had happened many years before. There are so many moments stored in our brains that can't be accessed without a trigger—a smell, a sound, a taste. My work with Ira largely consisted of cataloguing his lifetime of triggers. My great appreciation of the Gershwins' music only deepened as Ira talked about the creation of it. Then I'd find recordings I'd never heard (and couldn't have heard anywhere else) in the music closet, discoveries that gave me an exclusive education in the Gershwin oeuvre. That music was the bond that bridged our sixty-year difference in ages.

Through Ira I met many other songwriters. When I was with Ira, it seemed like anything could happen and anyone might walk through the door to visit the old master. Ira made sure I met everyone who did, and invited me to join in the conversation. Then I started playing at parties in Beverly Hills because people knew I was this young kid who worked with Ira Gershwin, and the association had a cachet that was important to the Beverly Hills hostesses. Sometimes they'd ask me to bring Ira along, but there was no chance of that happening. After I had played a party, Ira always liked to hear about my exploits the next day, and I tried to recount the previous evening's events with as much flourish and energy as I could muster.

I was also playing a couple of nights a week in piano bars around Los Angeles. Patrons sit very close as you play, making requests and conversation between songs. During these moments I'd talk a little about the history of each song. Today, people frequently introduce songs in this anecdotal way, but I think I was the first person to incorporate it to such an extent into my performances. This experience was the greatest training for what I do now. The first clubs I played were gay bars, because those were the places where my musical repertoire was appreciated. It's also where I started meeting celebrities who were interested in my music. Of course, playing in bars, I was liable to encounter the odd patron who'd drunk too much, but I quickly learned how to handle the hecklers.

For me, knowing about a song and where it came from always made it more interesting. If I heard one song from a show, I immediately wanted to know about the rest of the songs, and I found that other people wanted to know, too. Sharing this knowledge is like letting them in on a secret. I was lucky to have developed my style in piano bars, a venue that allowed me to connect with people in a humorous and lighthearted way. For example, I recently asked an audience if anyone knew what songwriter had the greatest number of hits in the twentieth century. People were yelling "George Gershwin!" and "Irving Berlin!" and "Cole Porter!" and "Harry Warren!" One lady shouted "Barry Manilow!" (The answer is Harry Warren, who had the greatest number of "charted" hit songs.) It is a fun moment to interact with the audience that way, but it is also an educational moment in the guise of entertainment. Championing the other writers is as important to me as is promoting the Gershwins, especially when it comes to Harry Warren, who was a magnificent man and another musical genius.

Ira told me so many stories that my time with him made me a better storyteller. He and George wrote a song called "The Babbitt and the Bromide," which was about two people exchanging pleasantries but saying nothing substantive to each other: "Hello, how are you?" "How's the folks?" and other such inanities. They meet twenty years later and have the same mindless conversation. The last line is "Ta, ta, olive oil, goodbye." Ira asked me, "You know what 'olive oil' means?" and I said, "Yeah, she's the character in *Popeye*." He laughed gently, but not in a belittling way—he was never unkind. "Olive oil," he explained, was twenties slang for "au revoir." So many clever references in lyrics become obscure as time passes.

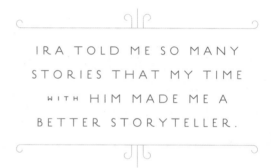

IRA TOLD ME SO MANY STORIES THAT MY TIME WITH HIM MADE ME A BETTER STORYTELLER.

Ira had a very mischievous sense of humor. I have a copy of a letter Ira received in 1957 from one A. Clarey, recently arrived in New York from France with songs for sale. "Dear Miss Gershwin," the letter begins. Would she be interested in writing lyrics for a couple of songs, and could they meet, preferably after 7 P.M.? A postscript notes, alluringly, "I have a pretty good baby-grand at my place."

Ira replied, "Dear Mr. Clarey, I'm very sorry but I couldn't possibly see you after 7 P.M. as I am engaged to a very jealous young man who wouldn't like it. Sincerely, (Miss) I.G."

Eventually I finished cataloguing Ira's closet, but Leonore pulled me aside and told me I had given Ira a new lease on life: "I know one day you are going to go off and do things on your own.

(OPPOSITE) *Ira's humorous reply to a request to collaborate.*

A.Clarey
610.West.145 str.
N.Y.31.. N.Y.
Tel.TOmpkims-2-8623   19 Oct. 1957

Dear Miss Gershwine

          I came in this country from France and I have
absolutely no connection among song-writers.
          Recently I presenter two (out of 25) melodies
of mine to Shapiro-Bernstein Music Publishers, and I
have been told that the the Company would publish them...
....if I have good lyrics for these melodies. Just to
say that probably these melodies are not too bad.
          Would you mind listen to them?
If so, please, give me an appointment. Naturally, your
hour will be my hour, but, since I am working, I would be
very pleased to meet You after 7 p.m., IF POSSIBLE.

              Hoping hear from You soon,
                 I remain,
                    Sincerely Yours

                                        A. Clarey

P.S.

I have a pretty good baby-grand at my place.

Dear Mr. Clarey,
            I'm very sorry but I couldn't
possibly see you after 7 P.M. as I am engaged to
a very jealous young man who wouldn't like it
                    Sincerely
            (Miss) I. G.

I think you have a very bright future. But I'd like to ask you to stay as long as you can and, while you're here, I'm going to open every closet and drawer in this house. Keep yourself busy and keep my husband happy."

So I stayed on.

I worked for Ira for six years. When I first went to work for him, he was depressed over the death of his friend Eddie Carter. Eddie had been a literary agent—one of his clients long before was Raymond Chandler. When Eddie retired, he went to work for Ira for fun, and the two men were more buddies than anything else. Ira felt Eddie's loss deeply and my presence helped to give him a lift. In time, our relationship evolved greatly. Ira

was, to all intents and purposes, house-bound, and I became his eyes and ears—his means of contact with the outside world.

Monday to Friday I would arrive at Ira's around one in the afternoon. Being nocturnal, Ira was a late riser. He stayed up most of the night by design or due to the repeated failure of his sleeping pill du jour. Part of my work was to spend time with him, so there was sometimes a blurred division between work time and social time. As Ira became more infirm, Lee was most concerned about keeping him vital and connected to the world, and it became my job to keep him amused in between my other assigned chores. Eventually he became bedroom- and then bed-bound and a

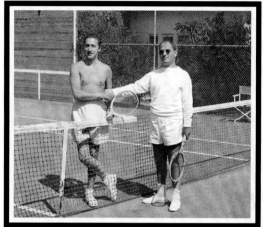

piano was moved into the room, where I would play for him daily. When Ira eventually took a nap, usually late in the afternoon, it was incumbent upon me to entertain Lee, who, as time progressed, became needier than Ira.

He hadn't always been so reclusive. He had never been a great partygoer, and rarely went out, but still he loved to see people. Visitors would drop by his home at two in the morning for a chat or to have a sandwich. To see Ira, you had to go to his house. If the porch light at the house on Roxbury Drive was on, it meant that he was up and you could stop by. For decades, his home was a Hollywood place of pilgrimage. In 1939, William Holden came to town to make the movie

Golden Boy. He was introduced to the Gershwins and stayed at their house for a while. Elaine Stritch showed up to do Oscar Levant's TV show, and after the live broadcast Levant brought her over.

Lee also loved to entertain and be the perfect hostess, so for years she and Ira ran their own exclusive salon. Judy Garland, Humphrey Bogart, Shelley Winters, Louis Calhern, Angie Dickinson, Zero Mostel, Gene Kelly, and every other big name you can think of paid their respects. Irving Lazar, Hollywood super-agent, closed some of his big deals at the Roxbury house. Harold Arlen and Yip Harburg wrote part of "Over the Rainbow" on George's piano. Sinatra played pool there alongside Groucho. You get the idea.

(LEFT) *Vernon Duke and Ira in 1936.* • (RIGHT) *Harold Arlen and Ira on the tennis court.*

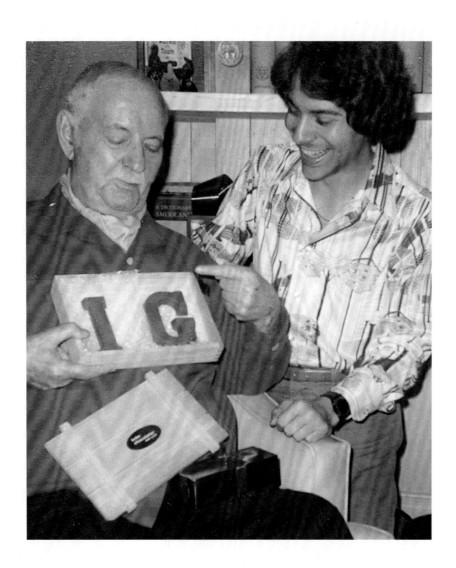

Ira and Michael on Ira's 81st birthday.

Ira never liked to dress up or make small talk, but Lee enjoyed formal dinner parties and hobnobbing with the "right" people, as she felt it was something she could bring into Ira's life that he could not supply for himself. While she wanted to make sure he was happy and stimulated, she also better perceived the advantages of inviting the right people to the house and knew what it did for business, something that Ira never would have thought about. When Ira and Lee first paired off, Ira would go to the family get-togethers, or opening night events, and he enjoyed the big soirees at the house, where George would entertain the crowd from the piano. But he never went to the swanky circuit parties on Park Avenue that George relished so much. In 1965, Angie Dickinson and Burt Bacharach threw an engagement party for themselves—and this was pretty much the last time Ira attended that kind of formal event. After that, if Lee wanted to go to a party—and she often did—she went on her own, later reporting in detail to Ira everything he had missed.

Ira was a great putterer, doing crosswords, listening to the radio, playing records, reading, making a giant "Dagwood" sandwich. He remained interested in the world—as well as reading the *New York Times* every day, he watched the news and *60 Minutes* on Sunday nights when family friend Shana Alexander was on the "Point/Counterpoint" segment. He'd listen to gossip sometimes as a diversion. (Lee devoured it like a cat with a bird.) He loved movies on TV. He had no interest in contemporary music. He had a lifetime of his own music for company and was curiously unruffled by the new music that his own contemporaries were angrily denouncing.

Ira's ability to focus was declining when I knew him. He'd get frustrated when he had trouble concentrating. I remember Lee saying, "Oh, Ira has lost his ability for self-amusement." Which was where I came in. Lee couldn't occupy Ira—that was up to other people. She couldn't play the piano and she didn't like to dwell on the past—or talk about it at all, in fact—and this was precisely where Ira wanted to be. I came to figure out that she carried guilt about the way she had interacted with George in his last

> IRA NEVER LIKED TO MAKE SMALL TALK, BUT LEE ENJOYED PARTIES AND HOBNOBBING WITH THE "RIGHT" PEOPLE.

months, and besides, she felt that not living in the present was a character flaw. She was not given to self-examination. She also was impatient and irritated because Ira was not well—Lee was easily upset by any signs of weakness and often responded with an apparent lack of sympathy—though she made sure that he always had the best care. Lee would make sure not to reveal Ira's illnesses even though he had been inactive for years. (His songs had ended but the malady lingered on.) Once when he had to go to the hospital she had him transported in a vehicle that appeared to be a limousine from the outside but was a fully equipped ambulance on the inside so no one would see or know what was happening. She fiercely protected him, and if someone was hurt along the way, it wasn't intentional, just fallout from what needed to be done.

IRA WASN'T THE EMOTIONALLY demonstrative type who would share his inner feelings, but I'd sometimes ask him questions about George indirectly, and it was clear to me that he was still tormented by his brother's death. In 1954, Ira wrote the lyrics to Harold Arlen's music for the movie *A Star Is Born*, Judy Garland's triumphant return to the screen. He painstakingly and brilliantly crafted the lyric to "The Man That Got Away," the song many consider Ira's "last great standard," coming thirty years after the first, "The Man I Love." "The Man That Got Away" was treated with respect by Garland and by the movie's director, George Cukor, who ran up twenty-seven takes over three days until he had it how he wanted it. (The song later completed Ira's trifecta of Oscar nonwinners, losing out to "Three Coins in the Fountain.")

Some thought that Ira had drawn from his well of personal suffering in writing the lyric for that song—although the song is called "The Man That Got Away," I never felt there was any personal connection. The lyric seems to convey some bitterness and loneliness, but the song is clearly referring to a woman who has lost a lover. Still, I asked Ira if he'd suffered writing that song and he said, "I was doing my job." I pressed a little: "But it's so deeply emotional and so connected to very dark feelings." He said, "Then I did my job well."

> I'D ASK HIM QUESTIONS ABOUT GEORGE, AND IT WAS CLEAR THAT HE WAS STILL TORMENTED BY HIS BROTHER'S DEATH.

I once showed Ira a roll of color film that included some images of George, and he started talking about his brother's death. The photographs were taken in Mexico in 1935, when George took a trip after writing *Porgy and Bess*. On the roll were two snapshots of George—the only color photographs taken of him to my knowledge. I had prints made and showed them to Ira and I asked him if the photographs were an accurate representation of his brother's appearance. He said the tint was not quite the same—George's skin had been a little redder—and the beard was very heavy. He talked about how George sometimes had to shave a couple of times a day because his beard came in so quickly. Ira sat there looking at the photograph of George and he finally said, "How is it that somebody who looked so young, so youthful . . .

Ira working on A Star Is Born *in 1954.*

how is it possible that he could have died?" As he stared at the image he went into what I can only describe as a state of shock. He seemed to be reliving it all again. How could this have happened? I wish I had asked Ira to talk about George more deeply when I had the chance, but it seemed insensitive to pry.

Ira's life changed so radically with George's death because the two were not only brothers, but also work partners. Of all the legendary people whom Ira worked with after George's death—Kurt Weill, Jerome Kern, Aaron Copland, and Harold Arlen, among others—George was the only one he considered a true genius.

Ira remained George's great champion. He wanted to prove that George was better than anyone else. Lauren Bacall had told him Stephen Sondheim's 1979 *Sweeney Todd* was a real opera. When I played some of it for Ira, he asked, "Did Sondheim orchestrate it?" I said no. The implication

George in Mexico in 1935, with Rosa and Miguel Covarrubias.

GEORGE AND IRA BY THE PING-PONG TABLE
IN THEIR RIVERSIDE DRIVE APARTMENT IN 1931.

was that because Sondheim hadn't orchestrated *Sweeney Todd*, it wasn't a true opera. George had spent so many months orchestrating *Porgy and Bess*—something he was extremely proud of—and Ira felt Sondheim had fallen short of the gold standard as represented by George. Ira admired Leonard Bernstein and considered him a friend, but also felt that Lennie was a pale imitation of George. I consider that harsh, but I understand Ira's perspective. I believe Bernstein was dogged by the ghost of Gershwin and sometimes retaliated by criticizing him in print and lectures, while still conducting his music, as his audiences demanded.

IRA FELT SONDHEIM HAD FALLEN SHORT OF THE GOLD STANDARD AS REPRESENTED BY GEORGE.

Ira would get depressed about his brother now and then. He got very down while listening to a radio broadcast, *Gershwin at 80*, in 1978. Yip Harburg was on the program, talking about George's demise. Yip was a somewhat melodramatic man, and he described George's death very emotionally and graphically. He said Harold Arlen had vomited when he heard that George had died—a story that was deeply upsetting to Ira. He stayed in bed for a couple of days after that. How many times did Ira relive those terrible days? How much survivor's guilt did he bear?

IN 1982 I BOUGHT a new car. I wanted to get a license plate that honored George and Ira, so I settled on SWNDRFL, as in "'S Wonderful." When I showed it to Ira, he said, "If you show it to five people in a row, and if they know what it means, I'll buy it for you." So I showed the plate to five people. Admittedly, I stacked the deck by showing it to people like Rosemary Clooney, but when they all got the joke, Ira, who was always a man of his word, bought the license plate for me.

One day I was at Elizabeth Taylor's house in Bel Air and I parked in the driveway. While I was there, she got a call from the Bel Air Police Patrol asking if everything was all right. She told them that everything was fine and inquired as to why they were asking. They said, "Well, there's a car parked in your driveway with the license plate SWINDLER. We thought somebody was trying to take advantage of you."

"'S Wonderful" is very evocative of the period of my life I spent with Ira. The song was written in 1927 for a Broadway show called *Smarty* that was renamed *Funny Face*. It wasn't unusual for show names to change at that time. In 1925, George and Ira wrote a score for a show called *My Fair Lady*, but the title was changed to *Tell Me More* because the original wasn't deemed strong enough. *My Fair Lady/Tell Me More* included a song called "Why Do I Love You?" which is the name of a very famous, and different, song in *Show Boat*. It's easy to win a bet if you assert that George Gershwin wrote a show called *My Fair Lady* featuring a song called "Why Do I Love You?" because people will just think you've had too many drinks and mixed up Gershwin with *Show Boat* and *My Fair Lady*.

Funny Face was Fred and Adele Astaire's last musical together for the Gershwins. In its multiple tryouts (Philadelphia, Washington, D.C., Atlantic City, and Wilmington), the show seemed beset with problems. The brothers wrote a lot of material that was thrown out or changed, and it looked like the show was never going to come together. But upon arriving in New York *Funny Face*, the first musical to be performed at the Alvin Theatre, was a hit, running for 244 performances.

"'S Wonderful" is a great example of Ira's ability to play with words, create catchphrases, and capture the slang of the day. In the second verse, Adele as Frankie, singing with Allen Kearns's Peter, rhymes "fash" with "pash" (fashion

ance of "'S wonderful, 'S marvelous, you should care for me." Fred and Adele Astaire made a recording of the song in England in 1928 and, at one point toward the end of the song, Adele sings, "It's wonderful . . ." This drove Ira mad. Adele had been singing the song onstage for more than a year at the point when she made that recording, so perhaps it's not surprising that she took some liberties.

Also from the 1927 show *Funny Face* was a humorous song called "Tell the Doc." In his later years it took on an ironic note for Ira, as he believed that no matter what he did tell the doc, it fell on deaf ears. Ira's health was always precarious in the time I spent with him, and was the source of some friction in his home. I didn't think Ira's doctor was

> "'S WONDERFUL" IS A GREAT EXAMPLE OF IRA'S ABILITY TO PLAY WITH WORDS, CREATE CATCHPHRASES, AND CAPTURE THE SLANG OF THE DAY.

and passion) and "emosh" and "devosh" (emotion and devotion). Ira had used the same technique in the song "Sunny Disposish" for the revue *Americana* the previous year ("For life can be delish / With a sunny disposish"). He loved word games and puzzles and was very precise about the correct usage of his made-up words.

On the original lyric sheet for "'S Wonderful," which is at the Library of Congress, there is an emphatic note from Ira telling the sheet music typesetter to be sure to print the apostrophe before the *S*. Ira always bristled if someone sang "It's wonderful." The whole point was the specific rhythm and bal-

a good practitioner at all, but Lee loved him. Ira once said, "My doctor doesn't understand me," and Lee laughed and said, "Don't be silly, he's the best doctor in the world." End of discussion.

That doctor supplied Lee with a plethora of pills, and it wasn't until several years later that I put all the pieces together and came to understand that she had much more of a substance abuse problem than I realized. I was fooled in part because Lee had tremendous disdain for anyone who was addicted to anything. The only person for whom she had enduring compassion was her friend Judy Garland, whom she adored. Vincente

Minnelli (Garland's husband) once said, "Lee Gershwin cheers you up when you're feeling good," which was very accurate, because she could be an excellent cheerleader. Sometimes she was extremely solicitous and caring, but her mood could change in an instant. When anyone disagreed with her, she took it as a personal attack.

After Ira died, Lee asked me, "Is there anything in the house that you'd like left to you?" I said, "I'd love the piano." And without a beat she said, "Anything else?" It was George's favorite piano and he had it moved to California from New York when he traveled to Hollywood in 1936. Thus he wrote most of *Porgy and Bess* on it as well as most of the songs composed in the last year of his life. The piano is now in the Library of Congress, displayed in their George and Ira Gershwin room.

It's behind a rope, so no one gets to play it without permission, except perhaps for an occasional special event when it is carefully moved for a unique performance. I'm glad I got to play it daily for six years. I donated some items to that room to help them re-create George and Ira's working environment, including an old electric pencil sharpener Ira gave me, now reunited with his desk and typewriter. I still love that piano. Once in a while the staff gives me permission to come by, slip under the rope, and play on it again.

A guy from the Smithsonian Institution once came by while Ira was still alive to look at his memorabilia. He seemed impressed with various things in the house, but Ira had an old pinball machine in the downstairs billiard room, and after looking at practically everything the man said, "You know, we really would love to have that." How could this man have not expressed interest in any of the Gershwin memorabilia? Lee was so irritated that she made sure the Smithsonian got nothing. She also had a habit of tearing up anything negative about the Gershwins out of Ira's scrapbooks, destroying history and leaving gaps in the archive. Even a bad review of a show from 1932 was not acceptable, history be damned. Photos were also rejected if they did not display any of the principal Gershwin players in the best possible light. I learned to stop showing her things.

Lee was sometimes angry about this or that and she had a very acerbic tongue. She was, in her own words, a barracuda. She would often speak for Ira. I'd go into the music room and say, "How are you, Mr. Gershwin?" and she'd respond, "Oh, he's fine." Ira complained that she had never acted this way during his younger working years,

Funny Face *program cover from London, 1928, with caricatures of Fred and Adele Astaire and comedian Leslie Henson.*

ISIDOR GERSHVIN.

SCRAP BOOK

[The Coal Regions]

Coal Miners at Work

Anthracite coal as it comes out of the mines contains great quantities of stone, slate, and dust. It has to be broken up and picked over before it can be used. This is done in what are known as coal breakers. A coal breaker is a building almost as big as one of the grain elevators we saw at Duluth. The coal is taken to the top, and by machinery the lumps are separated into different sizes. They are then run through inclined troughs, or chutes, and boys, who are paid about fifty cents a day, pick out the slate and other rubbish as the coal goes by.

TROLLEY CAR

XI.—Trolley Car.

In 1881 an electric tramway one and a half miles long was built in Lichterfelde (Berlin). The first trolley car line operated with success in America was built in Richmond, Va., by Lieutenant Sprague, in 1887. There is no considerable city in the world to-day without its electric traction service.

The Chinese seem to have been the first to discover the directive power of the magnet. According to Chinese books an instrument like the mariner's compass was made by the emperor Hoang-ti, in the year 2634 B. C. It seems to have been used only for land-travel until about 300 A. D.

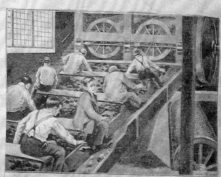

A Coal Breaker.

Periodic Comets.

Name.	Perihelion Passage.	Period (Years)	Perihel. Dist. Earth's orbit=1.	Eccen- tricity.	Name.	Perihelion Passage.	Period (Years)	Perihel. Dist. Earth's orbit=1.	Eccen- tricity.
Encke.....	1885, Mar. 7	3.3	0.34	0.846	Biela.	1832, Sept. 26	6.6	0.86	0.755
Tempel....	1884, Nov. 20	5.2	1.34	0.55	D'Arrest.	1884, Jan. 13	6.7	1.33	0.639
Barnard....	1890, Feb. 17	5.4	1.28	0.682	Faye.....	1881, Jan. 22	7.5	1.74	0.649
Tempel-Swift	1886, May 9	5.5	1.07	0.656	Tuttle.	1885, Sept. 11	13.8	1.04	0.821
Brorsen....	1879, Mar. 30	5.5	0.59	0.810	Pons-Brook	1884, Jan. 25	71.5	0.77	0.954
Winnecke...	1886, Sept. 8	5.8	0.89	0.727	Olbers....	1888, Oct. 8	72.6	1.20	0.931
Tempel.....	1885, Sept. 25	6.5	2.07	0.405	Halley.	1835, Nov. 16	76.4	0.59	0.967

certainly not when George was around. She, however, felt the need to take over and handle things, feeling that Ira must not be burdened. I remember Ira asking me what was wrong one time when I must have seemed down. I said, "Ah, I said such-and-such to Lee and she gave me a withering look." He said, "My wife gives everybody withering looks; why should that bother you? What's the big deal?"

LEE WAS PROBABLY IN LOVE WITH GEORGE FIRST BUT GEORGE DIDN'T HAVE WARM FEELINGS FOR HER.

Ira thought he had been very lucky to win Lee because she was beautiful and charming—a real live wire, and she did care for him deeply. Lee Strunsky met Ira at her sister Emily's wedding in 1920. Emily and her husband, Lou Paley, held a lot of parties that her friend George would attend, and Ira would come along, too. This was where Ira and Lee got to know each other. Lee was a flapper from a well-to-do family, so she must have seemed exciting and exotic to Ira. (Lee's first comment on hearing *Rhapsody in Blue* was, "You can't dance to it. What good is it?")

When Ira and Lee got engaged, she was the one who told him they should get married, which they did in 1926, with George playing piano at the wedding. Ira was so shy and insecure he probably would never have gotten around to proposing.

Lee was probably in love with George first— everyone was in love with George—but George didn't have warm feelings for her. Perhaps he was put off by the fake English accent (Lee was born in San Francisco), the clothes, the jewelry. But when his brother married her, that no longer mattered and he accepted her.

Ira and Lee were together fifty-seven years. There's nothing as unknowable as other people's marriages, but I thought it was an odd match because Ira was so guileless and fundamentally different from his wife in the most basic ways. Ira viewed Lee's behavior as amusing, baffling, brilliant, outrageous, cute, cunning, and cumbersome. He wrote her sentimental anniversary cards, and Lee was also outwardly affectionate toward her husband. She'd come in the room, give him a big kiss, and say, "I love you, dearie. Are you okay?" She was very proud of his work and proud of being Mrs. Ira Gershwin. Lawrence Stewart, who worked for Ira for years, said that Lee prized the Gershwin name more than Ira did.

When Ira was healthy, Lee traveled all over the world on her own. In later years she didn't go away as much because Ira was more dependent on her and she wouldn't leave him. Once in a while, though, she would take a much-needed trip. If Ira didn't hear from her for a while, he became very agitated. When she called, he would say, "Oh, thank God, Lee, thank God you're all right." One day, after his health was declining, he found her reading an issue of a travel magazine called *Passport*. When he casually said, "I didn't know you still get *Passport*," she said, "Well, even if I can't travel anymore I can still read about it." She resented the fact that she had to curtail her trips because of his illness.

(PREVIOUS PAGES) *Ira's scrapbook from 1908–1910.*

IRA AND LEE IN 1960.

Ira at a party for the Porgy and Bess *cast at the 1021 North Roxbury Drive residence in 1954.*

Unlike Ira, Lee was not afraid to show her anger. My fights with Lee eventually got so bad that I wouldn't go to the house for a couple of days because I couldn't bear to be around her. After a few days, she would call and say, "Ira needs you. You can't do this to Ira." She never apologized. I was too stubborn in those days and couldn't say sorry either, until I'd make a sincere effort to heal things, which she always accepted with open arms, and we would move forward. We had an odd dependency that neither wanted to admit. As the pattern went, we'd have a great time

for a while until something would set her off. A couple of months before Ira died I had to have an emergency appendectomy. Lee visited me in the hospital every day to tell me in detail how depressed Ira was that I wasn't there and how he needed me. She'd come in, berate me for abandoning Ira, and then go on her merry way. Now I understand about addiction and I curse the doctor who turned her life upside down.

Eventually I was privy to all the family business. I knew when Ira revised his will, naming his attorney, Ronald Blanc, and the author and academic Robert Kimball as executors. With uncharacteristic courage, I went to Ira and told him I'd like to be involved in his affairs after he was gone. Using one of Ira's favorite words, I said I would "assiduously" devote myself to the preservation of his work. Ira, with Lee's blessing, named me his literary executor alongside Kimball and Blanc. My ultimate dream was to spend the rest of my life caring for and propagating the Gershwin legacy. With Ron and Bob, I knew I'd have good allies as we strove to do the great things Ira would have wanted done.

It didn't turn out that way. After Ira died, I sadly fell out with Leonore over something that was trivial. Once she inherited everything, she changed her will to cut me out of the estate. Lee's attorney scared me into signing a piece of paper that removed any residual claims I might have had, and that was that. I almost instantly regretted signing it, but I was a twenty-six-year-old kid and this was a very powerful lawyer. His job was to get rid of me and he succeeded.

Lee and I were out of touch for some time because of the fallout over Ira's will, but in the late eighties I had a rapprochement with her. I had appeared on a TV show where I talked at length about Ira and his lyrics with great affection. Lee saw that show and immediately sent an effusive telegram saying she wanted to see me. We met and reconciled, and I was happily back in her world again. By this time, Lee was in declining health herself and she had mellowed. Her desire to forgive and move forward was something I never expected to witness. It was remarkable. Whenever there was any artistic question about the business she'd say, "Ask Michael. Michael knows. Michael will tell

you." But she'd forgotten I wasn't legally part of the estate, and I was never reinstated. While I felt for a time that I had been deprived of what I was supposed to do for Ira, I now see how things truly evolved as they were supposed to. His estate is run in a way that is a model for others and something that makes me proud and happy to watch. My career has been on a trajectory that implies I have been destined to perform rather than be behind the scenes, and I accept that with gratitude.

Lee lived until 1991, continuing to work on George's and Ira's estates up to the end. She remained as quixotic as ever, yet in her heart desired to do the best she knew to preserve the Gershwin legacy, feeling that nobody would know or care about her in the future except by association. She was laid to rest in the same place as George and Ira, at the Westchester Hills Cem-

IRA GERSHWIN
1021 NORTH ROXBURY DRIVE
BEVERLY HILLS, CALIFORNIA 90210

May 18, 1978

To Whom It May Concern:

Michael Feinstein, the bearer of this letter, has my permission to examine and to receive duplications of any material relating to my brother, George Gershwin, and to me that may be contained in your library or archives.

He is an employe of mine, working in a cataloguing and research capacity.

Thank you for your consideration and courtesy.

Sincerely,

Ira Gershwin

Ira's letter granting the author permission to examine and receive duplications of any George Gershwin–related material.

etery in Hastings-on-Hudson, New York. Lee was wrong about not being remembered or well thought of. Every time I go to the theater I remember her rules. Never nod your head from side to side, only up and down when inside. When you leave the theater, there is the "two-block rule"—that you don't talk about a show until you're that distance away. She taught me etiquette, manners, how to escort a lady, how to write a thank-you note. It was the way she truly knew to show kindness, by teaching. She was not sentimental, but practical. I miss her.

I wish that I'd had a better understanding of Leonore over the time that we were together. In retrospect, I think I sometimes saw her as the villain unnecessarily. She was an oddly principled woman who didn't always mean what she said in anger, but I was young, self-righteous, and very protective of Ira, not seeing then that the dynamic in their relationship long pre-existed my entrance on the scene.

ONCE MY INVOLVEMENT WITH the Gershwin estate was over, I became a full-time performer. I worked at a restaurant called 385 North on North La Cienega Boulevard in L.A. that was open from 1984 to 1987. Early on, they wanted to fire me because I only played old music, but then they saw how many people came for my show. In the fall of 1984, I started working at the Mondrian Hotel, on the Sunset Strip, and thanks to Liza Minnelli received my first national attention with television appearances and feature stories in national publications. She threw me an opening night party attended by Elizabeth Taylor, Joan Collins, Henry Mancini,

and a virtual *Who's Who* of Hollywood. How can I adequately thank her for that? Then I did my first real show—not the casual piano bar set—at the Plush Room in San Francisco.

Things really turned for me with my debut at New York's Algonquin Hotel in 1986. Back then, the Oak Room at the Algonquin was the most important cabaret venue in New York. The Oak Room is now closed, but for me it will forever be populated by the ghosts of performers who have graced the room. The gig was supposed to last for a month, but my engagement was extended to twelve weeks and every show sold out. I came back the next year and played another sixteen weeks, and my life changed. I shifted to concerts and recordings and laid the foundation for what I am doing now.

I wonder what Ira would make of me today. He never saw me perform onstage in person, but he did see me once on television. Lee came to see me play a couple of times, and was very supportive in her own tough-love way. I was her creation as far as she was concerned. And as I look back I'm confounded to realize that she was right.

I am thankful I got to spend so much time with Ira Gershwin. Working with him opened doors for me, and my first recording inevitably consisted of Gershwin songs. In the late eighties, very few people my age were singing these songs, so I was considered a novelty. But even after the novelty wore off, the songs played on. Unknowingly, I'd helped create a revival that is prospering to this day. As a child, how could I have dreamed that my obsession with ancient thirty-two-bar songs would evolve into an opportunity to help perpetuate them? I only hope that somewhere Ira and Lee are smiling, as I am when I think of them. ·

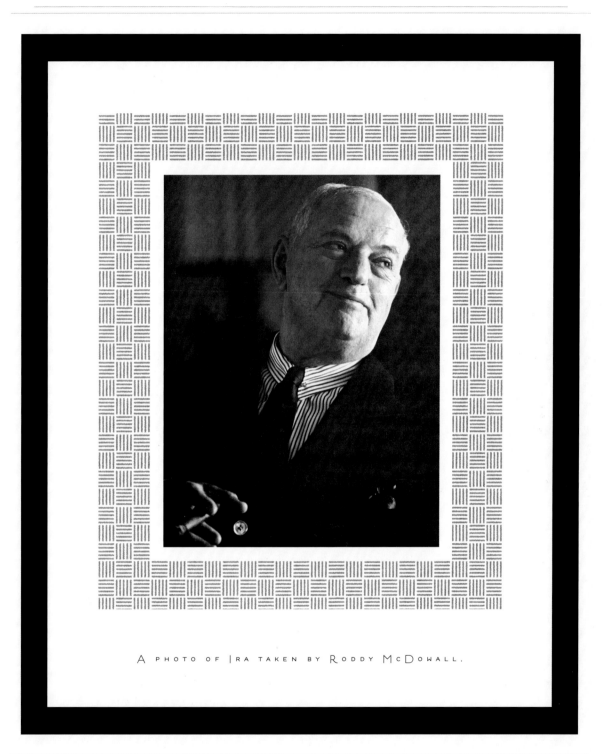

A PHOTO OF IRA TAKEN BY RODDY McDOWALL.

"I'VE GOT A CRUSH ON YOU"

from *Treasure Girl,* 1928

VERSE

NAT:

How glad the many millions
Of Annabelles and Lillians
Would be
To capture me.
But you had such persistence
You wore down my resistance;
I fell—
And it was swell.

POLLY:

You're my big and brave and handsome Romeo.
How I won you I shall never, never know.

NAT:

It's not that you're
attractive—
But oh, my heart grew active
When you
Came into view.

REFRAIN 1

I've got a crush on you,
Sweetie Pie.
All the day and nighttime
Hear me sigh.
I never had the least notion
That I could fall with so much
emotion.

Could you coo,
Could you care
For a cunning cottage we
could share?
The world will pardon my mush
'Cause I've got a crush,
My baby, on you.

REFRAIN 2

POLLY:

I've got a crush on you,
Sweetie Pie.
All the day and nighttime
Hear me sigh.
This isn't just a flirtation:
We're proving that there's
predestination.

I could coo,
I could care
For that cunning cottage we could share.
Your mush I never shall shush
'Cause I've got a crush,
My baby, on you.

· CHAPTER 4 ·

MICHAEL AND GEORGE

MY OBSESSION with George Gershwin started the same way it did for millions of other people—with *Rhapsody in Blue*. The first time I heard the piece—when I was twelve or thirteen—there was a sudden quickening of my heartbeat and a tingling in the *kishkes*, in my stomach. *Rhapsody in Blue* was like nothing I'd ever heard. I listened to it again and again after that, trying to figure out what made this music so powerful, so distinctive, so wonderful. I was instantly captivated by George Gershwin the composer. If this sounds like a coming-of-age love story, that's because it is.

As is the case with an affair of the heart, separation creates longing. If I hear *Rhapsody in Blue*

after missing it for a while, that first thrill is always there for me. That seminal excitement is the mark of Gershwin's genius, so deftly encapsulated in that early opus. It cannot be accounted for by studying the notes on paper, as his music is tied up with an energy that transcends the printed page. The *Rhapsody* is a joyous colossus that has survived all the petty jealousies of others who failed to comprehend George's achievement and tried to either diminish or studiously copy what he originated. It has also survived its own premature birth after not enjoying a full gestation period.

I was familiar with Gershwin the composer, but when I was in high school, I heard Gershwin's 1926 recording of "Fascinating Rhythm," which

George rehearsing with the Los Angeles Philharmonic in 1937.

GEORGE GERSHWIN IN 1937.

featured George at the piano with Fred and Adele Astaire singing, and that turned me on to Gershwin the performer. When I tried to play piano like George Gershwin I soon realized that he was inimitable. Like many other aspects of his art, his piano playing was created from an amalgam of his New York musical influences, which ranged from carnival music he heard at Coney Island through the Yiddish-inspired music of his neighborhoods to the jazz and blues of Harlem. The classics also insinuated themselves into his youthful brain, and he would sometimes quote from them in his playing. The brash authority in his keyboard style spills through the grooves of his early records and reveals much about his personality. Gershwin changed mu-

jukebox, and he'd listen to the tunes over and over again until he knew every word and every note of every song. My dad is still the one I call when I need to know a lyric, and he still charms the ladies when he bursts into song, much to my mother's consternation. (After he met the famously acerbic actress Elaine Stritch, Elaine called to tell me how much she enjoyed meeting my father. When I responded that my mother was sorry not to have met her as well, there was a pregnant pause and she replied, "Damn, I was hoping she was dead.")

My parents always encouraged my brother, my sister, and me to sing and play instruments, and I started taking piano lessons when I was five. We had previously lived in a house that had an

HIS PIANO PLAYING WAS CREATED FROM an AMALGAM of HIS NEW YORK MUSICAL INFLUENCES.

sic for me. He made me play differently, and he made me listen to other composers differently. My musical life changed so drastically with Gershwin that I thought of everything as either B.G. or A.G.: Before George or After George. Pardon the analogy, but he has comparatively brought a lot more joy to the planet than many religions.

I was predisposed to fall in love with George Gershwin's music, and Ira's lyrics came later, when I had more maturity. There was a lot of music around the house when I was growing up. My mother was a tap dancer, and my father loved to sing. He'd performed with local big bands around town, but never professionally. When he was a kid, he sold newspapers in front of a bar that had a

ancient upright in the basement, but I only remember crayoning on it and never playing it. After a piano was delivered to our home I discovered I had a talent for it, much like discovering the joyful taste of a favorite food. It was an instantaneous connection with the piano and I could play by ear with both hands, and was as surprised as my parents when it happened.

We'd often take in entertainment as a family, watching variety shows on television, traveling to see nearby summer stock together. We'd go see an old movie at the Ohio Theatre or the Palace in downtown Columbus, both giant movie palaces built in the twenties that are still operating as theaters today. My favorite films were the children's matinees on Saturdays, when they would show kid-friendly films like *Fantastic Voyage* or *Trog*, with Joan Crawford. "What an actress," my juvenile mind thought!

I remember that when I was twelve or so, my parents took me on another Saturday to the Center of Science and Industry to see *Top Hat*, the classic Fred Astaire and Ginger Rogers film. It was my first conscious introduction to classic Hollywood musicals, to Irving Berlin as well as to Fred and Ginger. I loved everything about that movie and was deeply moved by the orchestrations and deco style of the 1935 classic. My mom talked about how her mother used to make knockoffs of Ginger's costumes when she was little and my dad sang the songs all

such as Carole King's album *Tapestry,* which my sister wore out soon after it was released in 1971. That recording remains a favorite of mine because of its heartfelt simplicity and beautiful combination of piano and voice. There was no artifice and I could relate to the purity, or honesty, of the music. Years later I was proud to record an album with *Tapestry*'s original recording engineer, Hank Cicalo, a great talent himself.

Generally speaking I never liked rock 'n' roll; I didn't like the Rolling Stones then and I don't particularly like them now. I'm talking about feeling a deep affinity for such music. It doesn't move me for the most part, though I can appreciate it in a broader cultural sense and might even enjoy

WHENEVER I SAY, "GEORGE AND IRA GERSHWIN,"
I GET A SPECIAL REACTION.

the way home. As soon we got home I figured out how to play many of the songs on the piano.

Because I was by now showing a keen interest in music, I went with my parents to shows and movies like this without my brother and sister, who might have been bored or uninterested. Later, I'd spend hours down in our basement, listening to my ever-growing collection of 78s. "Go outside and play," my parents would beg, but I was happier in my own world. Little did I know that my life was already moving in a trajectory over which I had seemingly no control. Music was becoming my driving factor.

Occasionally, very occasionally, some contemporary music would take a spin on my turntable,

the presentation once in a while. Yes, I understand the animal appeal of rock 'n' roll for people, but I don't feel it as such. The revolutionary aspects, the sixties exhortations to be radical and different, always had an idiotic childishness and vulgarity that lacked any appeal for my teen sensibilities. It always seemed heavy-handed and sophomoric, with blasting sounds that somehow were supposed to be more effective if the music was turned up louder. To my ears, rock 'n' roll still sounds boring and repetitive, yet I see my friends go into paroxysms of blissful nostalgia with a glimpse of Keith Richards on TV. So I guess the lesson is: thank goodness we don't all like the same things, because life would be rather dull.

*R*HAPSODY IN BLUE is now one of the most performed pieces for piano and orchestra in the world, and I'm blessed that I get to witness the emotional power Gershwin has over so many people. I relish the chance to share my love of his music with my audiences. When I'm performing, a charge courses through the crowd when I say I'm going to sing some Gershwin—whether it's at Carnegie Hall in New York City or a nightclub in Tokyo. I perform (and praise) the works of other greats: Irving Berlin, Cole Porter, Jerome Kern, and many others. But whenever I say, "George and Ira Gershwin," I get a special reaction. People say, "I *love* Gershwin."

In my concerts I often set aside time for Gershwin requests. Most often, I hear the familiar titles and I'm happy to oblige—"Love Is Here to Stay," "Embraceable You," "Someone to Watch over Me," "A Foggy Day," "Love Walked In." . . . Some

people ask for less well-known numbers—"Isn't It a Pity" or "Ask Me Again." Inevitably, someone will try to trip me up with a really obscure song—"Blue, Blue, Blue"—or even a hokey one, such as "There's More to the Kiss than the XXX." Despite his genius, Gershwin was fallible—he did write some bad songs, and more than one or two in his early years. And occasionally, I'll get a request for one of them— the person just wants to see if I know it. Usually I'll play a few bars to prove that I'm not going to be stumped that easily. Or I'll launch into the song: "There's more to the kiss than—" and I'll stop in the middle of a line and say something like, "No, sorry, I like you too much to subject you to pain" or "There's no accounting for taste." Groucho Marx used to torture Irving Berlin by constantly singing an early song of his about the Devil called "Stay Down Where You Belong." Finally Berlin offered to pay him not to sing it. Sometimes I wonder what might be in the mind of someone who has requested a creaky song and try and consider if they really, truly like the thing they shouted out. Nah, my audiences are too sophisticated, right?

Once I get the audience comfortable enough to yell out something they'd like to hear, it can be like the proverbial floodgates opening, and the mass of yelling could be misinterpreted as something dangerous if I didn't know better. The fans are passionate about what they want to hear and will keep calling out until they're heard, no matter how far back they might be seated. Sometimes when two people from different parts of the house shout the same thing at the same time, I try to get them to exchange numbers, or least consider that they might be part of that Shakespeare "star-crossed" experience, but usually their spouses won't allow it.

George in the mid-thirties.

Then there are the folks who shout out something written by Berlin or another writer and have no regard that it's a Gershwin request segment. I sometimes ask them to leave, which gets a rise out of the assemblage. But heck, everyone else is paying attention and following directions, right? Then I try to placate them by explaining that their errant request will have some of the same notes as the other Gershwin requests and quote my grandmother, who would say, "You should be happy." The truth is that I understand that some people just might not know who wrote all of the songs they love and I'm just making merry out of it all. Others still will request a very contemporary song, perhaps sarcastically, and once in a while I can play it in the style of a standard. That can be fun.

Rhapsody in Blue lasts more than fifteen minutes, so it doesn't fit into my request sessions (and it isn't a song, so it's not on this volume's CD), but I've played it in concert many times. The first time was at the Hollywood Bowl in 1987. The combination of that piece in that setting was a frightening experience, because I'd never tackled anything so ambitious before. The Hollywood Bowl, with its tradition and aura—and great size—can be intimidating. *Everyone* has played there.

On my first night on that legendary stage, I was nervous and didn't play the piece as well as I could. I'm glad that this was more a case of first-night nerves than a consistent problem for me. On the Bowl stage in particular I have heard *Rhapsody* rendered many times and have seen great pianists occasionally blow it. Dudley Moore, who was a fine jazz pianist, never quite conquered the piece, and I heard Bernstein play it there as if he were on sleeping pills. But nerves have to be taken into

account. There have been legions of artists who possessed the musical talent to be great performers but weren't able to express themselves in public. Pianist Leopold Godowsky (considered the greatest of his generation) suffered tremendously from stage fright and is said never to have been heard publicly to his best advantage. (And there is a link here—Godowsky's son, Leopold Godowsky, Jr., married George and Ira's sister, Frances.)

A couple of years ago I got to play *Rhapsody in Blue*—or at least a six-minute condensed version of the piece—with the National Symphony for a televised Fourth of July celebration in Washington on the lawn of the Capitol. The event was attended by over a hundred thousand people, spread out for as far as the eye could see. There was a second pianist, the very gifted young classical artist Andrew von Oeyen. When we ran through the show the day before, I was introduced to actor Jimmy Smits, who was hosting. In a strange coincidence, it turned out that he was a graduate of George Gershwin Junior High School in Brooklyn. Even the association of the name with school hadn't put him off the music, as it might have for some—he said he loves George Gershwin.

On the day of the celebration, as soon as the announcer mentioned Gershwin, people in the audience started cheering. The clamor got even louder when they heard what we were going to play. *Rhapsody in Blue* is closely associated with July Fourth celebrations and has become a piece of Americana, like popcorn and hot dogs and baseball. Patriotic events like that one are designed to swell the heart, and when I watched a recording of the show later I could see how the people in the crowd, waving flags and swaying to the beat, were drawn

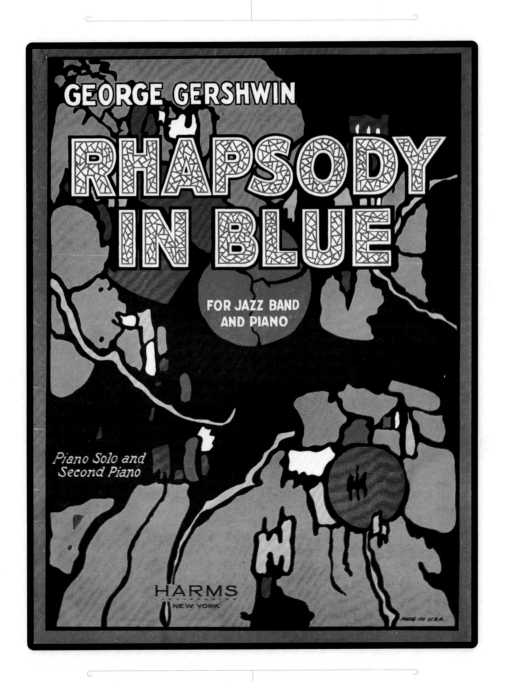

Artwork for the first edition of Rhapsody in Blue *(1924).*

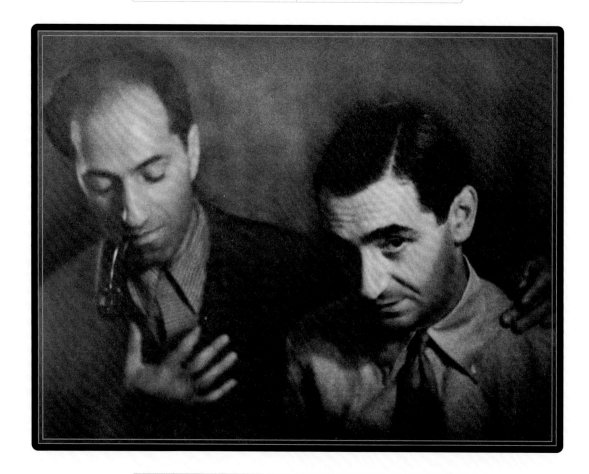

in and then carried along by the magnificence of music, which matched the occasion and the setting so perfectly. There was a real community, a profound sense of sharing in a musical experience, that I hadn't felt on such a scale in a long time. It was a reminder of what this street kid from Brooklyn had come to represent: the personification of America. And Ira wisely recognized it in his kid brother long before anyone else.

What audiences feel when they listen to *Rhapsody in Blue* is the essence of Gershwin's spirit, and his genius. *Rhapsody in Blue* embodies Gershwin's feverish industriousness, and I've always felt that as a piece of music it came at a particularly apt time for America, still a relatively young country when George composed it in 1924. There is beauty there, but also nervy jazz rhythms that offer hints of our great achievements and our great

George and Irving Berlin; photo taken by George with a camera timer.

promise—this was new, young, fresh, hopeful music, quintessentially American music.

We can't be complacent about our national treasures. This sentiment applies as much to Glacier National Park or the Florida Everglades as it does to a Mark Rothko painting or a piece of George Gershwin's music. We have to protect these extraordinary assets. Sometimes we don't do such a great job (look at the Everglades). For as long as I perform music, I'll play and sing Gershwin and do my best to ensure it remains in our nation's pantheon.

THE STORIED CIRCUMSTANCES of how George Gershwin wrote *Rhapsody in Blue* have a whiff of mythology about them, some of it created by George himself, who once said he wrote his masterpiece in just ten days. Given the brilliance of the piece, and his considerably deft natural talent, I guess it's possible, but not likely given the overall facts. There still are questions about the timeline that have never been definitively answered.

In November 1923, the singer Eva Gauthier performed a "Recital of Ancient and Modern Music for the Voice" at Aeolian Hall, one of New York's most prestigious venues, then housed in what is now the SUNY State College of Optometry building opposite Bryant Park in Midtown. Gauthier had a very eclectic program that ranged from Bartók and Schoenberg to Irving Berlin and Jerome Kern. She sang three songs by George Gershwin, including "(I'll Build a) Stairway to Paradise" and "Do It Again," and she was accompanied by him on the piano.

After attending this event, and sensing an opportunity, bandleader Paul Whiteman asked George to write something for a jazz concert.

Whiteman knew his rival, Vincent Lopez, was planning a high-profile jazz concert and Whiteman was eager to beat Lopez to the punch, so he gave George a deadline of the following February, just three months hence.

In early January of 1924, George was playing pool with Buddy DeSylva, with whom he was writing the musical *Sweet Little Devil*. Ira picked up that day's *New York Herald Tribune* and read a piece promoting Whiteman's concert, scheduled for February 12. In a great show of bravado, Whiteman had announced he would be premiering new works by Irving Berlin ("a syncopated tone poem") and the popular composer Victor Herbert. Whiteman also told the paper that George Gershwin was hard at work writing a jazz symphony for him. Only he wasn't, or so the story goes. George had forgotten that Whiteman had asked him to write a piece. Or maybe George and Whiteman had had one of those "Wouldn't it be fun if . . . ?" conversations that one side took seriously and the other didn't. In retrospect, the latter scenario is most likely.

PAUL WHITEMAN

and his

PALAIS ROYAL ORCHESTRA

will offer

An Experiment in Modern Music

assisted by

ZEZ CONFREY AND GEORGE GERSHWIN

New typically American Compositions by Messrs. VICTOR HERBERT, ZEZ CONFREY and GEORGE GERSHWIN will be played for the first time.

Aeolian Concert Hall
Entrance and Box Office
34 West 43rd Street

Tuesday, February 12th, 1924
—Lincoln's Birthday—
at 3 p. m.

TICKETS ON SALE NOW: From 55c to $2.20

Paul Whiteman's concert that introduced Rhapsody in Blue.

We can imagine the different reactions that Irving Berlin and George Gershwin may have had on reading this announcement in the newspaper: Gershwin saying, "Okay then," and Berlin, "Who does this guy think he is?" Whatever the case, after speaking to Whiteman, Gershwin got busy, and between January 4, when that story ran in the *Herald Tribune,* and February 12, when Whiteman's "Experiment in Modern Music" was performed in Aeolian Hall, George wrote *Rhapsody in Blue* and Whiteman's orchestrator, Ferde Grofé, arranged it for Whiteman's band. The amount of time it took to write may not have been "just ten days," but by any standard, that was quick work by George.

THE NEWSPAPER PIECE MAY HAVE ACTED AS A STIMULUS, ENCOURAGING GEORGE TO HURRY UP.

Another element of the genesis myth for this piece is the part played by the rattle of a New York–to-Boston steam engine. In December 1923, George went to Boston to attend the premiere of *Sweet Little Devil.* I've already mentioned how George found tunes in the noise of the streets of New York. On this occasion, the train ride, and what he called its "rattle-ty-bang" rhythm, supposedly spurred him to visualize the complete piece as if it were already written. "I heard it as a sort of musical kaleidoscope of America—of our vast melting pot, of our unduplicated national pep, of our metropolitan mad-

ness," he later wrote. Some of the serious academic debate on the writing of the *Rhapsody* has centered on the date of this train ride to Boston.

Gershwin biographer Howard Pollack believes George may have worked on the piece for two months, before and after the *Herald Tribune* story. The newspaper piece may have acted as a stimulus, encouraging George to hurry up, rather than being the first time he'd heard that the concert was actually going ahead. It's very mysterious, because Ira clearly recalled the pool hall incident to me and insisted that George hadn't known about the piece earlier. It is also possible that George started his conception of the piece before he was actually approached by Whiteman, as he already had stated his ambition to write larger-scale works. Maybe there was some kind of synchronicity in the timing of it all?

What no one disputes is the crucial role played by the bandleader Paul Whiteman, the self-proclaimed "King of Jazz." Whiteman was a fascinating figure, a very smart businessman who was a better showman than musician. Born in 1890 in Denver, Whiteman came to New York with his band in 1920 and enjoyed huge success in the twenties and thirties. He was a big, bluff man, married four times. After his career as a bandleader foundered, he went on to be music director for ABC Radio and until 1954 hosted *Paul Whiteman's TV Teen Club,* a talent show on ABC that featured as an announcer a young man named Dick Clark.

At the height of Whiteman's popularity there were several bands bearing his name touring the country, like regional productions of *Jersey Boys.* Whiteman made sure he surrounded himself with the best talent for his Palais Royal Orchestra,

(OPPOSITE) *1924 caricature of Paul Whiteman by Miguel Covarrubias.*

named after the club where he catapulted to fame. His arranger, Ferde Grofé, became an acclaimed composer, best remembered for his *Grand Canyon* and *Mississippi* suites. (When the pieces are played now they are usually heard in the composer's later orchestrations for symphony orchestra—although they sound wonderful in their original settings for a smaller band like Whiteman's.)

Despite his bombastic image and limited musical talent, Whiteman was an innovative force. Although his band didn't actually play a lot of what we would today consider jazz, the King of Jazz combined elements of popular, classical, and jazz music in his concerts in a well-marketed and very popular package. Musicians of the caliber of Bix Beiderbecke, Charlie Margolis, Jack Teagarden, and Tommy Dorsey played in Whiteman's band. Bing Crosby made his first significant records singing with Whiteman—with the Rhythm Boys and as a soloist. Whiteman paid his musicians very well, but the top earner in his band at one point was a trombonist who could play "Stars and Stripes Forever" on a bicycle pump. There was always the element of a novelty act with Whiteman.

Whiteman and Gershwin had worked together on the *Scandals* of 1922, for which George wrote his jazz-inspired piece, *Blue Monday*. *Blue Monday* was a thirty-minute one-act operetta set in Harlem, written for black characters and performed in its one-night run in the *Scandals* by white singers in blackface. Buddy DeSylva wrote the libretto and Will Vodery, the African-American musical colleague of Duke Ellington's, orchestrated it. (In spite of the ironic blackface onstage, Gershwin was characteristically colorblind regard-

ing the musicians with whom he worked.) As often happened with a new piece by Gershwin, critics were cool to it on opening night. They didn't know what to make of *Blue Monday*, not having heard anything quite like it before. The piece was immediately pulled from the show, which was supposed to be primarily light and sexy entertainment, not highbrow or weighty. The lingering question is how it made its way into the show to begin with. Did George convince the producer, with whom he had worked for three years, or was it the other way around? The composer Saul Chaplin once stated that the traditional response to a show on opening night is that the score isn't memorable, until it becomes memorable.

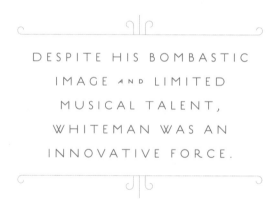

DESPITE HIS BOMBASTIC IMAGE AND LIMITED MUSICAL TALENT, WHITEMAN WAS AN INNOVATIVE FORCE.

Something else hurt *Blue Monday* on its opening (and closing) night. I learned about that "something" from the unpublished memoir of one of Whiteman's band members, Don Clark.

In the operetta's climactic scene, the character named Vi shoots her lover, Joe, because she believes a telegram Joe has received is from another woman. (She is right . . . and wrong. The telegram is from Joe's sister.) Clark writes that at the climactic moment on opening night, Vi pointed the gun at Joe, pulled the trigger, and nothing happened—the blank cartridge didn't fire. So Vi had to shout out, "Bang!" to let the audience know she'd shot Joe. It's hard for a show to recover from such a gaffe. The audience is supposed to be shocked, but instead they're laughing. That's deadly.

Despite its failure, *Blue Monday* was very rich musically and it marked the first key step forward for George on his long road to *Porgy and Bess*. Whiteman obviously knew there was something special in *Blue Monday*. He retitled it *135th Street*, after the piece's setting, and put it in his repertoire, playing it twice in Carnegie Hall concerts at the turn of 1925–26.

Listening to *Blue Monday* today, it is easy to hear the underpinnings that were the germ for *Porgy and Bess*. When you compare it to the relatively light Tin Pan Alley songs that Gershwin wrote for the rest of the score, it becomes evident that he always had a duality of musical expression, an expansive and larger-form sensibility that could not be solely satisfied by his thirty-two-bar creations. The harmonic advancement of *Blue Monday* would not have fit comfortably into popular songs of the time and Gershwin knew it. He had already told Ira about his aspirations to write in a greater musical form, and while the failure of *Blue Monday* was heartbreaking, it did nothing to weaken his confidence in his ability to write music of unique significance. His muse was strong and spoke to him clearly.

Whiteman envisioned his 1924 Aeolian Hall concert as a marketing vehicle rather than a money spinner. Promotional posters gave joint top billing to the pianist and composer Zez Confrey along with George, and Whiteman invited critics to rehearsals

so they could become familiar with the new works before the show opened. Ira also recalled that Confrey expectantly had peppered the town with posters heralding his appearance in the Whiteman show, sans any mention of other artists. Whiteman gave away a lot of tickets and lost money on the event, but he attracted an audience for his afternoon extravaganza that was studded with celebrities: composer Sergei Rachmaninoff; the great violinists Jascha Heifetz and Fritz Kreisler; conductors Leopold Stokowski and Walter Damrosch; writers Gilbert Seldes and Carl Van Vechten.

George's piece was essentially a work in progress when it was first performed. His working title had been *American Rhapsody*, but the wordsmith Ira, having seen an exhibition of paintings by James McNeill Whistler, including his *Nocturne in Blue and Silver*, suggested *Rhapsody in Blue* quite spontaneously at a party in Greenwich Village after George had played portions of his uncompleted opus.

George wrote the original score for two pianos, one being the solo instrument and the other to represent the orchestral part that would be scored by Grofé for Whiteman's jazz band. Perhaps the most famous feature of the piece, the clarinet glissando that opens the work—now one of the most recognizable snatches of music ever played—is also the subject of myth and conjecture. Some claim that it was extemporized and added by Whiteman's clarinetist Ross Gorman before the first performance, totally of his own volition. As Ira recalled to me, George heard Gorman fooling around before a rehearsal, playing a clarinet run up the scale in a smooth, uninterrupted fashion that was counterintuitive to the way the instrument was normally played. Upon hearing his extemporaneous exercise, George specifically requested that Gorman play the riff as a glissando to open the *Rhapsody*.

The title was far from Ira's only contribution. Another popular section, the famous E major theme that has moved listeners to tears, wasn't part of George's original conception of the piece. While working on the *Rhapsody*, George played some of what he had written to Ira, who said, "It would be nice to hear you break it up with something beautiful." Ira recalled an unused theme that George had written a few years earlier that was lying around waiting for a setting. He hummed it to George, who responded, "Oh, that corny thing?" George thought the segment was too maudlin for the piece, but Ira argued with him, in his sweet way, and tried to convince him to use it. Arranger Ferde Grofé also lobbied for its inclusion, and George added it to the mix.

If only the premiere had been recorded, then we'd know what was actually played! There is a famous note in the manuscript score, "Wait for nod," meaning the conductor should wait for a cue from the pianist while George extemporized onstage. In the manuscript there are two passages that were deleted when the sheet music was published. So nobody knows what *exactly* George played at the premiere. Portions of the piano part weren't written down and he may well have embellished what was on the page—that would have been characteristic. Shortly after the first performance, George conformed his performances to the published music and played the piece pretty much the same thereafter. While he might have sometimes played certain passages with different

PROGRAM

First Half

1. **TRUE FORM OF JAZZ**
   a. Ten Years Ago—"Livery Stable Blues" .... *LaRocca*
   b. With Modern Embellishment—"Mama Loves Papa" .... *Baer*

2. **COMEDY SELECTIONS**
   a. Origin of "Yes, We Have No Bananas" .... *Silver*
   b. Instrumental Comedy—"So This Is Venice" .... *Thomas*
      (Featuring Ross Gorman) (Adapted from "The Carnival of Venice")

3. **CONTRAST—LEGITIMATE SCORING VS. JAZZING**
   a. Selection in True Form—"Whispering" .... *Schonberger*
   b. Same Selection with Jazz Treatment

4. **RECENT COMPOSITIONS WITH MODERN SCORE**
   a. "Limehouse Blues" .... *Braham*
   b. "I Love You" .... *Archer*
   c. "Raggedy Ann" .... *Kern*

5. **ZEZ CONFREY** (Piano)
   a. Medley Popular Airs
   b. "Kitten on the Keys" .... *Confrey*
   c. "Ice Cream and Art"
   d. "Nickel in the Slot" .... *Confrey*
      Accompanied by the Orchestra

6. **FLAVORING A SELECTION WITH BORROWED THEMES**
   "Russian Rose" .... *Grofé*
      (Based on "The Volga Boat Song")

THE CONCERT MARKED A DEFIN
SHOWCASED GERSHWIN'S FIRST GR

Program from the concert featuring the first performance of Rhapsody in Blue.

(Program continued)

7. SEMI SYMPHONIC ARRANGEMENT OF POPULAR MELODIES

Consisting of

"Alexander's Ragtime Band"...⎫

"A Pretty Girl is Like a Melody"...................................⎬ *Berlin*

"Orange Blossoms in California"....................................⎭

SECOND HALF

8. A SUITE OF SERENADES...*Herbert*

    a. Spanish

    b. Chinese

    c. Cuban

    d. Oriental

9. ADAPTATION OF STANDARD SELECTIONS TO DANCE RHYTHM

    a. "Pale Moon" ....*Logan*

    b. "To a Wild Rose"..............................*McDowell*

    c. "Chansonette" ....*Friml*

10. GEORGE GERSHWIN (Piano)

    "A Rhapsody in Blue".........................*Gershwin*

        Accompanied by the Orchestra

11. IN THE FIELD OF CLASSICS

    "Pomp and Circumstance"...................*Elgar*

        Chickering Piano Used.

SING OF THE BATON, SINCE IT

ASSICAL PIECE AND HERBERT'S LAST.

voicing or slightly different phrasing, the overall form didn't change.

Rhapsody in Blue was scheduled to be the next-to-last of all of the pieces performed at Aeolian Hall that day, and the concert ended with the imperious strains of Edward Elgar. Whiteman's intention was to show how far jazz had come from its disreputable roots, and his band first played the 1917 hit "Livery Stable Blues" by the Original Dixieland Jass Band, ostensibly as a deliberately unflattering point of reference for what was to come.

The concert featured only two new pieces—*Rhapsody in Blue* and Victor Herbert's *Suite of Serenades* (yet no tone poem by Irving Berlin as Whiteman had promised). Victor Herbert had been one of the most important forces in American popular music for decades, but his piece was rather conventional.

After the concert, Herbert hosted a dinner at the Lamb's Club for Whiteman and Gershwin and others. Herbert offered Gershwin some advice about *Rhapsody*: "If I'd written that piece, I would have done this and would have done that . . ." George didn't really need Herbert's help, though Herbert was the revered elder statesman of American music and a larger-than-life legend. The concert marked a definite passing of the baton, since it showcased Gershwin's first great classical piece and Herbert's last—he died just three months later. A statue of Herbert stands in New York's Central Park, reflecting his immense contribution to American music.

I have spoken over the years with many people who attended that concert and, not surprisingly, their memories of the event differ. Since George's was the penultimate work in a long

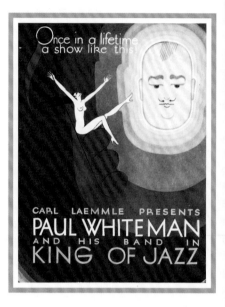

concert, some say that the audience was restless by the time he played. Composer and then–Harvard student Johnny Green said it was very hot in the auditorium and that was the biggest problem. (Johnny possessed a prodigious musical memory, but even he could not reproduce what tantalizing extra passages George played that afternoon.) I didn't get many details when I asked composer Harry Warren about it—he had written a piece called "So This Is Venice" for the concert but hadn't received a credit in the program, and he was still mad about it sixty years later.

Others say that the audience sat in rapt attention throughout. In the *New York Times*, the critic Olin Downes wrote about how much he liked "Livery Stable Blues," whatever the reason for its inclusion in the show, and he praised the contribution of black musicians to jazz, this uniquely American form of music. Downes only mentioned two composers in his review: Victor Herbert, briefly, and George Gershwin ("a lank and dark young man") at some length. Downes said *Rhapsody* revealed a great and ambitious talent who hadn't yet mastered writing for piano or for piano and orchestra. While he picked away at what he took to be Gershwin's deficits of structure and lack of preparation, he acknowledged that his piece was a welcome contrast to the drab sameness of the rest of the concert. He wrote that the audience appreciated what they heard and was "stirred"

(LEFT) *George working with Paul Whiteman and Dana Seusse in 1932.*
(RIGHT) *A program for Paul Whiteman's film,* King of Jazz *(1930).*

and "excited" by the new voice, one "likely to say something personally and racially important to the world. . . . There was tumultuous applause for Mr. Gershwin's composition."

My friend Johnny Green sat in the rafters and never forgot what he witnessed. To the end of his days, he remembered the physical sensation he experienced when he first heard the Andante theme from the *Rhapsody*. "It was so beautiful, I died," he said. Ira sat with friend Cecelia Ager, who kept her fingernails dug into his wrist as they watched. Ira was so nervous at the first performance that he doodled in pen all over the program, thus defacing what later became one of the most collectible pieces of Gershwin ephemera. Thirty years later his friend Sam Marx gave him his pristine copy, which is now housed in the Gershwin collection at the Library of Congress.

THE CONCERT PAID OFF handsomely for Paul Whiteman. He took his band on a six-week tour of the country only a few months after his initial triumph and *Rhapsody in Blue* became a fixture in his repertoire. George repeated his performance with Whiteman for some of the shows and when unavailable was replaced by Harry Perella and Roy Bargy, who played in the band. There was quite a furor over the piece and a demand for it to be recorded. In June 1924, George did so, with Paul Whiteman's band. Then George's music publisher said he wanted to print it, the whole thing, and Ira, wondering who would buy such an odd little mongrel, asked George, "In all seriousness, who's going to play it?"

But play it they did and buy it they did. The sheet music sold well. After Universal Studios paid

George a small fortune for the rights, Whiteman also played *Rhapsody in Blue* in his self-promoting movie, *The King of Jazz* of 1930. It offered plenty of good exposure for Gershwin, but Whiteman wasn't a great musician, and George hated the way he conducted *Rhapsody in Blue*, though the piano part was ably handled by Roy Bargy. He was a cartoonishly bad conductor (in his *New York Times* review of the Aeolian Hall concert, Downes wrote that Whiteman doesn't conduct, "he trembles, wabbles, quivers—a piece of jazz jelly"). When Whiteman traveled to London in 1926 and gave a highly touted performance of the piece, Adele Astaire wrote George a letter complaining that Paul Whiteman had massacred *Rhapsody in Blue* again.

Ferde Grofé's first orchestration of *Rhapsody* was for the unconventional twenty-three-piece band Whiteman used for his Aeolian Hall concert. Then he rearranged the piece for a slightly larger concert orchestra, a lusher version that smoothed out some of the jazziness; he rearranged it again in 1942 for a larger, symphony orchestra (with a minimum of forty-two players), which is the version that is commonly heard today.

Some prefer the second, smaller orchestration, which is the one George played throughout his lifetime—this is the version the Boston Pops plays, for example, finding it closer in spirit to the original. George always intended to go back and orchestrate the piece himself but never found the time. It would have been most interesting to hear what changes he might have made in the orchestration, especially after playing it hundreds upon hundreds of times. Would he have gone back to the more primitive jazz sounds of the Whiteman original, or would he have succumbed to the deco styles of the thirties, with muted instruments playing in a more subdued and streamlined style? While many purists insist that the *Rhapsody* should only be heard in the first jazz band arrangement, I always remind them that Gershwin himself always used a larger orchestration.

George recorded *Rhapsody* with Whiteman again in 1927, after the invention of the microphone prompted the Victor Company to produce a new edition in improved fidelity. At least the record label said "Whiteman." The two men argued over Whiteman's melodramatic interpretation. During the famous Andante section, Whiteman put in a great big *luftpause* (breath), which drove George crazy. (The following year he privately complained about an emasculated adaptation of his Concerto in F Whiteman had had Grofé create, and didn't want to autograph a copy of the record for a friend.) So the stalwart Nathaniel Shilkret (director of Victor's light music department), not Whiteman, conducted the work for the 1927 recording, although the bandleader's name still appeared on the record.

(This ghostly credit was by no means unprecedented. In the early days of the LP in the fifties, Capitol Records wanted Whiteman to re-record *Rhapsody in Blue* in high fidelity, featuring the young pianist Leonard Pennario. I asked Pennario what it had been like to work with the legendary Whiteman and he said, "I never met Paul Whiteman." Whiteman sent his associate, Roy Bargy, to conduct the piece, although when the record came out, Whiteman's and Gershwin's photos were emblazoned on the cover. Another example: a well-known Columbia recording from the mid-fifties called *Richard Rodgers Conducts Rodgers with the New York Philharmonic* was actually conducted by Robert Russell Bennett.)

These days there are a number of Gershwin performances of the *Rhapsody* available to the public, but many have pedigree problems of having been manipulated in one way or another, either in sound reproduction or by more nefarious means. In the 1970s there was much made about a new recording of the *Rhapsody* utilizing the original Whiteman Jazz Band arrangement, performed with the 1925 piano roll of the composer playing the solo part—in theory an exciting and fun idea. The jacket of the record was emblazoned with a beautiful Hirschfeld drawing of a ghostly Gershwin at the keyboard with lithe Michael Tilson Thomas conducting the band.

According to my close friend Stan Freeman, who was a dazzlingly talented pianist and Gershwin interpreter, he received an SOS to come in and secretly fix several sections of the "Gershwin" performance because they could not get it to synchronize with the orchestra, as the piano roll was simply too fast to keep up with, and they were at their wits' end. Stan said he went in and discreetly played the problematic sections, and the recording was saved.

The veracity of this claim was bolstered by Gershwin authority Edward Jablonski, who in a 2003 letter to me corroborated the story as told to him by legendary Columbia record producer John Hammond, so I believe it. The recording was nonetheless nominated for a Grammy, but when I played it for Ira, he resolutely insisted that George never played the *Rhapsody* at the breakneck tempos on the Tilson Thomas disc and considered it nothing more than a stunt. Still, the *Rhapsody* lives on unbended, unbowed, and youthful as Dorian Gray.

(OPPOSITE) *Sheet music cover for "Where's the Boy? Here's the Girl!" from* Treasure Girl.

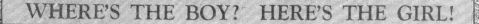

WHERE'S THE BOY? HERE'S THE GIRL!

ALEX A. AARONS & VINTON FREEDLEY

PRESENT

GERTRUDE LAWRENCE

IN A NEW MUSICAL COMEDY

TREASURE GIRL

BOOK BY

FRED THOMPSON

AND

VINCENT LAWRENCE

LYRICS BY

IRA GERSHWIN

MUSIC BY

GEORGE GERSHWIN

I Don't Think I'll Fall In
Love To-day
Where's The Boy?
Here's The Girl!
Oh, So Nice
What Are We Here For?
Got A Rainbow
K-ra-(?) I Love You
Feeling I'm Falling

MUSICAL NUMBERS STAGED BY
ROBERT CONNOLLY

NEW WORLD MUSIC
CORPORATION
HARMS
NEW YORK

THE SONG "I'VE GOT A CRUSH ON YOU" bears one of the essential properties of a Gershwin classic: flexibility. Like *Rhapsody in Blue*, "I've Got a Crush on You" has such great underlying DNA that you can change it significantly without altering its brilliant essence. Even radically altered, most interpretations of Gershwin songs cannot obscure evidence of the genius of the mind that crafted them. It's not an immutable fact, mind you, but the odds are pretty good in Gershwin's favor.

It's not just an ability to withstand a wide variety of interpretations that made these works so enduring: they also have in common a more fundamental adaptability of form. All the themes

As effectively as any other song, "I've Got a Crush on You" illustrates the extraordinary breadth of George's focus, from this versatile popular song to the groundbreaking orchestral piece. But still, why *this* song? Because it represents a significant period in his career with Ira and reflects changing styles in the way it transformed through the years to become an evergreen standard. And of course, musically speaking, I have the biggest crush on George and Ira. But I guess I have to stand in line.

In the fall of 1928, a year after *Funny Face* was produced, the Gershwins wrote a show called *Treasure Girl*. The star was Gertrude Lawrence, who had been a big success when she'd starred in *Oh, Kay!* a couple of years earlier, and it was anticipated that

BLURRING THE DISTINCTION BETWEEN HIGH ART AND ENTERTAINMENT, BETWEEN CLASSICAL AND JAZZ AND POP STYLES, WAS AT THE HEART OF HIS VISION FOR THE UNIFYING POWER OF MUSIC.

in *Rhapsody in Blue* are melodies George could easily have used in his songs. The Andante, in fact, was originally intended as the melody for a song. It is not a coincidence that the line between George's concert works and popular songs is such a fine one: erasing that line was one of the overarching goals of his creative endeavor. Blurring the distinction between high art and entertainment, between classical music and the jazz and pop styles, was at the heart of his vision for the unifying power of music and its ability to bring different kinds of people together.

Treasure Girl would be a hit. (Eight or nine songs from the show were individually published as it was opening—more than usual.)

But *Treasure Girl* ran at the Alvin Theatre for just sixty-eight performances. The problem was that Lawrence was asked to play a heel, what Ira called an "unsavory character," a completely unsympathetic gold digger. No one—neither the critics nor the public—could buy Gertrude Lawrence in an unpleasant role like this. It was similar to when Gene Kelly played bad guy Joey Evans in *Pal Joey*, the Rodgers and Hart musical of John

O'Hara's novel, which opened in 1940. Critic Brooks Atkinson asked if you can draw sweet water from a foul well. *Pal Joey* was certainly more of a success than *Treasure Girl*, but oddly *Pal Joey* broke records as a revival in 1952, with Harold Lang in the title role, in a later decade when the character was finally accepted by theater attendees.

In the original show, "I've Got a Crush on You" was an up-tempo dance number performed by Clifton Webb as Nat and Mary Hay as Polly. It was a fast and furious one-step, a one-step being the fastest tempo in which you could successfully maintain a dance. The emphasis is strongly on the beat, with perhaps a very similar feel to a seventies disco record.

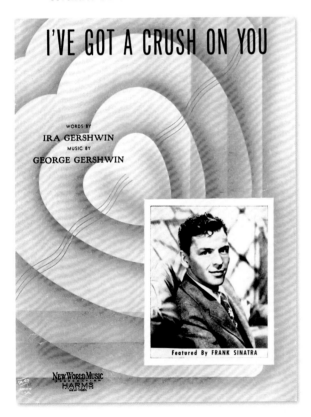

"I've Got a Crush on You" was still played fast when it was rescued from *Treasure Girl* and added to *Strike Up the Band* for that show's second incarnation in 1930. Ira Gershwin wrote that it was sung by Gordon Smith and Doris Carson and danced by them "at about the fastest $2/4$ I ever heard." But that is not how the song is sung today. "I've Got a Crush on You" survives (and thrives) as a radical reinterpretation, perhaps the most changed song in the Gershwin songbook.

Lee Wiley was a popular jazz singer from Oklahoma who performed with Paul Whiteman. In 1939 she recorded a set of 78s of Gershwin songs, including a version of "I've Got a Crush on You" that slowed the song down dramatically. She was the first artist to record the song at *any* tempo, so there was nothing to compete with her rendition except in the memories of those who'd seen the song performed on Broadway. In 1947, Frank Sinatra recorded the song the same way, and that sealed the deal for "I've Got a Crush on You." Slow it was to be.

When Ira first heard Lee Wiley's recording he felt thwarted and irritated, because he didn't think the lyrics worked well in a slow ballad setting. "What have they done to my song?" he said. But Ira listened to the song again, and the third time he listened to it, he decided he liked it. The lyrics actually did fit—the rhymes of "Pie" and "sigh" ("Sweetie Pie / . . . Hear me sigh") and alliteration of "coo" and "care" ("Could you coo, Could you care") worked well when slowed down.

Frank Sinatra is responsible for the continued popularity of "I've Got a Crush on You" as a ballad. After he recorded it, it became one of his most requested numbers. In the forties, the

GEORGE AND JEROME KERN IN 1933.

sheet music for it was printed with a new piano accompaniment that matched the general way Sinatra sang it. He recorded the song several times, the last time with Barbra Streisand for his *Duets* album in 1993. (Well, not actually "with," because they weren't in the same room when they sang their respective parts.) Gertrude Lawrence finally recorded an up-tempo version of the song a few years before her death in 1951, but by that time, "I've Got a Crush on You" was established as a ballad. To the end, Lawrence proprietarily insisted it must be sung as a faster song; she didn't like the slow version at all.

Stalwart Bobby Short was the only other soul to make a faithful up-tempo version of the song, for his 1973 double LP tribute to Gershwin, and was the first to record some previously unheard extra lyrics. When I played that recording for Ira he was so unfamiliar with those additional words that he insisted he hadn't written them until a scurried trip to his lyric file produced the evidence that indeed he had! There is also a spurious lyric that found its way into print courtesy of a former publisher, Herman Starr, who took it upon himself to change some of the lines for the 1948 publication so that they could be sung by either gender. In the process, where the original verse went, "How glad the many millions / Of Annabelles and Lillians," he paired "millions" with "Williams," which doesn't rhyme. This mistake was immortalized on Ella Fitzgerald's gargantuan five-disc Gershwin tribute in 1959. Ira was not amused. (Ira did write the feminine version, "How glad a million laddies / from millionaires to caddies. . ." and also offered "although I'm no du Barry, how glad Tom, Dick, and Harry. . .")

The 1948 corrected printing also offered a substitute for "You're my big and brave and handsome Romeo" with the lines "You're a treat, my sweet, you set my heart aglow," lines Ira approved so the lyrics could be sung from a solo male perspective, thus with all of these other lines offering a variety of choices to the research-minded interpreter.

I recorded the song in 2008 as part of my Sinatra Project, it being so singularly associated with Ol' Blue Eyes. In that context it was appropriate that I sing it the way Sinatra did, but I also like it up-tempo and, indeed, I love some of the harmonies Gershwin had in the original version. Even when I slow down the tempo, I try to incorporate harmonic choices George made.

The first time I heard "Crush" performed at a quick tempo it was a true revelation and made me love it deeply that way. I have also sung it at the faster tempo but find that most folks want to hear it slower. Sometimes in performance I'll do the up-tempo rendition and then embrace the sexy tempo, and people actually laugh at the foreign experience of hearing it at a gallop, almost like cartoon music. It was while listening to a recording of overtures from Gershwin shows that I discovered the fast version; it was played as part of the *Strike Up the Band* overture (arranged by the facile and talented Don Rose). For a while I only wanted to hear it up-tempo after that and for a period didn't like the slower renditions, feeling that they had bowdlerized the original. Ira ultimately liked it both ways and was grateful for its climbing status as another standard that was earning him a good deal of money, to boot.

The song might have become better known even faster if producer Arthur Freed hadn't chopped it out of the Oscar-winning 1951 film *An American in Paris*. It was sung and danced by Gene Kelly at medium tempo and had a charming swing to it, and was orchestrated by the legendary Conrad Salinger. The number was one of the songs hand-picked by Ira as a favorite to include in the film, and Kelly felt that it was one of his best numbers in the picture, but it was cut for pacing when the film was deemed to be too long. Kelly was devastated at its loss.

Some thirty years later I tried to find the deleted number, hoping to reclaim it for Ira and Kelly, but tragically it had been destroyed and was lost forever along with hundreds of other unused clips that had been trashed by MGM a decade earlier. Ira was genuinely sad when I delivered the news. The only thing that remains is the soundtrack, and if you close your eyes you can try to imagine what Kelly's choreography might have been like. Another treasure lost forever.

> KELLY FELT THAT IT WAS ONE OF HIS BEST NUMBERS IN THE PICTURE, BUT IT WAS CUT FOR PACING.

Returning for a moment to the lyric of "I've Got a Crush on You," it is significant to recognize that the words have the same potency that they had in 1928, in that their meaning still shines through as a fresh expression of a romantic notion. Whether it is sung fast or slow the sensibility of the words does not change. That's unusual, because often the tempo can give different emphasis or meaning to a lyric when it is altered.

It was written in the latter part of the twenties, and Ira had spent many years at that point trying to come up with fresh ideas for love songs and must have been tickled when he hit upon the idea of interpolating the thought of having a "crush" on someone into a lyric. In the mid-1800s the term "crush" referred to a social gathering or dance, and it is perhaps from that meaning that the use of it as an infatuation evolved. Sadly I never asked him specifically what his inspiration might have been and how popular the term was at that time. Sometimes he was ahead of the curve in using such popular phrases and other times helped create a few himself. Clearly George and Ira thought highly of the song, because it was the only number from the entire score of *Treasure Girl* that they reused later, and it was a full score indeed, with many first-rate numbers.

BY THE TIME THE BROTHERS had created "Crush" and the score of *Treasure Girl*, George had already composed several significant concert works, taking time to write them between (or during) his next Broadway assignments. After the success of *Rhapsody in Blue*, George was commissioned by conductor Walter Damrosch to write a piano concerto for his New York Symphony Orchestra. The Concerto in F premiered at Carnegie Hall under Damrosch in December 1925. The concerto was written much more methodically than the *Rhapsody*, over a period of months rather than weeks. He was eager to advance and write in a more structured form and was careful not to accept any challenge until he felt ready for it.

(OPPOSITE) *Royalty statement from Harms in 1929 for* Rhapsody in Blue.

ROYALTY STATEMENT
FROM
HARMS, Inc.
62-64 WEST 45TH ST., N. Y.

For GEORGE GERSHWIN

Below will be found the number of copies sold, and the amount of royalty due, for the <u>three</u> *months*

ending March 31, 1929

NUMBER OF COPIES	TITLES	SOLD	COPIES RETD.	RATE	AMOUNT	TOTAL
	RHAPSODY IN BLUE					
17 ·	ORCHESTRATIONS			.24	4.08	
15 ·	"			.30	4.50	
3 ·	"			1.00	3.00	
2,464 ·	PIANO SOLO			1.25	3,080.00	
26 ·	ORGAN			1.25	32.50	
16 ·	ORCHESTRATIONS			1.25	20.00	
125 ·	PIANO SOLO - FOUR HANDS			3.00	375.00	
44 ·	ORCHESTRATIONS			3.50	154.00	
14 ·	"			4.50	63.00	
2 ·	"			5.00	10.00	
2 ·	"			6.50	13.00	
	EXTRA PARTS				34.47	
					3,793.55	
		15% of....................				$569.03

Composing a formal concerto was a learning process for Gershwin; once he agreed to the commission he bought books and read up on the history and structure of the form. If he was going to write a concerto, he wanted to make sure he knew the classical definition. (With the *Rhapsody,* the very name relieved him of the requirement to write in a strict classical form.) George said his first movement utilized the Charleston rhythm, the second the blues, and the third was "an orgy of rhythm"—he was bringing a modern interpretation to a musical form that had been around for more than 150 years. Oscar Levant was one of the first pianists to embrace the new work and he performed the third movement on a 1934 radio show. He had met George in 1925 during the creation of the concerto and had the temerity to notice the manuscript in progress sitting on

Lobby card for the George Gershwin biopic, Rhapsody in Blue, *1945.*

George's piano and start to play through it. Levant said that George liked the slow second movement, the Andante, best of the three and played that single movement more often than any other portion of the work when time would permit only the performance of an excerpt on a broadcast. The piece was Ira's favorite work of his brother's.

I've never played the Concerto in F in public, but I adore the piece. In many ways I find it more musically fulfilling than the *Rhapsody*. Perhaps it's the expansive nature of the work and the more mournful thematic material that attract me. The electrifying and vigorous last movement, the Agitato, is very famous—it was used in the movie *An American in Paris*. It was based on an

composed his *Ragtime* in 1918, but George was the first to organically combine jazz and classical genres. Yet when he was asked by a major classical music figure to write a concerto, a piece with an established template, one interpreted by composers such as Chopin, Liszt, Brahms, and Beethoven, George simply did a little homework and went out and aced the test. I'm echoing what Ira often said, but I don't believe there was anything in music he couldn't have done had he put his mind to it.

George was also an unusually talented pianist, capable of successfully improvising in any situation, as he did with the debut of *Rhapsody in Blue*. He was a far better player than his popular music peers. Cole Porter couldn't play the piano well; Harry War-

BUT THE ONLY VIRTUOSO PIANIST WITH SUCH A RANGE OF COMPOSING ACCOMPLISHMENTS WAS GEORGE.

unfinished piano prelude George had begun right before he started work on the concerto. How wise of him to recognize the staying power of that theme as well as the possible ways he could imaginatively expand it. The pages of the unfinished prelude are held in the Library of Congress.

The breadth of George's talent continues to astound me. His ambition was limitless, as was his confidence. *Rhapsody in Blue* was a musical genre in itself, wholly created by George. He worked from no blueprint. There was no previous composition that so successfully and popularly combined jazz and symphonic music. George singlehandedly created a new genre. Stravinsky had

ren could only play in the most basic fashion. Warren had tremendous ability when it came to conceiving musical ideas, but they happened in his head—he couldn't translate them to the keyboard. Jerome Kern is considered perhaps the master of them all as a songwriter, but he was an erratic pianist—oddly so, considering the exacting nature of his music and its requirements. Irving Berlin was a double threat: a poor pianist and singer. An exception was Harold Arlen, who was a good player as well as singer and could extemporize from his songs. Rube Bloom was a great pianist who also wrote hit songs (as opposed to a songwriter who could play piano). Some of his hits were "Fools Rush In,"

"Here's to My Lady" (with Johnny Mercer), and "Don't Worry 'Bout Me" (with Ted Koehler).

But the only virtuoso pianist with such a range of composing accomplishments was George. Ralph Rainger was a dazzling second and seriously studied with Schoenberg, but sadly he never realized his loftier composing ambitions. Nor did the heavenly Johnny Green fulfill his larger-form compositional dreams. George's friend Fats Waller could dazzle at a party as well as George could—he could play anything in any key and he was a great songwriter, but his output was small compared with George's. Duke Ellington was also a wonderful songwriter, but his method of composition was quite different. Except perhaps for the several piano pieces he composed

for a series of demo recordings of the score of *Delicious* that were made with George at the piano with a then somewhat unknown singer named Bing Crosby. These would be an extraordinary find. So many of the recordings made by George are gone; tests he made for the Victor label in 1920 are listed in the record company logs, but no one can find them. Radio broadcasts once listed in the archives of CBS Radio were long ago destroyed. Had they survived we would be able to hear how Gershwin played many of his songs, often right after he had written them.

There exists a 1936 broadcast of a Paul Whiteman show announcing Gershwin as a guest, but only the first four minutes of that show survive,

BY THE TIME ONE OF HIS SONGS HAD BEEN DOCUMENTED AS A PIECE OF SHEET MUSIC, GEORGE'S FRILLS WERE LOST BECAUSE THE MUSIC HAD MOST OFTEN BEEN SIMPLIFIED FOR THE AVERAGE PIANIST.

early in his career, Ellington wrote everything with his band in mind. He played the piano extremely well but it was of secondary importance to him, as perhaps he had become spoiled by the muse of his band. On the other hand, of course, practically all of his recordings are supreme and unique, and his legacy is secure. His longer works are pungent and memorable, but as far as combining great writing and playing, George had no equal.

Unfortunately, there is but a slim archive that survives of the super-confident George playing his own work. For many years, I've searched

and sadly Gershwin does not feature in them. While a complete rehearsal recording of the *Second Rhapsody* does exist, there was an earlier original soundtrack recording of what became the *Second Rhapsody*, then called *New York Rhapsody*, prerecorded for the 1931 film *Delicious*. The shortened performance, as used on the finished soundtrack, was replete with cacophonous New York City sound effects, because the music was to accompany a girl's wanderings through the city. It disappeared in the sixties. And I desperately wish someone could find the complete recording of the 1936 concert in

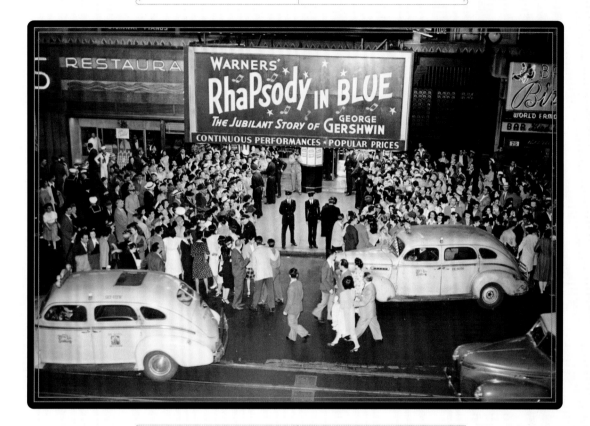

which George played *Rhapsody in Blue* and Concerto in F, as only a fragment survives.

Occasionally great finds are still being made, such as an air check of one of his 1934 *Music by Gershwin* shows that turned up in the possession of the relatives of one of the guests on the show, harpist Casper Reardon. Pianist and musicological wonder Peter Mintun made that discovery. Peter is one of those chosen people to whom the universe entrusts such things. Prior to his discovery only two episodes of that series existed, and this third episode has George playing "My Cousin in Milwaukee," a superior later creation from *Pardon My English* (1933), as well as part of the Concerto in F.

People who knew George said he would play a passage in a different tempo or a different style just for the fun of it. It would be wonderful to hear his improvisational genius. By the time one of his songs had been documented as a piece of sheet music, George's frills were lost because the music had most often been simplified for the average pianist. Those elusive original recordings would be priceless, because George performed his songs differently every time he played them.

The Rhapsody in Blue *New York movie premiere in 1945.*

F I HAD TO NAME ONE OTHER composer who affects me as much as George Gershwin, I would pick Erich Wolfgang Korngold (1897–1957). Korngold may not be as familiar a name, but when I hear his music it goes right to my heart just as George's does. A Central European composer born in what is now the Czech Republic, Korngold became best known to Americans when he worked in Hollywood in the thirties, writing scores for movies. But by that time, he was already well known in Europe as a classical composer, especially of operettas.

Korngold was a child prodigy, probably the only true musical prodigy since Mozart. I don't say that lightly. He paralleled Mozart in that at the age of six or seven he was writing longer-form pieces of music. In 1906, Korngold's father, Julius,

Anthony Adverse (1936) and *The Adventures of Robin Hood* (1938), and was nominated for *The Private Lives of Elizabeth and Essex* (1939) and *The Sea Hawk* (1940). His musical style essentially did not change throughout his life, and that was a common criticism, that he didn't "grow." But how much growing did he need to do? He mastered opera, and his film scores were really operas without words. In fact, he used some of his movie music in his classical works, a right he made sure he protected in his contracts. One of the themes from *Robin Hood* he later used in the last movement of his violin concerto, for example.

Gershwin had a similar facility for moving among genres and styles, and they evidently knew each other because Korngold attended George's 1936 performance with the Los Angeles Philhar-

IT WAS, ESSENTIALLY, THE INVENTION OF A NEW TYPE OF AMERICAN MUSIC.

took the boy to see Mahler to play the great composer his cantata, and Mahler proclaimed the boy a genius. He wrote a ballet when he was eleven, and his Sinfonietta in B Major was premiered by the Vienna Philharmonic and Felix Weingartner in 1913, when the composer was sixteen.

In adulthood, Korngold wrote piano music and a string of operas until the Nazis came to power. Then he initially split his time between Vienna and Hollywood, where he wrote his first film score, *A Midsummer Night's Dream*, in 1934. In all he wrote more than twenty scores for Warner Brothers. His music won Academy Awards, for

monic. Oh, what I wouldn't give to hear a conversation shared by the two of them! But there's no real musical comparison between the two men: there's no jazz in Korngold, for one thing. The similarity for me is the emotional experience I have listening to their music. Both composers did suffer from the unfair taint of association with Hollywood, Korngold much more than Gershwin. Korngold's movie score success made him less of a figure in the classical music world, and after the Second World War, when he went back to Europe, he was considered passé because he'd "sold out" and also because operettas were going out of fashion and his romantic style was considered part of the past. Clearly the problem of hasty and narrow-minded judgments plagued all of the most versatile composers, regardless of whether they wrote in the classical, jazz, or popular idiom.

The same fate befell Spanish classical pianist José Iturbi (1895–1980), who appeared in Hollywood musicals in the forties like *Anchors Aweigh* (with Frank Sinatra and Gene Kelly), and was never taken quite as seriously again. One of the more peculiar performances of the *Rhapsody* was given by Iturbi at the Gershwin Memorial Concert broadcast live from the Hollywood Bowl on Sep-

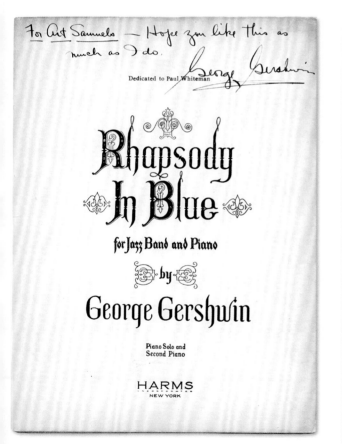

tember 8, 1937. Ira was present and was bemused by Iturbi's improvisation. I met the great pianist shortly before his passing, but I didn't have the temerity to ask if he improvised by choice or from loss of memory, as I once witnessed Van Cliburn do in a Chopin encore, also at the Hollywood Bowl, and he fooled most of the attendees.

I don't agree with such snobbery regarding great musical endeavors. The success of Korngold's film scores shouldn't detract from the value of his operas. Few people would think of denigrating a film score merely because it had been written by a composer of operas. But this came up constantly for Gershwin—it seemed inconceivable to some critics that he could be a wonderful writer of piano concertos, pop songs, operas, musicals, film music, and also something as singular and wonderful as the *Rhapsody in Blue*. Rather than bow before that level of genius, it's easier to say that the music is overrated.

I T'S TRUE, OF COURSE, that not everything George wrote was a success. But the breadth of what he was trying to achieve—and what he did achieve— was extraordinary. It was, essentially, the invention of a new type of American music, one that melded the old and the new, the street and the concert hall, the classical, the popular, and the jazz-infused.

There's no composer alive with the stature Gershwin had in his lifetime. He was the most popular composer in America, giving the lie to the notion that true quality can only flourish in obscurity. He was a phenomenon everyone wanted to meet, and great classical composers, including Maurice Ravel, Alban Berg, and Ralph Vaughan Williams, were fans. *Rhapsody in Blue* was con-

Autographed title page of Rhapsody in Blue, *one of two existing first editions signed by Gershwin.*

stantly on the radio when George was alive. He toured frequently, conducting and playing with orchestras, but he was best known for his musicals and the hit songs that came out of them. The songs touch me in the same way the more "serious" music does, a depth of emotion that is evident in everything from *Rhapsody in Blue* to a song like "I've Got a Crush on You." Oddly it was his former collaborator Irving Caesar who felt that George had sold out and not followed his true path. In reference to George he once told me, "You cannot please the muses and the masses." Of course, in my opinion George did just that.

With *Rhapsody in Blue*, George Gershwin made a quantum leap in American music. Before *Rhapsody in Blue*, American concert music was stolid and largely devoid of personality and copied from European traditions. People were looking for the true American voice and Gershwin had a clear vision of what that voice should be. He wanted to extend jazz beyond the limits of the three-minute song. In an article published in *Theatre Magazine* in 1926, he said his best works were the *Rhapsody* and Concerto in F. The *Rhapsody*, he said, "succeeded in showing that jazz is not merely a dance; it comprises bigger themes and purposes. It may have the quality of an epic. I wrote it in ten days; it has lived for three years, and is healthy and growing."

Still, it was only after George's death that pianist Oscar Levant insistently integrated Gershwin into the standard orchestral repertoire. Today, his music remains as thrilling as ever. Gershwin might have used the same language and the same notes as other musicians, but he created unique music—music with a spiritual quality, a warmth, a humanity to it. Any great art inspires us to dream of achieving greater heights. With its extra magic, Gershwin's music enthralls and touches people in a way that is unlike the effect of any other composer. The experience of performing his music countless times leads me to this conclusion.

Of all the songs that give me the feeling of being closest to Ira, "I've Got a Crush on You" is one of the most resonant. In my mind's eye I can see his face intently listening as I play the song for him on the piano, his eyes shut, a Mona Lisa smile on his face, silently mouthing the words as I sing them, retreating to his happy times of yesterday and the resplendent memories brought back by George's music. How his world had changed in the intervening decades, and looking at him then, I wished to be able to transport him back to his treasured past. When the song finishes he pauses for only a moment before opening his eyes and returning to the present. Then with a characteristic tongue-in-cheek manner he grins and says, "Very good Gershwin!" I couldn't agree more. ·

(ABOVE) *First recording of* Rhapsody in Blue *(1924).* • (OPPOSITE) *George's self-portrait, 1933.*

"THEY ALL LAUGHED"

from *Shall We Dance*, 1937

VERSE

The odds were a hundred to one against me,
The world thought the heights were too high to
climb.
But people from Missouri never incensed me:
Oh, I wasn't a bit concerned,
For from hist'ry I had learned
How many, many times the worm had turned.

REFRAIN 1

They all laughed at Christopher Columbus
When he said the world was round;
They all laughed when Edison recorded sound.

They all laughed at Wilbur and his brother
When they said that man could fly;
They told Marconi
Wireless was a phony—
It's the same old cry!

They laughed at me wanting you,
Said I was reaching for the moon;
But oh, you came through—
Now they'll have to change their tune.

They all said we never could be happy,
They laughed at us—and how!
But ho, ho, ho—
Who's got the last laugh now?

REFRAIN 2

They all laughed at Rockefeller Center—
Now they're fighting to get in;
They all laughed at Whitney and his cotton gin.

They all laughed at Fulton and his steamboat,
Hershey and his choc'late bar.
Ford and his Lizzie
Kept the laughers busy—
That's how people are!

They laughed at me wanting you—
Said it would be Hello! Good-bye!
But oh, you came through—
Now they're eating humble pie.

They all said we'd never get together—
Darling, let's take a bow,
For ho, ho, ho—
Who's got the last laugh—
He, he, he—
Let's at the past laugh—
Ha, ha, ha—
Who's got the last laugh now?

· C H A P T E R 5 ·

MUSIC AND SOCIETY

I N 1927, IN "JAZZ IS THE VOICE OF THE American Soul" written for *Theatre Magazine*, George Gershwin said no one knew what the next decade held in music. "But to be true music it must repeat the thoughts and aspirations of the people and the time. My people are Americans. My time is today." George's America was very different from today's. In 1930 the census counted 123 million Americans; there were close to 309 million in 2010. About half the population lived in rural areas then; now less than 20 percent does. In 1934, with the country struggling through the Depression, a quarter of the American workforce was unemployed. Women had gained the right to vote in

1920, but Jim Crow laws were still in force in much of the country, and African-Americans remained effectively disenfranchised for another forty-five years.

Some of those newly enfranchised young women flaunted custom by wearing drop-waisted skirts, stockings, and makeup. They smoked and drank, did the Charleston in dance halls and nightclubs, and generally had a high old time. One of those flappers was Ellin Mackay, the Catholic debutante daughter of multimillionaire Clarence Mackay. She repudiated what she described as the "dull old days" ruled over by the Gilded Age society of Mrs. Jacob Astor's exclusive "400"—the number of socially acceptable New York families

George painting Ruby Elzy, Serena *in* Porgy and Bess*, 1935.*

identified by Mrs. Astor in the 1870s—and scandalously married a Jewish immigrant named Irving Berlin in 1926. Ellin Mackay was disinherited for her impudence. The 400 were intended to be bastions of old money standing firm against the rising tide of arrivistes who had actually made rather than inherited their own fortunes. In the twenties the dam finally broke.

The "Roaring Twenties"—also called "the Jazz Age"—were a giddy time of shortening skirts and social experimentation, as chronicled in the short stories and novels of F. Scott Fitzgerald. Jazz, the exciting new musical style, came to New York City in 1917—just as George was coming of age—when the Original Dixieland Jass Band, a group

of white musicians from New Orleans, played Reisenweber's Club at 58th Street and Eighth Avenue. The band made what are recognized as the first jazz recordings that same year and spawned a musical movement that George would tap into.

The Morton Gould, Betty Comden, and Adolph Green show *Billion Dollar Baby* was produced in 1945 and was set in the twenties as an homage to that period, and Comden and Green, although very young, lived through the Jazz Age. I once asked Betty what the twenties were actually like, and she said, "Oh, it was horrible," meaning it was so excessive. Because of Prohibition, which was in effect from 1920 till 1933, there was rampant lawlessness and degeneracy. There were also

(LEFT) *George as Groucho Marx at a costume party. Richard Rodgers as Zeppo is at far left.*
(RIGHT) *George at two other costume parties.*

extraordinary cultural achievements, as many different types of American music melded. Artistically and otherwise, the twenties were a time of great invention, from *The New Yorker* to Mickey Mouse. Of the iconic names from that era, those of greatest interest to me are the likes of Robert Benchley and Dorothy Parker; James Weldon Johnson, Duke Ellington, and the Harlem Renaissance; and most of all, George Gershwin, whose music helped define the twenties and who rubbed shoulders with all of the other important artistic forces, both black and white, in that era.

Future composer Jule Styne was working in Chicago during that period in a speakeasy, and a patron insistently requested that he play *Rhapsody in Blue*. Styne kept telling the guy that he didn't know it and was about to tell the guy off when a sympathetic onlooker whispered in his ear that he was talking to Al Capone. Jule instantly learned how to play *Rhapsody in Blue*. It seems everybody was a Gershwin fan back then.

The twenties were the only complete decade during which George was active as a professional composer. When they began, he already had a Broadway score, *La La Lucille* (1919), and his hit song "Swanee" under his belt. (In 1920, Ira was still Arthur Francis, but his time was coming, too.) The emerging genius of the Gershwin brothers soon brought them in contact with a vibrant New York social scene. George and Ira, the sons of Russian immigrants, were not born into this scene: they were introduced to New York's smart set when they were very young men by the Paley brothers, Herman and Lou. Herman was a composer and knew George when he worked as a song plugger at Remick's. Lou, a high school English teacher, became what his wife, Emily—Lee Gershwin's sister—described as George's literary mentor. (It might have been the Paleys who introduced George to DuBose Heyward's novel *Porgy*.) Lou Paley wrote words to some of George's tunes ("Something About Love" in 1919, and also songs for the *Scandals*). Lou must have been quite a special guy, because his wife, Emily, was perhaps the kindest and sweetest person I ever knew.

THE TWENTIES WAS THE ONLY COMPLETE DECADE DURING WHICH GEORGE WAS ACTIVE AS A PROFESSIONAL COMPOSER.

For years, Lou and Emily Paley opened their West Village home on Saturday nights, serving Prohibition-compliant tea and cookies. Some of the regulars were Buddy DeSylva, Howard Dietz, Morrie Ryskind, Vincent Youmans, Oscar Levant, playwright S. N. Behrman, screenwriter Arthur Caesar (brother of Irving), and Hollywood luminaries John Huston, Groucho Marx, and Edward G. Robinson. Emily Paley said Ira never missed one of the Saturday night parties and George, who relished spending time with other creative minds, whether they were musical or literary or scientific, often came as well when he didn't have other commitments. "Our house was even a testing ground for George's dates," Emily recalled. "If one of George's girls didn't like the atmosphere, he gave her up."

Gregarious George, comfortable in any company, was always ready to play a new song for crowds of any size. Funny, handsome, and charming, he must have been a great guest. He never felt out of place in even the highest society. He was confident of his talent, and once he became famous he was fawned over. When he was in London or Paris, the smoke signals would go up—"George Gershwin's in town"—and people would clamor to meet him.

George was a frequent attendee at parties held by Cartier vice president and relentless socialite Jules Glaenzer. In 1938, *Life* magazine published a picture of Glaenzer with film star Loretta Young and said he was "rich and social . . . twice married and divorced. [He] is an excellent dancer and has a great flair for arranging parties." The wattage of Glaenzer's celebrity friends was somewhat higher than that of the Paleys'.

George recalled one of Glaenzer's parties from 1922 ("one of his usual parties," as he put it). Charlie Chaplin was there, along with musical entrepreneurs Florenz Ziegfeld and Paul Whiteman, the theater's Fanny Brice and Noel

Coward, and Fred and Adele Astaire. George had just written a song with Buddy DeSylva called "Do It Again." (According to George, he and DeSylva had knocked out the song in the office of George's publisher, Max Dreyfus, in no time.) "Do It Again" received its first public airing when George played it that night at the party. The French singer Irene Bordoni immediately rushed across the room, saying she must have it. And so the song became the centerpiece for her Broadway show *The French Doll*. Ira used to do an adorable impression of Bordoni's thick French accent—"I must 'ave zat song."

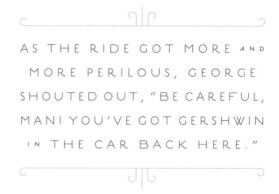

AS THE RIDE GOT MORE and MORE PERILOUS, GEORGE SHOUTED OUT, "BE CAREFUL, MAN! YOU'VE GOT GERSHWIN in THE CAR BACK HERE."

Relating this story is classic George. He didn't tell stories like this to brag. As far as he was concerned, he was merely pointing out the facts. *New Yorker* critic Alexander Woollcott said of George, "He was above and beyond posing. He said exactly what he thought, without window-dressing it to make an impression favorable or otherwise." He was by no means modest. Take the famous yarn of George getting a ride with an unusually reckless cabbie. As the ride got more and more perilous, George shouted out, "Be careful, man! You've got Gershwin in the car back here."

Jerome Kern, Dorothy Fields, and George at the Ambassador Hotel in Los Angeles in 1937.

George's self-assurance, though never mean-spirited, could sometimes ruffle feathers. One such story involved his friend Harry Ruby, a songwriter and screenwriter. He had written hit songs ("Three Little Words," with Bert Kalmar) and worked on the *Ziegfeld Follies* and also a number of the classic Marx Brothers movies, including *Animal Crackers, Horse Feathers,* and *Duck Soup.* Ruby had this very successful career in show business, but what he'd really wanted to be was a baseball player. One day he said to George, "Let's play some baseball," and George said, "I can't, I'm worried about my hands." So Harry said, "What about my hands?" and George paused for a moment and said, "It's not the same thing."

Harry called George up the next day. "George, you know, I just have to tell you I was really hurt. We were talking yesterday and I said, 'You know,

Ira, Lee, George, and Ellin and Irving Berlin on board a ship to Nassau in 1933.

what about my hands?' and you said, 'It's not the same thing.' That really hurt my feelings." There was a long pause and then George said, "But it isn't." Of course, George was right, but who else would have said it? He made his living playing *Rhapsody in Blue*, and it was hardly a diplomatic remark yet was guilelessly delivered.

There was a comic charm to George's self-adoration. His friends Emily Paley and Mabel Schirmer were invited by George to lunch at a

Having George Gershwin play at your party was a coup, something even the wealthiest hostess couldn't buy. And perhaps, once in a blue moon, a particular hostess would not have wanted to buy it if there were other pianists present, since George developed a reputation for not ceding the stage at parties. Abraham Chasens, a chronicler of the classical music world, recounted a party thick with musicians at which George was holding court from the keyboard. Sergei Rachmaninoff

AS MUCH AS GEORGE LIKED THE ATTENTION OF THE GIRLS, IT WAS PERFORMING THAT EXCITED HIM MOST.

new home he was eager to show off. The girls dressed up for the occasion, but so did George, who wore a new suit he had bought in London. When he answered the door the first thing he said was, "Well, girls, how do I look?" In his book *A Smattering of Ignorance*, Oscar Levant recalls playing with George at a concert at Lewisohn Stadium on the campus of City College in New York in 1932. "It was hardly over when one of his truly well-disposed friends rushed back, wrung his hand, and said, 'George, it was wonderful!' 'That's all?' said George, with characteristic abstraction. 'Just "wonderful"?'"

Another anecdote finds George at a party with a showgirl sitting on his lap. The hostess asks George to perform, and he's so excited at the prospect of playing that he gets up before the girl has a chance to move and she spills onto the floor. As much as George liked the attention of the girls, it was performing that excited him most.

had brought with him the great Vladimir Horowitz as his guest, and Rachmaninoff wanted Horowitz to be given a chance to play a piece he had written, *Danse Excentrique*. Of the handful of pianists who might actually have been able to play with more brilliance and verve than Gershwin, Horowitz would be one. But George played and played with no sign of letting up. Eventually Rachmaninoff lost patience and asked George to get up. "Horowitz," he said in his thick Russian accent, "play your dance."

George was always extremely enthusiastic about his own music. While it seemed that he'd rather listen to himself play than listen to anyone else, he was also interested greatly in the work of those whom he admired, writers like Harold Arlen (who considered George a mentor). But when he was at a party, the temptation of the spotlight was simply too great. Every moment at the piano, not least of all in a public setting, was an opportunity for a new creation. What emerged through his fingertips fascinated him, and he loved to share his excitement. George would say to the company, "Listen, do you want to hear my new score?" And then he'd sit down and play the whole thing from memory. George S. Kaufman said that by the opening night of any Gershwin show, George had already played the score so much around town that the musical would seem like a revival.

Some of George's contemporaries—people he knew from parties—even caricatured and parodied him in their works. George S. Kaufman's 1934 play *Merrily We Roll Along*, written with Moss Hart, includes a character, Max Frankl, who is widely assumed to be based on George Gershwin (there is another character reportedly based on Dorothy Parker). Frankl, a shockingly immodest young composer, calls Kern and Berlin washed-up "old hacks" and says that the only name worth remembering would be his own. George was not offended by the idea that he was being represented like this—apparently he thought Frankl was the only normal character in the whole play. (It's important to note that Gershwin revered both Kern and Berlin and did not ascribe those aspects of Frankl's character to his own.) In 1935, Cole Porter, in *Jubilee*, called out George by name for his habit of hogging the piano. In the song "My Most Intimate Friend," the hostess of a party boasts of her event, "'Twill be new in ev'ry way / Gershwin's promised not to play."

The caliber of talent George was playing for at these New York parties was sometimes extraordinary. The photographer Carl Van Vechten wrote about a party he gave in January 1926 at which Adele Astaire danced, the British opera singer Marguerite d'Alvarez sang Gershwin songs, Paul Robeson sang spirituals, James Weldon Johnson recited his poem "The Creation," and George played *Rhapsody in Blue*. (After moving into my first apartment in New York and getting unpacked, I started to read Van Vechten's introduction to the book *The Gershwin Years,* in which he quotes from his diary, to eerily discover that his glittering parties with Gershwin had taken place in the very building where I had just settled.) While Moss Hart was working with George S. Kaufman at Kaufman's home one afternoon (a regular occurrence in the thirties, when the two men created several Broadway hits together), he took a break for tea and found Alexander Woollcott, Dorothy Parker, and George Gershwin gathered all in one room. Hart confessed he was terrified.

WHAT BETTER TITLE TO CELEBRATE this very high society than "They All Laughed," written in 1936. As with many of Ira's creations, there's more going on in the song than is implied by the title. "They All Laughed" is from *Shall We Dance*, and is another of literally dozens of songs that I like best when sung by Fred Astaire, which is particularly appropriate in this case because the music was inspired by Fred's dancing, one of George's favorite muses.

The genesis for the melody was in something George had written years earlier, a short instrumental piece for Astaire that was intended to be a dance number for the 1927 musical *Funny Face*. It didn't make it into that show but appeared a year later in another play, *Rosalie*, and was called "Setting Up Exercises." To add to the confusion, the title on the manuscript was "Merry Andrew,"

which was restored when it was published thirty-five years after George's death. The first five notes of the piece were recycled as the opening of "They All Laughed." (In another odd synchronistic experience, shortly after musing over "Merry Andrew" and its origins, I was given the original manuscript for the piece by a nice woman who had rescued it from the super of her New York apartment building, who found it when cleaning out an abandoned unit. I subsequently donated it to the Library of Congress.)

Ira's inspiration for the lyric had been percolating for a dozen years, since he had seen an advertisement for a self-taught piano course. "They all laughed when I sat down at the piano," the ad said. This is yet another wonderful example of a love song that doesn't seem to be a love song until it ambushes the listener. Ira was proud of this bit of misdirection. He recalled that he and George played the tune for their friend and colleague George S. Kaufman, who liked a mushy love song about as much as Ira did. There's nothing alarming for Kaufman in the opening. So far, so unsentimental until, "It's the same old cry!" But Kaufman knew better. "Don't tell me this is going to be a love song!" he said. And sure enough, the next line confirmed his suspicions. As soon as he heard "wanting you," Kaufman shook his head and said, "Oh, well."

George and Ira were proud of the fact that this was a love song cloaked in a lively, up-tempo dance number and with playful, equally upbeat lyrics. The name checks include the Wright brothers, Guglielmo Marconi (inventor of the radio telegraph), Rockefeller Center (built over the course of the thirties), inventors Eli Whitney (the cotton gin) and Robert Fulton (the steamboat), chocolate pioneer Milton Hershey, and Henry Ford. Inventors, business tycoons, and real estate developments are hardly the fare of a conventional love song.

A S WITH "I'VE GOT A CRUSH ON YOU" and so many songs in the Gershwin canon, "They All Laughed" proved compatible with a wide variety of sounds and styles of performance. Even though Fred Astaire was the inspiration for the song, it is Ginger who sings it in the movie *Shall We Dance*, backed by Jimmy Dorsey's famous swing orchestra, before she and Fred dance to the music. Dorsey's orchestra, which plays uncredited on some songs, augmented the RKO studio band. Bands, if they could be persuaded to play without a credit, cost the studios less. It was a matter of controversy for years whether or not Duke Elling-

ton's band played without billing on the soundtrack of the Marx Brothers' *A Day at the Races*. Studio records eventually proved that Ellington did play, and for half what he would have been paid had he been given billing. He wasn't going to get the credit, and he was happy to take the money.

Dorsey's swing musicians, combined with the RKO fifty-piece orchestra, bring a big-band feel to "They All Laughed" that was very contemporary in 1937, when the film was released. While some songwriters might have been intimidated by the big bands and swing, George, as ever, embraced the new and smoothly incorporated the changing tastes and styles. When I first recorded the song, I performed it at the same tempo as the original Astaire waxing. George has placed in the piano accompaniment a descending figure that approximates the sound of derisive laughter, and I miss that phrase in most versions, as it is usually eliminated for being old-fashioned. Not to my ears.

"They All Laughed" is one of the earliest George Gershwin songs to enter my repertoire. Perhaps the highest praise I've heard for this song came unwittingly after I performed it at a nightclub on Sunset Boulevard one evening. It was a showcase where anyone could sign up to sing, and I was one of a number of young hopefuls looking for a break. My choice of an old song might not have been the best way to get noticed by an agent, but at least one person was impressed by it. A very young man came up to me after the show and said, "That's a wonderful song. Did you write it?" That someone would think this song was a contemporary number demonstrates its timelessness. I disabused the young man of his notion and told him "They All Laughed" was written in the thirties by George and Ira Gershwin. Sadly, he'd never heard of George and Ira Gershwin.

The first major recording of the song was by its muse, Fred Astaire, accompanied by the Johnny Green Orchestra, and the effervescence of that first waxing remains as potent as ever. Fred rerecorded a lot of his hits in a gargantuan multi-record set in 1952 and was accompanied by a group of jazz greats led by the impossibly talented Oscar Peterson, but that later rendition is lacking its joyous abandon as far as I'm concerned. It takes the song at a much more languid pace and has lost some of the essential Gershwin snap that makes that first recording sublime.

WHILE IT'S TRUE THAT MANY GERSHWIN SONGS HAVE FARED WELL AT A SLOWER TEMPO, CERTAIN ONES CRY OUT FOR A MORE ENERGETIC OR CHARGED PACE.

While it's true that many Gershwin songs have fared well at a slower tempo, especially the love songs, certain ones cry out for a more energetic or charged pace. The other thing I like about that original record is that Johnny Green's piano solo reminds me of what George might have sounded like playing it. Since we don't have a recording of George, Johnny acts as a virtual surrogate, since he was just as gifted at the keyboard as Gershwin. Years later when I told Green

how much I loved his playing on that particular track, he sat down at the piano. He had heart trouble and other health challenges, but he managed to once again play it in the difficult key of G flat, the same key in which he had recorded it with Astaire fifty years before. He recounted the circumstances surrounding his *Shall We Dance* recordings with Fred and said that he had studied the rough cut of the film performances first and then went away and slaved for days over the arrangements to make them as perfect as possible. The patina remains all of these years later.

Ginger Rogers also made records, but they did not sell well because her singing voice was not her strong suit. Ginger carried an insecurity about her singing and she refused to allow several of her earlier records to be released. Somehow they were released anyway in England, and she was furious. Thus by 1937 she was not making records and made only one more in the course of the rest of the entire 78 rpm era. While she remains magic on the screen, divorced of her visual persona the voice alone, alas, falls short of alchemy.

These days, the song is not as well known as it was only a few years ago. The historical references in the song get more obscure with each passing year. Unfortunately, the same name dropping that lends this lyric its originality and inventiveness now makes the song increasingly inaccessible to generations of kids who are no longer taught who Whitney or Fulton were. As much as it saddens me to see a classic song lose ground for such incidental reasons, I've been encouraged to find that a little education goes a long way toward solving the problem.

I once performed this song at a private high school in Los Angeles made up of particularly bright

and talented youths, most of whom had never heard the name Gershwin. Before launching into "They All Laughed," I explained the historical references in the song and was rewarded with an enthusiastic ovation at its conclusion. Sometimes it only takes a half a minute and a little patience to restore life to a mysterious line in a song. Rewardingly, illuminating the song's original meaning provides a lesson in history through the animating lens of music. In this way, the songs whose references now seem obscure can reanimate the past, actively igniting young imaginations. If you ask a group of kids to watch an old newsreel, it has far less impact. In spite of the decreasing presence of the arts in school curricula, I've been happy to find that when a group of kids are exposed to these classic works and given all the necessary context to appreciate them, they invariably respond positively.

George and Ira on the set of Shall We Dance *with Astaire and Rogers (seated) and Hermes Pan, Mark Sandrich, and Nathaniel Shilkret in 1936.*

Dear Michael:

A friend, Mrs. Mildred Knopf, a noted author of many cookbooks (her late husband was Eddie Knopf, the MGM producer), has some Gershwin memorabilia on her den walls - autographed photos of Gershwin (George) and notes from him....as well as Piatogorsky, Kern, etc. etc.

One of these is a page written in pencil. These are the exact words:

G. G.

I Do Like

1. sun bathing
2. A good book
3. seeing great paintings
4. a tolerant woman
5. exercise
6. A Hudson River sunset
7. noodle soup
8. a good shave
9. Doing someone a good turn.
10. The things said about Irving Thalberg

I Do Not Like

1. Icy winds
2. women's stocking with seams off center
3. B Pictures
4. cheap women
5. sentimental tripe
6. oysters
7. long speeches
8. bad losres (losers)
9. dead cigars
10. anything phoney.

Best,

Frank

a ya call me when you el ...?
276-1943

FROM THE FIRST TIME he sat down at the piano, no one laughed at George's music. It opened many doors for him and was a gift that set him apart from the multitudes of other aspiring songwriters. Very quickly, and at a young age, George became a famous personality. He was on the cover of the July 20, 1925, issue of *Time* magazine. He was twenty-six and was then the youngest person to have been so featured. George was sandwiched between a couple of real heavyweights of the age: Alfred E. Smith, the governor of New York, had been the cover boy the week before, and Henry Ford got top billing the week after.

George was a symbol of the supremely confident young creative talent that was sprouting from America's fertile cultural soil, and he attracted other successful men and women in all different fields. George made friends with stockbrokers and bankers such as Emil Mosbacher and Otto Kahn. The actress Sylvia Sidney recalled George playing at Kahn's massive (127 rooms) estate called Oheka Castle in Huntington, Long Island, where the music echoed down the endless halls. She said that the music filled that cavernous expanse from the moment she arrived on Friday until the Sunday night she left. He was the guest of honor at a party at the Kit Kat Club in London that was attended by the Prince of Wales—later, briefly, Edward VIII. The Prince of Wales was kind enough to attend, but Ira, to George's slight consternation, was not. One of George's favorite souvenirs of his travels was a signed photograph Edward's brother Prince George, the Duke of Kent, had given him that was inscribed, "From George to George."

For such a well-known and well-connected single man about town, there was always a party to go to. There was almost always something to celebrate, and it seems George was out almost every night. For the opening night of *Porgy and Bess* on October 10, 1935, a group of men, "all very well off," in Kay Swift's phrase, financed a lavish white-tie fete for 430 guests at publisher Condé Nast's house, where a Spanish orchestra played selections from the opera and the party went on all night.

George went to a lot of shows, in part because he was interested in hearing what other musicians were working on. Among Ira's trove of mementos were drawers of dusty business records, and among them I found a canceled check George wrote for opening night tickets to the Rodgers and Hart musical *Jumbo*, which played at the Hippodrome on Sixth Avenue from November 1935. George must have brought along a sizable group of people, because there was a list of names attached to the check. It wasn't unusual for one artist to pay another the professional courtesy of purchasing tickets, and Rodgers had attended the opening of *Porgy and Bess* only a month earlier, writing George a letter of high praise thereafter.

The way professional musicians engaged with one another's work was very different in the Gershwins' time. Paul Whiteman's "Experiment in Modern Music" concert in 1924, where *Rhapsody in Blue* premiered, was packed with musical luminaries curious to see what Whiteman (and George and Victor Herbert, the other composer debuting a work) were pulling out of their hats. Cole Porter was also a big supporter of his professional colleagues. Like George, Porter didn't feel threatened by his talented contemporaries. In the Gershwins' circle, the songwriters all hung out, playing their songs for each other and sharing

(OPPOSITE) *Note to author from publicist Frank Liberman.*

ideas. At one point, George said to Cole Porter, "Let's write a song together," and Porter said, "Well, I would, except writing lyrics is easy for me. The music is the hard part and I don't want to deprive myself of the delicious struggle."

The tremendous camaraderie of these artists continues to amaze me. Most people are significantly more jealous and paranoid today. In addition to regularly attending performances of one another's work, musicians congregated to play together and entertain one another. The thought of a group of creative artists getting together to play and sing their work is exhilarating, but I don't think this kind of casual performing milieu exists today. It all happened regularly at

that time; no one thought it unusual. Then as things gradually changed, the surviving attendees of such soirees would shake their heads in awe at the mere memory of such gatherings.

There are a couple of home recordings from the late thirties in which you can hear Ira having fun, joking, laughing, engaging in bit of dialogue from a show, and speaking in musical shorthand. Present along with Ira were Yip Harburg, Harold Arlen, Robert "Doc" McGonigle (who wrote comedy sketches for Bea Lillie), Milton Ager, the lyricist Ted Koehler, and Alexander Steinert, who was the vocal coach for *Porgy and Bess*. Listening to these brief fragments makes the listener want to leap into a time machine and join the fun.

(CLOCKWISE FROM TOP LEFT) *George playing golf* • *At the beach in 1927* • *At the gym.*

Sometimes I would sit alone in Ira's living room, narrow my eyes, and squint at the surroundings, trying to visualize all of those marvelous talents gathered together making music. (Liza Minnelli and I tried to revive the tradition many years later, but people were reticent about going to the piano and performing, myself included. One night Madonna basically ordered me to the piano, saying, "I want to hear you play." I replied that sometimes there is a feeling of self-consciousness that gets in the way and I didn't feel up to performing that night, not being at my best. She haughtily replied, "Oh, then I should lower my expectations?" and I replied, "I think it's a good idea to do that generally.")

> ORIGINALLY A SONG WAS INTRODUCED TO THE FAMILY AROUND THE PIANO LIKE A VISITING RELATIVE WHO CAME TO STAY FOR A WHILE.

The decline of domestic musical gatherings is just one part of the way the communal experience of music has waned. People still go to concerts, and a few rock and pop acts like the Rolling Stones, Madonna, U2, Lady Gaga, and Bruce Springsteen can sell out tours playing in huge, impersonal stadiums, yet even these stalwarts are facing more challenges, with economics making attendance at live shows more and more rarefied.

Though the protagonist in the original ad inspiration for "They All Laughed" garnered skepticism when he sat down to play, it still was the way most people heard a lot of music. Originally a song was introduced to the family around the piano like a visiting relative who came to stay for a while. But fewer and fewer people make music at home now. And the technology that has brought us together in so many realms has also torn us apart, beginning with the Walkman and reaching a new level with the ubiquitous iPod.

It may be that new technologies have enabled this change, but the real reason for it is a different sensibility about the role of music, which informs the way people make use of this technology. As I've said, I cling to the hope that our sensibility will someday be more communal, and that music will be the uniting force in our social lives that it once was.

AS SOON AS THEY WERE ABLE, George and Ira started hosting parties—first at the homes they shared, and later at the separate residences they acquired when they became more established. Party or no party, these homes were often full of people. Even as he gained fame and success, George stayed true to his roots. He was never embarrassed to have his parents in the room, though they spoke with noticeable accents and were not glamorous people. He especially enjoyed his father, a master of malapropisms with a corny sense of humor. Once I found a piece of paper upon which Ira had jotted in shorthand many of the funny things that his father said. He seemed fearless and was fueled by appreciation for the simple blessings of life. Certainly the amazing things he had witnessed through George and Ira had transformed his world in undreamed-of ways.

The shining light of the Jewish musical world, George was also proud of his Jewish heritage. He was a great supporter of Jewish charities, but he was not religious. Nor were his parents—they would draw the blinds during the Jewish holidays so the neighbors couldn't see they were not observing. One of the projects George never finished was an opera based on a play by Russian playwright S. Ansky called *The Dybbuk*. The suggestion to musicalize this play, about an evil spirit that is a key figure in Jewish mythology, came from Otto Kahn. Many Jewish music scholars have written about George's connection with Yiddish musical theater. George could speak Yiddish (and Ira, a *bissel*), and

he went to Yiddish shows, but the truth is that he was no more influenced by Jewish music than by any other kind of folk music.

Of the three boys, only Ira was bar mitzvahed, though Lee and Ira had a traditional Jewish marriage service. Ira went a step further than his skeptical brother and was an avowed atheist. And although George moved easily in a WASPy world of privilege, he wasn't totally isolated from the endemic anti-Semitism of the era. He once went up to Lake Placid to visit his girlfriend and wasn't allowed into the Lake Placid Club because he was Jewish. He was denied a hotel room in Toronto in 1934 for the same reason. Cole Porter got similar treatment—the same people who embraced his brilliance at parties and performances called him a "pansy" behind his back. Or worse. This was a time of great double standards.

As adults, George and Ira changed residences quite frequently, trading up in real estate as they became more successful. George wrote "Swanee" at the family's apartment on West 144th Street. In 1920 the Gershwins moved to an apartment at 110th Street and Amsterdam Avenue. In 1924, *Lady, Be Good!* was lucrative enough for the family to move to a five-floor townhouse on West 103rd Street, which had enough space for Ira, George, and their parents to each take a floor, with siblings Arthur and Frances between. It was here that Ira and Leonore were married and set up house together. Sometimes, the influx of family and friends at the 103rd Street house proved too distracting for George to work, so he took rooms at the Whitehall Hotel on 100th Street. Even there, George could be overwhelmed with the parade of visitors and hangers-on.

George with conductor Albert Coates at Lewisohn Stadium in New York in 1932.

In 1929 George and Ira took adjoining pent-houses at 33 Riverside Drive between West 75th and 76th streets. Finally, the brothers moved across town in 1933, when George bought a four-teen-room duplex at 132 East 72nd Street, and Ira and Lee bought a smaller apartment across the street at number 125. George's ever-changing in-terests were reflected in his homes. His later apart-ments had a gym, so he could work out privately, and this home had the luxury of three pianos, so he was never far from inspiration.

There was also space set aside for him to paint. (George became an accomplished portrait painter, often of major figures in his life, such as Arnold Schoenberg and Jerome Kern. Ira, who was thought by some to be a better artist than George, gave it up around 1932, at about the time it start-ed to consume George. He found painting to be a relaxing diversion. I believe George could have made it a full-time pursuit, having been praised by various critics.) There was plenty of wall space for his growing collection of art. In that later pe-riod, George sent his cousin Henry Botkin to Eu-rope to buy paintings for him, and Botkin spent about $50,000 (!) on artists such as Chagall, De-rain, Gauguin, Kandinsky, Leger, Modigliani, Picasso, Rouault, Rousseau, and Utrillo. George also had a passion for traditional African art, and Ira saved a great deal of it long after George's pass-ing. In my own collection, I have two of Ira's paintings, one memorializing the view from 33 Riverside Drive.

The most frequent guest at either Gershwin home must have been Oscar Levant, who spent so much time with the brothers that he was more a lodger than a visitor. Describing the Riverside Drive penthouses, Levant wrote, the place "was mostly filled with an element of parasites, both aesthetic and gustatory. . . . Here I discovered I was a born leader, for I soon took charge of this hitherto disorganized group." Lee Gershwin, who always proudly reminded me that she had brought him into the fold, adored Oscar and was more for-giving with him than most. If he insulted a guest, she'd throw him out, but he'd be back soon enough with her blessing. Somehow she had a psychic em-pathy for Oscar that made her tolerate behavior that she would not have abided in anyone else.

George's living room (LEFT) *and bedroom* (RIGHT) *at 33 Riverside Drive.*

Levant ate many meals with the Gershwins, sometimes sharing the ultra-bland toddler's diet George favored to combat his "composer's stomach": zwieback, rusks, Swedish bread, stewed fruit, and applesauce. Between meals, Oscar played hours of table tennis with whoever was around and made himself useful playing second piano, as when George scored his *Second Rhapsody* on the other instrument. The male-dominated talk went on, often all night. It was talk, Levant wrote, of "prize-fighting, music, painting, football, and sex." George was an enthusiastic sports fan: Kitty Carlisle spoke of once going to a prizefight with him and ending up as bruised as the fighters, because from his seat George rambunctiously moved in tandem with the choreography in the ring.

WHEN DISCUSSING GEORGE and his attitudes toward sex and romance, we're mostly guessing, as there is so much innuendo, legend, and gossip mixed up in his story. The authors of various biographies have unscrupulously pushed their own agendas. After his passing there was much gossip about George's sexuality—lyricist and early collaborator Irving Caesar thought he was gay, although that seems to have been a minority position. Irving would never elaborate on his reasons for saying this. He later carried with him a lasting jealousy over the fact that George had dropped him to write songs in favor of Ira. Still, I don't believe Irving told his story about George because he was annoyed with him, because he was a principled man who told the truth as he saw it. Nor do I feel that he would have wanted to hurt George, and perhaps that is why he did not say more.

There were a few others who felt that George was more interested in men than women. Cecelia Ager, wife of Milton, also insisted that George was gay, but like Irving Caesar, she would never elaborate. Milton, a roommate of George's in the early twenties, sputtered at the notion, and Cecelia cast him a cold glance, saying, "Milton, you don't know anything." In contrast we have the many stories of his womanizing and his mass of letters to various paramours. In explaining the rumors about George's sexuality, my armchair psychology, and take it for what it's worth, is that I think he had a large sex drive, as described to me by a few of his friends. They would also confide that he wasn't able to emotionally connect on a deep level with anyone. In short, George couldn't reconcile sex and love. He was conflicted to the point that he knew his mother wanted him to marry a Jewish girl but could only have satisfying sex with someone he didn't know well or at all.

An older gentleman I met in San Francisco named Tom Van Dyke was in Europe with George in 1928 and told me firsthand a story I had heard before. He observed George in a Parisian house of prostitution, watching him through the keyhole, and found George to be mechanical in his sexual performance. Whatever the case, it's clear that George wasn't a prude when generalizing about women—but it was different where his sister, Frances, was concerned. If Frances's skirt was pulled up too high, George would yank it down over her knees. He also monitored her language and made sure she didn't wear too much makeup.

George dated a lot of beautiful Gentile women, but he would never have married a woman who wasn't Jewish (unlike Irving Berlin, who twice married Catholics). George carried on his affair with Kay Swift for ten years, starting in 1925. When they met, she was married to banker James Warburg and George was dating Pauline Heifetz, sister of the violinist Jascha. Kay later told me that George was the best lover she ever had. This of course contradicts my general theory about his being unable to connect sexually with someone with whom he had a deep emotional tie. But Kay was pretty spectacular. An accomplished musician and composer, she was tremendously helpful to George with his music. Kay and James Warburg divorced in 1934, but although George was in love with Kay, according to Kitty Carlisle, he wouldn't marry her because she wasn't Jewish, while others said it was because she had three children. (Despite George's affair with Swift, he saw Rosamund Walling, a Swarthmore student and a cousin of Lee's, a few times between 1929 and 1931. He even proposed to Walling, but she felt George was more interested in the idea of being married than in her and she turned him down.)

(I understand about mothers and the hopes they have for their children. A friend who comes from a deeply Orthodox Jewish family told me that his mother was upset that he was dating a Gentile woman. My response was, "Do you know how happy my parents would be if I dated a Gentile woman?")

Lee Gershwin passed on to me a little charm that Kay gave George on the opening night of *Porgy and Bess* in 1935; it was a tiny gold dove with their birthstones in each eye, a diamond and a sapphire. When George went to California for what turned out to be the last time in August 1936, he and Kay agreed to take a break from each other for

a year. Near the end of that time, Kay sent a message to George, but he didn't respond. A short time later, she says, George said, "I'm coming back for both of us." This was just weeks before he died, and it was told by Kay after George's death.

ONE OF THE FIRST THINGS IRA DID AFTER GEORGE'S DEATH WAS TO SEND ALL OF KAY'S LETTERS BACK TO HER.

Ira did not recall that they were going to be reunited, and as much as I adored Kay, I wonder about the veracity of this story. Just stating this possibility makes me feel sheepish, as I know how much George meant to Kay and how devastating his death must have been to her. Still, it's possible that she created this thought as a coping mechanism, to think of what might have been, and "happily ever after." Her own romantic affairs after George died were never of the same caliber and it would be forgivable if she had changed the ending of their story. What could it hurt? One of the first things Ira did after George's death was to send all of Kay's letters back to her; she destroyed them, not wanting history to be privy to such intimate details. In any event, Kay was a remarkably kind, spiritual, and wonderful woman.

During the time when George and Kay were taking their break, friends say he was actively seeking a bride. George had many actresses to squire

(FOLLOWING PAGES) *A letter from George to Irving Caesar, written while he was working in Baltimore, 1918.*

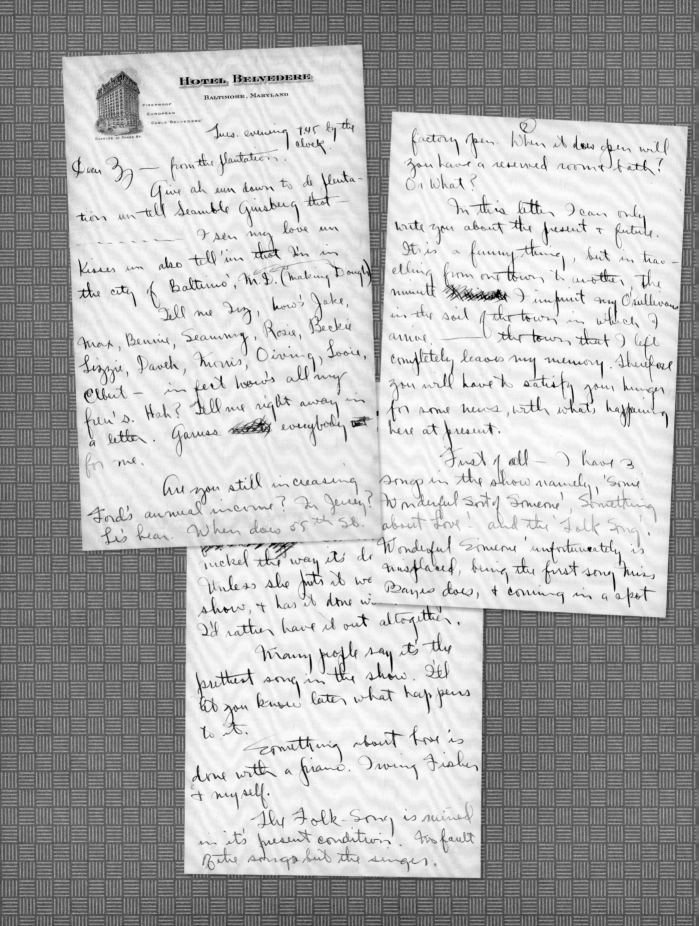

HOTEL BELVEDERE

BALTIMORE, MARYLAND

FIREPROOF
EUROPEAN
CABLE "BELVEDERE"

CHARLES AT CHASE ST.

Tues. evening 7.45 by the clock.

Dear Zy — from the plantation.

Give ah um down to de plantation un tell Seamble Ginsberg that —
—————— I sen my love un kisses un also tell 'im that I'm in the city of Baltimo', M.D. (Making Dough)

Tell me Izy, how's Jake, Max, Bennie, Seaming, Rosie, Beckie, Lizzie, Davek, Morris, Oiving, Looie, Albert — in fact how's all my feu's. Hah? Tell me right away in a letter. Garuss ~~everybody~~ everybody for me.

Are you still increasing Ford's annual income? In Jersey? Is bear. When does 55th St.

~~nickel~~ the way it's do ~~unless she puts it we~~ show, + has it done w~~ I'd rather have it out altogether.

Many people say it's the prettiest song in the show. I'll let you know later what happens to it.

Something about love is done with a piano. Irving Fisher + myself.

The Folk-Song is ruined in it's present condition. It's fault of the songs but the singer.

---

factory pen. When it does open will you have a reserved room + bath? Or What?

In this letter I can only write you about the present + future. It is a funny thing, but in travelling from one town to another, the ~~minute~~ ~~minute~~ I imprint my O'Sullivans in the soil of the town in which I arrive. ——— the town that I left completely leaves my memory. Therefore you will have to satisfy your hunger for some news, with what's happening here at present.

First of all — I have 3 songs in the show namely, 'Some Wonderful sort of Someone', 'Something about Love' and the 'Folk Song'. 'Wonderful Someone' unfortunately is misplaced, being the first song Miss Bayes does, + coming in a spot

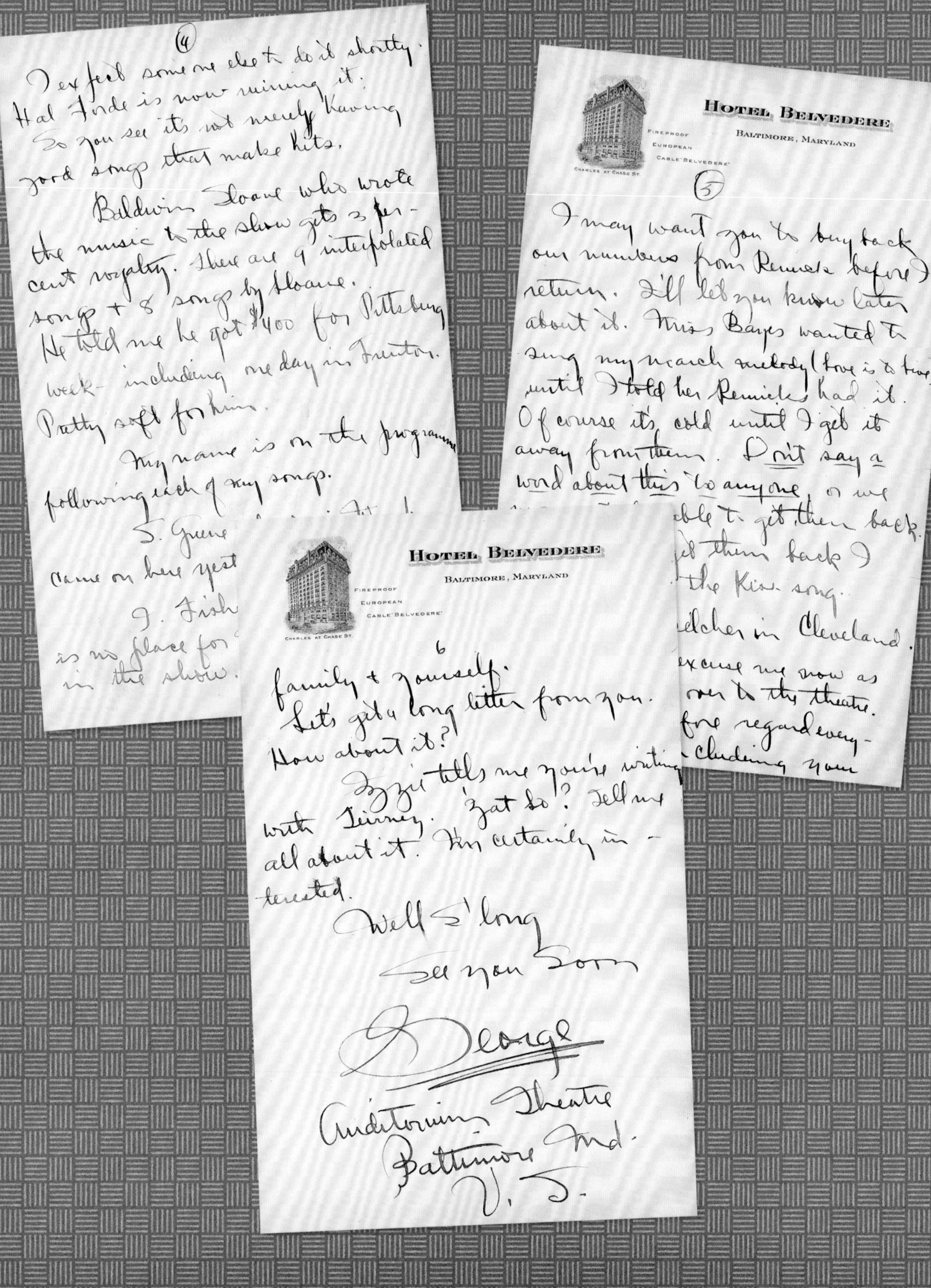

I expect some one else to do it shortly.
Hal Forde is now singing it.
So you see its not merely having
good songs that make hits.

Baldwin Sloane who wrote
the music to the show gets 3 percent royalty. There are 9 interpolated
songs + 8 songs by Sloane.
He told me he got $400 for Pittsburg
week - including one day in Trenton.
Pretty soft for him.

My name is on the programm
following each of my songs.

S. Guerce _____ Act 1.
Came on here yest _____
9. Fish _____
is no place for _____
in the show.

HOTEL BELVEDERE
BALTIMORE, MARYLAND
FIREPROOF
EUROPEAN
CABLE 'BELVEDERE'
CHARLES AT CHASE ST.

I may want you to buy back
our numbers from Remick before
return. I'll let you know later
about it. Miss Bayes wanted to
sing my march melody (Love is to live)
until I told her Remick had it.
Of course it's cold until I get it
away from them. Don't say a
word about this to anyone, or we
_____ able to get them back
_____ them back I
_____ the Kiss song.
_____ cher in Cleveland.
_____ excuse me now as
_____ over to this theatre.
_____ fore regard every-
_____ including you

HOTEL BELVEDERE
BALTIMORE, MARYLAND
FIREPROOF
EUROPEAN
CABLE 'BELVEDERE'
CHARLES AT CHASE ST.

6

family + yourself.
Let's get a long letter from you.
How about it?

Izzy tells me you're writing
with Terry. Zat so? Tell me
all about it. I'm certainly interested.

Well s'long
See you Soon

George

Auditorium Theatre
Baltimore, Md.
U. S.

around L.A.: Simone Simon was one of his targets, as was Ginger Rogers. In March 1937, he attended a dinner at Edward G. Robinson's house in honor of Stravinsky and he sat next to Paulette Goddard. Her contrary reactions to him at the party immediately attracted him. "Mmmmmm," he wrote his friend Mabel Schirmer of Goddard. "She's nice. Me likee."

George pursued Goddard hard, although she was married to Charlie Chaplin at the time. Sometimes Paulette did manage to break away from the controlling Chaplin for a secret liaison and there actually exists home-movie footage of George and Paulette taken at a getaway in Palm Springs, showing them relaxed and smiling.

Goddard's father was Jewish, which might have made her marriage material had circumstances been different. But I doubt that George really would have settled down with her. I think the fact that she was married, and therefore off-limits, was a big part of her appeal. George was perennially conflicted when it came to love—I think that if Goddard had said, "Hey, Charlie and I are divorced, I'm free," he probably would have fled in the other direction.

Goddard's lack of interest in George was further demonstrated to me eighty years after their affair, when I saw that the family of actor Burgess Meredith was selling a copy of *Porgy and Bess* that had been inscribed by Gershwin to Goddard. She

(CLOCKWISE FROM LEFT) *George's self-portait* • *George's portrait of DuBose Heyward.*
Ira's view from 33 Riverside Drive.

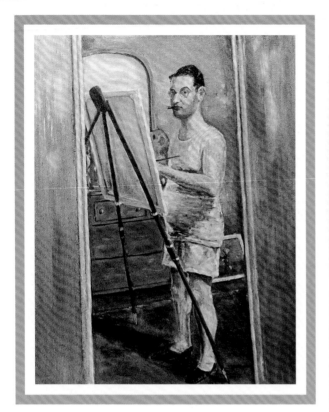

was later married to Meredith, and when they were divorced she did not bother to take her personally autographed copy of *Porgy* with her.

The woman who seemed to be the perfect partner for George was Kitty Carlisle. She was smart, glamorous, cultured, sophisticated—and she could sing. What's more, she was Jewish. She and George saw each other from late 1933 until George went to California. And yet she knew she couldn't marry George because, she said, George didn't really know what love was. Kitty used to get beautifully written love letters from grand literary types, and George would send notes like, "Well, I'm going to golf now." She felt that he wasn't really in love with her.

George, however, believed he was in love with Kitty and thought she'd be the ideal wife for him. She was certainly everything George's mother wanted in a daughter-in-law, so much so that after George died, Rose Gershwin asked Kitty to sit with the family at the funeral and pose as his fiancée. Kitty declined. Nine years later, she married Moss Hart.

Perhaps George's unhappy love life was part of the reason he went into analysis, which he underwent five times a week from the spring of 1934 to the fall of 1935. Unfortunately, he chose as his analyst Dr. Gregory Zilboorg, who was something of a shrink to the stars—and, sad to say, a quack. Psychoanalysis was in its infancy,

(CLOCKWISE FROM LEFT) *Ira's self-portrait, "My Body"* • *Ira's still life* • *George's self-portrait.*

and a devious character like Zilboorg could inveigle Gershwin into his exploitative operation. Zilboorg was a Russian émigré who had served in the cabinet of the doomed Kerensky government, which was overthrown by Lenin and the Bolsheviks. He and George became very close. When George went to Mexico for a vacation after *Porgy and Bess* debuted, Zilboorg went along, thus blurring the lines of their professional-personal relationship.

The consensus among George's friends was that Zilboorg wasn't good for George. Kitty Carlisle hated him. Still, after therapy, George's sister, Frances, said George was more thoughtful.

I met Zilboorg's widow many years ago. She was very defensive when she found out I had worked with Ira. The first thing that she said, without provocation, was, "My husband had nothing to do with George's death." If only the notes of his sessions with Gershwin had survived.

THE TWENTIES WERE the perfect time for George, and New York was the perfect setting, bursting with culture and at its apogee of national influence. There was live music everywhere—emanating from concert halls, band shells, hotels, bars, and schools. Every little church choir, opera company, Yiddish theater group, street corner musician, and ragtime pianist on Coney Island provided him with inspiration.

George's name appeared in the papers frequently, but the coverage was nothing compared to the scrutiny celebrities face today. Babe Ruth ran through a railway car full of journalists pursued by a naked woman holding a knife and nobody wrote about it. George was no Babe Ruth when it came to pursuing (or being pursued by) women, but it was to his benefit that he lived during a time when the media was more interested in lionizing celebrities than in going through their garbage.

Would George have had the same success in today's world? Sadly, I don't believe so. If he were alive today, George's genius would find an outlet, of course, but music was simply more important in his time—especially the making of music in private, which hardly takes place today. The job of a song plugger, the first rung on George's career ladder, doesn't even exist anymore. He would have loved technology today and made something interesting out of it. He would have embraced popular culture

Photo and message from Kitty Carlisle to the author.

and found a fresh way of expressing the music we take for granted, but the circumstances of media and celebrity seem to be such that he might not have been appreciated for his art, as art is no longer the way most artists are judged. It's all wild conjecture, and the fact that he was incarnated into a specific time is inseparable from his art.

BEFORE *PORGY AND BESS,* HE SUFFERED THROUGH SEVERAL YEARS OF FAILURE ON BROADWAY.

George was born ready to take on the world and draw from it. But the world wasn't always ready for him. Before *Porgy and Bess*, he suffered through several years of failure on Broadway, and he still hadn't written anything that had the impact of *Rhapsody in Blue*. But it's clear he was growing artistically even when the public didn't embrace what he was doing. The Concerto in F, written after *Rhapsody in Blue*, is now considered by most musical authorities to be the superior piece.

In 1928, George wrote *An American in Paris*, which is also a significantly original work. Commissioned, like the concerto, by Walter Damrosch, the piece was largely written by George in the French capital and orchestrated back in New York. Described as a "rhapsodic ballet" (that word again), *An American in Paris* premiered with Damrosch and the New York Philharmonic at Carnegie Hall on December 13, 1928. The band

consisted of large brass and woodwind sections, a lot of percussion (including "four taxi horns" that were used in the well-known "walking theme," personally supplied by George for the performance), and strings. Again, George mixed jazz with classical tropes and again, audiences were more responsive than many critics.

Of his other classical pieces, the *Second Rhapsody* was immediately obscure and the *Rumba*, or *Cuban Overture*, of 1932 received very little attention. The *"I Got Rhythm" Variations*, which he wrote in 1934, were performed during his lifetime only by George.

Live music was a less dominant cultural force in the thirties than it had been in the previous decade, in part because of the increasing power of Hollywood and the growth of media like radio and recorded music, yet it was still incalculably stronger than today. Live performance, on Broadway and in theater, was also becoming less significant back then. All of this may have contributed to the fact that George didn't have the same success in the thirties that he'd enjoyed in the twenties, or maybe he was diverging artistically in a way that could be likened to growing pains.

George and Ginger Rogers in 1936.

After *Porgy and Bess*, George and Ira went to Hollywood not only to make money, but to prove that they still could write pop songs together. They were engaged to write a score for Astaire and Rogers, and it was a plum assignment. But professionally, George had an increasingly horrible time, and the studios felt their songs were inferior to the material Jerome Kern had turned out the year before for the same team. Perhaps the understanding of the public had been outstripped by George's continually developing talents and ever expanding harmonic palette, which was influenced by Schoenberg and others. George was also interested in swing music, which was just coming into fashion, but many still wanted to hear *Rhapsody in Blue* more than his new songs. Now we look at the songs he and Ira wrote in this period—"They All Laughed," "They Can't Take That Away from Me," "A Foggy Day (in London Town)," "Love Is Here to Stay"—and we consider them among their finest and marvel that they were so prolific in such a short period of time. It's ironic to read reviews of his work at the time and note that his film music was not immediately lauded or appreciated.

GEORGE AND IRA WENT TO HOLLYWOOD NOT ONLY TO MAKE MONEY, BUT TO PROVE THAT THEY STILL COULD WRITE POP SONGS TOGETHER.

Time has an odd way of clarifying opinions that were once accepted as fact, and the passing years have been largely good to their work. Even though he might not have seen it that way, Ira was lucky to live into his eighties and witness the worldwide acceptance of George's work on a scale of massive proportion. My wish today is that Ira's own work be appreciated as deeply as his brother's, because there have been a few voices of late that I feel have not fairly assessed his talent. When inevitably those opinions are obscured with time, wherever their spirits cosmically repose, George and Ira will have the last laugh. ·

Sheet music cover for "They All Laughed" for Shall We Dance.

GEORGE IN A SELF-PORTRAIT.

"SOMEONE TO WATCH OVER ME"

from *Oh, Kay!*, 1926

VERSE

There's a saying old
Says that love is blind.
Still, we're often told
"Seek and ye shall find."
So I'm going to seek a certain lad I've had in mind.
Looking ev'rywhere,
Haven't found him yet;
He's the big affair
I cannot forget—
Only man I ever think of with regret.
I'd like to add his initial to my monogram.
Tell me, where is the shepherd for this lost lamb?

REFRAIN

There's a somebody I'm longing to see:
I hope that he
Turns out to be
Someone who'll watch over me.

I'm a little lamb who's lost in the wood;
I know I could
Always be good
To one who'll watch over me.

Although he may not be the man some
Girls think of as handsome,
To my heart he'll carry the key.

Won't you tell him, please, to put on some speed,
Follow my lead?
Oh, how I need
Someone to watch over me.

CHAPTER 6

"ONE PLUS ONE EQUALS THREE" —

Love Songs and How to Rewrite Them

HAVEN'T CONDUCTED A SCIENTIFIC SURVEY on this question, but I am pretty sure that 95 percent of all popular songs are about love. Even ones that on first listen don't appear to be concerned with that subject will eventually wend their way to that most basic emotion of our hearts. ("They All Laughed" is a case in point.)

Since they provide so much of their livelihood, where would songwriters be without love songs? And where would the rest of us be as well? After all, love songs make up an accompanying soundtrack for so many of our life's rituals, especially weddings and anniversaries, and they can be as necessary for the perfect romantic date as wine and candlelight. (One burning question has dogged me for years on this score: what did they play at Jewish weddings before Jerry Bock and Sheldon Harnick wrote "Sunrise, Sunset"?)

Love songs heighten our experience and connect to our hearts in a way that can only be achieved with music. The lyrics of a great versifier can allow us to express that which we cannot eloquently express ourselves, and make the world a more exciting, romantic, and safer place, if only for a short time. Love songs become our personal property and define important moments in our lives.

But writing such songs presents a serious challenge to a songwriter, most particularly to the lyricist. Not to minimize the plight of the composer, who must work with combinations of only twelve

A favorite photo of Ira's.

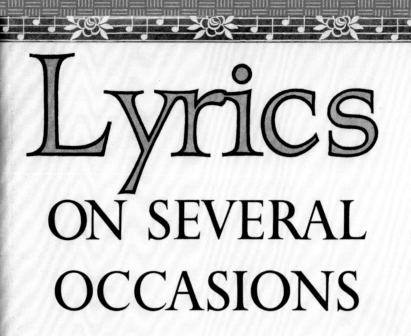

Lyrics
ON SEVERAL
OCCASIONS

A selection of Stage & Screen Lyrics Written for
Sundry Situations; and Now Arranged in Arbitrary
Categories. To Which Have Been Added Many
Informative Annotations & Disquisitions on Their
Why & Wherefore, Their Whom-For, Their How;
and Matters Associative.

by

IRA GERSHWIN
Gent.

notes, but it's the job of the lyricist to ensure that the meaning of the song is distinctive. How do you come up with an original idea to differentiate your song from the millions of love songs that have already been written? And if you have a catalogue of songs to your name, how do you make your next song different from the ones you've already written? And then how to write the one after that?

> IF A LYRICIST IS GOING TO IMPART CREDIBLE EMOTION, HE HAS TO AVOID THE CLICHÉS THAT ALREADY LITTER THE SONGBOOK.

Such was the quandary faced by Ira Gershwin. Because love takes on so many guises—passionate, unrequited, young, mature, ageless, lost, and so on—the composer is free to roam across the whole musical spectrum. But if a lyricist is going to impart credible emotion, he has to avoid the clichés that already litter the songbook. He must try to find new ways of saying the same thing, new ways to say "I love you" without using those three words. It's a devilishly difficult trick to pull off.

Ira, obviously, was a master at finding different ways of expressing the oft-expressed emotions of love. In his book, *Lyrics on Several Occasions,* Ira arranged his songs into loose categories: "The Not Impossible He," "Divers Duets," "The Possessive Case," "The Importunate Male," "The Importu-

nate Female," "Ladies in Lament," and so on. The word "love" doesn't appear in the section titles, and it only rarely appears in the song titles. Ira approached the subject gingerly, focusing not so much on love itself as on its many manifestations and symptoms.

Ira's work on *Lyrics on Several Occasions* is illustrative of how meticulously he labored at his craft. The book is a collection of his lyrics with a commentary accompanying the songs. It's not a long book, but with his young assistant, Lawrence Stewart, Ira worked on it for four years, from 1955 until its publication in 1959—writing, rewriting, tightening. Stewart later wrote that working with Ira (often accompanied by Oscar Levant) meant dealing with nonstop punning and banter, punctuated by frequent visits to Ira's thirteen-volume *Oxford English Dictionary.* Ira would endlessly rewrite Stewart's triple-spaced typescript. For Ira, no sentence was ever really finished. He felt the same way about his lyrics. When Ira looked over a lyric thirty, forty, or even fifty years after he had written it, he did so with a critical eye—*Perhaps this can still be made better,* he would think.

Ira chose the words for his lyrics with extreme care. For example, a favorite of mine is "Isn't It a Pity?" from 1933's *Pardon My English*:

> *Imagine all the lonely years we've wasted:*
> *You, with the neighbors—*
> *I, at silly labors;*
> *What joys untasted!*
> *You, reading Heine,*
> *I, somewhere in China.*

(OPPOSITE) *Cover of Ira's memoir,* Lyrics on Several Occasions, *published in 1959.*

With Ira, every syllable was gone over many times so that each line was the perfect expression of whatever it was he was trying to convey. He wanted to be witty but never at the expense of emotion. The goal always was to be fresh and inventive. Ira preferred to express himself in a whimsical way because he was not outwardly sentimental. For Ira, in writing a love song, wit would take the front seat over passion.

Ira understood what it took to create great expressive art—he could see it manifested right in front of him in his brother and could feel when inspiration was welling up inside of him. He strove to match the level George reached with his

Ira was different from George in that he operated in just one form. While George tried his hand at everything that had musical notes in it, Ira stuck to writing song lyrics, and that was fine by him. He had experimented with short stories as a young man—he wrote one called "A Harlem Idyll" that I found a copy of while going through Ira's papers with him one day. I started to read the story, but Ira took it from me and immediately ripped it to shreds, saying under his breath, "Does anyone mind if I tear this up?" He thought it was an awful literary attempt and didn't want anyone to see it. I wish I'd first read the story before I showed it to him, but I had no idea he was going to have that reaction.

BEFORE HE BEGAN WORKING ON A SONG IRA WOULD SHARPEN HIS BRAIN BY DOING CROSSWORD PUZZLES.

music and was spurred on by his brother's boundless energy. He took pride in taking his witty and clever lyrics as far as he could while still appealing to and touching the public. The trick was never to underestimate the audience but also never to overestimate it either. He understood that if he were too witty, the only person he'd impress would be himself, and maybe Oscar Levant. Writing for a character in a show of course dictated much of his output, and his first goal was always to create what was needed in the context of the production. Since romance was at the heart of every musical comedy, the subject matter of many Gershwin songs was predetermined. Commerciality was not paramount in the creative process, yet he had to stay mindful of it.

His wishes had to be respected, and while one could get into a debate about saving art from destruction at its own creator's hands, I will mercifully refrain.

Before he began working on a song Ira would sharpen his brain by doing crossword puzzles and reading arcane books about words. And then he would dive in . . . but in his own way. Ira was a world-class procrastinator. When he had to write something he would put it off and put it off. He'd finally start, probably late in the day, then he'd stop to have a sandwich and read the newspaper. Finally, he'd force himself to get down to business and work for a half-hour or so, and maybe he'd come up with a couple of good rhymes, and that would give him cause to celebrate. So he'd stop and have a cigar. Sometimes he would work all night like that.

The process was difficult partly because Ira was so hard on himself. He would discard lines that he'd later realize were perfectly okay. Ira was able to bear down better when he had a deadline. Sometimes George would ask his brother, "Okay, Ira, where's the lyric? I need the lyric." And if Ira needed to stay up all night to finish the job, he'd do it.

Achieving the right combination of words and music is a mysterious process. The husband-and-wife lyricists Marilyn and Alan Bergman say that when they hear a tune the words are already written; they just have to find them somewhere out in the world and bring them home to roost. Just as a sculptor can look at a piece of stone and see the outline of a figure, they see it as their job to merely "liberate" the lyric.

Ira always cautioned that he wrote his lyrics to fit the tune exactly and they shouldn't be heard without the melody, and he was right. It's true that like most lyrics, Ira's words by themselves sometimes don't amount to as much, and it's almost impossible to read them without the soundtrack of the music insinuating itself. Take "I Got Rhythm": "I got rhythm, I got music, I got my man, who could ask for anything more?" This lyric doesn't do much by itself, but it is perfectly fitted to the tune and, as with all great songs, each element makes the other immeasurably stronger. To use the words I once heard an agent use, it's a case of "one plus one equals three." It's the combination of words and music that creates the magical synergy that songwriters are looking for. Where a love song is concerned, the need for alchemy is greatest, as the songwriter is attempting to describe something that is abstract, a feeling— the act of falling in love or being in love or losing love. Words by their nature are specific, while music, like love itself, plays on our emotions. So a great love song creates elation and excitement out of this synergistic melding of abstract, undefined music and concrete, well-chosen words.

Which brings us back to the question: How do you write a great love song? Harry Warren spoke of how a stupid producer would sometimes tell him (his hired-hand songwriter) that he wanted him to create five hit songs for his movie. Don't write any song, write a hit! Easy for him to say. Only a very few writers like Warren could conjure up the emotional alchemy when it was demanded of them like that; he then relied on his lyricist, Al Dubin, to match the feat. Creativity strikes

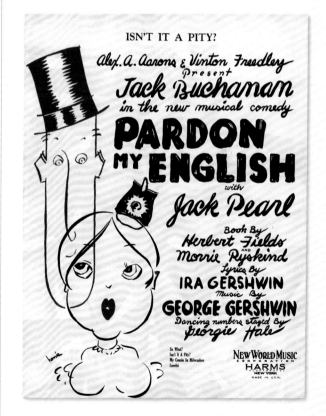

"Isn't It a Pity?" sheet music cover from the show Pardon My English.

composers and writers (and painters and novelists and playwrights) in many ways. George was endlessly and easily creative; Ira had to work and work to find inspiration. Had it not been for George, Ira would have been far less productive. He loved the results, but he hated the work. How these two siblings turned out so vastly different is one of the mysteries of the ages.

For Ira, writing a lyric was like doing a puzzle. In any puzzle you have only so many pieces to work with and there are strict rules, for good reason. Ira's principal constraint besides the tune itself was that, as all first-class lyric writers did, he had to use a perfect rhyme scheme. Of course, once you've zeroed in on one word to end a line, you are limited by sound to what you can use to complete the rhyme. (In these days of nonrhyming songs, it is necessary to explain this basic tenet of classic song versifying.) While working on "I Got Rhythm," Ira had seemingly exhausted all the possibilities in rhyme, and they sounded uncharacteristically prosaic and unexciting. They were expected and clichéd. Once he had exhausted everything he could think of, he was left with a seemingly impossible task. He found rhymes, all right, but they didn't give the tune wings and uplift it into the celestial glory it deserved.

So Ira came up with the absurd notion of writing a lyric that didn't rhyme. It was against convention and everything Ira believed in. Without form, what is a song? Yet here, it felt right. He trusted his instinct—as he had when he created the phrase "'s wonderful"—and then stood by it with the same attitude you take when you dare someone to contradict your immutable opinion: "Just try and challenge me!" Not only was he

not challenged, he was acclaimed for the simple approach, an approach that he sweated bullets to achieve. Go figure.

Ira and I once talked about the song "Sing Me Not a Ballad," which he wrote with Kurt Weill and which was published in 1945. Ira felt it was a bit smutty, though by today's standards it's very tame. The song ends with,

> *Spare me your advances*
> *Just, oh just make love.*

Ira was always a little disturbed by the song. He felt that it was maybe a little too "on the nose," that it was basically saying, "Let's do it." As a love song it was far more direct than Ira's usual tone. In that case, I asked him, "Why did you write it?" And he answered, in a very exasperated tone, "I couldn't help it. That's where it took me." Just as the Bergmans described their pre-existing lyrics as waiting to be discovered, this is what can happen in the creative process. Sometimes you are led down a path, and where you end up is not always where you thought you were going. The whole process is mysterious, as if the song were finding its own way into the light, whether the writer likes it or not.

WRITING A GOOD SONG is devilishly hard, but even doing so doesn't guarantee success, because the right person has to be found to sing the song. Many great songs have languished because they never found the right voice to bring them to life. Ethel Merman, the star of *Girl Crazy*, had a voice that fit the pre-amplified Broadway stage beautifully, but having a big voice alone has never been a prerequisite for starring in a musical.

More important, singers need to convincingly inhabit the character and transfix the audience with their performance. In other words, they need charisma. No amount of bravura singing can compensate for a lack of stage presence. The converse, however, isn't always true: an actor can dominate a scene while delivering a song without singing brilliantly. Gertrude Lawrence was such a performer, and Ira tried to explain her magical appeal to me after I expressed disdain for her recorded singing voice. "Pure magic" was the phrase he used to describe her stage persona.

The London-born Lawrence introduced "Someone to Watch over Me" in George and Ira's Broadway musical *Oh, Kay!* in 1926. The book for *Oh, Kay!* was written by Guy Bolton and English

though, her performance was mesmerizing. And so the words of the love song on the page were given life through interpretation and performance.

Gertrude Lawrence and George Gershwin knew each other from the Manhattan party circuit. She had been a West End chorus girl and nightclub singer, and first appeared on Broadway in transplanted revues created by London producer André Charlot in 1924 and 1926. Her first Broadway musical in which she was a solo star was a triumph: *Oh, Kay!* was a hit in New York and the West End. Her second musical, *Treasure Girl*, in 1928, suffered a different fate entirely, but that didn't stop her, and Lawrence was a star for decades on both sides of the Atlantic. Lawrence triumphed in 1931's *Private Lives* (which was written for her by

SO IRA CAME UP WITH THE ABSURD NOTION OF WRITING A LYRIC THAT DIDN'T RHYME.

novelist P. G. Wodehouse (Bolton was a Gershwin regular, and he and Wodehouse had worked as librettist and lyricist with Jerome Kern starting in 1917 on a famous series of hit shows at the Princess Theatre). In 1925, *Sunny*, Kern's first show with lyrics by Oscar Hammerstein, had opened.

The show had a tryout in Philadelphia, where George bought a cheap rag doll for Lawrence to use as a prop during this number. She stood onstage alone and sang to the doll. In a photograph of the scene, she looks impossibly coy, something she was not outside the theater. By all accounts,

Noel Coward), first in the U.K. and later on Broadway, and she starred in Ira's *Lady in the Dark* in 1941. In 1952, while starring in Rodgers and Hammerstein's *The King and I* with Yul Brynner, she fell ill and succumbed to undiagnosed liver cancer at the age of fifty-four.

"Someone to Watch over Me" is now a staple of George and Ira's canon. The song began its life as an up-tempo dance number, with its musical phrases clipped shorter and the lyrics run together. Unlike with "I've Got a Crush on You," which was later slowed down in interpretation,

it was George and Ira who repurposed "Someone to Watch over Me."

Here's where luck came in, as it so often does in the creation of a successful song. As George was playing the up-tempo tune for Ira so that he could think about a lyric, he was distracted by their sister, Frances. While George attended to whatever it was Frances was saying, he kept playing but slowed down as he listened. Ira then said, "Wait a minute, play it slower. This works better as a ballad." George agreed, and "Someone to Watch over Me" took on its almost mournful mien. George took out the jagged syncopated phrases and rhythmic ideas originally encoded in the tune and used them instead in the song "Fidgety Feet," which now filled

the dance song slot that the tune for "Someone to Watch over Me" had originally occupied.

> *I've got fidgety feet, fidgety feet,*
> *fidgety feet!*
> *Oh, what fidgety feet, fidgety feet,*
> *fidgety feet!*
> *Say, mate, come and be my sway mate;*
> *How can anyone resist that*
> *rhythmical beat?*

Ira mentions the "fast and jazzy" origins of "Someone to Watch over Me" in *Lyrics on Several Occasions.* He also writes about being rushed to the hospital for an emergency appendectomy in

Gertrude Lawrence in Oh, Kay! (RIGHT) *Lawrence holding the rag doll given to her by George Gershwin.*

the middle of writing *Oh, Kay!* In 1926 this was a much more serious medical situation than it is today, and Ira was in New York's Mount Sinai Hospital for six weeks, by which time the musical needed his lyrics. In the pinch, Ira's friend Howard Dietz, a lyricist (and later the head of publicity at MGM), offered to help. He came up with the title "Someone to Watch over Me." Dietz had nothing to do with the writing of that lyric but did lend a hand to a few other efforts for the show. Ira later became irritated that every time he received a royalty check for the songs from *Oh, Kay!*, he had to figure out a small stipend based on the percentage of income and send it on to Dietz. Finally, Dietz

the mood, and moves the story along; a great show to set it in; and a great star to sing it. One plus one equals three. The fact that the song was written to be an entirely different animal is merely a curiosity now. The stars aligned and a standard was born.

THE QUESTION OF WHERE music comes from within a writer is fascinating to me. You might wonder if the romantic notions expressed by George, Ira, and their contemporaries bore any resemblance to their real-life experiences. George had a love life that has been much written about but is still shrouded in mystery, probably

WE DO KNOW THAT HE COMPOSED A SPECIAL WALTZ THAT HE WOULD PLAY FOR HIS ROMANTIC PROSPECTS.

agreed to be paid off in a lump sum and Ira happily put away his calculator.

Gertrude Lawrence played Kay, the sister of a British toff caught up in a liquor-running operation (this was the age of Prohibition). Kay has to pretend to be married in order to maintain the caper. She isn't married but longs to be.

For "Someone to Watch over Me," Ira created an original love lyric with straightforward expressions of longing. And yet it is full of invention, from the two well-known aphorisms cleverly juxtaposed in the first two lines to the made-up rhyme of "man some" and "handsome."

Here the elements of a great love song come together: a memorable and emotionally affecting tune; a lyric that amplifies the music, captures

because it appears that he was never able to sustain true love. We do know that he composed a special waltz that he would play for his romantic prospects, inserting their name at the appropriate spot so they would believe he wrote it just for them. It often helped seal the deal. (Kitty Carlisle claimed that George gave her a copy of the music, but she was never able to locate it.) So whether or not he personally believed in what he wrote, he certainly believed in its power to bed.

Ira couldn't mine *his* love life for broad inspiration because his experience of the travails and triumphs of the heart was limited, since he'd been married, and mostly happily, for almost all of his adult life. Ira repressed a great deal of emotion and I doubt anyone ever knew how he truly felt about his romantic life, perhaps on some level even his wife. Lee did once say that Ira was a voyeur and that would make sense. He observed the way others experienced romance and channeled it into his work.

Ira emphatically denied that any song bore any resemblance to his real life. However, Ira told me he wrote, "He may not be the man some girls think of as handsome," in "Someone to Watch over Me" because he felt so lucky to be marrying Lee, which happened as the song was created. His own shyness precluded further expression of what he personally felt, yet he well understood the many permutations of love, even if he never truly experienced love as he might have desired. Once I was talking to someone on the phone, and after I hung up I realized that Ira was nearby. He said, "You were talking to a sweetheart, weren't you? I could tell by the sound of your voice." To no avail I had tried to cover up that fact.

Of course, love songs don't have to be autobiographical at all, and the relationship between lyrics and a songwriter's experience is often ambiguous, and sometimes nonexistent. The lyricist Edward Heyman, who kept his homosexuality under the radar, wrote a tremendous number of hits about love, and I often wonder if any of his lyrics were autobiographical. One of his biggest songs, with Johnny Green's music, was the great standard "Body and Soul" from 1930:

I'm all for you
Body and soul.

I've met and known many of the classic songwriters, and they didn't look like a very romantic bunch. Of course I encountered most of them in their autumnal years, but to a man they resembled businessmen rather than artists, which proves again that appearances are deceiving. It was hard to reconcile the bespectacled and age-spotted exteriors with the sparkling inner souls that had created countless songs that launched a million affairs. Some of the men were content in relationships, while others were restless and romantically disillusioned, fated to live the rest of their days in an existence that offered them little hope of enjoying what they had propagated their entire lives in song.

There were exceptions to this sad rule. Burton Lane was contented, deeply happy with his wife, Lynn, and I daresay he believed in the philosophies he expressed in the songs he wrote with Yip Harburg. The whimsy of "Old Devil Moon" intermingles poetic passion with an honesty that rings true. Lyricist Yip Harburg actually fell for the wife of his collaborator Jay Gorney (with whom he wrote "Brother, Can You Spare a Dime"), and after marrying her, he lived the rest of his days in sweet contentment and true devotion to his Edaline. "Eddy" Harburg's comment was, "I won't marry a man who hasn't written 'Brother, Can You Spare a Dime.'"

Composer Hugh Martin found deep and true love late in life after a rocky road along the way. He, probably more than any other songwriter, wrote true to life and in what he believed, even though most of what was written was on assignment. His songs are a tantalizing mix of optimism, hope, and insecurity that often says, "I am not worthy, but maybe you'll like me anyway." His classic "The Boy Next Door" is a great example.

Herman Hupfeld wrote one of the most famous love songs of all time, "As Time Goes By."

(OPPOSITE) *Original souvenir program cover for* Lady in the Dark.

Hupfeld was, in the parlance of the times (his times were 1894–1951), a confirmed bachelor. He lived his entire life with his mother and died in the same Montclair, New Jersey, house where he was born. Most of the other Hupfeld songs of which I am aware are not about romance, and perhaps that accounts for why they never became as popular as his greatest creation.

Cole Porter wrote in the same sexy fashion that he secretly lived, and expressed a unique sensual passion in his output of that era. His own private life probably fueled the way he deftly expressed the excitement of a relationship that was taboo and "too hot not to cool down."

The disparity between Richard Rodgers the man and his melodies is fascinating, as he was very businesslike and rarely demonstrated the kind of sentimentality that made his songs beloved the

of its bittersweet complexity and was capable of gorgeous sentiment when he desired it, in songs like "Isn't It Romantic" and "My Funny Valentine." Perhaps his truest songs are "It Never Entered My Mind," "Nobody's Heart," and "Why Can't I?" Oh, yes, he understood those words.

Jerome Kern was described paradoxically as being tough as a martinet but also a pixie who loved practical jokes. When it came to his music he, too, was all business while those sinuous, free-flowing streams of inspiration poured forth. Recently discovered early letters to his father-in-law to-be reveal a soul who is hopelessly in love with his intended. He promises to build a life of security and caring for his Eva, and when he died four decades later they were still deeply in love. After his passing Eva platonically remarried a gay singer named George Byron (with a prenuptial agreement

SOME of the MEN WERE CONTENT in RELATIONSHIPS, WHILE OTHERS WERE RESTLESS and ROMANTICALLY DISILLUSIONED.

world over. He was known as a notorious womanizer who freely grabbed the derriere of any beautiful chorus girl close at hand. These were days of male dominance, long before the concept of sexual harassment was conceived. It would be hard to credit Rodgers with believing in the philosophy of his work, especially when one listens to interviews with him as he pragmatically discusses his output. The heart-touching tunes just flowed out of him.

Rodgers's first collaborator, Lorenz Hart, was a tragic, lonely genius who wrote about love in all

in place) so she could have companionship, but no one could ever replace her "Jerry."

Johnny Mercer wrote everything from songs of requited passion like "Out of This World" and "Come Rain or Come Shine" to the wistful "When the World Was Young," the fervent nostalgia of "I Remember You," the agonizing "One for My Baby," and the vengeful "I Wanna Be Around." I believe that he lived all of them and believed all of them, too. His alcoholism couldn't take away the pain of the human condition nor the tragedy of unfulfilled desire, but he also knew that life was ever evolving and still held hope for fledgling hearts, even if at the same time it was winding to its inevitable conclusion. His songs became darker at the end of his life, but he never stopped believing in the possibilities that love could offer.

FOR THESE MEN, AND MEN LIKE THEM, WRITING A SONG WAS A JOB WITH A POTENTIALLY HUGE COMMERCIAL PROFIT AT THE END OF IT.

For these men, and men like them, writing a song was a job with a potentially huge commercial profit at the end of it. How often did the writers write for themselves and believe in what they wrote? Probably not very often, as there were deadlines to be met, characters' points of view to be expressed, specific requirements called for by producers that were no different from ordering a suit in a certain size and color. The Tin Pan Alley guys who worked free-form were even more mercenary in their desire to generate a title that would keep the printing presses going night and day.

However, from that pressure-cooker climate of toil a body of work emerged that contains truth and a resonance that have helped sustain it for decades. Ira and George knew in retrospect that they had created art that meant a great deal to the world. If they didn't always feel it when they wrote it, they must have perceived it later, when they looked at the damp and misty eyes of the masses who responded to the simple emotions they expressed. These are feelings that will never leave us, no matter how much the world changes. Perhaps such a clichéd statement is yet another idea for a popular song?

'M ALWAYS INTRIGUED when I hear a very simple melody that becomes a huge pop hit—I wonder how many times that tune has been used in another context. (This section is subtitled "Love Songs and How to Rewrite Them.") If you are "recycling" a melody, you have to have a different rhythm and, of course, a different lyric. One of the things that makes Sondheim so distinctive is that his harmonic palette is so advanced, he is able to cloak his tunes in a multitude of guises.

Gershwin did have patterns, elements he would employ over and over again, such as certain intervals at the piano, noted in the similarities of several songs from *Oh, Kay!* that all begin with the same basic melody, cleverly disguised one from the other. But he used them in such a way that they didn't sound like they were copies of anything. With so many songs out there, it's a miracle that anything sounds original. (There was one person who believed Gershwin songs were copies—Vincent Youmans, who insisted that Gershwin stole from him. If you listen to Youmans's "Oh Me, Oh My, Oh You," written in 1921 with lyrics by Arthur Francis, it does sound very much like "Funny Face," written in 1927. But George certainly didn't need to steal.)

When I was doing the show *All About Me* with Dame Edna, we cowrote and performed "The

Gladdy Song," and I know its melody has been used many times. If I were ever sued, I'm sure I could find a half-dozen versions of that melody. Our show didn't run long enough for anyone to care, perhaps, yet we were proud of our musical contribution to light pastiche.

Harry Warren wrote "Lullaby of Broadway," which in 1935 won him his first Academy Award. Then Harry got sued, accused of having plagiarized from a song called "All About Broadway," and he was pretty upset. As he vividly recounted it to me years later, Harry went to his close friend Jerome Kern and said, "Jerry, what do I do?" Kern (who had earlier dealt with his own plagiarism suit) said, "Play me the tune." Kern listened for a minute, then went over to a filing cabinet where he kept a copy of all the songs he'd written, published and unpublished, literally hundreds of them. He pulled out a song he'd written twenty years earlier and threw it over to Harry. He said, "Here's your 'Lullaby of Broadway.'" Case dismissed.

The fact that there was an earlier song with the same melodic structure made anything that followed it a copy of what already had been conceived by Kern, thus nullifying any claims to infringement. One could also, I believe, dig up an earlier song or theme that was utilized similarly in an even earlier context. Kern was unconcerned about such things, recognizing that there is nothing new under the sun, for only the way it is altered is what makes a melody or song fresh.

So many songs were inspired by other songs. When Burton Lane's show *On a Clear Day You Can See Forever* opened in 1965, it included a comedic song called "On the S.S. Bernard Cohn," which made it into the 2011 revival. When

Sondheim's *Company* opened in 1970, the title song was one Burton found particularly delightful, so he told Sondheim, "I love that song." And Sondheim laughingly said, "Well, you should. You wrote it." Sondheim had been able to morph it into something sufficiently different.

KERN WAS UNCONCERNED ABOUT SUCH THINGS, RECOGNIZING THAT THERE *is* NOTHING NEW UNDER *the* SUN.

I once performed a song called "This Heart of Mine," by Harry Warren and Arthur Freed, in a nightclub. Sondheim was in the room. He later told me, "I love that song," then added, "I love it so much that I found myself writing it three or four times."

Ira and Burton Lane.

It's easy to change a few notes to make a song different. For example, Harry Warren wrote a song called "The Only, Only One (for Me)," published in 1924. Then he discovered it was very similar to "Tea for Two," which over the course of a year evolved into a big hit in 1925 but had been written and published at the same time as Harry's tune. Who actually wrote it first is not as important for the legal system as who copyrighted it first. So he made a few changes in the notes and his song survived. David Raksin wrote a theme for a Vincente Minnelli movie called *Two Weeks in Another Town* in 1962, and discovered it was very similar to a movie theme written by Bronislaw Kaper (composer of the music for the 1962 movie *Mutiny on the Bounty*). Raksin changed a few notes and his theme became perfectly acceptable.

A SONG IN A SHOW HAS TO EXPRESS WHAT CAN'T BE RELATED ANY OTHER WAY AND CREATE DRAMA AT THE SAME TIME.

A title cannot be copyrighted. For example, and unsurprisingly, there have been dozens of songs written called "I Love You," including one by Harry Archer and Harlan Thompson that was a big hit in 1923 for the show *Little Jessie James.* Two decades later, on a bet that he couldn't come up with a decent lyric for such a clichéd title, Cole Porter wrote a song with the same moniker

and it indeed became mildly popular. Before George and Ira wrote *Strike Up the Band,* there was a turn-of-the-century song with such a title that eventually has been forgotten yet was at one time immensely popular.

HOWEVER THEY CHOOSE to go about it, songwriters face the extremely difficult task of drilling down on the numerous but scattered ideas they may have and crafting something for the broader context of a show. It is difficult to integrate music and dialogue so that one element seamlessly leads into and out of the other. A song in a show has to express what can't be related any other way and create drama at the same time. When this is done improperly, a song can become absurd, or it just gets in the way. The great theater directors can sense the inappropriate placing of a song in a show and ruthlessly reject it, no matter how good it is on its own. Composers and lyricists aren't always as clear-eyed.

Remember that most show tunes are written for specific moments in a musical. As musicals evolved and became more sophisticated, the subject of the songs became increasingly integrated into the plot, whereas many earlier musicals had very little plot to speak of. Some songs, such as "Embraceable You," started life in one musical (*East Is West*) and ended up in another (*Girl Crazy*). Songs like these are specific to a mood rather than to a point in a plot. (That mood is usually some shade of love, of course, which does help.) This is why I like to know, whenever possible, the circumstances of the writing of a song. I want to know why it's not just another love song. I think that the only way it can be properly judged is in context.

Recently I was at a club and a performer did a number from a show. Afterward, one person I was with turned to me and said, "Well, that was terrible." I had thought the song was wonderful because, when I listened to it, I was thinking about the composer's intention for it and thus heard it in a different context. The people I was with just heard it as a song.

At one time the hit records heard and embraced by the public were from shows that shared perhaps it was easier in the days of loose plots for shows. As most writers evolve, their style of writing becomes more clear and streamlined as their craft allows them to express an idea with less effort and more accessibility.

As with any other creative endeavor, there are no rules that determine the process of writing any kind of song. Endless crafting will work for one writer, while another may be able to knock off a song in an hour, and as previously stated, Ira and

> EVEN FOR AN ACKNOWLEDGED GREAT LIKE STEPHEN SONDHEIM, IT CAN TAKE TIME, AND MANY REVERSALS, TO GET TO WHERE ONE WANTS TO BE.

their place equally on the charts with pop creations, a practice that continued heavily through the sixties. Now that most recordings are by singer-songwriters and are crafted as recordings that are popular for their sound and production more than the musical or lyrical content, Broadway songs can sound passé in comparison.

When Burton Lane was working on *Finian's Rainbow,* he decided to write a score that was integrated into the book and not think about writing hits. He ended up with five hit songs, including "How Are Things in Glocca Morra?" Irving Berlin conversely always tried to write hits but balanced with the pure book songs. With his genius he could also make those book songs into hits. That's the key to it all: making the songs resonate in a clear and simple way so they fulfill the plot and can step out for other use as well, perhaps as a stand-alone love song. That's why

George were on opposite ends of the spectrum. Within the constraints of the genre, you can do anything. Do you want this note to go up a half-step or down a half-step and up an octave? Each choice can be a technically correct solution, but what's the right choice for the song's context? What's the right choice for its lyric? Breaking the rules may be the way to solve the problem and usher in a new sound along with it. Burt Bacharach did it and legitimized a mongrel pop sound. He had been working for many years before he discovered his sound, or it discovered him.

Even for an acknowledged great like Stephen Sondheim, it can take time, and many reversals, to get to where one wants to be. Sondheim always followed his own path and he sometimes paid a price for it. When he was a young man, he wanted to write the music and the lyrics for *Gypsy*. But the star of the show, Ethel Merman, didn't want him

to write the music. This was almost thirty years after *Girl Crazy*, and Merman was a major star, so she got her way and Jule Styne was hired.

At first, Sondheim wanted to drop out of the project, but his mentor, Oscar Hammerstein, said, "Do it." Hammerstein thought it would be instructive for Sondheim to write for a big star like Ethel Merman, so he did. Still, he didn't like compromising. *Gypsy* was a huge hit and gave Sondheim's

career a big boost. (As of this writing it has been announced that Streisand will play the role originated by Merman in a revival, and it reminds me that no matter who else plays the role, for my money, no one will ever sing it better than Merman did, if only because it was written for her voice specifically. Just as I don't ever want to hear anyone but Streisand sing "Don't Rain on My Parade," because they always in some way copy her.)

Advertisement for A Damsel in Distress.

Still, it wasn't until 1962, with *A Funny Thing Happened on the Way to the Forum,* that Sondheim wrote both the music and lyrics for a Broadway show. *Forum* ran even longer than *Gypsy*. But his next show, 1964's *Anyone Can Whistle,* ran 955 times fewer than *Forum*: 964 performances to nine. Musically, up to that time it was perhaps his truest voice, but the show bombed. When revived recently in concert, it revealed an incomprehensible book and ambitious and sometimes perplexing musicalization that tried to make sense of the libretto, an impossible task.

Making sense of a libretto is a task sometimes faced by songwriters, but making sense of their own songs could be equally daunting when inspiration offered too many options. Often,

still wasn't sure what he wanted. Some choices are just impossible to make.

OCCASIONALLY I'LL HEAR A NEW SONG that has an effect on me, but it happens more often with instrumental music, because most songs today have lyrics that don't rhyme. Sometimes I'll sing a song with some phrases that don't perfectly rhyme because the whole song is otherwise great, but it's hard to accommodate. For me, nonrhyming is often a deal-breaker when I hear a song: the lyrics have to rhyme.

Here's why rhyme is necessary: the essence of what is celebrated in the songs written by the classic songwriters is their ability to work within a very constrained form. The templates and limitations

YOU CAN'T FOOL WITH AN EVOLVED TRADITION THAT GOES BACK CENTURIES, EVEN THOUGH TO MILLIONS IT MATTERS NOT A WHIT.

George would get the song right the first time, but even he couldn't do it every time. There is a song called "Pay Some Attention to Me" that George and Ira worked on for the movie *A Damsel in Distress* in 1937 but remains unfinished and unpublished. It actually started life in 1930 with a different melody. George and Ira could never decide whether they wanted the chorus to be "Please pay some attention to me" or "Please pay some attention, some attention to me," the choice being the addition of several notes, giving the end of each phrase a different feeling. Decades later, Ira and I talked about that song—and he

force the writers to work much harder and mine the breadth and depth of their creativity, and it just wouldn't be the same if they had carte blanche to do whatever they wanted. It's much harder to create something original when you have to keep drawing within the lines.

The expression of an idea is so much easier in free-form and nonrhyming songs. While I may love the idea, I can't appreciate the "craft" in a song like that because in comparison to tradition, there's no craft at all. Sondheim feels that it's all over where perfect rhymes are concerned, and I don't know if he's right or not. Discipline is the key, and the sloppy expression of thought with near or not-so-near rhymes is pedestrian to my ears. To me, you can't fool with an evolved tradition that goes back centuries, even though to millions it matters not a whit.

Harking back to the last century of creative work, it's true that there are many standards that miss a pure rhyme here and there, or don't rhyme at all. Some lyrics in *Funny Girl* don't perfectly rhyme, and lots of Tin Pan Alley hits strayed from clean coalescence. A huge hit from the twenties called "Love Nest" rhymed "warm" with "farm." Perhaps in some tiny corner of the country, that rhymes. Later editions of the song mysteriously contained "charm" as a replacement for "warm." "Penthouse Serenade" rhymes "jazz pattern" with "Manhattan." Benny Davis, writer of "Baby Face" and countless other songs that made him rich, was known for his use of near rhymes. The impeccable Howard Dietz, upon hearing a slipshod assembly of Davis lyrics, quipped, "Heaven save us from Benny Davis."

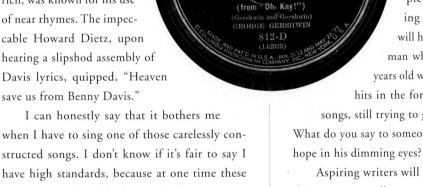

I can honestly say that it bothers me when I have to sing one of those carelessly constructed songs. I don't know if it's fair to say I have high standards, because at one time these were everyone's standards, even in the more commercial environs of Hollywood. It would bemuse songwriters and lyricists from the twenties and thirties that this subject would even be a topic of conversation. No rhyme; no lyric. No lyric; no song. I think it's like doing a crossword where you don't have to get all the letters right to complete the puzzle. What's the point?

Having said all this, there are contemporary writers who I think are simply great. John Bucchino (*A Catered Affair*) is a unique and original songwriter. Adam Guettel, who wrote *The Light in the Piazza* and *Floyd Collins*, is so very talented and digs deep with his rich expression. Ditto Susan Werner and Lindy Robbins, who write pop songs and can easily stretch into the theater if they so desire. There are many more. But for most, their work isn't usually heard on the radio, so their songs have less reach. How many of them will have the chance to be heard or the break they need? How much of it is fate, karma, good luck, or bad breaks?

Despite the desperate state of popular music today, there are still people plugging away, writing songs in the hope they will hit gold. I know a gentleman who is almost a hundred years old who had a couple of mild hits in the forties and is still writing songs, still trying to get his songs out there. What do you say to someone who still carries this hope in his dimming eyes?

Aspiring writers will send me recordings of their songs as well, sometimes several a month. Rosemary Clooney used to get piles of submissions from hopefuls who would send their offerings on tapes. She and I were rehearsing one day and I told her my tape had run out. She said,

Gershwin's own recording of "Someone to Watch Over Me" played in strict dance tempo.

"Oh, I've got tape," and pulled out a box filled with cassettes of songs she'd been sent. You might strike gold, but once you've listened to twenty awful songs, it's hard to sit through more. To do it, you'd need to have the musical version of a food taster, someone whose job is to make sure you don't get too badly poisoned.

> IN 2010, LADY GAGA SANG IT ON THE *TODAY* SHOW AND I WAS AT FIRST SHOCKED, THEN THRILLED TO HEAR HER RICH PERFORMANCE OF IT.

Aspiring songwriters would do well to study "Someone to Watch over Me" for all that is contained in it. Just as I always find something fresh in singing it, likewise a student would doubtless find layer upon layer of inspiration and knowledge contained within. There is a reason it is sung by many contemporary performers as well as classic ones. In 2010, Lady Gaga sang it on the *Today* show and I was at first shocked, then thrilled to hear her rich performance of it.

The classic American song has been more than just a favorite art form to me—it's been an education in its own right. I've immersed myself in the world of the song and amassed a lot of arcane information about it. I've listened to and sung thousands of love songs and learned countless volumes about the universe of emotion that exists within

their strict boundaries. I was never a good student—I lacked the discipline to study academically. Like George, who left school at fifteen, and Ira, who dropped out of college after a year, I sought my schooling out in the world, albeit a very different world from that of the Gershwins.

Nothing interests me more than love songs—listening to them, singing them, collecting them, preserving them. Most of that isn't something you can learn in a classroom, and I feel my very personal education has stood me in good stead, both professionally and academically. And although I never went to college, knowing it would be futile on many levels, to my own considerable shock—and much to my parents' delight—I've been awarded three honorary doctorates, from Cal State L.A., Five Towns College, and Allegheny College. Finally, my mom can say she has a doctor in the family. And it's the love songs that helped get me there. •

(ABOVE) *British sheet music cover for "Someone to Watch over Me" from* Oh, Kay!
(OPPOSITE) *Handwritten lyrics for songs from* Lady in the Dark; *the lower half is for "My Ship."*

198

Cowboy Song (?)   Harlem Row   East Georgia

The grass is just as green here as in Arizona)
On sunny days the sky is just as blue
The stars are no dimmer, the river's got that shimmer

But I'm afraid there's no maid to take the place of Linda Lou
It's a toss up of choice excepting for the voice of Linda Lou

When things get tough it's no better back in Georgia
The pavements' just as hard back there, it's true
The rocky fields are just as rocky
And the ~~firemen~~ just as cocky
But there I can stare at that angel Linda Lou

                                But write as I will
                            A song — I still
But   And I'll wait   For that one fine day one Spring
Oh, I'll wait for years
         Till my ship appears
    One fine day one Spring
(on a fine day one fine Spring)   ?
    But the diamonds + such
    all wont mean much
If that day lacks just one thing
But my ship need never sail the foam
Oh, my ship need never be
                              to share with me

But my ship need'nt ever sail the foam (blue)
My treasure needn't
My ship doesn't ever ever be
If when she arrives she doesn't bring home
         If my ship that day doesn't bring home
my love, My love, to me / a sweet, sweet love

"EMBRACEABLE YOU"

from *Girl Crazy*, 1930

VERSE 1
DANNY:

Dozens of girls would storm up;
I had to lock my door.
Somehow I couldn't warm up
To one before.
What was it that controlled me?
What kept my love life lean?
My intuition told me
You'd come on the scene.
Lady, listen to the rhythm of my heartbeat,
And you'll get just what I mean.

REFRAIN 1

Embrace me,
My sweet embraceable you.
Embrace me,
You irreplaceable you.
Just one look at you—my heart grew tipsy in me;
You and you alone bring out the gypsy in me.
I love all
The many charms about you;
Above all,
I want my arms about you.
Don't be a naughty baby,
Come to papa—come to papa—do!
My sweet embraceable you.

VERSE 2
MOLLY:

I went about reciting,
"Here's one who'll never fall!"
But I'm afraid the writing
Is on the wall.
My nose I used to turn up
When you'd besiege my heart;
Now I completely burn up

When you're slow to start.
I'm afraid you'll have to take the consequences;
You upset the apple cart.

REFRAIN 2

Embrace me,
My sweet embraceable you.
Embrace me,
You irreplaceable you.
In your arms I find love so delectable, dear,
I'm afraid it isn't quite respectable, dear.
But hang it!
Come on, let's glorify love!
Ding dang it!
You'll shout "Encore!" if I love.
Don't be a naughty papa,
Come to baby—come to baby—do!
My sweet embraceable you.

ENCORE REFRAIN
DANNY:

Dear lady,
My silk-and-lace-able you;
Dear lady,
Be my embraceable you.
You're the only I love, yes, verily so!
But you're much too shy, unnecessarily so!
MOLLY:
I'll try not
To be so formal, my dear.
DANNY:
Am I not
A man who's normal, my dear?
There's just one way to cheer me;
Come to papa—come to papa—do!
My sweet embraceable you.

· C H A P T E R 7 ·

PERFORMING AND INTERPRETING THE SONG

MUSIC IS UNIVERSAL. Whatever the genre, whether the music is played by a rock 'n' roll band in a basement, by a full orchestra at Carnegie Hall, or on a tin flute at a street corner, the performer uses combinations of notes, rhythms, and tempos to express herself and to elicit a response, to create a dialogue with an engaged audience. Even though some people are more musically fluent than others, nearly everyone can listen and react in some way, because we all understand the basic sounds of a musical alphabet.

But when words are added to the music, the situation gets more complicated. A lyric requires a more thoughtful or knowing response. Some-times it's as simple as asking, *What does that mean? Or, Have I grasped the nuances of the words? Does the lyric complement and reinforce the music and vice versa?* A lot of it can be simple instinct, but that might come only after years of experience, being immersed in the music. Often, there's no right answer to these questions or any like them. It's a left-brain/right-brain distinction: music appeals to us on an instinctive, emotional level, while words demand an intellectual response.

George and Ira worked tirelessly to make songs that were a perfect whole, words and music fused together in glorious synergy. While George sometimes played his songs in public, like most songwriters who aren't singers, the Gershwins

The author in the recording studio.

needed an interpreter to give life to their work. To borrow a metaphor from another art form, George and Ira started with a blank canvas and painted their picture, and what they created was a second canvas for a separate artist to work with. This canvas is not blank but still not prescriptive in any meaningful way, and thus leaves almost infinite room for creative decision making. Just as a lyricist's jeweler-like act of interpretation works within the structure of a melody, a performer's art is no less creative for the fact that it works within the bounds of the whole song. Both interpretive acts transform the song from an abstract form (naked melody for the lyricist, mere idea of a song written on a page for the singer) into an actualized and well-defined one: they make it a reality. From literature comes the idea of the so-called intentional fallacy—the author's intent is not the most important factor in interpreting a work, since it can never be known completely or with perfect certainty—which means, if this idea is applied to a song, it's all in the singing of it. Even knowing the circumstances under which a song was created, or even knowing the author, ultimately only gives clues, albeit important ones, of how to bring through their intentions.

However they go about it, singers are trying to establish a connection when they reach out to their audience. And as performers, we are breathing life into a song when we sing it. Otherwise, it's nothing more than scratches on a page. Artists express themselves by trying to interpret a song in their own way—to add to what the composer and lyricist set on paper and not take away from it. (At least I hope this is the case.) If a singer can't bring his own style to a song, his craft is lacking; if he

simply imitates another singer, it's karaoke. Sometimes the composer expresses a desire to have his song performed one way or another, and a singer must balance this with his own artistic impulse. But if he is skillful, the singer can still make his distinctive mark on the song.

Singers perform for the same reason that songwriters compose: they want to make a connection with an audience. In other words, they crave a reaction. It can be an immediate and visceral reaction if they are playing live, which is what can make singing before a crowd so powerful and exciting for a performer. But you can never predict what will happen. That's why it's art, not science. No one expects every viewer of Picasso's *Les Demoiselles d'Avignon* to have the same reaction to it—that's an absurd thought. And so is the idea that everyone has to perform or listen to a song the same way.

Performers will want to take on the great songs because it is their artistic obligation as a singer to work with the best material. But speaking of material, it's sometimes the case that just because you paid a hundred bucks a yard for the silk, it doesn't mean you shouldn't have picked the polyester. Take "Summertime" (George's music, DuBose Heyward's lyric). If you look up "Summertime" online you'll find a list of a hundred artists who have recorded it—Louis Armstrong, Chet Baker, Bing Crosby, Miles Davis, Duke Ellington, Ella Fitzgerald—and that's only a few. Some know Duke Ellington's 1943 recording best, or Janis Joplin's version, or Sarah Vaughan's. Each iteration is different. Each version has its admirers and champions, which is how it should be, of course.

Once a song is recorded, any artist can perform it, but there are certain restrictions. Legally, you're not supposed to change the melody without the permission of the publisher (although people do it all the time) and you can't change the lyrics (and that law was once strictly enforced by publishers, decades ago). Otherwise, you're free to do your best, and your worst. But just because you can perform the song any way you like doesn't mean you should. My philosophy is very simple: if a change adds something to a song, good. If not, don't do it. There is no reason to change something just for the sake of leaving your mark on it. If a singer made a change to one of Ira's songs that improved it, he was all for it, being surprisingly liberal. But in his opinion, that seldom happened.

its essence. I suspect that this adaptation wouldn't have bothered George either, as the evolution was organic. George himself famously enjoyed playing variations of his own songs, not only playing them in different keys but drastically altering them in other ways to stay fresh in his improvisational skills, yet he always knew which essential elements had to be retained for a song to work.

The best songs are played over and over because they have these unbreakable defining elements and they can withstand the variety of interpretive shades and nuances that different performers bring to them. That's what makes these songs standards, something we'll talk more

IF A CHANGE ADDS SOMETHING TO A SONG, GOOD. IF NOT, DON'T DO IT.

Of course, what counts as adding to or improving a song is as much a matter of taste as it is which songs are the best in the repertoire. But in both cases, there are some useful ways to approach these questions so that our choices are meaningful rather than arbitrary. This chapter is about the different ways interpreters make these decisions and the standards I use in my own performances when choosing among the many ways to sing and play each song.

Songs do evolve over time, of course. "'S Wonderful" was changed forever after Gene Kelly and Georges Guétary duetted it differently in the film *An American in Paris.* The song has been sung with that syncopation in the final phrase ever since. (The arrangers at MGM made this change.) Ira was fine with that; it loosened the song up without altering

about in the next chapter. But some singers can work alchemy even on a less resilient song and turn lead into gold. An example of a song that the creator thought was far from his best work is "Ain't That a Kick in the Head," by Sammy Cahn and Jimmy Van Heusen. Cahn felt that it was an uninspired lyric, yet it became immensely popular due to a great performance by Dean Martin, assisted by Nelson Riddle, whose arrangement is what I maintain made the record addictive. In a similar vein, while I've always felt that the lyric to the standard "Stardust" is treacly, the Nat Cole version is sublime. So regardless of whether a song is a standard or not, a single, standout performance can make a song come across better than it might have originally sounded.

So WHAT MAKES A GREAT SINGER? As I've written elsewhere, I believe life experience is very important. When it comes to classic songs and not the pop stuff disseminated for the moment, nineteen-year-olds have a hard time singing convincingly about the heartache of an affair that has ended (unless of course, the listener is another nineteen-year-old). The very premise of a song like "How Do You Keep the Music Playing" is that it is about a couple who have been together for a while. Justin Bieber ain't gonna cut it (or feel free to insert here the name of any prepubescent pop idol). Not that it can't be done—the best singers are storytellers, and if the story rings true, that's half the battle. The best singers also make songs conversational and intimate, no matter the size of the stage they are on. And to return to the idea of the intentional fallacy, sometimes a great singer can reinterpret a song to reveal something not even the writer knew was there.

When Hugh Martin wrote "Have Yourself a Merry Little Christmas," he ended up rewriting the lyric at Judy Garland's behest and ultimately felt that she better understood what was needed to be expressed in that song than he did. They later clashed when working together on the film *A Star Is Born*, when Hugh as vocal coach tried to get her to sing "The Man That Got Away" more quietly and she had him fired. Hugh always maintained that he was right, in spite of her rendition's being considered a true classic.

A good voice is important, but it's not everything, or even indispensable. Stephen Sondheim has said he doesn't care about the voice—he cares about the interpretation of the lyric. Mabel Mercer was a terrific storyteller and still one of the great interpreters of lyrics when she was in her seventies and eighties. It wasn't about the voice, but rather her ability to inhabit a lyric. In her last years, she was to perform in San Francisco and, becoming ill, had lost what little voice she had. In desperation she went to see the best throat doctor available. He gently said, "Miss Mercer, may I ask your age?" She replied that she was well into her eighties. He then responded, "Well, you have the vocal cords of a much older woman." Mercer was revered by many, including Sinatra. (Interestingly, it seems that Sondheim couldn't bear Mabel Mercer's singing. I don't know why, but when asked to say something about Mabel he responded, "I have nothing to say about Mabel Mercer.") So how does a singer give the impression of being "in" the lyric? To quote Oscar Hammerstein, "How do you hold a moonbeam in your hand?"

George and Ira arriving in Los Angeles in 1936.

As in all things, interpretation comes down to a matter of taste, on the part of both the performer and the audience, and some people enjoy a wider variety of interpretations than others. For example, George liked interpretations besides his original one much more than Ira did. This is why George loved to hear other people play variations of his songs as much as he liked to play them himself.

Ira and I agreed on most things. Like me, Ira loved the way Judy Garland sang his songs—especially when she did it in his living room, though he did comment that she had periods where she sounded more quavery, especially in the forties. But we didn't agree about everything. Like Ella Fitzgerald. Ella made what many consider one of the iconic Gershwin recordings, *Ella Fitzgerald Sings the George and Ira Gershwin Songbook,* with the Nelson Riddle Orchestra. It was a deluxe boxed set, five LPs with liner notes, released in 1959, and Ira was crazy about it while I was not. Riddle is considered today to be the most important popular song arranger of the fifties and sixties, and yet, much as I agree with that assessment and revere him, I find many of his Gershwin arrangements disappointing. They are brilliant arrangements, of course, but in many instances he dispensed with the original harmonies, and I miss them. Riddle's version of "Love Is Here to Stay" uses a repeating six- or seven-note phrase, a bluesy riff, throughout as accompaniment. It works well, but I still long for what Gershwin wrote for that number. It's a matter of how one is reared on the songs to begin with and what other renditions are compared with what we know. Most people wouldn't know what the original harmonies are anyway and therefore have nothing to compare to.

While both Ella Fitzgerald and Nelson Riddle are iconic figures, my preference with Ella and Gershwin is for her earlier and simpler renderings with Ellis Larkins at the piano. I once worked up the temerity to tell her so. She said, "I understand. They're more intimate." (I also think the Sarah Vaughan Gershwin interpretations are more interesting and spontaneous as jazz renderings than Fitzgerald's, but Ira strongly disagreed about that, too. He didn't even want to listen to the rest of her double Gershwin LP when I started to play the tracks for him. For me Hal Mooney's arrangements on that collection are lovely and underrated.)

WHEN ELLA WAS AT HER MOST FREE AND UNENCUMBERED, SHE WAS AT HER BEST.

I don't think Ella Fitzgerald was always a deep interpreter of lyrics. She was often inside the song musically but not lyrically, yet she was so talented that it didn't always matter. Listen to the 2009 box set of unreleased live recordings from 1961 and 1962 called *Twelve Nights in Hollywood* and prepare to be dazzled. Like all of her recordings before a live audience, these are the pinnacle of extraordinary spontaneous and joyful expressions of her art. Her voice was a marvelous instrument, but when it comes to certain emotional places that naturally come out of the lyric, to me, she's just sometimes not there. Her recording of "The Man That Got Away" on *The Harold Arlen Songbook* is cold as ice.

Then again, there's her "Cry Me a River." Arthur Hamilton wrote the song for Ella to sing in a movie released in 1955 called *Pete Kelly's Blues,* but Jack Webb, the director and star of the film, cut it because he didn't think she could "handle it." Ella later made one of the great recordings of the song, first released in 1961, and Hamilton felt vindicated. When Ella was at her most free and unencumbered, she was at her best.

When I listen to a performance, I always compare it with that of the great singers of the material. There aren't too many contemporary interpreters of classic songs who can stand with Peggy Lee, Nat Cole, Rosemary Clooney, Buddy Clark, and,

a Sinatra-esque big band. He created the definitive version of so many great songs, including Gershwin's "I've Got a Crush on You." (When a version of a song is labeled as definitive, it means that it is generally accepted as the correct version by the creator, the public, and the critics.)

In the fifties he strove to reinvent the standards and did it irrevocably. So many of these songs are ones that I like to hear the way he did them, yet sometimes I wish he hadn't gotten so hip with some of them, pulling a little too far away from the songs' beginnings. This is just a matter of taste, and is the thing that does sometimes help sustain a song. But it can also eclipse the original.

ONCE PEOPLE HEARD THE SINATRA VERSION, IT BECAME DEFINITIVE.

going back further, Ethel Waters, Cliff Edwards, Sophie Tucker, and the young, jazzy Bing Crosby. And every singer has to be compared to Frank Sinatra, because he immortalized a lot of songs.

Having said that, I have views about Sinatra that are colored by the way I approach the songs themselves and what is important about preserving the original blueprint of them. So I might as well just say it.

Let's start with the given that he is one of the greatest singers of the twentieth century. Yes, I feel that in so many ways he is sensational. I admire him so much that I have made two albums—*The Sinatra Project* and a sequel featuring songs he helped make famous: "The Song Is You," "There's a Small Hotel," "Fools Rush In"—performed with

Sinatra was so influential that he could recast a song and single-handedly change the way it was sung. "They Can't Take That Away from Me" was written by George and Ira for the movie *Shall We Dance* in 1937. In the film, Fred Astaire is wearing his heart on his sleeve, singing the song to Ginger Rogers as a gently undulating ballad.

Later, Sinatra swung the song with a big, cocky swagger that I think diminishes the plaintive essence of the original. ("Swing" music began in the mid-thirties and was a style of big band music with strong, urgent rhythms peppered with virtuoso solos. Think Count Basie or Benny Goodman.) Once people heard the Sinatra version, it became definitive. (Another song I can't stand "swung" is Jerome Kern and Dorothy Fields's "The

Way You Look Tonight." Written for the 1936 movie *Swing Time,* it was also sung by Fred to Ginger as a ballad, only to be shifted out of its harmonic shape down the road. It was Sinatra who swung "The Way You Look Tonight," but in my tribute album I performed it as a bossa nova, imagining what it might have sounded like had he recorded it with Antonio Carlos Jobim, the bossa nova pioneer and composer of "The Girl from Ipanema.")

There many things I adore about Sinatra, and the above comments are simply a matter of taste, but knowing how much he revered the songwriters, this is where I really feel that he could veer way out of line: he changed the lyric in some songs. Sinatra always said the lyric was the most important thing to him, but then he would sometimes make gratuitous changes to the words, changes that seem nonsensical. People bristle when I bring this up and I don't understand why. One night when I was sharing this opinion with Quincy Jones, who worked with Frank a lot, he got so angry that he yelled at me, "Well, it's too bad that you weren't around to tell Frank how to sing the songs." Sheesh! I started out by saying he was great, didn't I?

Another of my heretical opinions about Sinatra is that he shouldn't have sung this line in "A Foggy Day":

> *I viewed the morning with much alarm.*
> *The British Museum had lost its charm.*

Ira's original was "I viewed the morning with alarm." You might think, "What's one word between friends?" But Frank's version has a different meaning, and the change disrupts the flow of the line. At

his best, Sinatra is unbeatable, so it pains me to see the ruining of an otherwise perfect interpretation with an interpolation of less lofty proportions.

Another example: in "New York, New York," Sinatra might sing, "If I can make it there, I can make it any goddamn where." Any *goddamn* where? Really? Forgive me, Sinatraphiles, but I don't feel that this makes the song any better. So where Frank changed a lyric, I change it back.

If a song is written in the first person, of course, and the "I" is a woman, it is permissible to change the words, such as in "The Lady Is a Tramp"—"She gets too hungry for dinner at eight." But I don't interpolate words like "sharkies," "frauds," and "broads" as he did in this song, because this would come off as phony if I did it. (If Sammy Cahn, who wrote so many lyrics to order, were still alive, I'd call him for help. He did write some great extra lyrics for me on occasion.)

It would have been great to hear Sinatra sing some of the additional words and verses for some songs. Often he would repeat the first chorus even if the second chorus had a different lyric. Perhaps he didn't know there were more words. Also, he would sometimes omit perfectly good verses or choruses. Maybe they wanted the records to be shorter for potential airplay. For Cole Porter's "At Long Last Love," he sang the first chorus twice and that was it. It's only about a third of the song! Some songs are so often shortened it's as if the full version doesn't exist. (For instance, there is an alternate bridge lyric to "Over the Rainbow" that was cut out of the movie *The Wizard of Oz.* I've only recently heard anyone sing the full version of "Over the Rainbow," and it's unlikely to get widespread exposure.)

OF COURSE, SINATRA IS ONE of the immortals, and I'd put Peggy Lee in that company as well; in many ways I think of her as his female counterpart. She wasn't afraid to radically change the basic shape of a song. She was fearless, yet she was always working with a clear intention of what she was trying to achieve, and did it with an emotional reason and always with thought. Sometimes, when hearing one of her interpretations for the first time, my reaction was, "Oh, my God, listen to that!" She illuminates the bones of a song in a unique way.

Nat "King" Cole was usually a great singer of lyrics, dazzlingly great. Rosemary Clooney said that Nat "King" Cole could sing so well he could make a bad song sound good. His voice was extraordinary and he almost always sounded like he was 100 percent connected to the words. With someone like Nat Cole, the expectations are so high you're surprised when he makes what seems like a misstep, even one time. A friend of mine recalled seeing him on television singing "The Party's Over." It's a very sad song, but when he got to the line, "The party's over, the candles flicker and die," Cole was singing with a big, beautiful grin on his face, moving his fingers in a seductive little hand movement as if to mimic the flicker of the candle. He was countermanding the lyric to such an extent that I think he might have missed the point.

Tony Bennett has a great ear for a good song, and I wish he sang more of the unusual ones that he discovered along the way. He did, for example, a couple of songs Jule Styne wrote with Stephen Sondheim that otherwise would have fallen through the cracks, and we should be grateful for that. He still has an insatiable hunger to hear the next great one.

When I hear Julie Wilson sing a Gershwin song or any other song that I may be a little tired of, she makes it fresh for me. Her tireless work to find the core of a song shines through. She doesn't perform much anymore, but her live recordings really give a sense of her uniqueness. The sudden loss of Mary Clere Haran from the performing scene was a devastating one, as she brought brainy freshness, love, and exuberance to her shows. Barbara Cook sings every song thoughtfully—she has a character and a scenario built around each interpretation that are not spoken to the audience, but are felt in the way the song is sung. Her master classes have imparted information to aspiring singers that is worth a million bucks. Some of the male classic lions are Steve Lawrence, Vic Damone, Jack Jones, Tony Martin. All blessed with perfect voices, each unique and timeless.

In my first book, I wrote about some other singers I like. One of the people I mentioned was Weslia Whitfield. (She now spells her name "Wesla." This is how it was always supposed to be pronounced, but no one ever said it that way.) She is a fascinatingly talented interpreter. Marilyn Maye, who is now in her eighties, provides a veritable primer on how to sing and swing American popular music. John Pizzarelli does great jazz renditions of songs. Guitar wizardry is his main talent, but he's a wonderful interpreter and a fantastic entertainer.

Of the younger generation, there's John Proulx, who at this writing is not as well known but is a very talented singer of pop songs with a fresh and contemporary sensibility. The San Francisco jazz singer Paula West is very talented and another one of the great ones. Rebecca Kilgore, based in Portland, Oregon, has made some definitive recordings with Dave Frishberg and others. She is always fresh and surprising, yet very true to the song. Her song choices are always the freshest of anyone around. And speaking of that, Catherine Russell really sends me the way she gives out. k.d. lang is another singer who performs the standards very well, but she doesn't necessarily know (or care) about the background of the songs, as she comes from a different place. She once said singing standards was easy for her, and she has a certain facility that certainly makes it seem easy. It's just innate for her. She feels it; she understands it; it comes flowing out of her. Lang's interpretations are more connected and more successful than those of most of her contemporaries.

NONE OF WHAT I'VE SAID ABOUT PERFORMING PRECLUDES A SINGER'S FAKING IT.

None of what I've said about performing precludes a singer's faking it. Many extraordinarily gifted singers with beautiful voices bring to their interpretations something that can't be classified as actual feelings. A singer has to carry within him or her a backstory, an image, or a scenario that is internalized yet hopefully comes through in the interpretation. Without that, the song might as well be a grocery list. Sarah Vaughan

was a marvelous singer. On her mid-fifties Gershwin album, she sang "Aren't You Kinda Glad We Did?" (a tune of George's from the thirties to which Ira added a lyric for the 1946 movie *The Shocking Miss Pilgrim*). The song has the bridge "Socially I'll be an outcast: / Obviously we dined alone. / On my good name there will be doubt cast— / With never a sign of any chaperone." She didn't know what she was singing, so she misread the words on the page and sang, "On your good name there will be doubt cast— / With never a sign of any Chapter One." Perhaps there's some oblique meaning to that phrase, but I don't know what it is. She sang music instinctively and beautifully, but the lyrics and what they meant were of secondary importance. Nevertheless, I've heard a number of her recordings that are fantastic interpretations—dazzling, visceral, and natural, and you wouldn't know that she wasn't feeling or understanding the words.

There are also some pop singers who have recorded albums of standards who don't have a clue—not that it's hurt their sales in many cases. I don't have anything against pop or rock singers as a breed—how could I, as so many are formidable? I like Bryan Ferry's interpretations on *As Time Goes By* (1999), particularly his version of "Lover, Come Back to Me." The song was written by Sigmund Romberg and Oscar Hammerstein for the Broadway show *The New Moon* in 1928, and was sung in a very operatic, stentorian fashion by Evelyn Herbert and Robert Halliday. Most versions, though, follow the Les Paul–Mary Ford version, to which Bryan Ferry is much closer. Ferry's idiosyncratic voice worked brilliantly with that song, and I was struck by his connection to it, sung in the same Texas swing style as Paul and Ford, but with a weathered rockabilly edge.

Being very close to my subject, I have a passion for these songs that may seem extreme. But you've probably figured out by now that I'm an extreme kind of guy.

IFIRST FELL IN LOVE WITH "Embraceable You" when I was growing up in Columbus. I was the young guy who collected 78s (an unusual thing for a teen to do, as I've said, but I was an unusual and, I guess, nerdy teen). I found a 1944 Decca Records collection of three 78s from the Judy Garland–Mickey Rooney movie version of the Gershwin musical *Girl Crazy*. The Judy Garland performance of "Embraceable You" was wonderful. Her version had something of a lilt, establishing a pace that is often lacking in contemporary performances. It's an unfortunate trend that sees old ballads, slow songs by definition, played much more slowly these days, as if singing a song more slowly makes it carry more sincerity. It's perhaps the only aspect of society where something is slowing down.

The melody for "Embraceable You" was written with a pulse, a somewhat insistent beat that matches the joyousness of the lyric. Contemporary versions—the slowed-down ones—can be lugubrious, wallowing in the romantic aspects of the song at the expense of the tongue-in-cheek quality of the lyric. To my mind, it dangerously borders on taking interpretative license too far. It might reveal only that performers lack the real connection they have to have with a song before they can connect with an audience. It's become formulaic singing and formulaic thinking, as if reducing a song to an equation: slowly = profound; very slowly = profound squared.

Singers who approach a lyric intelligently can prove they understand it and take it somewhere different. But too often singers are faking it. They'll seek gravitas in the words when it isn't there and try to bring it to their performance, as if closing your eyes and emoting histrionically made a banal song more meaningful. They'll sing it faster, or in a different key, or they'll change harmonies, a melody, or even some of the words. Sometimes the song is improved, but more often these are just tricks, and the result is a regrettable misstatement of what the songwriters created.

Take George's song "Do It Again," which has a lyric by Buddy DeSylva. It was originally a cajoling, pleading song that was meant to be humorous: "Oh, do it again . . ." "I may say no, no, no, no, no. But do it again." And now it's always

taken far too seriously, with comically erotic accents making it an ultra-sexy, slow, and sultry number. When the artist gets to "Do it again" it's more like heavy breathing than singing. Not everyone can be Marilyn Monroe.

When singers of standards say they love this or that writer, but then change the words and ruin the rhyme in one of his songs, to me that's either arrogance or ignorance or both. There must always be craft and there are dues that have to be paid before taking certain liberties. Perhaps the

Songs must have fresh interpretations to survive, and this is where the subject of taste enters once more. I have finally come to trust my instinct in matters of taste, as a result of years of experience studying and performing this music. Great artists often reach a plateau where the subject of taste is instinctive and a part of their overall artistic approach. Singers can also become caricatures of themselves, especially as they sing the same songs decade after decade, thus showing that it is not always ultimate maturity that spawns the greatest

A SINGER WHO APPROACHES A LYRIC INTELLIGENTLY CAN PROVE THEY UNDERSTAND IT AND TAKE IT SOMEWHERE DIFFERENT.

key quality a singer must have is integrity, an elusive combination of skill, empathy, and fortitude. Like honesty and experience, integrity can't be bought; it has to be hard-earned. Artistic integrity is the result of all of life's circumstances, good and bad. The age-old question is: does an artist have to suffer in order to become a great artist? Not necessarily, but if he doesn't, it might be the audience that suffers.

Another pet peeve of mine comes when singers close their eyes when performing, thus disconnecting themselves from the very people they're supposed to be singing to. It reminds me of an old joke the comedian Eddie Cantor used to tell about the violinist David Rubinoff. "Why does Rubinoff close his eyes when he plays? Because he can't stand to see an audience suffer." (Cymbal crash, please.)

interpretations. While I take a great many liberties in my renderings, there are certain aspects of a song that I will not change because they are the essence of what made the thing famous in the first place, and if I start to go too far afield in my interpretations and don't have the good sense to do it myself, I hope that my loved ones will tell me when it's time to stop.

ALTHOUGH "EMBRACEABLE YOU" debuted on Broadway in 1930, the song was written in 1928, when George and Ira were working on an operetta for Florenz Ziegfeld called *East Is West*. The show was going to be a great extravaganza of the Far East, and Ziegfeld had dispatched minions to buy silks and Asian objects for costumes and sets. As Ira tells it, they'd written about half the show when Ziegfeld got sidetracked by a book he'd read called *Show Girl* and told George and Ira to abandon *East Is West* and produce a musical based on the book. In the tune notebook I own there's a list of pieces George had finished for *East Is West*. Many of the songs were very specifically Asian-themed, but others were more generic. Ira said that many of their songs, even the ones that seemed like all-purpose love songs—"Someone to Watch over Me" or "Love Walked In" or "He Loves and She Loves"—were written for a particular character at a particular emotional point in a show. "Embraceable You" was written for a plot situation in a musical that was never made, but it was recycled—and saved—for *Girl Crazy*, the first new musical the brothers worked on after *Show Girl*.

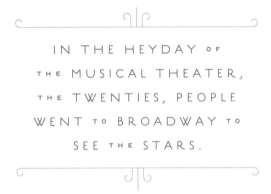

IN THE HEYDAY of the MUSICAL THEATER, the TWENTIES, PEOPLE WENT to BROADWAY to SEE the STARS.

A favorite version of "Embraceable You," a song written for Broadway, comes from the forties Hollywood version of the musical, with its lush production and large string section. *Girl Crazy* was staged on Broadway just as Hollywood was surpassing it in importance and just before George and Ira took on their first Hollywood assignment, the movie *Delicious*. Broadway performers have always been unique animals because they have to reignite the magic of a song seven, eight, some-times nine times a week. In the heyday of the musical theater, the twenties, people went to Broadway to see the stars. They went to see Fred and Adele Astaire's new show and to hear the Gershwins' new songs, and not because the show had an interesting story. Often the best interpreters on Broadway back then wouldn't sing the songs note-perfectly because they were focused on delivering the song to the audience by force of their personalities, which is a different art.

Some of the performers on Broadway at this time were old vaudevillians, denizens of the variety shows that were largely made redundant by the advent of cinema. William Gaxton, who starred in *Of Thee I Sing* in 1931, was one such artist. I've heard a radio recording from the fifties of him singing "Who Cares?" from that show, and he was definitely *performing* the song, booming it out in a scenery-chewing style with more concern for effect than for the precise value of each note. *Of Thee I Sing* is not an easy score to sing, so I wish there existed more than this brief sound bite of Gaxton performing it to hear what he did with the rest of it.

The choruses in musicals did not always enunciate the words, and Ira complained about it. Oscar Hammerstein, on the other hand, knowing that the choruses could not be well understood, didn't bother to write words of consequence for them, and when he went to London to hear one of his shows staged there, he discovered that with their superior diction, the British choristers revealed all of his verbal dirty laundry. He wanted to crawl under his seat out of embarrassment.

"Embraceable You" is a jaunty song, a joyful expression of love. "Don't be a naughty baby, /

Come to papa—come to papa—do." When George sang the song and his father was in the room, Morris would pound his chest proudly and say, "That's me. I'm the papa." If a woman is performing the song she might wrongly sing, "Don't be a naughty baby, / Come to mama—come to mama—do," which just isn't as effective. When Ginger Rogers, as Molly, singing with Allen Kearns's Danny, introduced the song on Broadway in 1930, Ira's original lyric was "Don't be a naughty papa, / Come to baby—come to baby—do," a more sur-

prising version than the more mundane "Come to mama." The whole lyric was couched, of course, in the lyrical and cultural conventions of the time. "Just one look at you—my heart grew tipsy in me./ You and you alone bring out the gypsy in me." It's quite tongue-in-cheek if it's delivered with that original lilt—remembering that Ira was always more whimsical than lugubrious or sentimental.

This is one of those occasions where too much background knowledge can be a curse. Or at least a mixed blessing. Even though it doesn't

Ethel Merman and chorus girls in Girl Crazy *in 1930.*

appear that it would be difficult to sing, "Embraceable You" is a song that I find hard to interpret. My problem is, do I want to do it right, or should I do it the way most people expect to hear it? Doing it right means singing its strict rhythmic values at a faster pace, which, filtered through today's sensibility, seems at odds with the romantic nature of the words. I'm always grappling with the way Gershwin wrote it and the way it's interpreted now, trying to find the middle ground between the two. When I recorded it for my first album, *Pure Gershwin*, I sang it slower than I do in live performances. If I can perform "Embraceable You" as a ballad, retain its original lilt, and still have it come off as the romantic song that contemporary audiences are looking for, that's the best interpretation I can give it.

There's no recording of Ginger Rogers singing the song in 1930, the year she introduced it, although she did record it decades later. There is a surviving recording of a Phil Ohman/Victor Arden Orchestra version (Ohman and Arden were a piano duo and close associates of the composer, playing in the pit at many of his shows, but not, however, at this one), but it isn't quite as interesting, because it's a dance band version and glosses over the lyric and renders it secondary to the music, as the purpose of the recording was more for dancing than listening.

When Ginger finally made a proper recording of the song in the sixties it bore no resemblance to her original approach, and was accompanied by a contemporary-sounding arrangement. A few years ago I found a radio recording of her from 1931, while she was still in *Girl Crazy*, but alas, it featured only the briefest part of "Embraceable

You." Happily, there was an extended version of "But Not for Me," which she also introduced in the same show.

When Judy Garland recorded what I believe to be the definitive performance of "Embraceable You," it was more than a dozen years past the first production of *Girl Crazy*. Garland's version added to the harmonies, trappings that don't detract from the original even though it's proudly a forties creation. Many classic songs of the twenties and thirties, including "Embraceable You," are today performed from the perspective of their reimagining from a later time. It's fascinating to hear how artists from previous eras treat a song, and very often with these songs of the Gershwin era, I find that I prefer versions created nearer the time that the piece was written. There is a seminal feeling that comes from an earlier interpretation, perhaps, because the interpreter is coming from the same cultural and artistic world as the composer. A later interpretation can be effective in new ways but often lacks the submerged sociological point of view and thus loses some of its resonance. Or maybe music making was just more fun back then. And it shows.

I've engaged in some musical time travel of my own. We followed a fifties sensibility on my album *The Sinatra Project,* which was arranged by Bill Elliott. In the fifties, Nelson Riddle and Billy May, Skip Martin, and so many other great arrangers would augment the original songs harmonically and rhythmically, thus adding something without diminishing the essence. Bill called it "putting the tail fins on." Years before, Judy Garland had certainly put the tail fins on her Cadillac with the help of the geniuses from the MGM music department. Mickey Rooney told me that George Gershwin was often on the set when he and Judy were making *Girl Crazy*. "That's interesting," I replied, "because George Gershwin died six years before the film was made." Unflappable, he bellowed back, "He was there, dammit, he was there!"

MANY OF MY FAVORITE PERFORMANCES of George and Ira's songs were done by Fred Astaire. When I'm deciding how I want to sing a song, I go back to the source, and often it's the freshness and excitement of the original I like best, as with "Fascinating Rhythm." That recording by Fred and Adele Astaire with George at the piano was made in London in 1926, two years after the song was written, and I have never heard it performed better, with the jazzy rhythms and harmonies intact, just as George wrote them.

> MANY OF MY FAVORITE PERFORMANCES OF GEORGE AND IRA'S SONGS WERE DONE BY FRED ASTAIRE.

Fred and Adele Astaire embodied two distinct types of Broadway performers. The last thing Fred ever sounded was staid, but he sang the songs close to the original, to how the music was written, while Adele took more liberties. If you listen to that 1926 recording of "Fascinating Rhythm," Adele is stretching the notes and Fred is not, and

I noted earlier how Adele made a recording of "'S Wonderful" in which she sings "It's wonderful" at one point, to Ira's dismay. The legendary dancer John Bubbles (the original Sportin' Life in *Porgy and Bess*) invented the modern style of tap dancing, and everyone wanted to learn from him. Fred asked Bubbles to teach him some steps, but Bubbles said that Fred was too slow, so he taught Adele, who in turn later taught Fred.

Ira's appreciation of the way a song was interpreted changed over the years. He was content to let contemporary influences enter into an interpretation as long as they didn't mess with the original too much. Late in life, he got bored with the slow and treacly versions of Gershwin songs that were already popular, but was equally vexed by anything that went too far in the other direction.

One of Ira's disappointments was with a later recording made by Ella Fitzgerald and André Previn of his songs. The glow of Ella's voice had diminished, and for whatever reason the recording somehow just didn't gel. The producer Norman Granz came over to play the roughs for him fresh from the studio, and Granz watched Ira like a hawk to gauge his reaction. Not wanting to hurt Norman in any way, Ira smiled, nodded, and gesticulated in feigned appreciation all the way through the session.

After Norman left, I asked Ira if he was hungry, and he said, "No, I have to go to bed. With those puppy eyes staring at me, Norman was begging for approval and I'm exhausted." Norman was famous for spending major money to fix even a minuscule error on a recording, which Ira had learned from a past experience. Ira knew that if he didn't appear to love it, Norman might not release the record.

When he produced a recording of Cleo Laine and Ray Charles performing *Porgy and Bess*, that too did not please Ira, and Norman sensed it. Later he came to Ira and said that he had made a mistake and had poorly produced it, in spite of the remarkable talent involved. Ira's acceptance of jazz was limited anyway, and he sometimes found humor in that. In the early fifties, when Mel Tormé and Frances Faye made the first full-length recording of *Porgy* in a jazz setting, Ira quipped that Frances should have sung Porgy and Mel should have sung Bess.

George didn't live long enough to hear how changing tastes affected interpretation of his songs through multiple decades. He barely made it into the era of swing music and died before the form reached its apex, so he only briefly heard how his songs could be swung. He had a great appreciation for jazz musicians and their ability to extemporize an interpretation that would take a song to a different place. One of the greatest improvisers of his era was Art Tatum. George saw him play at a nightclub one night, when (according to Oscar Levant) he played the equivalent of Beethoven's eighteen piano variations on the melody of George's song "Liza," which delighted the composer as if he were a little child. When Tatum finished, George begged for more.

That said, in a show George preferred to hear his songs the way he wrote them, especially when they were first heard on the stage. The initial presentation as he conceived it was very important to him. Kay Swift once complained to George about the way Ruth Etting was singing one of her songs in a show: "After Ruth sings the first chorus, she takes so many liberties with the song I can't

recognize it." Even the composer couldn't force a star to sing the song they way he wanted. So George replied, "Just be happy she's singing it straight in the first chorus."

AMONG THE TREASURES I FOUND at the Warner Bros. warehouse in Secaucus in 1982 was the original manuscript of "Embraceable You" from *Girl Crazy*, along with eighty-six other original Gershwin manuscripts.

At the time, I was friendly with Ginger Rogers, who'd first sung "Embraceable You" on Broadway more than fifty years earlier. When I told her about my discovery of the manuscript she said, "Oh, can I have it?" I had to tell her it was destined for the Library of Congress with the rest of the Gershwin material. Ginger said, "But George wrote it for me." She was adamant that George had composed it for her, so she deserved to have the original manuscript. I didn't have the heart to tell Ginger that the song was written for *East Is West*, not *Girl Crazy*.

When I told Ira the story, he said that this stubbornness wasn't uncharacteristic of Ginger. For someone to survive as long as she did in show business, they have to have an iron will. Ginger was a lovely woman, but she was no shrinking violet. At times, she could be emotionally guarded, but she was solicitous, too, always taking time to answer letters and correspondence from her fans. I never saw her act unkindly toward anyone in any situation.

Even though at age nineteen Ginger was already well known, Ira told me that during the *Girl Crazy* tryouts out of town, Ginger's voice was weak, and it was hard to hear her over the footlights. The producers wanted to fire Ginger, but George insisted on keeping her because she was beautiful, and all the college boys were going gaga over her. She never knew that George saved her job. (Forty years later, I said something to Ginger about college boys being crazy about her and she said, "Wheeee!")

I met Ginger in 1978, when I was invited to be part of a Gershwin tribute at Carnegie Hall—a benefit concert for the American Cinematheque—and we clicked for some reason. After one rehearsal for the show, we were standing together on an intersection along 45th Street and I was trying to flag down a taxi. Finding a cab is not the easiest thing to do in Midtown Manhattan. I'd only been in New York a handful of times and I guess it was clear I didn't have the knack. Ginger said, "Honey, move over," and stepped into the street, stuck two fingers in the corner of her mouth, and issued a piercing wolf whistle. A taxi stopped immediately. She gave me a sweet little smile, got in the cab, and off she went.

THE MOST IMPORTANT PART ABOUT PERFORMING A SONG WELL IS ABOUT INHABITING IT.

Ginger was one of the women George was romantically interested in when he was in Hollywood during the final year of his life, although Lee Gershwin said George could never get to first base with Ginger and George himself stated, "She

has a little love for a lot of people." By this time George was taking his hobby of painting seriously, and when Ginger told him she was interested in taking it up herself, he took her to an art supply store in Beverly Hills and bought her a small painting kit. Poignantly, when she finally opened the box shortly after George died, she discovered that he had done a little drawing of her and left it in the kit for her to find. It ended up being a gift from George from beyond the grave.

Ginger and Ethel and all the others when performing a song effectively could somehow channel their life experience into it, even at an early age. The most important part about performing a song well is about inhabiting it. To do this, I believe you must also know a song's history: when it was written, why it was written, who it was written for, and how it was first performed. Although we can never have perfect knowledge of a composer's intentions, learning whatever I can about original context is essential to me. Otherwise, it's like tasting someone's soup: you might think, "Oh, I can make that," but if you try to reproduce it without knowing the recipe, who knows what you'll end up with?

I don't know the intimate history of every song, but I can always find clues—the writer, the year, the show. Do you have to know everything? No. Ultimately it is about the music and the lyric on the piece of paper. That's where experience and instincts come in. You can sing a song well knowing nothing about it, but knowing the background will make you sing it differently.

This is something I take into account when I plan out a program for a performance. I know what songs an audience is anticipating when they

(FOLLOWING PAGES) *George's notebook pages for songs from* Girl Crazy.

217

Verse - Embrace me

not for the

Barbary Coast (Verse)

"Embrace Me" (Verse)

come to see me, so I make sure when I map out the set list that I'm giving people what they want. But I also like to introduce songs that an audience may not be familiar with, singing, for example, "Easy Come, Easy Go," a great song by Johnny Green and Edward Heyman that few people know. Sometimes I will take a lesser-known song and pair it with something better-known—I've coupled a Marshall Barer/Duke Ellington song, "C'est Comme Ça," with an Ellington standard, "I Got It Bad (and That Ain't Good)"—and it takes the audience on a journey.

Especially with these less familiar songs, I make a point to share some background with the audience. When I tell stories and provide the marginalia as a lead-in to a song, it's a part of the performance of the song. Some people have made jokes about me because of this, and I've even been parodied on TV a few times, so I try to do it whimsically because the audience is there to be entertained, not educated. (However, I loved that *The Simpsons* joked at my expense.) This is my way of tapping into the essence of the song, which is what any singer must do if he's to perform a song convincingly.

Knowing "Love Is Here to Stay" was the last song George wrote, with Ira completing the lyrics after his brother's death, is essential to me for singing it well. The song has been slowed down over the years until it's almost stationary, but it doesn't need to be sung like a dirge to have the feeling of poignancy that should come with appreciating the circumstances of its writing.

Being attentive to the history of a song doesn't mean I'm slavish to the original, but it does give me fodder for deeper interpretations.

Much of the wider songbook of the musical theater—George and Ira's songs included—can sound staid in the Broadway versions. It might be constrained by the limitations of the pit orchestra, or I might not like the arrangement. The size of band makes a difference, too: a big band is going to make different demands on me than if I choose to perform a piece alone sitting at the piano.

(It's not just the poor old singer who can mess up a song. When arrangers try to be too creative, they can detract from a song. Take the verse of "How Are Things in Glocca Morra?": "I hear a bird, Londonderry bird. / It well may be he's bringing me a cheering word . . ." Burton Lane wrote a wonderful harmonic progression for it, without which the song just isn't as good. When arrangers leave it out, it's like leaving the house without wearing socks. Something's missing. People might not always be musically attuned enough to hear the difference consciously or might not know the original harmonies, but they can instinctively feel the difference; I'm convinced of it.)

The key for me is to retain the integrity of the original while taking advantage of the freedom I have to interpret the song in a way that will make it sound fresh. I have recorded Gershwin songs in many different ways, sometimes in a more contemporary musical style. In retrospect I regret some of the choices I've made, because choosing a contemporary style can destroy the timelessness that made the song a classic in the first place. This is different from offering an interpretation that has both contemporary and classic appeal thanks to its universal essence.

As I mentioned, I may choose to revisit an era when I perform a song. This kind of dexterity is difficult for many singers, but I've never found it so because I grew up with this music and feel I understand it so well. Generally, I know where that middle ground between original and updated is going to be, whether it's in a Nelson Riddle–style arrangement, a forties version, a sixties homage, a simple rendition at the piano, Latin-infused, with electric bass underpinnings, or whatever. Finding the freshness is what makes what I do so exciting. How am I going to successfully reintro-

used it as the sound track for his classic cinematic homage to the Big Apple, *Manhattan*. That sound evokes so much that is New York.

This sound is so often imitated that its knockoff version has become clichéd and is sometimes used for comic effect. On the other hand, many interpretations of Gershwin's songs are so far removed from the original that the harmonies, a key feature of the best songs, are dispensed with entirely. In this way, the Gershwin sound, the sound that first drew me to his music, is diluted. If I don't hear some semblance of that sound, I

BEING ATTENTIVE TO THE HISTORY OF A SONG DOESN'T MEAN I'M SLAVISH TO THE ORIGINAL, BUT IT DOES GIVE ME FODDER FOR DEEPER INTERPRETATION.

duce a song that will be known to many but to others will be heard for the first time? It can come in a flash or take a week. Or I might hand off the most vague of ideas to a trusted arranger like John Oddo and ask him to arrange it.

As a young man, after I had listened to a lot of George's music, I learned to identify that specific "Gershwin sound." It's extremely difficult to articulate how music sounds, but in essence, I found a totality to his rhythmic ideas, a set of schemes that ranges across his music and unites it with a common thread. There are also certain harmonies that make his songs identifiable, which appear in orchestral works such as *Rhapsody in Blue* and Concerto in F, as well as the songs. You'll hear a passage that's so dazzling and distinctive it can only be Gershwin. That's why Woody Allen

miss it badly. It's like the telephone game (where one person hears a story and passes it on to the next, and so on): what emerges at the end bears no relation to what went in at the start. It means that the song has been interpreted to death.

I've been labeled a "purist," but if I were a purist, I'd sing the song exactly as it was written in the sheet music and it would die a slow, straitjacketed death. A prime example of taking liberties is the way I do Irving Berlin's "Alexander's Ragtime Band." I start slowly and build to a furious tempo. That's a radical reinterpretation of the song, but I think it works brilliantly. Please forgive me for trumpeting this, but one of my happiest moments was when Jack Lemmon told me that he felt that this was the greatest reinterpretation of a classic song that he'd heard.

My taste is expressed in the way I sing this or any other song. It's also expressed in what I enjoy listening to, including many nonpurist versions of songs—even jazz, the least "pure" form of all. Peggy Lee's version of the Rodgers and Hart song "Lover," which was a hit in the fifties, angered Richard Rodgers. His "Lover" was a waltz, and Peggy turned it into a mambo swing number with bongos and strings like whirling dervishes accompanying her bravura vocals. When he encountered her shortly after the release of her recording, Rodgers's succinct but unforgiving words were, "It's a waltz." I like what she did, but it bears no relation to what Rodgers wrote. In fact, I like Peggy's jazz take alongside the original tempo. Similarly, "My Man" was always a torch song, but Peggy sang it with a drumbeat that wouldn't have sounded out of place in a strip club. It was great storytelling.

SOMETIME EVERYTHING CLICKS MAGICALLY AND THE EXCITEMENT GOES TO ANOTHER LEVEL.

And then, on the other hand, I'll hear gifted singers do things that I find puzzling. After Patti LaBelle sang "Over the Rainbow" her way, Sam Harris also sang it her way, and then finally Mandy Patinkin did "Over the Rainbow" and sang it like it was *Medea*. Well, maybe he was right. I did want to commit murder after I heard it. Yet they are all talented artists.

IN ORDER FOR A PERFORMER TO GIVE LIFE to the song, there must also be an audience. You might think there would be uniformity to how audiences react to a show, with perhaps some variation between countries or coasts, or matinees and evenings, but each separate group responds in a very different way, because audiences are made up of very different groupings of people. Sometimes everything clicks magically and the excitement goes to another level. I believe it's true that some nights, there's just something in the air. I remember reading years ago about an experiment that compared the reactions of audiences in various Broadway houses. The conclusion was that if an audience in one house was a little less responsive than average, it would be that way in the other houses, too. Maybe it's the tides, or the moon, or the weather, or that day's performance of the stock market.

If I get that wonderful, responsive audience, I feel my performance changing. I might be able to take a risk here and there, feeling that the audience is going to come with me. The mysterious nature of live performance creates many interpretative surprises along the way, and even with a song performed many times, something fresh can come of it, buoyed by the energy of a particular audience.

This reminds me of my friend the tremendously talented lyricist and sometime composer Marshall Barer, whom I once observed say the following at a show: "Every once in a while, a performer has the privilege of appearing in front of an audience that is so connected and responsive to his every moment, it makes you want to give them every ounce of what you've got. This is not one of those audiences."

IT'S TOUGH TO MAKE generalizations about audiences in different cities. New York audiences seem to have more knowledge of certain music, for example, New York–themed compositions or songs by writers who were themselves urban animals like Rodgers and Hart or Cole Porter. This is not to say that people everywhere don't appreciate the work of those writers. However, many of their references are so New York–centric that the geographic life experience makes the songs more salient. Again, it's not that the audience is more sophisticated, but they might have experienced more shows because they live in New York City, where such things are more readily available. It's a subtle distinction, such as the standard of French spoken by someone who was born in France versus that of someone who may be fluent but hasn't lived in France her whole life.

You can find a fantastic audience anywhere. I was recently in Florida performing a show based on my *Sinatra Project* CD. The best show of the tour was in Naples, one of the best audiences I have ever had, and it was simply the pinnacle. The next night, in another city, it was a very good show, but it wasn't Naples. Why it happened that night and in that place, I do not know.

I've had terrific audiences in other countries. The appreciation for American music is great in Japan. You can go there and find hundreds of reissues of old records on CD, many by jazz singers I've never heard of who only sold a few records the first time around. The CDs will sometimes be issued in limited editions of as few as twenty-five. I always wonder who is going to buy them, but someone does.

I thought I had a copy of every record that Rosemary Clooney ever made, but a friend of mine bought me a single that Rosemary made in Japan in 1978 that I didn't know existed. Many American performers have gone to Japan and given their careers a bounce. Carmen Cavallaro was a big star in this country from the thirties through the sixties. He was a technically brilliant pianist, as good as anyone. His music was more Latin than jazz. In the sixties and seventies, he toured Japan frequently and made records exclusively for the Japanese market. In the end he was a bigger star in Japan than he was at home. The singer Johnnie Ray had an unprecedented stack of hits in the early fifties and remained very popular outside the United States for decades, in the U.K. and Brazil, for example. Women would try to tear off his clothes even when he was getting on in years, an experience he found alternately hysterical and terrifying. He would laugh and say, "At my age?"

The Japanese have appreciated the great ones over the years. The Sinatra Society there is avid and has its own record label. Sinatra, Ella Fitzgerald, Mel Tormé, Peggy Lee, and my beloved Rosemary Clooney—they all played huge venues in Japan. There's an excellent jazz club scene there, and not just in Tokyo.

Music truly is the universal language. I was in Kathmandu on vacation, the epitome of the back of beyond. There I met a man called Dhubby, an expat from India who loved Cole Porter and really knew his songbook. We met in a restaurant with a piano and I sat down and played some Cole Porter for him. It was one of the thrills of his life. If you can find a Cole Porter fan in Kathmandu, you can find one anywhere. Of course, Gershwin is known around the world. Music has always been one of America's most influential exports.

IN MY INTERPRETIVE STYLE, I haven't been greatly influenced by any one male singer. I learned more from the songs. I evolved my own style, although early on some said I was copying the great Johnny Mathis. That was taken as a compliment, yet I'd never heard much of him outside the radio hits, and when I did, I realized my approach was fundamentally different. Mathis was with a major record label, and they had him recording songs for the purpose of creating hits (not that there's anything wrong with that), with the attendant pop arrangements in place to help achieve the desired result. My approach has always started with the songwriters and following through their intentions before any other considerations. I wasn't a great singer when I started out and had a lot to learn. While I still have much to learn, I hope I've become a stylist who doesn't sound like anyone else. Even me.

Nowadays many singers try to sound like the most successful artists of the moment, which is futile. Many singers want to sound like Sinatra, and, of course, he casts a shadow over the whole profession. Michael Bublé was in that camp initially. On his first album, there were several Sinatra tracks for which his producer, David Foster, reproduced the arrangements Sinatra used. Bublé's first appearance in the United States was at a nightclub I owned in Los Angeles and I asked Foster, "What made you do that?" "Well, if you're going to sing the songs," he said, "how else would you do them?" And I thought to myself, "Well, let me count the ways." Now Michael is doing more original songs, and he's evolved into a unique stylist with a distinctive voice. He's got showmanship and a whole lot more going for him. Slowly he's leaving the classic songbook behind, for better or for worse.

Collaborating on a song with another singer is another type of performance. It's not like playing with a band—theoretically, they are following you. When you sing with someone, you have to create a tight team and not a two-headed monster. Success largely depends on the sensibilities of the two artists. Much of it is nuts and bolts, like the key. If you don't sing in the same key, you have to work out the harmony. When I used to appear on *Live with Regis and Kathie Lee* I would often be told, "Kathie Lee wants to sing a duet." I was happy about that, but inevitably she'd have to sing the song in *her* key. She'd sing the melody, and it was up to me to come up with the harmony. She always sounded great, and I was always searching for the note, which was frustrating. It wasn't Kathie Lee's doing—this is what the producers wanted.

For a man singing with a woman there's often an accommodation that has to be made because the two ranges are different. You have to work out a routine where each singer shows his or her best suit. Many times, when I hear duets, they sound so shoehorned together that it's not pleasant. When Tony Bennett made his first duets album, it sounded like more thought needed to be given to the dividing of the range and the harmonies between him and his partners. His more recent effort had more time, money, and planning put into its production, and it shows. Sinatra's late duets albums were made with him singing the songs all the way through in the studio, after which other singers were brought in and their voices added where Sinatra's was removed. For me, these recordings were at times embarrassing, and yet they were among his best-selling.

I've sung with many people: Barbara Cook, Liza Minnelli, Tony Bennett, Nancy Wilson, Melissa Etheridge, Mary Martin, Elaine Stritch, and the sublime Christine Ebersole. The person I most loved singing with was Rosemary Clooney, mostly because of the way she interpreted songs and partly because of how much I adored her and her sense of humor. John Oddo, who arranged for both of us, would work out routines that worked for both of our ranges. It took some doing at times.

Cheyenne Jackson is fun to collaborate with because of his extraordinary musical range. I enjoyed making our album *The Power of Two* in 2009 very much, and we included two George and Ira standards—"A Foggy Day" and "Someone to Watch over Me." For these two songs, Cheyenne sang solo to my accompaniment, and in the latter he decided not to change the pronouns in the song. The decision was made spontaneously, yet for many it became a highlight of the album. For

Irving Berlin photographed by George Gershwin.

the duets we sang together, he and I can trade the melody back and forth, and sing harmonies above or below each other with great ease. He also has great musical instincts. His abilities to phrase, be in harmony, and stay connected are innate.

On the other hand, singing with Nancy Wilson, one of the great voices of any generation, was like walking a tightrope because she didn't want to rehearse. She liked to do it in the moment, which is how she always does it and why she is a legend. I would have enjoyed having the opportunity to go through the songs at least once with her—I was concerned about when I should sing and when she would respond—but we didn't. We went with the flow, even though there were times when I felt like, "Oh, my God, I'm going to go over the cliff here." It worked, though—so much so that after it was over she suggested going on tour together.

Debbie Reynolds had probably fifty ideas for duets that we could do, but we couldn't seem to settle on anything. She has creative sparks flying so fast you can't keep up with her. Initially, we rehearsed and worked on a routine, but when we got to the performance, she didn't follow the routine. I improvised with her, and it came off just great. With other singers, I've rehearsed a lot, and it hasn't come off as well.

As a performer, I've certainly made my share of mistakes. I've misread the music or made an error, and it hurts when it's going to be that way forever on a record. I've recorded things that were wrong for one reason or another, and there are parts in some of my records that I wish I could change. Not too many of late, I am pleased to say, but it has happened. I recorded Kern and Ham-

merstein's "The Song Is You" on *The Sinatra Project*. I had always sung the bridge melody that matches the words "I alone have heard this lovely phrase" one way, but Bill Elliott, the producer who did the orchestration, said Sinatra always sang it another way and since this was a tribute to Ol' Blue Eyes, I should do it that way, too. Bill was gently insistent, and I happily agreed, thinking it was correct, but I later realized that the way Sinatra sang it was not consistent with the original. I should have gone back to the primary source. It'll bother me every time I hear the song. To many this is a small point, but those are the things that keep me up at night.

If I'm working on a song, I might have to listen to an old recording to remember how it goes. Revisiting a recording can be painful because all I hear are the many problems. It's like looking at an old photograph—I might remember the circumstances of the recording, what was going on in my life at the time, but I don't recall all of the

The author at the piano in Venice, California, 1979.

details. With other cuts, I remember the specifics, but they don't evoke any significant memory. Some of these recordings I like; some I don't. (More often, it's the latter.) Perhaps I didn't sing the song as well as I might have. I often realize I wouldn't sing it the same way now.

Like many performers, I don't like to revisit old recordings, as it is a futile exercise. The odd and wonderful medium of recording captures a moment in time, and I've come to accept that moment as part of my evolution. Once in a while I'll listen to something and say, "Who is that person?" while other times I feel absolutely connected with what I expressed.

As an artist, it made me feel less alone on this to learn that Barbra Streisand hates all her early recordings, ones that most consider among

A recent encounter with Barbra came around to a conversation about a song I had introduced that she subsequently recorded. She said, "You sang a wrong note in that song." To which I replied, "I didn't know that. One of the songwriters was present and didn't say anything. That's going to bother me forever that there's a wrong note on that track and I can't fix it." Her rejoinder was, "Of course you can. Just go in and fix it." The thought of going back and fixing a mistake at what would be massive expense had never occurred to me, but to Barbra it was quite feasible.

Liza also hates her own early records. She and I were at a club in Sweden, and they played her "New York, New York." I said, "Gee, it's nice to hear that," and she said, "Oh, I'm just hearing someone who isn't always in tune." Liza has tre-

IT MADE ME FEEL LESS ALONE TO LEARN THAT BARBRA STREISAND HATES ALL HER EARLY RECORDINGS.

her best. They were recordings for which she sang live with an orchestra, which to me is the best way to make a record and was once the way it was always done. At one point, Barbra wanted to have her early stuff suppressed. Liza Minnelli said to her, "I'd like to remind you of one thing. Those are the records that made you famous." Maybe they aren't flawless, but they are throbbing with emotion, and some of the chances she takes are breathtaking. When she is reaching for a note with dramatic effect, even if to her ears it may not be perfect, to me it's all dazzling.

mendously sensitive ears that can pick up anything in an orchestra that might be the slightest bit off, things that many musicians cannot hear, including me. It's like witnessing human radar watching the way she finds anything that isn't perfect at an orchestra rehearsal. Must be in the genes.

THE SONGS OF GEORGE AND IRA GERSHWIN have survived as long as they have because successive generations of singers have continued to find fresh angles of approach, something in the song that resonates with their musical style. It might be the singular genius of George's music, which makes so many of his melodies live on, or the extraordinary precision and cleverness of Ira's words.

There is something mysterious, even magical, about the process of performing music. Much has been written about music from every vantage point: scientific, therapeutic, spiritual. Music is made up of vibrations and so, at the most basic, subatomic level, are we. When a body sympathet-

am at a loss to adequately verbalize what this music means to me as well as millions of others. Part of me bristles at such questions: I find myself reluctant to delve too deeply for fear of destroying the magic, or dipping into the well so often that it might run dry.

The fact remains, when all else falls apart, music is the refuge that rescues and revives the soul. David Raksin, composer of "Laura" and one

MUSIC IS AN ESSENTIAL PART of OUR EXISTENCE. NEITZSCHE WROTE: "WITHOUT MUSIC, LIFE WOULD BE a MISTAKE."

ically vibrates with the music, I can't help but feel there is a transformational effect. Music brings about undeniable changes to the mind and body alike. Elaine Stritch has arthritis, and told me the only time she's not in pain is when she's performing because she's not aware of her body.

Music is an essential part of our existence. Nietzsche agreed with me; he wrote: "Without music, life would be a mistake." (*Twilight of the Idols.*) Music is often considered the loftiest of the arts, the highest and rarest form of artistic and emotional expression. It is unique in that it directly affects the heart, pleases us on the intellectual plane, and yet also does something to us physically. A song moves us, makes us feel more alive. It can give us the gift of an experience; a life's journey in thirty-two bars. But those are just words. Words without music.

As one who has been interviewed countless times about the body of work that I perform, I still

of the finest musicians and composers I have ever had the privilege to know, completely rejected my notion that music comes from a divine place. As shattered as I was by his bursting of my idealized bubble, another part of me just thought, "Whatever it is, David, don't stop doing it. Please don't stop!" Amen to that.

Regardless of how I am feeling before I go onstage, I feel suffused with emotion and energy once I'm performing. Other sensations fade. When we sing, we go to a place where we leave behind everything that we don't need. When I perform in a venue, regardless of its size, I have a sense of expanding to reach everybody in the space. I feel as connected to a person in the back row as I am to a person sitting right in front of me. At the end of a concert, when it has gone well and someone comes up to me and says, "I thought you were singing just to me," I know I have done my job well. ·

MICHAEL AND BURTON LANE.

"WHO CARES?"

from *Of Thee I Sing*, 1931

REPORTERS:

We don't want to know about the moratorium,
Or how near we are to beer,
Or about the League of Nations,
Or the seventeen vacations
You have had since you've been here.

Here's the one thing that the people of America
Are beside themselves to know:
They would like to know what's doing
On the lady who is suing
You—Diana Devereaux!

Ev'rybody wants to know:
What about Miss Devereaux?
From the highest to the low:
What about Miss Devereaux?

WINTERGREEN:

It's a pleasant day—
That's all I can say!

MARY:

Here's the one thing we'll announce:
Love's the only thing that counts!

REPORTERS:

People want to know:
What of Devereaux?

WINTERGREEN:

When the one you love is near,
Nothing else can interfere.

ALL:

When the one you love is near,
Nothing else can interfere.

VERSE

WINTERGREEN:

Here's some information
I will gladly give the nation:
I am for the true love;
Here's the only girl I do love.

MARY:

I love him and he loves me,
And that's how it will always be,
So what care we about Miss Devereaux?

BOTH:

Who cares what the public chatters?
Love's the only thing that matters.

REFRAIN

Who cares
If the sky cares to fall in the sea?
Who cares what banks fail in Yonkers,
Long as you've got a kiss that conquers?
Why should I care?
Life is one long jubilee,
So long I as care for you—
And you care for me.

CHAPTER 8

WHY SOME SONGS SURVIVE
AND OTHERS DON'T

n his lifetime, George Gershwin saw the publication of over eight hundred of his songs, but he actually composed double that number, maybe just two dozen of which are well known today. And that number is getting smaller over time as tastes change. The survivors—the songs that are still listened to, sung, and recorded—are reduced to a core that includes many of the songs in this volume: "Love Is Here to Stay," "Someone to Watch over Me," "Embraceable You." Does this mean George only wrote twenty-four great songs? Of course not. A mysterious process of attrition consigns some songs to obscurity and anoints others as timeless classics, and whether a song ends up ignored or revered may have little to

do with its intrinsic quality. Sometimes odd twists of fate can rescue a song from obscurity, or banish another with equal force.

Responding to a song is a deeply personal experience that is like creating a friendship. You may relate to the lyric, you may like the tune, or you may connect with the song on a deeper emotional level. Most listeners think of specific songs in the frame of their favorite version: You think of "Singin' in the Rain," and you hear Gene Kelly singing it. You think of "Unchained Melody," and it's the Righteous Brothers. This is especially the case with more recent popular music because, whereas the great standards were recorded by many different artists, pop hits are covered somewhat

Ira and George at work in 1937.

infrequently. We store the song in our memory—this is a connection, a relationship we have with the song—and the memory is amazingly accurate about what it retains.

Relating to a song is not always instantaneous, and sometimes it takes active work on the listener's part. People don't always think of enjoying music as something that should require much attention or thought, but the beauty of great songs is that they reward a few minutes' focused reflection in incredible ways. Songwriters and artists put a tremendous amount of effort into their craft. If we as consumers listened a little more closely, we might get more out of the song and, perhaps, build a closer relationship with it. Some complex songs would gain more fans and prosper as a result.

Of course, there are different ways to listen to music. Having music on in the background can make certain activities much more enjoyable (ahem . . .), but by definition it's not the same thing as really listening (could you repeat that?). Listening with close attention to the lyrics as well as the music is a different activity altogether, as some people never click in. Those who do are likely to include fans of Gershwin and Berlin and Porter, since these composers wrote with the sort of detail that richly repays a careful listener and can become addictive to boot. Background music serves a purpose, and it as such should not be minimized. However, I'm reminded of an old *Mad* magazine gag in which they depicted an album title: *Music to Listen to Julie London By.* If you never pay attention to a lyric it's like admiring a flower from afar and never moving in close enough to discover the complexity and wonder of its deeper makeup and fragrance. You're missing out on a lot.

Revisiting a song can reveal new and previously unnoticed facets, even with songs you've known for years. Porter's "Begin the Beguine" is a song I heard for many years, but it wasn't until I heard Tony Martin sing it at my club and then sang the song myself that I paid any real attention to what the song is actually about. In it, the protagonist is practically schizophrenic over a lost love. While yearning for the love to come back, he sings, "So don't let them begin the beguine! / Let the love that was once a fire remain an ember." Yet two lines later he sings, "Oh yes, let them begin the beguine, make them play!" Suddenly it has become a song about a tremendously torn emotional journey. When I really looked at the lyric, I found so much more depth in the character and pondered what Porter must have been thinking when he wrote it somewhere in the South Pacific in 1935.

George singing Porgy and Bess *in 1935.*

232

Among songs, there is an unofficial and infinitely arguable hall of fame of sorts that includes a collection of enduring favorites, what we call "standards." What's known as the Great American Songbook mostly encompasses songs created by certain ordained writers from 1920 to 1960. Roughly. These are songs that are practically indestructible—a singer can tear the song apart, reinterpret it to within an inch of its life, and it will

THE BOTTOM LINE IS, HOW DOES THE SONG FEEL WHEN YOU HEAR IT, WHEN YOU SING IT?

still be recognizable. "Embraceable You" and the other Gershwin numbers just mentioned are such songs. It is this repeated reinterpretation that defines a standard. It's not necessary that every artist finds success with his reworking of a standard song; it's just a requirement that someone keep trying. (I do believe that there are songs being written today that might also join the hallowed ranks of the classic songbook, but only time will tell.)

Each of these great songs has the good bones that allow it to withstand decade after decade of artistic punishment (and much as I'd like to, I won't point any fingers at particular punishers). An artist might completely change the tempo, the mood, the feel, and we'll still know the song. It's like a great house that's remodeled but retains its classic structure. These songs have to be strong both lyrically

and musically so that a good singer can find a fresh way to interpret them. It's that malleability that gives these songs their deserved longevity.

As with everything in music, the notion of what makes a song great or good, or mediocre or terrible, is a matter of opinion. It's like Justice Potter Stewart's famous definition of pornography: "I know it when I see it." You might say about a great song, "I know it when I hear it." The point is that in order for someone making a judgment about a song to have credibility, he needs to demonstrate his experience and knowledge and understanding of the subject over and over (probably the opposite of what Justice Stewart had in mind when he stated how he recognized pornography). If one person says, "That's a great song," and another says, "No, it isn't," it's not easy for either side to prove its case. Perhaps what they are saying is, "My taste is better than yours."

Though I am loath to bring him into the fray, Alec Wilder, the composer, songwriter, and author of the hugely influential (and, in my opinion, terribly misguided and sometimes pompous) book *American Popular Song*, wrote repeatedly about his dislike of Gershwin's "repeated-note effect" (Wilder says Gershwin was "obsessed" with it) and all the technical devices Wilder was able to identify that George used, as if there were something inherently wrong with these things regardless of how they sound. When I read this stuff, I think, "Who cares?" The power of a song does not come from analysis of it; it comes through the emotional connection it creates.

However, to play at Wilder's game and challenge the theory: in the case of that repeated note effect, it is the addition of those notes at the start of the chorus of "They Can't Take That Away from Me" that launches the song magnificently. Think of that melody with only three notes at the start instead of five and you'll understand what I mean. The end of "Embraceable You" has the delicious lines, "Don't be a naughty baby, / Come to papa—come to papa—do." The lines use the supposedly dreaded repeated note effect, and again they accomplish a heightening of emotion. Gershwin knew what he was doing with every repeated note, note, note.

On the subject of analyzing songs, I have heard "Summertime" picked apart on NPR as well as being the subject of an hour-long documentary on BBC Radio. Usually I'm not interested when someone performs an autopsy on a song, because to be qualified for an autopsy you have to be dead. It doesn't matter to me that the G sharp is occurring on the fourth note of the eighth bar or whatever it is. The bottom line is, how does the song feel when you hear it, when you sing it? Alfred North Whitehead said, "It requires a very unusual mind to undertake the analysis of the obvious." (Author Ed Jablonski had that quote pasted in the front of his copy of the Alec Wilder book.)

· · · · ·

IT'S A CURIOUS FACT THAT TIME AND PASSING fancies change what is popular. Songs can fall out of the imaginary hall of fame of standards if they are no longer sung with any regularity. They can sit in limbo, awaiting reinterpretation.

Consider George and Ira's "But Not for Me," from *Girl Crazy*. Twenty years ago, it was one of the great standards. It was also the title of a movie from 1959 that starred Clark Gable and featured Ella Fitzgerald's take on the song. Today, it's not so well known, and the fans who revere "Love Is Here to Stay" won't necessarily be familiar with "But Not for Me." Because of the old-fashioned, pre-feminist nature of the lyric, "The Man I Love" is not as famous as it once was, but it continues to hold popularity among jazz musicians, who are less familiar, generally speaking, with the lyrics. Its place as one of the biggest songs in the catalogue has been taken by "Love Is Here to Stay," which was a late bloomer.

It's also true that a great song can fall out of favor and then get rediscovered. It might take just a new recording to allow a new generation of fans to hear the song. A good example of that is Harry Warren and Al Dubin's "I Only Have Eyes for You," which was written in 1934. It was a hit then, and it was a big hit for the Flamingos in 1959 and then again for Art Garfunkel in 1975. It's overdue for its once-a-generation reissue. "It Ain't Necessarily So" has been a hit several times, including a version by the British band Bronski Beat in 1984 that was almost unrecognizable as the original, with a synthesizer sound that was unmistakably of the eighties. I was talking with George Michael around this time and he didn't know "It Ain't Necessarily So" was written by George Gershwin, let alone that it was from *Porgy and Bess*. In the same vein, "I Got Rhythm" was a hit for the Happenings in 1967 (albeit with a changed melody) and sold more than a million singles, and the Hilltoppers put "Love Walked In" on the charts in 1953. And so on.

Another song that was made into something else entirely was Charles Strouse and Martin Charnin's "It's the Hard-Knock Life," from the

1977 musical *Annie*. Twenty years later, Jay-Z took the hook from "It's the Hard-Knock Life" and built a rap song ("Hard Knock Life (Ghetto Anthem)") around it. He had a big hit and made the writers of *Annie* a lot of money, probably more than they made on any other song, which brings up the issue of how much dough you need to let someone render your song unrecognizable. Something like this probably does no harm to the original song, because they are two completely different entities that appeal to two completely different audiences. It's like the punk version of "Over the Rainbow" (by Me First and the Gimme Gimmes). It's very tongue-in-cheek—horrible and funny at the same time. In the same vein, Hugh Martin said that he enjoyed the version by heavy metal band Twisted Sister of his song "Have Yourself a Merry Little Christmas."

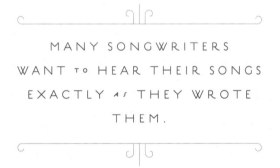

MANY SONGWRITERS WANT TO HEAR THEIR SONGS EXACTLY AS THEY WROTE THEM.

On the other hand, "Fly Me to the Moon" is just one of a myriad of songs that are dominated by one single interpretation. The song wasn't written by Frank Sinatra. It wasn't even called "Fly Me to the Moon"—Bart Howard's 1954 song was originally titled "In Other Words." Later versions of these songs invariably refer to the predominant interpretation, however much that differs from the original. The song was originally written as a waltz and Bart Howard preferred it in that meter. Kaye Ballard's introductory recording of "In Other Words" is very different from Sinatra's swinging take, but it demonstrates the quality of the song that it can bear both interpretations with ease. Many other singers sang it like a waltz—Peggy Lee and Mabel Mercer, among others. The composer, while telling me he was grateful for Sinatra's version and the income it generates, still preferred it the way he wrote it.

On the other hand, many songwriters want to hear their songs exactly as they wrote them, which might prejudice a song's chance of longevity. Richard Rodgers always wanted the version that played in the theater, with the original Robert Russell Bennett or Hans Spialek orchestrations. He hated the way Mel Tormé sang "Blue Moon," while in turn, Tormé was furious that Rodgers complained about how he sang the song.

Sondheim is in the Rodgers camp. If one note is displaced in the accompaniment, it's debilitating to him. It wouldn't matter to a listener whose ears aren't as sophisticated, which would be almost everyone. For Sondheim, it's not what he wrote. Sondheim once lamented that when "Send in the Clowns" was arranged for Frank Sinatra, a chord was changed in error. Unfortunately, that mistake was copied by singers who relied on Sinatra's version rather than consulting the sheet music.

Mel Tormé (with Bob Wells, aka Bob Levinson) wrote one of the classic holiday songs, "The Christmas Song" ("Chestnuts roasting on an open fire . . ."), which has been covered about a million times. Tormé said someone sent him a new recording made by the easy-listening arranger Hugo

Winterhalter called "The Christmas Song Cha Cha Cha." He said, "How do you think I felt about that?" And before anyone could answer, he said, "I loved it!" His point was that different interpretations keep a song like this alive.

If ever I'm lucky enough to have people do cover versions of songs I've written, I'll be thrilled—even if they stink. I once heard someone do an unrecognizable rock version of "What I Did for Love" at my club, Feinstein's. (Marvin Hamlisch composed the song and Edward Kleban wrote the lyrics; it's from *A Chorus Line.*) I sent a recording of it to Marvin for the shock value. Marvin is very much a "live and let live" kind of guy and seemed unfazed by the whole thing.

While interpretations needn't be slavish copies—they can change a song dramatically to great effect—they should retain what it is that makes a song distinctive. As I've pointed out, songs need to be reinterpreted to have life, but if a singer takes too much license, the songs themselves will suffer. This is a complex subject and a paradoxical one, because there is always the exception that proves the rule. And if no one took chances in a song interpretation we might be deprived of a new rendition that could have even pleased the original creator.

I felt the way Cole Porter's songs were performed in the movie *De-Lovely,* in which Kevin Kline played Porter, was a musical travesty. The makers of the movie tried to make the songs sound current by bending melody lines, adding more contemporary beats, and stylistically ignoring the period that was so meticulously depicted scenically. The songs were emasculated harmonically and lyrically. In trying to please everyone,

all they did was ensure that the songs missed both marks—Porter fans didn't appreciate the new interpretations and younger audiences didn't like them either. I doubt many new fans were made for these great songs.

Unfortunately, I unknowingly encountered the music producer of the score for that film and loudly complained about how I hated the arrangements. When the guy walked away without a word, bystanders told me who he was. Perhaps it was divine retribution, as I later found out that he had specifically criticized the way I sing standards. Okay, to each his own; but in some cases I feel a need to stand up for the departed, and defenseless, songwriter.

I FELT THE WAY COLE PORTER'S SONGS WERE PERFORMED IN THE MOVIE *DE-LOVELY* WAS A MUSICAL TRAVESTY.

In 1990 an album of Cole Porter covers called *Red Hot and Blue* benefiting AIDS charities was released. The performers were mostly rock stars—U2, David Byrne, Debbie Harry, and Iggy Pop. Some of the songs were changed in such a way that by comparison to the originals, they were stripped of their drama. Rock musicians will sometimes try to avoid sounding too "theatrical," because it's a pejorative in the pop world, and will simplify the complex chord changes to dumb down the music in a more fashionable pop style. As a result, rock versions of Broadway songs often sound the same. Rock lyrics are often delivered in aural 2D: completely flat and emotionless, perhaps with sardonic effect. This might be intentional when the lyric is supposed to be ironic or detached, but it doesn't work when the original is upbeat. My criterion always is: has anything been *added* with a new interpretation?

Sometimes songs survive despite our best-intended efforts. I remember finding in Ira's lyric file various revised versions of a song called "I Can't Get Started," which had music by Vernon Duke. Alec Wilder wrote Ira a letter saying he was working on an album with Sinatra and asked if Ira could update the lyric for the project. Ira did, but for some reason Sinatra used the original lyric and recorded a version of the song that Ira found dirgelike and lacking in the ego-deflating humor of the original.

I THINK "WHO CARES?" IS A CLASSIC, even if it wouldn't be the first song most Gershwin fans would mention in a list of favorites. It represents the heralding of a new style in music and lyric that is reflective of the era, as well as exhibiting a clear-eyed distillation of a beautiful economy of expression, perhaps mirroring the austerity of the times.

"Who Cares?" comes from *Of Thee I Sing*, the second of the three political plays that George and Ira wrote toward the end of their great run of musical comedies. These were quite different animals. In place of the romantic comedy came broad, non-denominational satires that took aim at the political system without pushing any specific agenda. The first ill-fated production of *Strike Up the Band* followed *Oh, Kay!*, beginning its unsuccessful

tryout run in Long Branch, New York, at the end of August 1927. Then came *Funny Face* (tryout in Philadelphia in October 1927). Hard on the heels of those shows came *Rosalie* (Boston, December '27; Broadway, January '28) and then the flop *Treasure Girl* (Philadelphia, October '28; Broadway, November '28). In 1929, *East Is West* morphed into *Show Girl* (Boston, June '29; Broadway, July '29) before the rejiggered *Strike Up the Band* returned, opening in Boston on Christmas Day 1929 and finally arriving in New York on January 14, 1930.

This great tangle of shows demonstrates, once again, the tremendous productivity of the brothers and the theatrical world as a whole. It also shows that it's not easy to divide George's and Ira's careers into convenient eras: musical comedies/political plays/the folk opera/Hollywood. But there are themes and trends. *Girl Crazy*, which moved from Philadelphia to Broadway in September/October of 1930, was the end of a run of musicals. Then came the movie *Delicious*. The second of the satires, *Of Thee I Sing*, followed.

Of Thee I Sing was a big hit, running for 441 performances, more than twice as many as *Strike Up the Band*. For that earlier show, George S. Kaufman's book was reworked by Morrie Ryskind. Kaufman and Ryskind worked together on *Of Thee I Sing* from the start. It was the first musical to win the Pulitzer Prize for Drama. Kaufman and Ryskind won for their work, as did Ira, who wrote the lyrics. But George, as composer of the music, wasn't eligible for a citation. Ira was so embarrassed by this that he kept his Pulitzer Prize on the back of his bathroom door. In 1998, George was awarded a Special Pulitzer commemorating the centennial of his birth. The prize, accepted by his sister, Frances, helped rectify the earlier omission, but it was a little late for the principal players.

I met Ryskind, who died in 1985, when I was working for Ira. When Ryskind came over to Ira and Lee's house, the two old friends hadn't seen each other for years. As a young man, Ryskind was thrown out of Columbia University's journalism school, which had been endowed by Joseph Pulitzer and which administers the prizes that bear his name. He wrote pieces for the *New York Evening Mail,* as did Ira and Kaufman, and was a frequent collaborator with Kaufman on Broadway and in Hollywood. Ryskind was a socialist when he was young, and a vigorous opponent of America's entry into World War I. He became very conservative later, voluntarily testifying before the House Un-American Activities Committee in 1947 and acting as a founding member of the board of William F. Buckley's influential conservative magazine *National Review.*

This did not sit well with Kaufman, and Ira, who never made enemies with anyone, simply kept his distance, as he'd lost touch with Morrie anyway.

Ryskind was about a year older than Ira, and they were both elderly men when I met him. For most of Ryskind's visit the two old colleagues competed with each other to see who was sicker. "Well, I've been in the hospital three times . . ." I think the contest ended in a tie—both men had a little of the hypochondriac in them, not that they weren't also quite frail by that time. Ironically, it could have been a watered-down Marx Brothers routine, the kind that Ryskind might have once concocted for them. To paraphrase the Irving Berlin song, "You're not in love, you're just sick."

George S. Kaufman was born in Pittsburgh in 1889 and, like Ira, worked a number of semi-menial jobs while trying to make it as a writer, first penning light verse for then well-known columnist Franklin P. Adams in the *Evening Mail.* Kaufman was multitalented, a playwright and screenwriter (The Marx Brothers' *A Night at the Opera*) and a charter member of the Algonquin Round Table. (He was also a critic, a different kind of talent.) Kaufman was a serial collaborator—with Moss Hart he wrote *The Man Who Came to Dinner* and *You Can't Take It with You*, which won the Pulitzer in 1937. The producer Edgar Selwyn put Kaufman together with George and Ira for *Strike Up the Band,* and when Kaufman and Ryskind decided to write *Of Thee I Sing*, they turned to George and Ira again.

Kaufman was the source of the deepest cynicism in these shows. He was a very acerbic guy and had a line for everything. What's satire? When *Strike Up the Band* was failing the first time, he

Published Of Thee I Sing *libretto dust jacket.*

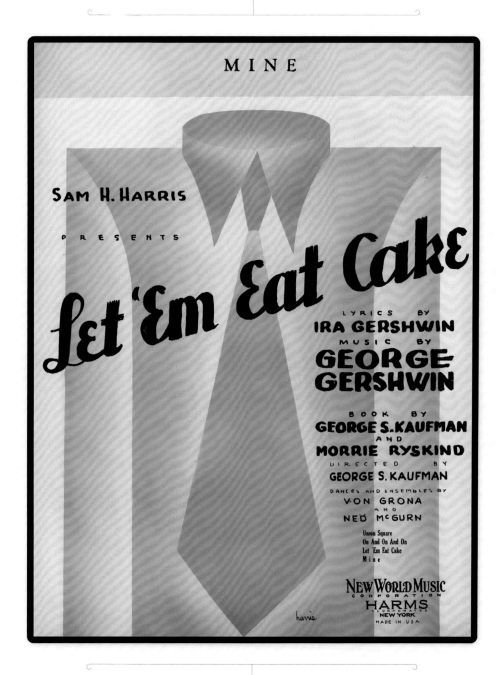

"Mine" sheet music cover from Let 'Em Eat Cake, *1933.*

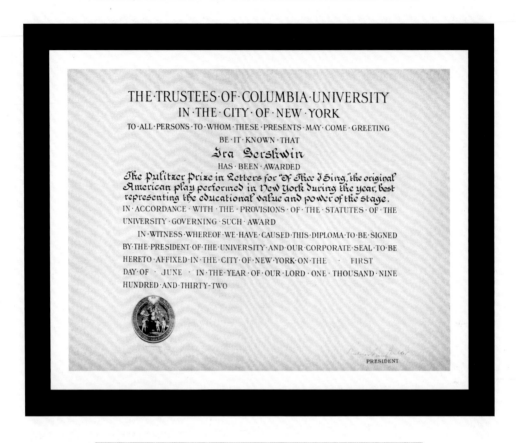

THE·TRUSTEES·OF·COLUMBIA·UNIVERSITY
IN·THE·CITY·OF·NEW·YORK
TO·ALL·PERSONS·TO·WHOM·THESE·PRESENTS·MAY·COME·GREETING
BE·IT·KNOWN·THAT
Ira Gershwin
HAS·BEEN·AWARDED
The Pulitzer Prize in Letters for "Of Thee I Sing," the original American play performed in New York during the year, best representing the educational value and power of the stage.
IN·ACCORDANCE·WITH·THE·PROVISIONS·OF·THE·STATUTES·OF·THE
UNIVERSITY·GOVERNING·SUCH·AWARD
IN·WITNESS·WHEREOF·WE·HAVE·CAUSED·THIS·DIPLOMA·TO·BE·SIGNED
BY·THE·PRESIDENT·OF·THE·UNIVERSITY·AND·OUR·CORPORATE·SEAL·TO·BE
HERETO·AFFIXED·IN·THE·CITY·OF·NEW·YORK·ON·THE   FIRST
DAY·OF   JUNE   ·IN·THE·YEAR·OF·OUR·LORD·ONE·THOUSAND·NINE
HUNDRED·AND·THIRTY-TWO

PRESIDENT

famously said: "Satire is what closes on Saturday night." He was terrifying to most people, because they were afraid they'd be demolished by him. And yet Leo Robin, who was a young lyricist with a one-way ticket from Pittsburgh trying to make his way on Broadway, went to visit Kaufman and he said Kaufman was very nice to him, perhaps sensing the extreme vulnerability of the soul. After telling Robin he should go back to Pittsburgh, Kaufman made an introduction for him that helped him start his career.

KAUFMAN GAINED SUCH A REPUTATION for being a wit that in his declining years he had trouble living up to it. Ira said he was at a gathering, a card game I think it was, late in Kaufman's life, and Kaufman kept throwing out "embarrassing" comments and lines that were meant to be funny but weren't. I think how difficult it must be for someone known for being funny to maintain it.

For *Of Thee I Sing*, Kaufman and Ryskind looked at the problematic state of the country and decided to write something that would make light

Ira's Pulitzer Prize.

of the situation. In 1931, the show was considered quite irreverent because it mocked the political system and the president, albeit a president who appeared in a completely imaginary story. What is fascinating about it today is how the story, for all of its absurdity, has more echoes in the current state of politics than it did when it was first created. Thus it is worth recounting the plot:

John P. Wintergreen is the presidential candidate. "He's the man the people choose; / Loves the Irish and the Jews." Wintergreen is thirty, "good-looking, magnetic." He's also a complete nincompoop. His vice president is Alexander Throttlebottom—a man so anonymous that no one ever recognizes him. The election is stage-managed by political bosses Louis Lippman ("alert, rather good-looking, Jewish") and Francis X. Gilhooley ("plausible, Irish"); by newspaper baron Matthew Arnold Fulton ("very stout, florid"); and by senators Carver and Lyons, representing the West and the South. It's never specified which party is being lampooned—we can safely assume each is as bad as the other.

In the play, every branch of government is made fun of. The president spends his time on vacation, opening speakeasies and asking governors for racing tips. Senators debate giving a pension to Paul Revere's horse. The vice president is a waste of space. The show had a definite edge.

At the outset, Lippman and Gilhooley are in a convention hotel, having just presided over the selection of candidate Wintergreen. Gilhooley is concerned the party is getting wise to the backroom convention fixes. And we never should have sold Rhode Island, Gilhooley says. The men decide they need something to take people's minds off

Rhode Island. Fulton has an idea—get the president to fall in love with an all-American girl and have a contest to find her. So the first lady will be chosen in a reality show of sorts, with the White House the prize.

Wintergreen runs on the love platform, and southern belle Diana Devereaux wins the beauty pageant to marry him. Alas, Wintergreen throws a wrench in the works by falling in love with Mary Turner, organizer of the pageant, because she makes fantastic corn muffins. Before Wintergreen and Mary can marry, however, Diana takes them to court for breach of promise, and the Supreme Court ("the super Solomons of this great nation")—notorious then as now for deciding presidential elections—sides with the Wintergreens, allowing them to marry, and he wins the election. But Diana gains support for her case in the court of public opinion, and the president and first lady, in distress, sing "Who Cares?" to each other.

George was proud of the song, and it's the first major tune heard in the original "Of Thee I Sing Overture," cleverly used in counterpoint to a rhythmic figure that delightfully propels it into our brains.

THE WRITER GEORGE FRAZIER, a frequent critic of Ira's lyrics, claimed that Ira stole the "Yonkers /conquers" rhyme from Rodgers and Hart. The third chorus of their song "Manhattan," from 1925, has the lyric: "We'll go to Yonkers, / Where true love conquers, / In the wilds." Ira was very irritated by this accusation and said that he very easily could have used some other rhyme, such as, "Who cares what banks fail in London. / We've a love that will not be undone." For a 1952 revival, Ira updated the lyric for audiences that knew nothing of banks failing by writing, "Who cares how history rates me / Long as your kiss intoxicates me."

Although "Who Cares?" was one of the more popular songs to come out of *Of Thee I Sing*, it was never a huge hit. Still, it was a big favorite of George and Ira's. It's a song closely tied to the plot of its show, but it also works well independently of the show. (In 1940 Fred Astaire recorded "Who Cares?" with Benny Goodman and his orchestra. This is one of the few Gershwin songs that Astaire didn't introduce but went on to record.)

As was customary in those days, when "Who Cares?" was published, the original lyrics were altered for words that were less tied to the show's plot. In place of the verse "Here's some information . . ." the published version went,

> Let it rain and thunder!
> Let a million firms go under!
> I am not concerned with
> Stocks and bonds I've been burned with.

BESIDES ITS INNOVATIONS in music and lyrics and its value as a period piece, another thing I love about "Who Cares?" is just how well it resonates with our own historical moment. The satirical attitude of the show, which this song encapsulates, is one of total disillusionment with endless war and political chaos. Decades before anyone had heard the slogan "Make love, not war," "Who Cares?" made a clever musical plea for exactly that. The song was born out of a time of hardship that, sadly, is not dissimilar to current times. Under the lighthearted exhortation to forget about the political turmoil and embrace personal well-being and relationships is the pain of an often hopeless reality. In other words, it tells us, let's wave the white flag and retreat to the bedroom.

THE SONG WAS BORN OUT OF A TIME OF HARDSHIP THAT, SADLY, IS NOT DISSIMILAR TO CURRENT TIMES.

THE BIGGEST SONG TO EMERGE FROM the score of *Of Thee I Sing* was the title song, Wintergreen's campaign number and the last song heard as diplomatic and constitutional crises are averted.

> Of thee I sing, baby—
> Summer, autumn, winter, spring, baby.
> You're my silver lining,
> You're my sky of blue;
> There's a love-light shining
> Just because of you.

> Of thee I sing, baby—
> You have got that certain thing, baby!
> Shining star and inspiration,
> Worthy of a mighty nation—
> Of thee I sing!

The song has an anthemic feel, but it also has the wink-of-the-eye satire of the show. This is created in large part by Ira's clever use of the word "baby." It was quite daring of Ira to take part of the national lyrical fabric—"My country 'tis of thee, / sweet land of liberty, / of thee I sing" —and add the slangy "baby." Ira was aware of the danger and wrote that if the audience had showed disfavor at the perceived slight, he'd have changed the lyric. But he recounted that at the intermission of the show on opening night, audience members were marveling at "Of Thee I Sing" and about how clever and delightful it was with the new appendage.

I have recorded both of these songs. I included "Who Cares?" on my album *Nice Work If You Can Get It* and "Of Thee I Sing" on my 1998 Gershwin recording called *Michael and George.* On that CD, I used electronic instruments to augment

the acoustic section. I thought it would be interesting to do that because, had George lived, he would have experimented with modern musical technology as he did in his own time. George once wrote a piece for a quarter-tone piano (a special instrument invented by Hans Barth that used half the standard semitone scale) and was one of the first Americans to play a Hammond organ. In my version of "Of Thee I Sing" we used a synthesizer bed that doesn't exactly sound like strings—it sounds like what it is. That album was deeply offensive to some people, who thought I had sold out. Other people liked it a lot, which is always the way of things. The aforementioned are two of three Gershwin discs not available on iTunes, thus rendering my complete recorded Gershwin output unattainable for download. Of course, who am I to judge the wisdom of excluding the thing that made me famous in the first place?

N 1952, *OF THEE I SING* WAS REVIVED ON Broadway, starring film actor Jack Carson, but it only lasted a couple of months. Ira had worked on the production, in spite of the fact that he had doubts about its efficacy those many years after the original. Ira dutifully rewrote many lyrics for the revival, and it turned out to be the last time he ever had anything to do with Broadway: times were changing, and as he got older and more resistant to that change, Ira's interest was waning. He never wanted to work that hard and Broadway had become confounding.

Also in 1952, fact mirrored fiction when Ira rewrote the words of "Love Is Sweeping the Country" from *Of Thee I Sing* and "It Ain't Necessarily So" to create campaign songs for Democrat Adlai

Ira and George with George S. Kaufman and Morris Ryskind, in 1933.

Stevenson, who was running against Dwight Eisenhower for president. Ira was a Democrat but quietly so, and some of his more political friends put pressure on him to contribute the new words. For "It Ain't Necessarily So" he wrote,

> They say Ike's arranging for things to be changing
> But it ain't necessarily so.

And based on "Love Is Sweeping the Country,"

> Adlai's sweeping the country!
> He will be the next prez.
> We'll be leaning
> On words with meaning,
> For he means every word he says.

Political satire is always hard to revive, because it dates so fast. Songs with very time-specific lyrics often struggle to survive long. *Strike Up the Band* doesn't have the same bite it had in the twenties. In 2006, there was a concert performance of *Of Thee I Sing* in the Encores! series at City Center, with Victor Garber as Wintergreen and Jennifer Laura Thompson as Mary. It was well done and well received. Whether it would have sustained audiences in a longer run on Broadway, I don't know. Attitudes are now different in fundamental ways, and a lot of what seemed so irreverent when the show came out can feel tame today unless one takes a deeper look.

Still, *Of Thee I Sing* is a wonderful show. It can be viewed as a precursor to *Porgy and Bess* because of the thematic unity of the music. Musi-

cally, George was flexing his muscles and writing in a larger form that unified the score through clever reuse of various basic themes that gave the show a beautiful arc. Melodies were reprised in different contexts and in different styles. It's also not a traditional musical studded with songs, but a highly sophisticated musical play, closer to the manner of *Show Boat* than a pure song vehicle like a twenties musical. The show was so integrated musically speaking that its innovation in the thirties might have made it a failure in the twenties. The hybrid nature would be more familiar to contemporary audiences, and the energy of the score is decidedly fresher these many decades later than much of what followed it.

ONE SONG DOESN'T AFFECT MY REVERENCE FOR PORTER'S ABILITY AS A WRITER.

JUST BECAUSE A SONG HAS BEEN designated by fate as a classic doesn't mean we all have to like it. Thankfully, our tastes are different. I have written disapprovingly about "Night and Day," and some people got very upset. Tony Bennett was particularly offended that I would say anything negative about Cole Porter. "I find it boring. . . ," I wrote of the song. "I don't have a feeling of completeness or resolution when I sing 'Night and Day.'" The way the melody jumps around "leaves me hanging there feeling like I've just been taken on a bum cab ride and then dumped." My opinion of this one song doesn't affect my reverence for Porter's ability as a writer. I just feel that certain Porter songs are more successful than others, and "Night and Day" has always left me cold. It's a great song in its construction, yet it somehow doesn't move me much on other levels.

I sang "Night and Day" at Carnegie Hall for a Frank Sinatra tribute. The song was part of Sinatra's first solo recording session, and I was asked to re-create it. I didn't think that his recording was a particularly deep rendition of the song, though perhaps it was more deeply stated than most contemporary singers' versions of the time. It was from the big band era—a lot of recordings from that time are more about the singer trying to keep up with the band and maintain tempo than about interpreting the song. I have sung "Night and Day" and "gotten into it." Emotionally I'm able to deliver even if intellectually I don't like the material. It's an interesting process, because when I finish, I find that I like the song better than I did before. Being forced to inhabit a song's perspective often generates greater sympathy with it. Perhaps if I sing it enough, I'll change my mind.

When I accept song requests from an audience, someone may select a song to which they are deeply attached but I am not. One night when someone yelled out "Stardust," my kneejerk response was, "Sawdust?" Musically speaking, I like Hoagy Carmichael's melody, which is considered to be one of the best ever. It's one of the most revered, certainly one of the most recorded songs. Lyrically, it's hard for me to connect to Mitchell Parish's ephemeral and quaint poetic allusions. The song was originally conceived as an up-tempo jazz number and might not have become a standard in that form, but to me it is more interesting when closer to its roots.

For reasons I can't explain (and perhaps that's good), certain other great standards I just don't always connect with. "All the Things You Are" is a beautiful song. Many believe it to be Kern and Hammerstein's greatest achievement, but I don't think it's nearly as magnetic as other songs of theirs. Funny thing—I love the music better without the lyric and vice versa. Together, not so much!

Nor do I have unequivocal affection for every song that I love. "Blues in the Night" is a beloved song, and I love and appreciate it when Johnny Mercer sings it, but I don't think I could sing it convincingly. There's no place I could go emotionally that would make it possible for me to sing "Blues in the Night." For me, the song goes on a little too long, and I'm slightly bored by the end of it. (Johnny Mercer fans, please don't take offense.)

"Over the Rainbow" is also a fantastic song, but I played that song so often during my years of nights spent in piano bars, I just can't get any joy out of hearing it again, no matter which end of the song I'm on, listening to it or performing it. The thrill has gone. If I never hear it again, I'm fine.

And many who have played in a piano bar in the seventies and eighties would rather take cyanide than sing "New York, New York." It can still bring me a thrill when I hear it done well, but a standard like that has a ratio of bad performances that outnumber the good ones. Liza creates the goose bumps every time, but I wish many others would lay off. Dale Gonyea wrote a parody about the millions of times he's heard "New York, New York," and it concludes with hearing it in a public restroom, spurring him to say, "If they can play it there, they'll play it anywhere."

Having previously mentioned my feelings about hearing some songs too often, I have faced some repercussions as a result of it. In my first book, when I wrote that I was tired of "Over the Rainbow," I didn't suspect that such words could possibly cause such deep offense, but they did on the part of at least one person who was angry with my blasphemous comments. I was signing CDs at a store in Cincinnati and a woman said to me, "How dare you say that about 'Over the Rainbow'!" I said, "Excuse me?" and she said, "How *dare* you!" She was very deeply upset—it was as if I had mocked the pope. The look of rage on her face and her physical trembling caused me to consider asking for security to step in. I wondered if I might be assassinated for criticizing "Over the Rainbow," surely a first.

I still remember to look over my shoulder whenever I'm in Cincinnati.

I N 1933 CAME THE SEQUEL to *Of Thee I Sing—Let 'Em Eat Cake,* which was a flop. It was considered too acerbic and dark and only lasted ninety performances. In the show, John Wintergreen loses his re-election bid to John P. Tweedledee, outfits his supporters in blue shirts, and takes over the government with the help of the army. It was the kind of coup that was actually taking place in parts of Europe at the time, only with goons in brown or black shirts. Everyone gets stamped on (one song proclaims "Down with Everything That's Up"), and there's no leavening love story, as there had been between Wintergreen and Mary in *Of Thee I Sing.* It's so dark that Wintergreen

and Throttlebottom almost get hanged at the end of the show—something even poor dumb Throttlebottom doesn't deserve. So he's saved and ends up as president, a fate only slightly better than death. The authors must have thought at the time, "This'll get 'em." But Ira said that it just never gelled as had their first combined venture, and once a show starts off on the wrong foot, it can sometimes never find its way back.

There was one standout song in *Let 'Em Eat Cake,* "Mine," which was sung in counterpoint. It's a love song Wintergreen sings to Mary, with the ensemble acting as a Greek chorus, singing directly to the audience while John and Mary sing to each other.

The point they're making in the song
Is that they more than get along;
And he is not ashamed to say
She made him what he is today.

It does a person good to see
Such happy domesticity;
The way they're making love, you'd swear
They're not a married pair.

He says, no matter what occurs,
Whatever he may have is hers;
The point that she is making is
Whatever she may have is his.

ALL: *Mine, more than divine*
To know that love like yours is mine!

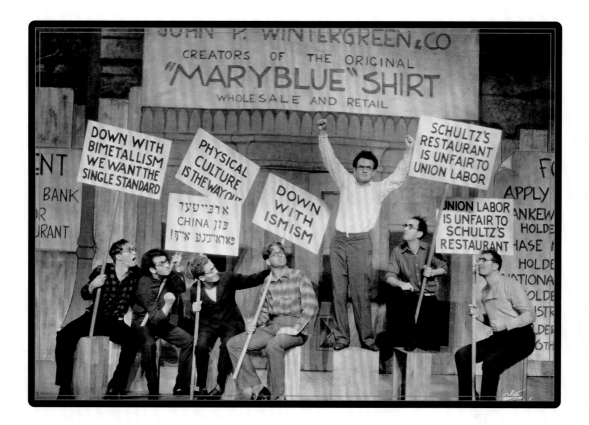

For me, this song is an enduring standard and another leap forward in the Gershwin creative arsenal. It's often cited by many as a perfect duet-counterpoint song that was the precursor to better-known ditties like Irving Berlin's iconic effort "You're Just in Love," though Berlin had experimented with counterpoint earlier. "Mine" is a love song with a timeless appeal that lives on while the show is mostly forgotten (although Opera North in the U.K. staged both *Of Thee I Sing* and *Let 'Em Eat Cake* in 2008–09.)

There was just too much reality in *Let 'Em Eat Cake.* George and Ira's run of Broadway success had ended. Before *Let 'Em Eat Cake* came *Pardon My English,* which opened on January 20, 1933. It was a plagued show for many reasons, with pretensions of being an operetta. The biggest problem was the book, which could never be settled on. (I have a copy of the original script, which is covered with haphazard notations.) Ira described the whole experience as a "headache." George and Ira only took the job (Ira wrote) to help out producer Alex

Philip Loeb and ensemble in a scene from Let 'Em Eat Cake.

Aarons, who badly needed the money. *Pardon My English* couldn't save him—it ran for only forty-six performances. The show was put together during the heart of the Depression, and business on Broadway was terrible. The subject matter didn't help. If ever there was a good time for a musical about schizophrenia, this wasn't it. (Well, at least part of me feels that way.) George's music did show his growth as a composer. There is some extraordinary thematic material that reflects his studies in harmony and composition. Some of it borders on being atonal, yet it is the most creative use of such an anti-popular sound.

S O FAR, I'VE BEEN TALKING about the survival of songs in terms of their reputation and popularity, especially whether they become standards, but before a song has a chance at becoming a classic, it has to survive in the much more basic sense of not disappearing from the historical record altogether. Many songs have never been recorded, published, or written down at all. Unless these songs are remembered by someone who wrote or heard them, they have already vanished into the ether. Some unheard-of treasures may be waiting in obscurity to be rediscovered; others already have lost that opportunity.

It was a different matter for a song to survive in the era before phonograph records were universal. Songs were distributed mainly by sales of their sheet music, and fans played the songs they liked rather than just listened to them, a more active and dynamic relationship than we share with the material today. Sheet music remained popular as long as people gathered to play music but our consumption has gotten more and more solitary over time.

I collect sheet music for two reasons: first, it helps me trace the lineage of a song—through all its various interpretations and versions—back to the show from which it originated. Second, I'm always looking for great songs that as chance would have it didn't make it into the ranks of the standards. That's why I have a collection of over thirty thousand pieces of sheet music together with an almost equal number of recordings. And that's why I get very little sleep when I'm not working.

I could spend the rest of my life going through my collection of sheet music, which is made up of other collections I've inherited or purchased, and probably find a thousand great songs. I have a better chance of finding an unknown gem by Kurt Weill or Cole Porter or Johnny Green than I have of loving something on the radio today.

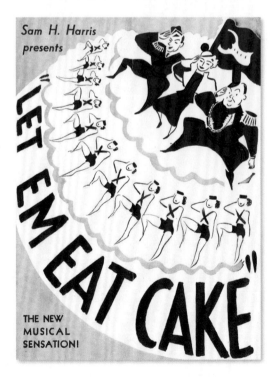

Let 'Em Eat Cake *advertising herald.*

The dissemination of a song as sheet music is largely a lost form, but it can reveal the commercial journey taken by a song when one examines the various editions created through the years. In many instances, we can look back and credit the original sheet music publishers for confusion about what is the true version of a song. From the version performed onstage, the publisher would create a sheet music edition for the consumer. If a song became a hit, it would go through many editions and when reprinted could be revamped in length, lyric content, or overall style in order

edition with the lyrics in French or in Spanish; versions of the song transcribed in different keys, which were designed for home singers with "high," "medium," or "low" voices. Again, the songs that last are endlessly adaptable and can survive being dissected in all these ways.

To reveal a little of my eccentricity (if you haven't already gleaned enough in these pages), I have an unceasing fervor for knowing, learning, preserving, and sharing songs. Songs are my currency, my way of life. I'm doing my best to keep as many of these songs alive as I can. When it

THE DISSEMINATION OF A SONG AS SHEET MUSIC IS LARGELY A LOST FORM.

to perpetuate its sales potential, and the songwriters might not have any knowledge of their actions nor the authority to control them. Or a publisher would reprint a song to reflect the arrangement on the latest hit record so anyone who bought the sheet music could try to re-create that specific version. So different editions might hold information about the genesis of a song.

Publishers always worked hard to appeal to as many people as possible with their songs. Originally a song would be published with the name of the show it came from on the cover. The names of the other published songs from that show would also be listed, linking the songs with the show. Once the song was a hit and had a life of its own, it would be published with a generic cover—just "Embraceable You," by George and Ira Gershwin. There would be more versions—an

comes to finding new songs, I feel a great enthusiasm, a burning desire to know more. Whenever I pick up a song, I'm curious as to where it came from. Who wrote it? If it's a movie, what is the movie? Or what is the show? Who were these writers? What are the references in the lyric? What color socks were they wearing?

I'm constantly finding songs that surprise me and I'm always hopeful I can unearth a hidden gem. There have been discoveries of lost songs and lyrics by Porter, Mercer, Rodgers, Kern, and others that seem to have been hurled through the universe with careful aim to land on my doorstep. Somehow these songs know that if they can find their way to my door they have a better chance of surviving and thriving than otherwise. It's true that I am always on the lookout for music and records, and the process of the search and discovery sets my mind on a path of contemplation akin to meditation.

I was at a flea market recently and spotted a stack of sheet music. I found a song unknown to me by Walter Donaldson and Gus Kahn for sale for two dollars. Such moments are ones of silent rejoicing, even though the price was probably appropriate for the common garden-variety Tin Pan Alley fare. Donaldson was one of the most prolific American popular songwriters and he had numerous hits (including Jolson's "My Mammy"), many of them written with Kahn.

As I was looking at the music, I thought about how Donaldson had written what seems like thousands of melodies. And also how Kahn as a lyricist had to keep coming up with yet another way of expressing love. How did they do it? How did they keep going back to the well and so often come up with freshness and quality?

There are certain names I always look for when I'm song hunting. One for example is Bud

Green, who also had a song in that flea market stack. Green's biggest hit was "Sentimental Journey" in 1941. He'd written songs in the twenties and thirties like "I Love My Baby, My Baby Loves Me" and "Once in a While." Green is an example of a lyricist who was considered a good Tin Pan Alley journeyman who turned out a lot of solid songs, but didn't have the luster, the genius, of a Johnny Mercer or Yip Harburg or Oscar Hammerstein or Ira Gershwin.

I sometimes try to imagine what it was like for these writers to create in a time when there were other lyricists and composers who were clearly superior to them. Did they perceive themselves as guys who just worked in the Tin Pan Alley trenches, trying to churn out a hit? Or did they feel they were equal in talent to their peers but hadn't gotten the same breaks? I was with Harry Warren the day his old friend Bud Green died, and he accepted it with the numb familiarity that such news had come to represent to a man who had lived into his late eighties and was still hanging on. "Poor Bud," Harry said, seeing one of the last of his generation pass.

There's a great deal of luck involved in the survival of one song over another. A lot of songs never get published, including many written by the greats like Cole Porter or Burton Lane, for example. Ralph Rainger, the film composer who died in a plane crash in 1942, left a great stack of unpublished songs. Most often, those songs remain unheard.

It's not just in unpublished music that treasures await—there are albums full of neglected songs. In 1957, Page Cavanaugh, the great pianist, made an album called *Fats Sent Me,* which was

The author with composer Harry Warren, 1980.

made up almost entirely of Fats Waller tunes that had never been heard at the time. It's a marvelous recording, but it's obscure.

Some years ago, I recorded an unpublished Gershwin song, "Ask Me Again." To me, that song wasn't as good as the classic Gershwin songs that we remember. But if that song had been premiered in 1937 by Fred Astaire, perhaps people would say, "That's one of the great classics." That song didn't get that lucky break.

It dogged Ira that he had a stack of unpublished Gershwin songs and tunes. He was always trying to find ways to get those songs out there; he would save them for nameless future projects that

might fit. He kept songs like this in his head because he didn't want anyone to know about them. These hidden songs will die with him if he doesn't write them down.

The song he played me I can remember, and while I've never written it down, at least there's now a recording of it, and our session was also videotaped. Jerry gave me the song because he decided that it was okay for it to be heard, and so I will sing and share it with others, to set it on its flight. There's another song—one that Harry Warren wrote with Ira Gershwin that was never written down called "For the Life of Me" that they put away and I found. Ira reused the title later with

I'M CONSTANTLY FINDING SONGS THAT SURPRISE ME AND I'M ALWAYS HOPEFUL I CAN UNEARTH A HIDDEN GEM.

never developed, much to his conflicted relief as he grew older. Songwriters never want to waste anything. They want to put their work out in the world when they think it has its best shot, and they never lose faith that their song's time is coming. Arthur Schwartz, who had many hits throughout his career, including "Dancing in the Dark" and "That's Entertainment," doggedly kept plugging a song he wrote with Leo Robin through the last two decades of his existence. While he felt the song could be a hit, it seems that no one else agreed.

Jerry Herman played and sang for me a song he'd written for a musical (which was supposed to star Chita Rivera) that never happened. He'd held on to the song for maybe twenty-five years just in case he came across a project where it

Arthur Schwartz and was none too pleased when I turned up the earlier effort, not wanting to be accused of repeating himself. The early one was at least preserved on a home recording made by Harry Warren, but another called "Taking No Chances with You" is missing the notated music. Harry Warren once had it and played it for me, but since his death the music just disappeared. No search has ever located it, but I still remember the tune and I guess I had better preserve it somewhere.

There must have been a lot of great songs that went down with their composer. Ira could remember George's early instrumental composition "Tango," which he wrote in 1913. Ira would hum it for me. And it was frustrating for him, because he could hear the whole damn thing in his head but nobody could get it out of his brain sufficiently complete to write it down. There's a fragment of "Tango" that exists on a 1936 radio broadcast—about four bars of it. Better than nothing, I guess.

The conductor Michael Tilson Thomas's father, Teddy Thomas, recalled attending a Gershwin revue in a nightclub on the roof of the New Amsterdam Theatre (perhaps *Morris Gests's Midnight Whirl*) in the late teens, early twenties. Gershwin had written songs for the show and Teddy Thomas remembered one: "Let a Cutie Cut Your Cuticle," which he played and Michael Tilson Thomas taped. That song only existed because Teddy Thomas remembered it, and hopefully still does if Michael still has the fragile cassette he recorded it on. Kay Swift remembered and notated a number of Gershwin melodies that otherwise were forgotten. In some cases where there were only single-line lead sheets, she was able to harmonize and remember the songs. In a couple of cases, when Kay notated songs that were lost that later turned up, she was inevitably correct in what she remembered. (In one case, however, for "The Union League" from *Let 'Em Eat Cake*, she wrote down two completely different harmonizations at two different times that both sounded Gershwinesque. Flip a coin, anyone?)

Ira tried to rescue the walking-the-dog music from the movie *Shall We Dance*. In 1940, he contacted RKO Studios and asked if they had the music, and they said they didn't. In 1958, Ira was in New York visiting his publisher, and a talented musician named Hal Borne walked into the office and Ira said, "Weren't you the rehearsal pianist on *Shall We Dance*?" And Borne said,

"Yeah." Ira said, "Do you remember the walking-the-dog music?" And Hal said, "Yes, I do." Hal Borne played it, and someone took it down, and it was subsequently published.

The odd thing is that in 1977, I found the orchestration of the walking-the-dog music, and it had been at RKO all along. It wasn't in Gershwin's manuscript copy, but the orchestration was there and could have been extracted from it. But Hal Borne remembered it, and it was published, as a piano solo, and it existed only because of him.

KAY SWIFT REMEMBERED AND NOTATED A NUMBER OF GERSHWIN MELODIES THAT OTHERWISE WERE FORGOTTEN.

But getting back to one of my flea market sojourns, in all there were three pieces of music that I almost bought at my recent visit there. But I looked at them and thought, well, these are songs that I'm never going to sing. There was a song written by Harold A. Levey and the lyricist Zelda Sears, who wrote with Vincent Youmans. The title of it was "Love Has No Words" from a 1922 Broadway musical, I think called *The Clinging Vine*. And inside, even though the title on the cover was "Love Has No Words" the phrase used in the song was "Love has no word." It was a song about the fact we are unable to express what we feel when we're in love. After "love has no word" there were bars and bars of humming to make the point. (No words, get it?) So it's a novelty song in that respect. And I thought, well, I could buy it for the sake of completeness or as a possible demonstration of the maudlin in twenties theater songs, but I thought the better of it.

Sometimes I'll buy a song because the writer on a sheet is a famous name, even though I don't like the song. Sometimes I'll buy the song because it's from a show that's of interest to me. And sometimes I buy something because of the absurdity of the lyric, and because I might be able to use it in a humorous way. It can be joy to find a copy of something like "Hungry Women" or "Where Did Robinson Crusoe Go with Friday on Saturday Night?" Again, it's all part of the exploration and my way of studying. For the songs themselves, it could mean the difference between new life and continued obscurity. Until the last copy of a song is lost, there's always the chance, no matter how slim, that someone will find it and sing it again.

I used to perform a song in my act called "China, We Owe a Lot to You," which I found on a 78 recorded by the Watson Sisters around 1920. I bought the record for a quarter, cheap because the disc had a big scratch in it. It was a very silly song written by Milton Ager and Howard Johnson in 1917. Milton Ager was the father of Shana Alexander, who was my close friend. Oddly, I found this record and then very soon after I was going through Milton Ager's sheet music after he died—his wife, Cecelia, and Shana asked me to go through his things—and I found the sheet music. And within a couple of days, when I got home to my apartment one night, a neighbor had slipped a photocopy of a song under my door with a note saying, "Do you know this song?" and of course it was "China . . ." The synchronicity was not unnoticed.

> *China, way out near Asia Minor, no*
> *country could be finer beneath the sun;*
> *You gave us silk to dress our lovely*
> *women, 'Twas worth the price.*
> *And when we couldn't get potatoes, you*
> *gave us rice.*
> *We mix chop suey with your chopsticks*
> *You've taught us quite a few tricks we*
> *never knew*
> *We take our hats off to one thing we've*
> *seen,*
> *Your laundries keep our country clean*
> *China we owe a lot to you.*

People used to scream with laughter because it was so silly. In this era there were hundreds of

The author with songwriter Jerry Herman.

Asian-themed songs like "Chong, He Come from Hong Kong" (1919), most of which don't bear too much inspection, lyrically speaking. As we've seen, George's "Swanee" was based on the popular hit "Hindustan." Everything adds a little bit to the picture of our country and the world through the eyes of Tin Pan Alley. These songs help connect us with a time that has passed, offering a glimpse at the mores and culture and hopes and aspirations of yesterday. When we sing that old song, we become one with the songwriter for three minutes.

It bears repeating that most of the standards in the Great American Songbook started life in some musical or revue. None of these shows was written for posterity. Each was a piece of popular entertainment, quickly produced. If a show failed, no one really gave it a second thought, and sometimes the music was destroyed on closing night, like burning a figure in effigy. This is why in some cases we don't have surviving music or orchestrations or the book. A lot of the early shows, even the successful ones, have never been revived. Yet still, some of the songs make it through.

> THESE SONGS HELP CONNECT US WITH A TIME THAT HAS PASSED, OFFERING A GLIMPSE AT THE MORES AND CULTURE AND HOPES AND ASPIRATIONS OF YESTERDAY.

There are any number of reasons why a song might remain alive. A song might survive because it's interpreted by a great artist like Sinatra who remains wildly popular. It might live on after one stunning interpretation that sets a new benchmark, or it might gain new life after being rediscovered by a contemporary artist. But I believe most of the great songs survive because they are great songs. There's that fate or karma once again coming into play. Perhaps it's the case that there are no accidents, as New Age thinkers like to say. This is where I return to the philosophy of "Who Cares?" as it gently reminds us that the ephemeral nature of our existence will be ever tempered not only by the glories of romance but also the music that doggedly and mystically survives. And all of us play a part. ·

George during a radio broadcast.

"Who Cares?" sheet music cover from Of Thee I Sing.

"I GOT PLENTY O' NUTTIN'"

— from *Porgy and Bess*, 1935 —

PORGY:

Oh, I got plenty o' nuttin',
An' nuttin's plenty for me.
I got no car, got no mule, I got no misery.
De folks wid plenty o' plenty
Got a lock on dey door,
'Fraid somebody's a-goin' to rob 'em
While dey's out a-makin' more.

What for?
I got no lock on de door,
(Dat's no way to be).
Dey can steal de rug from the floor,
Dat's O.K. wid me,
'Cause de things dat I prize,
Like de stars in de skies,
All are free.
Oh, I got plenty o' nuttin',
An' nuttin's plenty for me.
I got my gal, got my song,
Got Hebben de whole day long.
(No use complainin'!)
Got my gal, got my Lawd, got my song.

WOMEN:

Porgy change since dat woman come to live with he.

SERENA:

How he change?

ALL:

He ain' cross with chillen no more,
An' ain' you hear how
He an' Bess all de time singin' in their room?

MARIA:

I tells you that cripple's happy now.

ALL:

Happy.

PORGY:

I got plenty o' nuttin',
An' nuttin's plenty fo' me.
I got de sun, got de moon, got de deep blue sea.
De folks wid plenty o' plenty,
Got to pray all de day.
Seems wid plenty you sure got to worry
How to keep the Debble away,
A-way.
I ain't a-frettin' 'bout Hell
Till de time arrive.
Never worry long as I'm well,
Never one to strive
To be good, to be bad—
What the hell! I is glad
I's alive.
Oh, I got plenty o' nuttin'
An nuttin's plenty fo' me.
I got my gal, got my song,
Got Hebben de whole day long.
(No use complainin'!)
Got my gal.

ALL:

Got his gal.

PORGY:

Got my Lawd.

ALL:

Got his Lawd.

PORGY:

Got my song!

CHAPTER 9

THE TOP OF THE MOUNTAIN—

Porgy and Bess

FROM THE DISTANCE AFFORDED by three quarters of a century, it's clear to me that George Gershwin's 1935 opera, *Porgy and Bess,* is his masterpiece of masterpieces. (Ira's role in the creation of the work, while substantial, was less than their usual fifty-fifty partnership.) With the debut of *Porgy and Bess,* George had climbed to the top of his creative mountain, but in 1936, with *Porgy and Bess* having lost money on its Broadway run and on an equally financially draining two-month national tour, George was left with a somewhat diminished reputation and the need to find a paying gig in Hollywood. Imagine that. In spite of his unique standing, the public was just as fickle then as it is now and reduced him to a box office pariah.

Porgy and Bess had been gestating in George's brain for ten years. While today, most people have heard of the opera, it started life as a novel based on a real-life character. In 1925, DuBose Heyward, an insurance-salesman-turned-poet-turned-fiction-writer, published his first novel, *Porgy.* Heyward, born in Charleston, South Carolina, in 1885, knew southern life intimately, including that of the African-Americans who lived parallel but separate lives from most whites, practically invisible to them.

Heyward learned about Gullah life—the distinctive Low Country African-American culture—

A press shot of George, DuBose Heyward, and Ira in 1935.

when he worked in a cotton warehouse on the Charleston waterfront. He lived on Church Street, close to "Cabbage Row," a dilapidated stretch of buildings that housed a produce market. One well-known inhabitant of Cabbage Row was a disabled man named Samuel Smalls, aka Goat Sammy, who used to beg from a cart pulled by a goat. In 1924 Smalls was arrested for firing shots at a woman named Maggie Barnes, an incident Heyward read about in the newspaper. The characters and setting for a novel—"Porgy," "Bess," and "Catfish Row"— practically fell into Heyward's lap.

Porgy was published in 1925. George read the novel the following year during rehearsals for *Oh, Kay!*, and got in touch with Heyward right away to ask if he could adapt it. *Porgy* was a hot property— Cecil B. DeMille had bought the movie rights and, alas for George, Heyward's playwright wife, Dorothy, was already working on a theatrical version. For the Heywards, the play took priority, and the stage play, produced by the Theatre Guild, opened on Broadway in October 1927 and ran for more than three hundred performances in two engagements.

Following this stage success, Heyward was intrigued by the idea of working with George Gershwin, and the two men met for the first time in late 1927 in Atlantic City, where George was working on *Strike Up the Band*. Despite his long-time interest in the form, George didn't feel ready to commit to a full-scale opera, which was the treatment he believed suited *Porgy* best. While he knew that he could do it, he also felt that he needed a few more years of experience to be able to properly realize his gargantuan musical ambition.

Within a few years, however, New York City's Metropolitan Opera, in the form of George's

patron, Otto Kahn, approached George about writing an opera, and George decided that he was ready. This was when he investigated making an opera version of the stage play *The Dybbuk* but to George's dismay, he discovered that the music rights were held by an Italian composer. His first inclination for subject matter had always been a more native source of American music, and in a 1920 interview in *Along Broadway: The Edison Musical Magazine*, he expressed his desire to one day create a full-scale work based on the music of the "darky." (He used that term absolutely non-pejoratively, shocking though it sounds today. By 1935, the term had disappeared from his vocabulary.) Already in 1920, when he was best known for "Swanee," George was talking about writing operettas. "After that may come opera," he said, ". . . but I want all my work to have the one element of appealing to the great majority of our people." So it was not a surprise that George found his way back to the idea of *Porgy*.

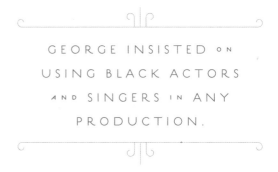

GEORGE INSISTED ON USING BLACK ACTORS AND SINGERS IN ANY PRODUCTION.

George insisted on using black actors and singers in any production, but the Met said they'd only put the show on with white performers in blackface. The Met also said it wouldn't use an all-black cast because there weren't enough black opera singers, but George wouldn't back down. (*Porgy and Bess* eventually went into repertory at the Met in 1985. The Met was able to fill most of the major parts with African-American members of its company.)

The Gershwin estate still requires that all productions must feature an all-black cast, save the few nonsinging white roles.

Other artists continued to show an interest in *Porgy*. At one point Al Jolson wanted to make a movie version in blackface, and then he proposed a musical to be written by Hammerstein and Kern, but the two men were too busy to start. How different social and musical history might have been had that come to fruition. . . .

Finally, in 1932, with Heyward hurting financially in the beginnings of the Depression, he was prompted to start work on a musical adaptation of his most valuable literary asset. George was finally able to commit himself to a *Porgy* made on his terms, on Broadway with the Theatre Guild producing and Rouben Mamoulian, who had directed the stage play, reprising the role for this version. The Theatre Guild was a far step down from the august power and prestige of the Met, but it was the only organization from which George could generate interest. So the opera would have to be produced with a carefully watched budget.

At the end of 1933, George and Ira were at a professional turning point, which is a polite way of saying they needed a hit. They were coming off back-to-back flops that year—*Pardon My English*, which ran for just forty-six performances at the beginning of the year, and *Let 'Em Eat Cake,* which lasted for just ninety. George knew that *Porgy* would require a considerable investment of his time and he was fortunately able to use the $2,000 a week he made from his *Music by Gershwin* radio shows (sponsored by Feen-A-Mint, an over-the-counter laxative) to fund his first attempt at writing an opera. Over the years his celebrity as an American musical icon had made him a desirable radio personality, and he accepted a lucrative contract to host his first-ever radio series. It was a financial boon in those hard times.

By the time *Porgy* was ready for George, George was ready for *Porgy*. His formal compositional education with the Russian émigré Joseph Schillinger, which began in 1932, was already bringing greater sophistication to George's musical palette, even though Ira later insisted that the influence of Schillinger was slight and had little impact on *Porgy*. The three operetta-like political satires the Gershwins had done between 1927 (if you count the first version of *Strike Up the Band*) and 1933 marked a progression away from musical comedy with their opera-like sequences that featured greater musical and dramatic gravitas. Each had been more complex and integrated in form than the previous one. George had tackled black themes with diligence and seriousness before, initially with *Blue Monday* (later renamed *135th Street*) in 1922.

That piece, with a small cast, was presented as part of a revue and only lasted one night, but now he was prepared to use a larger canvas with a more serious theme and fulfill the desire to literally and figuratively integrate his musical palette.

Porgy was a specific story in a specific place and time that was as mythical to blacks as it was to whites. The first scene on Catfish Row features a craps game with players like drug dealer Sportin'

Along Broadway

Reg. U.S. Pat. Off.

The Edison Musical Magazine

Marie Rappold

This issue has more than 1,250,000 readers

Tales of Tin Pan Alley

"Swanee" and Its Author

ANY of those who imagine that all the writers of popular songs are indifferent to the improvement of American musical taste, should have been present at this interview with George Gershwin.

His words seemed more suited to the learned lecturer than to a composer of popular hits. They would have sounded well in a college hall, and here were we in Tin Pan Alley, the thin walls scarcely keeping out the piano poundings of the "hit" seekers.

"Why if you were in Europe and heard the music of our supposedly native composers, you would be unable to say 'that work is American.' They no more voice the spirit of these United States than did Tchaikowsky represent Russia, or Puccini, Italy, when they wrote in styles of other lands. Do you know, I think Irving Berlin is more typically American than many of those whose works are heard in opera and concert halls."

"That is undoubtedly a fact," I responded, "but the question is whether American music will finally be a new idea like 'jazz' or a development of some phase of Indian or Negro song."

"We seem to have little in common with the Indian, or any sympathetic association that would cause the survival of music founded on tunes of that race," Mr. Gershwin answered. "He may be a picturesque character, but certainly the Redman is not representative of America today.

On the other hand, the darky is a very definite part of our life. His songs and spirituals, in my opinion, form the base upon which our permanent music will be built."

"Is your great song hit, 'Swanee,' a result of that theory?" I asked.

"Yes, I am glad to say that this most liked of my compositions is in accord with my consistent declarations. The very name 'Swanee' has always appealed to me, its easy, flowing sound having a real charm. It was in the spirit of the 'Swanee' and the Southland, and in the music of that section

George Gershwin Composing a Melody

that my song was written, and I am happy to be told that the romance of that land is felt in it, and that at the same time the spirit and energy of our United States is present. We are not all business or all romance, but a combination of the two, and real American music should represent these two characteristics which I tried to unite in 'Swanee' and make represent the soul of this country."

Of his many fine compositions, Mr. Gershwin regards "Swanee" as the best, which is high praise when we remember how popular his other works have been.

"What is your ambition in composing?" I asked.

"Operettas that represent the life and spirit of this country are decidedly my aim. After that may come opera, but I want all my work to have the one element of appealing to the great majority of our people."

Life and Porgy, Heyward's fictionalized beggar on the goat cart. Bess is the girlfriend of a man named Crown who kills another player, Robbins, when the game goes awry. Alone, Bess can only find shelter with Porgy. Life's hard on Catfish Row. There's not enough money to bury Robbins and the fishermen have to work despite oncoming storms which will eventually claim their lives.

Sportin' Life tries to get Bess to come with him to New York but she stays with Porgy, who seems content with his sorry lot ("I Got Plenty O' Nuttin'"). Crown reappears to reclaim his girl

necessarily so," sings Sportin' Life—that he died young. "Look what happened to him," he admonished.) It is true that the show did use the language of the era, including what is now referred to in polite company as the N-word (words Ira removed from later editions of the published score). But George was a liberal in a very segregated society who mixed socially and professionally with African-Americans and was more aware of the black world than most of his compatriots, in part because of his appreciation for the work of William Grant Still, Fats Waller, Art Tatum,

> ## PORGY AND BESS HAS BEEN CRITICIZED FOR ALLEGEDLY STEREOTYPED PORTRAYALS OF BLACK LIFE.

from Porgy, and in Act Three the men fight over Bess and Porgy kills Crown. Sportin' Life moves in on Bess, persuading her that Porgy will go to jail for killing Crown and telling Porgy that he'll be found out because murder victims bleed again when their murderer is present. Porgy refuses police requests to identify Crown's body and by the time he is released from jail, Sportin' Life has spirited Bess away to New York.

Porgy and Bess has been criticized for allegedly stereotyped portrayals of black life—Duke Ellington was complimentary about George's dramatic craft but criticized the inauthenticity of the language. Ellington was a paradox in many ways. In the sixties, he claimed that it was because of George's blaspheming of the Bible in "It Ain't Necessarily So"—"It ain't necessarily so. / De t'ings dat yo li'ble /To read in de Bible— / It ain't

James P. Johnson, and the many jazz artists he listened to in clubs.

W. C. Handy, often called "the father of the blues," had composed the groundbreaking "Memphis Blues" in 1912, a song described by Handy's biographer David Robertson as "the first nationally popular blues tune." George gave Handy a copy of the score of *Rhapsody in Blue* and inscribed it: "To Mr. Handy, Whose early 'blues' songs are the forefathers of this work. With admiration & best wishes, George Gershwin."

In 1926 Handy compiled a scholarly book called *Blues: An Anthology* that included compositions by George, thus acknowledging his prominence in American music and the fact that he had synthesized black music with his own. "[*Rhapsody in Blue*] conveys, and with the help of the blue note as well as by other means for

(OPPOSITE) *George's 1920 interview that reveals his intention to write opera.*

which Gershwin has no one else to thank, a rowdy, troubled humor as marked as that of the best of the old blues," Handy wrote.

Porgy and Bess was going to run on Broadway, which was still the Great White Way, although some strides had been made in integrating shows. The first time a black actor appeared on Broadway with white actors was in 1910, when comedian Bert Williams performed in the *Ziegfeld Follies,* though they were in separate segments and not onstage at the same time. The first integrated musical was *Great Day,* produced in 1929, and a failure. By the thirties there were several Broadway shows that featured black actors, like *The Green Pastures* in 1930, but often the shows were not

The thirties were a time of turmoil in our national history for many reasons, and the economic problems only intensified the racial divide that was becoming more evident in daily life. The NRA (National Recovery Administration) was run by white officials, and African-Americans were not treated fairly nor given the financial aid that they should have received. Blacks were still largely barred from white-run radio shows and yet their music was becoming more mainstream and popular. The stage and film roles afforded African-Americans were almost always stereotypes, and the calls from the black press that it was time for change went unheeded by white establishment.

GEORGE SAW THE STORY AS A LARGE AND COLORFUL CANVAS NOT UNLIKE THE CLASSIC OPERA STORIES THAT WERE STEREOTYPICAL IN MANY WAYS.

integrated—when black actors performed, all the actors on the stage were black.

The first black star to share top billing with white actors on Broadway was Ethel Waters, who appeared in Irving Berlin and Moss Hart's *As Thousands Cheer* in 1933. When the show was in tryouts in Philadelphia, the three white stars refused to take a curtain call with Waters. According to Berlin's daughter Mary Ellin, they were jealous of Waters, who was stealing the show. Berlin decreed that if the four stars couldn't do a curtain call together, there would be no curtain calls. Actors' egos being what they are, the three white actors took a bow alongside Waters the following night.

In 1942, Walter White, executive secretary of the NAACP, traveled to Hollywood and met with the major film producers, asking them to create more realistic and substantial roles for the Negro race, but it had little impact. Into all this entered the idealistic George Gershwin with a vision for an opera that he felt was a glorification of the African contribution to American music, but one that was fraught with controversy. His subject matter was offensively foreign to the northern black community, but George saw the story as a large and colorful canvas not unlike the classic opera stories that were stereotypical in many ways—a convention of the form.

A photo of George, DuBose Heyward, and Ira, signed by George and Heyward to Ira.

AFTER THINKING ABOUT IT FOR SIX YEARS, and dipping in and out intermittently for two more, George worked on *Porgy* solidly for twenty months, from February 1934 to October 1935—eleven on composing the music, and then nine on orchestration. He worked principally with Heyward, the author of the original work, rather than with Ira. Heyward adapted his prose for the recitative sections of the opera, and for the most part George set Heyward's words to music. This was largely the opposite of how he usually worked with Ira, who wrote lyrics to match his brother's melodies. George worked equally well either way. George mostly worked in New York, where he could do his radio show; Heyward was in Charleston; and when later asked to join the project, Ira mediated between them on the libretto and the words to the songs that needed conventional rhyming and helped provide his sheen to the finished version.

Of the songs in the show, using Ira's *Complete Lyrics* as a reference, the lyrics to "Bess, You Is My Woman Now," "I Loves You, Porgy," and "Oh, Heav'nly Father" are credited to DuBose Heyward and Ira Gershwin (not necessarily in that order), and the lyrics to "Oh, I Can't Sit Down!," "It Ain't Necessarily So," "A Redheaded Woman," "There's a Boat Dat's Leavin' Soon for New York," "Oh, Bess, Oh Where's My Bess?" to Ira alone. Credit in the remainder went to Heyward.

If you look up the songs on the ASCAP website (the American Society of Composers, Authors and Publishers), the situation is more confused, with Ira given a co-credit on "Summertime," not one of the songs he worked on, and a victim of music business politics that can muddy the waters. I have a letter (reproduced in this book) in which Ira delineates exactly which lyrics he wrote, as such credits were important personally and professionally. He never would take credit

for something he didn't do. Whatever the true division of labor, DuBose Heyward and Ira agreed to split the lyricist's royalties fifty-fifty.

Ira went to great lengths to share songwriting credit with Heyward in order for him to qualify for an annual royalty check from ASCAP. Heyward needed to have a minimum number of credited compositions (I think it was five or six) that would qualify him for membership. After his work with George on *Porgy and Bess*, Heyward was one song short, and Ira tried to give him a half-credit for "It Ain't Necessarily So," so he could reach the ASCAP minimum. Heyward told Ira he was very sweet to offer, "but no one will ever believe I had anything to do with that song."

(Another example of Ira's generosity in this regard: Yip Harburg suggested just the song title "Make Way for Tomorrow" for the 1944 film *Cover Girl*—Jerome Kern supplied the music—but Ira listed him as a collaborator on the entire song. Conversely, Ira never wanted credit for his lyrical contribution to the end of "Over the Rainbow," considering it to be inconsequential. It happened when Harburg and Arlen were trying to finish the song at Ira's home one night. When asked why he uncharacteristically chimed in and helped complete it, Ira said, "I wanted to make it a short evening.")

Ira also found the time to work on two full-scale revues during this period—*Life Begins at 8:40,* with lyrics written with his old friend Yip Harburg, which began a successful run at the Winter Garden Theatre in August 1934, and the *Ziegfeld Follies* of 1936, whose stars included Fanny Brice and Bob Hope. Vernon Duke wrote the music for the *Follies*, Harold Arlen for *Life Begins at*

George with his cousin, painter Henry Botkin, at Folly Island, South Carolina, in 1934.

8:40. It was Ira, riffing off the title of the best-selling book *Life Begins at Forty,* who suggested the title for the revue, referring to a time when curtains might be going up along Broadway.

> But they wake at eight-forty because—
> Actors love to get your applause—

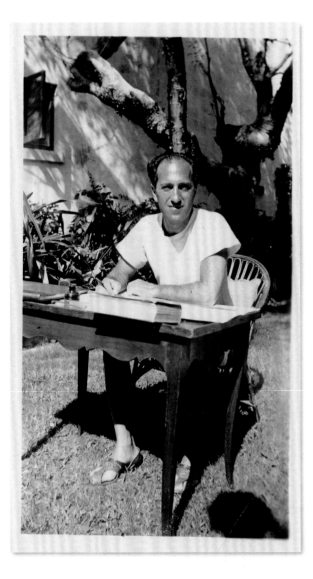

IN THE SUMMER OF 1934, George and his cousin, the artist Henry Botkin, traveled to Folly Island in South Carolina, where George stayed five weeks to work with Heyward. George and Henry shared a sparse cabin on the beach and Gershwin regularly got up hours earlier than he ever did in New York to work. (Even here, though, he found time to have a social life, often accompanying a young widow for walks along the beach.) During this visit, Heyward took George to St. James Island to visit the regional Gullah community at their worship. The ceremony involved rhythmic singing called "shouting" and at one point George joined in, shouting back and forth with the Gullahs. Heyward later said that George was "probably the only white man in America" who could have pulled that off.

George was developing all of his formal compositional skills and by the thirties had come a long way. All of his manuscripts, from *Rhapsody in Blue* to *Porgy and Bess,* are very deftly written out and they're all George. Earlier in his career, George could certainly have orchestrated the *Rhapsody* himself, but he simply didn't have time since it was due in less than a month; thus Ferde Grofé did the arranging chores, working hand in hand with George. Later in his life, George spoke of going back and orchestrating the *Rhapsody* himself, especially since it was now being played by symphony orchestras, but he never took the time to do it and also had become a bit weary of the piece by that point. He had played it more times than he cared to and sometimes seemed to give a perfunctory interpretation at the keys.

George had tremendous technical ability and a deep knowledge of music, but he never became as accomplished an orchestrator as he desired to

George orchestrating Porgy and Bess *in Florida in 1935.*

be, something he felt even more strongly as the swing era started to emerge. When George came to Hollywood in 1936, he requested that the Jimmy Dorsey band play on the soundtrack of *Shall We Dance*, liking the more contemporary evolving swing sound they would bring to his music. The orchestrator for the band, Fud Livingston, was in awe of George and almost imploded at a meeting with him.

A few months later, Gershwin met George Bassman, a wunderkind who was specifically hired to orchestrate the "Drum Dance" performed by Fred Astaire in the movie *A Damsel in Distress*. Seeing Bassman's work, George said, "I wish I could orchestrate like that." Bassman, who was very young, all of twenty-two, had studied at the Boston Conservatory and was a composer as well as an arranger. His biggest song, written in 1932, "I'm Getting Sentimental over You" (words by Ned Washington), was sold outright for twenty-five dollars and later became the theme song for Tommy Dorsey. When Bassman spoke of his meeting with Gershwin years later, he said, "Imagine George Gershwin wishing he could orchestrate like I did!" So although George had orchestrated *Porgy and Bess* brilliantly, he never stopped studying. He was always pushed by that intense desire to be better.

· · · · ·

T HE MET WAS WRONG—THERE WERE, of course, black opera singers who could sing *Porgy*, but they had to be found. Many had the talent and had tried to pursue careers in classical music, but doors were shut, forcing them to pursue other occupa-

tions. Gershwin was told about Todd Duncan, a music professor at Howard University in Washington, D.C., who had sung in *Cavalleria Rusticana* in New York in 1933 with an all-black opera company. George invited Duncan up to audition in his apartment, and George was staggered by what he heard. After a few bars, George offered Duncan the part of Porgy, a role he went on to perform with great success hundreds of times. Hearing the extraordinary voice of Duncan on the surviving recordings, many feel he remains the perfect voice to render the score. He certainly does for me.

When *Porgy and Bess* was tried out in Boston it was too long. Frantic cuts were made and by the time it came to New York, the opera was about forty-five minutes shorter but still lengthy at three and a half hours minus intermissions. *Porgy and Bess*'s opening night was October 10, 1935. George and Ira sat on either side of Kay Swift in a star-packed house. According to *Time* magazine, "half the Somebodies in town" were in attendance. In addition to a cadre of critics, there were movie stars like Leslie Howard, Joan Crawford, and Katharine Hepburn; writers Edna Ferber and J. B. Priestley; the great violinists Kreisler and Heifetz; publishers Condé Nast and Harold Ross; and George's old bandleader partner, Paul Whiteman. The audience loved it but, as always after a first night, everyone involved in the show waited anxiously for the reviews.

A new Gershwin show was an important event, so newspaper coverage was heavy, more so because no one was quite sure what they would be seeing. The *Times* sent both music critic Olin Downes and theater critic Brooks Atkinson. Atkinson wrote that this *Porgy* was a better play than the original *Porgy* and deferred to his colleague on the music. Downes complained that one minute he was watching an opera, then an operetta, then a Broadway entertainment. (George himself described his work as a "folk opera," which wasn't entirely helpful.) Ten days after the opening, Downes wrote a long follow-up piece in which he confirmed that *Porgy* was indeed an opera.

Composer Virgil Thomson, whose own opera with an all-black cast, *Four Saints in Three Acts* (with a libretto by Gertrude Stein), played on Broadway in 1934, was famously ungenerous. "I

In some cases they were unable to proffer much of an opinion.

Yet it is also true that many critics were positive in their reviews, and it's an exaggeration that the work was universally panned. Some understood and loved it from the start and accepted it in the same way we do today, but with all of the other issues swirling around the work and so many opinions, it seemed at times to be swallowed up in a mire of confusion that obscured its purity.

From today's perspective, the arguments about what kind of musical or dramatic work

NO ONE HAD TRIED TO COMBINE SO MANY DISPARATE MUSICAL STYLES INTO A SINGLE WORK.

don't like fake folklore, nor fidgety accompaniments, nor six-part choruses, nor bittersweet harmony, nor gefilte-fish orchestration." When his critique of *Porgy* was later reprinted in a collected book of his writings, Thomson expunged the gefilte fish reference for a less Semitic-specific slur.

Not for the first time, George's critics were suffering from what we might call category confusion. Simply put, no one had tried to combine so many disparate musical styles—American folk music, European-inspired opera, jazz—into a single work, and those who passed judgment on works of theater and music were confounded and angered by the lack of neat classification of styles that were required by the establishment of the time. Some of the critics were more concerned with labeling what they were watching than in trying to give an honest assessment of the work.

Porgy is seem unimportant when we remember what it achieves in the hearts and minds of the audience. While it is unequivocally regarded as an opera, it still causes debate among some who tiresomely question its place in the larger field of classical music. *Porgy* is filled with a power of inspiration and craft that elevates it into the pantheon of musical achievement. Gershwin's integration of musical and theatrical elements is so complex and astute that it has taken generations to fully grasp the enormity of his achievement. It is the precursor and inspiration for much that has come after. *West Side Story* and the works of Sondheim would not exist without *Porgy*. When Stephen Sondheim held in his hands the original manuscript of *Porgy*, he was moved to tears, and one of his tears spilled onto the fragile score, leaving a slight stain that will forever bind the two composers.

In a piece in the *Times* on October 20, 1935, George defended his description of *Porgy and Bess* as a folk opera. He explained that it was a folk tale whose characters would sing folk music, but rather than using existing folk tunes he wrote his spirituals and did so in the form of an opera. As far as George was concerned, DuBose Heyward's story had the dramatic intensity required of an opera but because he was writing an opera for the theater, George believed he was within his rights to write songs, albeit in an operatic form. George knew he was toying with an established tradition but was comfortable doing so. After all, he writes, "*Carmen* is almost a collection of song hits."

The term "folk opera" wasn't without precedent. In 1919, composer Reginald De Koven and playwright Percy MacKaye unveiled their *Rip Van Winkle: Folk-Opera in Three Acts*. De Koven wrote in a more traditional classical form, while

A later production of Porgy and Bess.

Gershwin created a new musical amalgam and knew he was breaking new ground. As George correctly noted in his *New York Times* article, no one had written an opera about "Negro life in America." He understood he was creating an entirely new genre—this "opera for the theatre"—one he hoped would have a broader appeal than regular opera. George was, as ever, aware of what an audience wanted. In the Rodgers and Hart song "The Lady Is a Tramp," one of the reasons that the song's protagonist is a "tramp" is because she goes to opera and "stays wide awake." Gershwin knew of what he spoke.

*P*ORGY AND BESS RAN at the Alvin Theatre for 124 performances. This was an excellent result when measured against the regular run of a new opera at the Met, but it wasn't sufficient to keep the opera playing on Broadway long enough for it to break even. The Theatre Guild cut ticket prices to try to prolong the run, but the production—and George, who with Ira had invested in it—lost money. Hoping to recoup some losses, the Guild sent the opera on tour to Philadelphia, Pittsburgh, Chicago, and Washington, D.C., and that was the end of the first production.

A year after George's death, his friend Merle Armitage mounted the first West Coast production, but by and large the work was heard by relatively few in the thirties. In 1940, Decca belatedly recorded an album of selections featuring members of the original 1935 cast, and that helped with *Porgy's* visibility. It was a well-, not best-, selling recording.

While *Porgy and Bess* has achieved immortality around the world, there are still many music fans who have never seen it, perhaps because it was created in the only medium in which Gershwin felt it would achieve its full expression: opera. Not everybody likes opera, and even if they do, productions of this one are not seen as often as revivals of any given classic Broadway musical.

A much shorter version of *Porgy* was created by director Cheryl Crawford in 1942, but it was not the original opera at all. Crawford cut the cast and orchestra, removed almost all the recitative, and turned *Porgy and Bess* into a more standard Broadway musical with dialogue and songs. This was the first successful production.

The changes were made with the blessing of Ira, and he was very fond of the new incarnation, feeling it worked well in that mode, though he missed much of the connecting music that was

(LEFT) *Todd Duncan and Anne Brown as Porgy and Bess.*
(RIGHT) *George taking a bow at the curtain call of the premiere.*

removed. This was the production for which Ira removed the N-word from the libretto, something he had wanted to do for a while, realizing that the world had already changed a great deal since 1935. He also expressed regret, saying that if he had realized how deeply hurtful the word was to black people, he never would have included it in the first place. The fact that George and Heyward were seemingly unaware of the way that word would deeply affect so many is in itself telling. Ira said he had to wait until Heyward died to remove the offensive word and replace it with various

Europe, making a stop on Broadway, and then traveling all over the world in an ambassadorial role courtesy of the U.S. State Department. This tour helped make *Porgy and Bess* a worldwide favorite. It also made stars of Price and Warfield. After a visit to the Soviet Union in 1955 (memorialized amusingly but inaccurately by the razor-sharp pen of Truman Capote in his book *The Muses Are Heard*), *Porgy* was mostly absent from the stage for two decades.

There was a movie version in 1959 directed by Otto Preminger (who replaced the original

> THIS WAS THE PRODUCTION FOR WHICH IRA REMOVED THE N-WORD FROM THE LIBRETTO, SOMETHING HE HAD WANTED TO DO FOR A WHILE.

other phrases that fit the scan of the music. It's a good thing he made those changes, because by the forties Etta Moten, then starring as Bess, refused to sing the original words anyway, and they would have lost their leading lady. In this attenuated form, *Porgy and Bess* was again more successful than the original opera.

In 1952 producer-director Robert Breen toured a production with some of the original recitatives restored, but the production was still more theatrically oriented than opera-like, with various dance sequences interpolated and much spoken dialogue remaining. The stars were Leontyne Price as Bess, William Warfield as Porgy, Cab Calloway as Sportin' Life, with Maya Angelou taking a role as a specialty dancer. It was a huge international success, touring the United States and

stage director, Rouben Mamoulian, at the helm), starring Sidney Poitier and Dorothy Dandridge. Though André Previn won an Oscar for his scoring of the film, it was a disaster—Catfish Row was given the Hollywood treatment and looked like a very pretty slum with inhabitants outfitted in lovely costumes. The failure of the film damaged the perception of the work, and it was eventually suppressed by Ira and the family. It took several years for the reputation of the opus to recover.

In 1976, Lorin Maazel and the Cleveland Orchestra recorded what he called "The World Premiere Complete Performance," the entire piece without the cuts made during the 1935 tryout in Boston. A year later, the opera was revived (and recorded) by the Houston Grand Opera, which also recorded the original, uncut version, which slipped back three uses of the N-word, something that distressed Ira greatly.

It was these recordings that Ira and I talked about the first time we met. The Houston Opera record had just been released and Ira was signing copies with wonder and satisfaction. Over forty years after he originally worked on it, there was finally a full document of what had been set down. It was hard for him to believe that it had come to pass. Ira and I agreed that we preferred Houston to Cleveland in this case, as they had the advantage of actually mounting their production and spending time to perform and hone the presentation. It was nirvana to watch Ira listen to it, as he was lost in a world of memory and melody.

In 2006, John Mauceri and the Nashville Symphony Orchestra presented a recording that preserved the cuts made for the 1935 Broadway run before it transferred from Boston. Mauceri argued that the longer Boston version was actually George's rehearsal score and was never intended for performance. He compared the surviving 1935 conductor's score, the cast's scores, and the original orchestra parts in order to, he said, "construct the version approved and supervised by George Gershwin." (Well, yes, he did approve it, but that doesn't mean he wouldn't have continued to make changes for subsequent productions.) This was a new *Porgy*, one that speeded up "Summertime" and slowed down "A Woman Is a Sometime Thing" so they were performed at the same tempo.

The Los Angeles Opera did a production, by the prolific Broadway and opera director and current head of the Glimmerglass Festival Francesca Zambello, that toured the United States. Director Trevor Nunn's *Porgy and Bess: The Musical* opened in London in 2006, which was ultimately a succès d'estime, which, to quote George S. Kaufman, means a success that runs out of steam.

It was in the spirit of the much altered 1942 version of which Ira approved that Mike Strunsky (Ira's nephew and heir) conceived the idea of creating a 2012 Broadway musical version, believing that it could stand alone as a separate work that wouldn't affect the original opera, which would continue on unfettered. After all, he reasoned, if it were successful more people could see *Porgy* on Broadway in a matter of months than could see it in years in an operatic form. Perhaps seeing it as a musical would spark people's interest in the original and steer them toward it. Ira and George would have approved of this concept—if not the execution.

The show opened in Cambridge, Massachusetts, for its pre-Broadway tryout, not far from where the full opera had its original tryout in Boston in 1935. Interestingly, there was an outcry about changes that had been made before anyone even saw the production, largely because of a *New York Times* interview with the principals of the creative team, in which they came off sounding as if they were fixing a long-flawed work. The alterations were far beyond simply dispensing with the recitative and creating dialogue, as had happened in 1942; they were changing the ending and creating new dialogue to flesh out the characters that they felt were not fully formed in the original.

On it went, and musical theater aficionados began to fret, and then to blog. Then Stephen Sondheim, in response to that interview, wrote an impassioned letter criticizing the team for meddling with a work that is his single favorite musical, one that he would take with him to a desert island before one of his own works. A public frenzy ensued, and the show was generally not well reviewed in that tryout.

There was an amazing metamorphosis that occurred between the troubled tryout and the opening on Broadway. I attended the opening of the tryout, and I liked many of the performers, their singing and their passion. However, the show was indeed flawed, primarily because of the orchestrations and alteration of Gershwin's score, which sometimes rendered it unrecognizable. The adaptor, Diedre Murray, a talented and well-respected musician, made offensive and emasculating alterations to Gershwin's beloved masterpiece, and I was confused. Remembering that Ira said he didn't mind changes if it made something better, I knew that this had the opposite effect and couldn't understand how anyone could come to these musical choices. They musically removed the drama and passion and left a mishmash to middling effect. If you're going to do *Porgy and Bess*, then why remove the thing that most moves the listener: the genius of Gershwin?

In their defense, the Gershwin family had given carte blanche to the producers to follow their vision without outside opinion until after it played in Cambridge; then they would discuss what needed to be done. So the free hand was used, the changes began, and when I was asked my opinion by several principals, I practically screamed that they had to go back to the original Gershwin harmonies. I was not the only one to express this; I was part of a Greek chorus. Change the style, the tempo, the feel, the instrumentation if you wish, but keep the essential harmonic palette; otherwise you're lost.

For the transfer to Broadway they did make massive alterations, and the show became a genuine box office hit, being extended and even garnering a cast recording. The audience felt the power of the show was preserved and stood up every night with heartfelt standing ovations. Now I hope that the dream of a viable Broadway version will live alongside the beloved original, and *Porgy and Bess* will continue to find new fans.

With the success of this Broadway *Porgy*, there's still room to create yet another version with 1940s-style Ellington arrangements or the sheen of Nelson Riddle's streamlined 1950s swing style. All of these could be melded to the story and music in a way that would resist comparison to the original and could stand mightily on its own. Maybe someday.

THINK THERE IS A PROBLEM with claiming to know the definitive version of any piece by a dead composer, *Porgy and Bess* or otherwise. Some people argue that George wanted his uncut opera to be heard, others that he made the cuts for Broadway, so we must listen to that version. Mauceri is adamant that his is the correct version and the last word of the composer, but it ain't necessarily so. Had he lived George undoubtedly would have made revisions to strengthen it dramatically and musically, but with his early demise we are left with many questions that will never be definitively answered.

I don't believe it's possible to claim that one production of *Porgy* is closer to what George intended than any other. Gershwin was constantly evolving as a writer and an artist. Had he lived, and *Porgy and Bess* been revived, George would have made changes and cuts and continued to refine and adapt and experiment with the work until he found a version that he liked. And then, with every succeeding production, he might have made more changes. I feel that neither the complete uncut version nor the Mauceri version is what George would have presented, because one is still too long and the other cuts music that he adored, like "The Buzzard Song" and the Jazzbo Brown music. He almost certainly would have fixed it. What we need is someone to channel George Gershwin and tell us what the hell he wants!

When it comes to choosing the production I like the best, or what length I'd prefer the opera to be, I'm going to sound like Switzerland. Why? Because I adore every note of the Houston Opera production as a recorded work when I have the time to relax and allow myself to be absorbed into

could live alongside the full operatic presentation. Ira approved such variations when he trusted those involved. I do not ever want to witness a hip-hop version of *Porgy* (as recently suggested by a famous Hollywood film director) or other such waterings down of his music. There is much room for creative expansion of what is there if one has the basic understanding of the composer's intention. Being a man of the theater, he understood the necessity of making changes, but we must never lose the essence of his opera, and regardless of how it is reimagined we must always come back to *Porgy* in its operatic form.

Tastes change, too. Sometimes *La Bohème* is performed in three acts, sometimes in two. That's just the way it is. Some great songs are cut from shows and then restored. "There Won't Be Trumpets"

THE ADAPTOR MADE OFFENSIVE AND EMASCULATING ALTERATIONS TO GERSHWIN'S BELOVED MASTERPIECE.

it. Seeing the Houston production onstage was exhilarating, but I confess that I was equally tired and felt at times that it was too long.

While I stand by Ira's desire that the opera be seen at its full length, I also know we live in a time when attention spans are getting shorter. The length of a classical concert in the 1800s was twice as long as our average performance is now, and audiences are starting to want more shows without intermissions. I am not against seeing *Porgy and Bess* as a musical (i.e., without the recitative) if it is handled carefully and lovingly, because I would consider this to be a different incarnation that

was cut from Stephen Sondheim and Arthur Laurents's show *Anyone Can Whistle* just before it opened on Broadway in 1964 (at the Neil Simon Theatre, the old Alvin). The show lasted for only twelve previews and nine performances, but Sondheim wanted the song restored for a recent revival and it was also included in the CD reissue of the original cast recording. But what would have happened if Sondheim hadn't been around to reinstate the song for the CD? The composer's wish would have been lost and whether we knew it or not, the true version of the musical would be denied us.

It's wrong to assume that the longest version of *Porgy* is the best version, or the version that George preferred. Songs get cut from shows all the time, and for many reasons. The most common reason is that the show is running too long (not many shows run short), but there are often complex artistic considerations to take into account. Sondheim has written that immediately before "There Won't Be Trumpets" was performed in *Anyone Can Whistle,* Lee Remick delivered a monologue that got such a terrific audience reception in previews that the song was overshadowed.

In some cases a song is cut because the featured performer is unable to sing it. Cole Porter wrote the standard "Easy to Love" for William Gaxton in his 1934 classic *Anything Goes.* But Gaxton couldn't sing it, so the song was cut in rehearsal. Two years later Porter put the song into an MGM movie, *Born to Dance.* The song finally

appeared onstage in *Anything Goes* in the 1987 Broadway revival.

The verse of the song "This Is New" was cut from *Lady in the Dark* because Victor Mature couldn't handle it. Perhaps the producers had thought Mature could sing because he sounded so wonderful in his Hollywood musicals. The only problem: it wasn't his voice. In another instance, Louis Jourdan, the original star of *On a Clear Day You Can See Forever,* was let go during out-of-town tryouts. He sounded wonderful in the musical film *Gigi,* and it was really his singing voice on the soundtrack. But the hours that the sound editors spent splicing together the countless takes to get a decent performance couldn't be duplicated live on the stage. So rather than cut the entire score, they had to replace the actor.

THERE ARE PERHAPS ONLY A HANDFUL of songs that can be extracted from *Porgy and Bess,* as most of the songs are so wedded to the plot that they don't stand up out of context. While the brothers often thought in terms of writing songs that were extractable from a score, *Porgy and Bess* was the exception. George did hope, of course, that the songs would have popularity outside of the theater, but he was less concerned about that than their suitability for the characters who sang them. Thus a song like "I Got Plenty O' Nuttin'" had slim chances of being a popular hit even from the outset.

Still, this is one of the most famous songs from *Porgy.* "I Got Plenty O' Nuttin'" was written differently from most of George and Ira's songs because of the contribution of DuBose Heyward. The three main creative talents working on the opera—George, Ira, and Heyward—were in the

Original cover art for Porgy and Bess *sheet music by Ben Harris.*

same room when the song was created. Ira and George had evolved a shorthand when writing songs, and it was not possible for Heyward to have the same ease of creation with George before Ira came on the scene. After Ira was asked to be involved to help lyrically smooth the way, he found that Heyward had good ideas and was easy to work with, sensing the synergy between the two and gently contributing where appropriate.

As Ira wrote in *Lyrics on Several Occasions*, there was a feeling that Porgy needed something "lighter and gayer" to sing than he had to that point in Act One. George started playing a melody and Ira and Heyward liked it at once. For the third or fourth time in his life, Ira thought of a title immediately—"I got plenty o' nuttin'"—and then he came up with the complementary line, too, "An' nuttin's plenty for me." Ira said he'd get to the rest of the song when he could, but Heyward asked if he might have a crack at finishing it because, thus far, he'd only written words which George had then set to music. Ira worked on what Heyward sent him two weeks later and "polished" it up, creating what Ira called in *Lyrics on Several Occasions* a "50-50 collaborative effort."

By 1959, when Ira's *Lyrics* was published, "Nuttin'" had become "Nuthin.'" Ira seemed uncertain when and how the change was made. In a letter about credits to *Porgy and Bess* songs to Alfred Simon of October 1971, Ira notes the spelling given in his own book. "Re 'I Got Plenty O' Nuttin',' " he writes Simon, "I believe, am not sure, that on later editions [of *Porgy*] I changed 'Nuttin'' to 'Nuthin'. . . .'" He refers in the first instance in the letter to "Nuttin'," and I prefer to use that spelling here.

George was very proud of this particular creation, as it was a grand realization of his desire to express something fresh in character development for the score. It was unconventional and deceptively folklike. When he played it for Todd Duncan, George remarked that it was his first great aria and called it his "banjo song." The orchestration was among the first that called for a banjo in the pit of an opera orchestra (Austrian composer Ernst Krenek's 1927 work *Jonny spielt auf—Johnny Plays On*—about the career of an African-American bandleader, has one too), and when George later created an orchestral suite from *Porgy*, he made the banjo part the solo in all its down-home glory.

A SONG LIKE "I GOT PLENTY O' NUTTIN'" HAD SLIM CHANCES OF BEING A POPULAR HIT EVEN FROM THE OUTSET.

This song has rarely received an individual pop recording because of its inseparability from the plot and the fact that it is not in the standard thirty-two-bar song form, since George didn't write it with thoughts of a pop career outside the walls of the theater. Because he wrote it with such specific harmonic requirements, once one has heard it in the original form, it sounds hollow without the full treatment.

There was a contemporary recording by none other than Bing Crosby, who was the most important pop singer of the thirties, and a dance band version by the Leo Reisman Orchestra featuring Broadway alumnus Edward Matthews, but recordings through the years have been few and far between. There is an amazing pop recording by Frank Sinatra that features a truly inspired Nelson Riddle arrangement, and a tour de force by Barbra Streisand with Peter Matz. Rosemary Clooney also sang it, as did Ella Fitzgerald, Sammy Davis, Jr., and, most recently, Brian Wilson, in a version that, sadly, is not likely destined for the ages.

My interest in performing the song has grown. I previously had no desire to hear the work out of the context of the original opera. I still think that the original setting is perfect. Then I started thinking about all the people who might never know the song, as they might not be likely ever to see *Porgy and Bess,* and how both Gershwins appreciated hearing different approaches to their songs. Indeed, I have a 1936 radio broadcast where George is introducing a marvelously gifted singer and pianist known by the single name Ramona and highly praises her rendition of another work from *Porgy,* "There's a Boat Dat's Leavin' Soon for New York."

Every time I approach a performance of a Gershwin song, I think about Ira and hope he would like what I'm doing. Even though he was very shy, we were close enough that he was not reticent about expressing his honest opinions about my performances, often with praise and sometimes the reverse, with devastating effect, when he didn't like a rendition. My fragile ego learned to become stronger from those experiences.

Expression of the jubilant nature of the lyric is essential to convey in order for the song to truly work. Ira and DuBose Heyward certainly captured a state of mind that makes having few worldly goods sound most attractive, and every time it's sung in the show, it never fails to move the audience with the simple heartfelt message of Porgy's "banjo song." "Plenty O' Nuttin'" will likely never be considered a great pop standard outside of *Porgy and Bess,* but in context it is an essential work, delightful and deeply fulfilling. And that's plenty enough for me.

THE ORCHESTRATION WAS AMONG THE FIRST THAT CALLED FOR A BANJO IN THE PIT OF AN OPERA ORCHESTRA.

While he loved "I Got Plenty O'Nuttin'," Ira's favorite piece of music from the opera is not one of the famous songs in it. There is a beautiful section in the first act that Porgy sings called "They Pass by Singing" that Ira liked the best.

They pass by singing, they pass by crying.
They look at my door and they keep on movin'.
When God made cripple, he made him to be lonely.
Night time, day time, you got to travel that lonesome road.
Night time, day time, you got to travel that lonesome road.

(OPPOSITE) *Ira's letter to Alfred Simon about whom to credit for which songs in* Porgy and Bess.

IRA GERSHWIN
1021 NORTH ROXBURY DRIVE
BEVERLY HILLS, CALIFORNIA 90210

October 25, 1971

Mr. Alfred E. Simon
400 East 59th Street
New York, N.Y. 10022

Dear Al,

I enclose the various Porgy and Bess credits you asked
for. Also a few notes at random - not for publication of course -
merely for your edification and, eventually, your wastebasket.

Re "I Got Plenty O' Nuttin'": I believe, am not sure,
that on later editions I changed "Nuttin'" to "Nuthin'"; certainly
that's the spelling I have in Lyrics O.S.O., p. 358.

Re "Bess, You Is My Woman Now": I worked out this duet
with George while DuBose was in Charleston. Since, however, I
used several of his lines from the libretto I thought it only
fair to give him full credit as col[...]

Re "Oh, Doctor Jesus": Du[...]
prayer which began either with "Oh[...]
Doctor Jesus" - I forget which. T[...]
to do six prayers to be sung pract[...]
wrote the additional five.

Re "A Red Headed Woman": [...]
had anything to do with this lady. [...]
Southern gent to tangle with her. [...]
charming men I ever knew.)

Re "Oh Bess, Oh Where's [...]
by George and me, including the in[...]
sung to Porgy by Serena and Maria[...]
its can be I.G. and G.G. (Later:[...]

Mr. Alfred E. Simon   -2-   October 25, 1971

[...]eet music some years ago - doubtless in connection
[...]oldwyn movie - I.G. alone is named, so perhaps let's
[...]hat way.)

[...]es, I realize what a back-breaker you and Dick are
[...] up-dating and expanding Encyclopedia of Theatre
[...]hether all the tough research is fully acclaimed or
[...]eat satisfaction is, or should be, that you two have
[...]cientious as is humanly possible. Anything more
[...]s, good statements) is velvet. My fingers are
[...]ots of "Anything more."

[...]ends her best, as does,

Always,

Ira

IRA GERSHWIN

LYRIC CREDITS FOR "PORGY AND BESS"

(First act lyrics by Heyward)..then:

IT TAKE A LONG PULL TO GET THERE (DuBose H.)
I GOT PLENTY O' NUTTIN' (I.G. + DuBose H.)
WOMAN TO LADY - (DuBose H.)
BESS, YOU IS MY WOMAN NOW (I.G. + DuBose H.)
OH, I CAN'T SIT DOWN - (I.G.)
IT AIN'T NECESSARILY SO (I.G.)
WHAT YOU WANT WITH BESS? (DuBose H.)
TIME AND TIME AGAIN (DuBose H.)
STREET CRIES (STRAWBERRY WOMAN, CRAB MAN) (DuBose H.)
I LOVES YOU, PORGY (I.G. + DuBose H.)
OH, DE LAWD SHAKE DE HEAVEN (DuBose H.)
A RED HEADED WOMAN (I.G.)
OH, DOCTOR JESUS (I.G. + DuBose)
CLARA, DON'T YOU BE DOWNHEARTED (DuBose H.)
THERE'S A BOAT DAT'S LEAVIN' SOON FOR NEW YORK (I.G.)
* OH, BESS, OH WHERE'S MY BESS? (I.G.) (This title correct)
I'M ON MY WAY (DuBose H.)

                              variously
*I've seen this title listed/as "Where's My Bess?" and
"Bess, Oh Where's My Bess?". Which do you prefer?
    See what I mean, Ira?!! ("Oh Bess, Oh Where's My Bess"
is the title on the sheet music. [No question mark])

I even have a home recording of Ira singing that passage in a full voice with uncharacteristic abandon, being carried away by its power.

My favorite parts of *Porgy* are many. "My Man's Gone Now"; "Bess, You Is My Woman Now"; "I Loves You, Porgy"; the Hurricane Fugue; the street cries; "Oh, I Can't Sit Down"; and on and on. It is a feast of musical riches and plumbs the depths of emotion and the highs and lows of the human condition. From the very first notes of the introduction through the establishing of Catfish Row, there are in the first thirty minutes alone a dizzying array of great melodies and themes that pour forth and continue through the whole exotic journey. The development of those themes and the varied ways in which George expresses subtle emotional nuances of character are magnificent and humbling.

When Gershwin was told by a friend that *Porgy and Bess* was a masterwork, he replied, "Thank you, I think so, too." That was not ego; it was his recognition that what he had created was channeled through him and that he was only the vessel. Perhaps that is why he called his publishing companies New World Music and later New Dawn Music.

As much as I deeply love "Summertime," it's one of the few Gershwin songs I'm not fond of singing. It's so perfect in *Porgy and Bess* that I don't like it nearly as much outside of the context for which Gershwin wrote it. The song appears early in the opera and is its first major aria. It is sung by Clara as a lullaby to her infant and is reprised twice. I do sing "Summertime" frequently, though, because people love to hear it, and I try to submerge myself in the spirit of the source. I'd sometimes rather listen to a particular song than sing it because I don't feel interpretatively I always have the correct sensibility or I'm vocally in the right place to sing it. After all, "Summertime" was written for a soaring soprano.

Also, the accompaniment written for the song is so specific, so delicate and beautiful and fragile, that divorced from that setting, the song instantly loses a lot of its force for me. The melody itself is clearly gorgeous, and that's why the song has become one of the most familiar and beloved Gershwin pieces, but one of my favorite

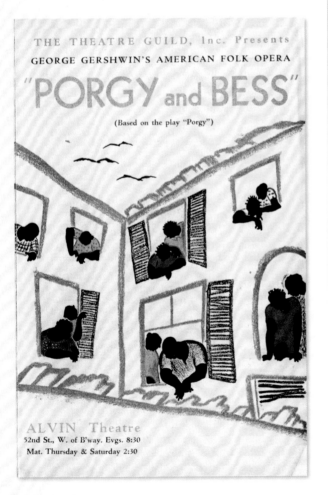

Advertising flyer for Porgy and Bess *at the Alvin Theatre.*

things about the song is Gershwin's original setting for the opera, a beautiful, alternating ostinato that undulates underneath the melody throughout the lullaby. Unfortunately, it is never or at least rarely performed that way outside of the opera. No one ever uses those specific harmonies and those figures, which to me deprives the song of what makes it most beautiful.

In my mind I hear "Summertime" sung in the original key, by a soprano crooning it to her babe in arms. That's why when I hear a singer in a jazz club belt it or bring out the embellished vocal roller coaster, it leaves me cold. Unfortunately that's the way most people like to hear it. There may be a time and a place for these vocal pyrotechnics, but

the existing treasury of American songs. They think of it as being like "Shenandoah" or "Deep River," a melody that evolved from the collective American experience, in this case sung by slaves in cotton fields. The song has that kind of timelessness and narrative power to it, which is a testament to the composer's genius.

SIXTEEN MONTHS AFTER the first incarnation of *Porgy and Bess* closed in Washington, D.C., George died. For a Tin Pan Alley songwriter to compose an opera was an ambitious enough feat, but to produce something as timeless as *Porgy and Bess* defies the odds and gives me absolute belief that music comes from a divine

THERE ARE IN THE FIRST THIRTY MINUTES ALONE A DIZZYING ARRAY OF GREAT MELODIES AND THEMES.

this isn't it. I even like Janis Joplin's version of "Summertime," in spite of the fact that it breaks the rules of how I normally want to hear it. Of course, there are many people who probably know Janis Joplin singing it but have never heard the original setting of "Summertime." It's one of George's greatest triumphs, with a wonderful lyric by Heyward. If ever you hear it playing, be sure to remind anyone who doesn't know who wrote it.

George said his goal with *Porgy* was to create his own folk tunes, authentic-sounding yet original, for his cripples, craps players, fishermen, and ne'er-do-wells. He was clearly successful at that, because it's often assumed, especially by non-Americans, that he borrowed "Summertime" from

source. Simply put, *Porgy and Bess* ranks as one of the great artistic achievements in twentieth-century music. And that was the bar George had set for himself. He said that *Porgy and Bess* would combine the drama and romance of *Carmen* with the beauty of *Die Meistersinger von Nürnberg*. Those comparisons are interesting in the context of the times, because at one point opera was as important a part of the average American household as popular music, and accounted for a large percentage of sales of recorded music. Today, people who know Gershwin and his "mongrel" opera have never heard *Carmen* or *Die Meistersinger*, so George has achieved his goal of reaching the people to that extent. And because George died so soon after *Porgy*, it plays a very prominent part in "what might have been" discussions.

In 1959, more than twenty years after George died, Leonard Bernstein wrote about *Porgy* in his book *The Joy of Music*. He praised some of George's recitatives, and said they indicate that George's music would have "reached *its own* perfection eventually." (My italics.)

With *Porgy* you suddenly realize that Gershwin was a great, great theater composer. Perhaps that's what was wrong with his concert music: it was really theater music thrust into a concert hall. What he would have done in the theater in another ten or twenty years! And then he would still have been a young man! What a loss! Will America ever realize the loss?

WHEN WRITING ABOUT SOMETHING as sublime as *Porgy and Bess*, I always feel a sense of the inability to express what makes it what it is. It's not simply the music in George's opera that has had such an impact; *Porgy* helps describe and represent a historic shift in our country's culture. The *Porgy* legacy is multilayered. One particular story that has never left me without a deep feeling of pathos and pride is the one I wish to recount.

Years ago I had the thrill of meeting many of the principals involved in the original 1935 production, among them Anne Brown, the original Bess. She recounted a story of the final days of the *Porgy* tour, when it was winding down as a financial disappointment but a great source of artistic pride. When the company was told that they would be appearing in Washington, D.C., Anne was thrilled because her family would be able to come and see the production, since they lived in nearby Baltimore. Then she

found out that the National Theatre, where they were set to play, was a segregated house and that no blacks would be allowed. She immediately went to George and told him that she wouldn't be continuing with the tour and when he asked why, she explained. He was mortified and told her he'd see what he could do. There was little hope that the situation would change, for it would be nothing short of a miracle to try and alter the long-held racist policy in effect at our nation's capital.

HE HAD THE NATIONAL THEATRE DESEGREGATED FOR THE SINGLE WEEK THAT *PORGY* WAS TO PLAY THERE.

Gershwin called Anne a few days later and triumphantly announced, "You're going to Washington!" She was confused until she realized what had happened. George had accomplished the impossible. He had the National Theatre desegregated for the single week that *Porgy* was to play there, and blacks and whites could sit together with equality. After *Porgy* departed, the National reverted to its segregationist policy, and eventually the owner of the theater closed it rather than bend to the demand that it be integrated.

When it finally reopened in 1952, the theater was at last fully integrated, and among the first shows to play there was the newly mounted revival of *Porgy and Bess*. •

Best wishes Todd Duncan Porgy 1935 1994

Of this limited first edition of

PORGY AND BESS

250 were printed

in October, 1935

this copy being number *48*

signed by

George Gershwin

DuBose Heyward

Ira Gershwin

Ruby Elzy

Georgette Harvey (Maria)

Anne Brown ("Bess")

John W. Bubbles (as "Sporting Life")

J. L. Buck as (Mingo)

Edward Matthews (Jake)

Helen Dowdy Strawberry Woman

John E. Garth III (Undertaker)

"THEY CAN'T TAKE THAT AWAY FROM ME"

from *Shall We Dance*, 1937

VERSE

Our romance won't end on a sorrowful note,
Though by tomorrow you're gone;
The song is ended, but as the songwriter wrote,
"The melody lingers on."
They may take you from me,
I'll miss your fond caress.
But though they take you from me,
I'll still possess:

REFRAIN

The way you wear your hat,
The way you sip your tea,
The mem'ry of all that—
No, no! They can't take that away from me!

The way your smile just beams,
The way you sing off key,
The way you haunt my dreams—
No, no! They can't take that away from me!

We may never, never meet again
On the bumpy road to love,
Still I'll always, always keep
The mem'ry of—

The way you hold your knife,
The way we danced till three,
The way you've changed my life—
No, no! They can't take that away from me!
No! They can't take that away from me!

· CHAPTER 10 ·

HOLLYWOOD AND THE END

OCTOBER 6, 1927, was the day the first talking feature film, Al Jolson's *The Jazz Singer,* was released. I will never forget that date—not because of *The Jazz Singer* but because it was the day my mother was born. (And no, she doesn't mind my saying so.) Every year on her birthday I have to resist breaking into a Jolson-infused rendition of "Happy Birthday." I have sung Jolson's "My Mammy" to her on numerous occasions, but less often since racial sensitivity made that song taboo. Jolson often performed in blackface, as he did in *The Jazz Singer* for "My Mammy," and the stereotypes that it perpetuated were terrible. (The phenomenon of blackface is a discussion for another book, but its heartrending impact on society should weigh heavily on the shoulders of anyone who celebrates entertainers of that era.) Still, Jolson was an incredibly dynamic performer. George Burns once told me Jolson was the finest entertainer he ever saw on a stage, and Burns saw thousands of acts over his one hundred years of life. That includes anyone you wish to name from the twentieth century, from Fred Astaire to Judy Garland to Frank Sinatra to Michael Jackson. Burns said electricity would run up your spine when you saw Jolson in action. He once was part of an audience in the Midwest that waited two hours for Jolson to show up because his train was late getting into town. Everyone stayed.

Ira, George, and Guy Bolton in a press shot for the film Delicious *in 1930.*

Jolson was probably the first superstar, as popular overseas as he was in America. The pairing of Jolson with the talking picture was genius. Although Jolson was, by all accounts, better live than in movies, the total number of people who'd seen him perform in person during his previous twenty years in the entertainment business was dwarfed instantly by the number of people who saw *The Jazz Singer*.

By today's standards *The Jazz Singer* seems maudlin, at times sophomoric, yet Jolson still displays a magnetism together with a personal humanity that he lacked in real life. In the movie, he sang six songs, including Irving Berlin's "Blue

Skies," "Mother of Mine, I Still Have You," and, at the end of the movie, "My Mammy," a song he first performed in his revue *Sinbad* (which also featured "Swanee," George Gershwin's first hit). Fans heard him emote, "I'd walk a million miles for one of your smiles . . ." This would become the iconic image of him, in blackface, down on one knee with his arms pleadingly outstretched, ". . . My Ma-mmy!" Jolson also improvised some lines of dialogue that stayed in the picture, though originally he was only supposed to sing.

The movie was a major hit for Warner Brothers. It was relatively cheap to make and earned more than $2 million, helping the studio increase its revenue five-fold for the year. *The Jazz Singer* started as a gimmick—sound—but when fans flocked to this new art form, studios raced to meet the demand. (The concept of talking pictures was so foreign to audiences of the time that critics of the brothers Warner referred to their upcoming talking film as "Warner's Folly.") Jolson then made a string of undistinguished films with diminishing success over the next ten years. By *The Singing Kid* in 1936, he was far from the biggest star in the movies. The medium he had pioneered soon made him obsolete, but he was still a huge star on Broadway.

Jolson's last Broadway show was in 1940, with *Hold On to Your Hats,* by Burton Lane and Yip Harburg. As was his habit, Jolson would say to the audience, "Do you want to see the rest of the show, or do you just want to hear Jolie sing?" Inevitably the audience would scream that they wanted Jolson to sing, and Jolson would demand that the rest of the cast be seated onstage while he'd entertain for the next half hour, the book be damned. Lane and Harburg wrote into the top of the show

Sheet music cover for "They Can't Take That Away from Me" from Shall We Dance.

a clever number where Jolson could sing extracts of his most famous songs, in hopes that it might deter the later hijacking of the plot. Still, inevitably, Jolson would later go down to the footlights and sing his hits directly to the audience. He couldn't be stopped and he couldn't be fired.

SEVERAL OF GEORGE AND IRA'S MUSICALS were made into silent movies around the time *The Jazz Singer* came out. That's right, there were *silent* versions of hit Broadway musicals, yet a poster I have of one such film trumpets it as a "gay musical comedy." (I can think of some current composers I wish had written in that period.) Contracts for musicals of the time included clauses offering terms for the sale of the show for motion pictures. The deal for *Funny Face* in 1927 even included a clause referring to television, then very much in its infancy. (I believe this was before anyone had completed an actual broadcast.) Film versions bearing little resemblance to the stage original were made of *Tip Toes* (1927) and *Lady, Be Good!* and *Oh, Kay!* (both 1928). Silent musicals would be played with live accompaniment: a piano or a theater organ in a small town; in larger cities, a live orchestra. (There were usually no vocals.) The bigger silent movies had special scores written for them; for others, the studios simply provided a cue sheet for a performer to play a piece of stock silent-movie music. It's odd that they didn't even retain the song hits from the stage versions to musically accompany the films.

When talkies came along they weren't without their teething pains. Producers, directors, actors—everyone—was figuring out how to make these films. The problem of how to hide the mic so that a performer could still be heard is depicted well in the movie *Singin' in the Rain*. At first, producers didn't hire the best musical talent; they used the people they had under contract. Then the big names started coming—Cole Porter was hired to write the songs for *The Battle of Paris* (starring Gertrude Lawrence) in 1929. Irving Berlin purportedly wrote ten or so songs for *Reaching for the Moon* (1930) but had a terrible experience—all but one of his songs ("When the Folks High Up Do the Mean Low-Down") were cut in previews. This was a stunning humiliation for a man who was idolized on Broadway and had autonomy in all his stage projects.

THERE WERE SILENT VERSIONS OF HIT BROADWAY MUSICALS.

After three or four years, the novelty of actors talking and singing wore off. The story material and the songs were often substandard and the films were relatively artless—the cameras never moved and there were no close-ups or cutaways, so there was little to maintain the audience's visual interest. It would be a few years before Busby Berkeley came along to reinvent Hollywood musicals, and in the interim they lost their allure at the box office. It was at this point that the Gershwins came to Hollywood.

George and Ira worked together in Hollywood twice, in 1931 and in 1936–37. The first time, they were hired to write songs for a movie called *Delicious.* The second time, they came to write a musical for Fred Astaire and Ginger Rogers after the pair's most brilliant moment together had already come in Irving Berlin's *Top Hat* (1935). The songs they wrote for Hollywood during this extended trip would be the last they would create together.

· · · · ·

AFTER SOME FALSE STARTS with the studios, George and Ira were hired by Fox in 1930 to write songs for *Delicious,* which was to feature frequent co-stars Charles Farrell and Janet Gaynor, a successful star of musical films despite her very small voice. The Gershwins made $100,000 for fourteen weeks of work. (George and Ira split the money seventy-thirty.) This wasn't the first time they had benefited from the largesse of the movie business. The brothers wrote the title song to accompany a movie called *The Sunshine Trail* in the pre–*Jazz Singer* era (1923), when Ira was still Arthur Francis. (The sheet music for a song written for a silent movie would be sold in the theater so the audience could play it for themselves at home.) The song was a somewhat pedestrian effort, and Ira was always embarrassed when I would bring it up to playfully nettle him. In 1930 George received the royal sum of $50,000 for the rights to use *Rhapsody in Blue* for the Paul Whiteman movie *King of Jazz,* a staggering amount in the Depression era.

The Gershwins were part of a parade of songwriters, artists, composers, and writers that passed through Hollywood plying their trade like latter-day troubadours. Among the writers were literary luminaries such as Raymond Chandler, Nathanael West, Aldous Huxley, Dorothy Parker, William Faulkner, and F. Scott Fitzgerald. Fitzgerald was famously miserable working in Hollywood in the late thirties. Everyone came for the money and sold a little of their souls. Writers were moved from project to project and were paid by the week. Some lowly scribes were paid by the day so they could be laid off on a holiday and rehired the day after so the studio could save a day of wages.

On Broadway, George's and Ira's earnings were usually derived from song royalties, which

> THE GERSHWINS WERE PART OF A PARADE OF SONGWRITERS, ARTISTS, COMPOSERS, AND WRITERS THAT PASSED THROUGH HOLLYWOOD PLYING THEIR TRADE.

were very unpredictable. If a song was a hit, the writers would make good money from sheet music and record royalties and from performance fees, but a hit was usually only a hit for a short time. Ira was famously frugal among his friends and always managed George's money as well as his own. With a movie contract, on the other hand, the money was usually a fixed payment. Only a few creative stars, men of the stature of Jerome Kern and Irving Berlin, received a percentage of a movie's profits. (How ironic, given that the Gershwin name has now eclipsed those of Kern and Berlin, two of George's idols.)

Another lure of Hollywood for the Gershwins was that movies, with their vast audiences and affordable tickets, created more hit songs than Broadway shows. The extraordinarily prolific Harry Warren had several number-one hits with songs from movies, three of which won Oscars: "Lullaby of Broadway" (1935), "You'll Never Know" (1943), and "On the Atchison, Topeka and the Santa Fe" (1946). Harry said that George once lamented to him, "Oh, my God, what I would give to have the kind of hits that you have." George had hits, but

far more Broadway hits than Hollywood, and movie hits usually generated much bigger money even if writers like Harry received less income because the lion's share of the profit was kept by the studio.

When creating a song for Hollywood, writers knew that what worked on the screen was generally less sophisticated than what pleased an audience on Broadway. Once he'd finished a song for a movie, it didn't pay for the writer to get too attached to his work. George and Ira could sit in the orchestra pit during rehearsals of a Broadway show and help fix a song if it wasn't working or have a say in how a scene might be changed to help the show move along. In Hollywood, a producer or director could play sound effects over a song, attach it to any kind of action, cut it down, or, worse, cut it entirely. On Broadway, music was the point of a show, but in Hollywood it was just one element among many needed to make a film. Composer André Previn said that in Hollywood the Music Department was no more or less important to the studio than the Department of Fake Lawns. He likened songwriters and composers to truckers delivering furniture or tomatoes. Songwriters usually didn't like the producers and the producers didn't care. Oscar Levant commented on the producer Sol Wurtzel, saying, "I know why Sol makes instantaneous decisions; he's not deflected by thought."

George and Ira had to know that. Each time, they came west for the money and their plan was to do their job as professionally as ever, then go back to their real work, on Broadway. George could earn enough money working on movies to comfortably focus on other projects, like his first symphony, planned for 1937.

Advertisement for Delicious *from* Photoplay Magazine, *1932.*

WHEN THEY ARRIVED IN HOLLYWOOD to work on *Delicious*, George and Ira took up residence in a Beverly Hills house once occupied by Greta Garbo. The musical world out west was a relatively small one but, as usual, George never had any difficulty filling his social diary. His early collaborator, Buddy DeSylva, lived in Los Angeles—he later became head of production at Paramount. The Gershwins were certainly familiar with Guy Bolton, one of *Delicious*'s screenwriters, whom they'd known since 1924, when Bolton wrote the book for their London show, *Primrose*. Another of *Delicious*'s screenwriters, Sonya Levien, later wrote the unreliable Gershwin biopic *Rhapsody in Blue*, released in 1945, after Clifford

midstream in favor of the more conventional and less expensive *Show Girl*. The tune of "Lady of the Moon" didn't make the cut for *Show Girl*, but reemerged in *Delicious* as "Blah, Blah, Blah." In another example of repurposing, a fragment of music from *Funny Face* became background music in *Delicious*. Later Ira wondered if he shouldn't have saved the tune for use as a real love song instead of one that parodied them.

George worked constantly while he was in California. He spent much of his time writing a piece for *Delicious* originally called the *New York Rhapsody*, which was not quite as long as *Rhapsody in Blue* but was unusual for its integrated purpose and ambition. The music was intended

THE TITLE WAS SOMETHING THEIR FATHER, MORRIS, MIGHT SAY ON COMPLETING A SATISFYING DINNER.

Odets's script was rejected. (Odets's script wasn't wasted, though, as it was later reworked to become a Joan Crawford vehicle called *Humoresque*.)

George and Ira contributed six numbers to the movie. They'd already written "Delishious" months before they came west. The title was something their father, Morris, might say on completing a satisfying dinner, with the extra syllable inserted for comic effect. The song "Blah, Blah, Blah" was what Ira called a "palimpsest melody," meaning that at least one other set of words had been set to the same music and then rewritten. In this case, the tune belonged to a song called "Lady of the Moon" from *East Is West,* the 1928 operetta that producer Florenz Ziegfeld called off in

to play as the wide-eyed Scottish immigrant (Janet Gaynor) took in the sights and sounds of Manhattan, both pleasant and menacing. George and Ira also wrote "Welcome to the Melting Pot," which was a cut above the standard movie musical fare, but it went largely unnoticed by audiences and critics at the time. (This piece is quite exciting and deserving of a contemporary hearing.)

Only part of the *New York Rhapsody* made it to the screen. George eventually adapted the piece into his *Second Rhapsody* (a name that he chose over *Rhapsody in Rivets*, *New York Rhapsody*, and *Manhattan Rhapsody*). Perhaps George retitled this new work the *Second Rhapsody* hoping to capitalize on the iconic status his first attempt had achieved. The

GEORGE, GUY BOLTON, AND IRA IN A
PUBLICITY SHOT FOR *DELICIOUS* IN 1930.

Second Rhapsody made its premiere in January 1932 via the Boston Symphony Orchestra, which was conducted by Serge Koussevitzky, with George at the piano. The piece is now a part of the Gershwin orchestral repertoire and is the one enduring, almost incidental, legacy of *Delicious*. While it couldn't possibly possess the resonance of *Rhapsody in Blue*, it does contain a heartrending, sentimental theme of which Ira was quite fond.

IT WAS SOON CLEAR THAT THEIR SECOND HOLLYWOOD STAY WOULD BE LONGER THAN THEIR FIRST.

By the time George and Ira left Hollywood in 1931, *Delicious* was dead in the water because musicals had become box-office poison between the time the movie was written and when it was released. There was nothing the brothers could have done to save it or any of the musicals of 1931 or 1932. Alas for George and Ira, no one figured out how to successfully translate music and movement to the screen until Busby Berkeley choreographed *42nd Street* in 1933. Berkeley's famous geometric combinations of ranks of chorines were imaginatively staged and seamlessly filmed and brought Harry Warren and Al Dubin's songs to life. When *42nd Street* premiered, the movie musical was revitalized and it went on its way, without the Gershwins for now.

IN JANUARY 1936, George's masterpiece, *Porgy and Bess,* closed on Broadway after 124 performances. By March, the opera had completed its modest four-city tour. George's faith in the enduring quality of what he'd achieved with his folk opera would eventually be justified, but not in his lifetime. Meantime, he turned back to Hollywood, where the musical was continuing to enjoy the popularity reignited by *42nd Street*.

George had gone to Mexico for some much needed R&R after his hard work on *Porgy and Bess*, and his agent, Arthur Lyons, found that Hollywood was now a little wary of the Gershwin name. Extraordinary though it may seem today, George's career had been temporarily damaged by *Porgy and Bess*. There was confusion about his future: Had he left popular music behind in favor of classical and symphonic works? Would he want to write songs anymore? There was a famous exchange of telegrams in the summer of 1936—producer Archie Selwyn, brother of Edgar, writing to George that he'd heard Gershwin was only interested in "highbrow" music. George shot back, ". . . rumors about highbrow music ridiculous. Am out to write hits."

While George had no intention of abandoning popular songs in favor of "highbrow" music, he did look to Hollywood to finance his work on some classical projects, like another opera and his never-completed string quartet. And while Ira had made a little money from his work on *Porgy and Bess*—about $2,000—George lost more. Whatever money George made was used to pay the copyists hired to prepare the score. *Porgy* took a long time to write, and George had relied on the money he made from his laxative-sponsored radio show. He did make some money from his royalties, but he hadn't had a new show in three years. In 1934 he went on a concert tour with the Leo Reisman Orchestra, playing twenty-eight gigs in twenty-eight days across the Northeast and Midwest of the country, but the tour lost money by being booked in theaters that were too small to recoup the expenses.

George also spent a lot—he was generous with family and friends, he gave to charities, and he enjoyed an expensive lifestyle. In short, George looked to Hollywood because he needed the money. (The usually careful Ira had previously lost his *Delicious* money to the stock market.)

It took months for Arthur Lyons to get George and Ira a decent deal in Hollywood. The country was in the middle of the Great Depression and even the most successful songwriters were getting paid less. Eventually George and Ira took a flat $55,000 fee from RKO for a Fred Astaire–Ginger Rogers picture, ultimately titled *Shall We Dance*. It was a good paycheck, of course, but about half what they'd made in 1931.

George and Ira returned to Los Angeles in August of 1936. They had traveled west by train the first time; this time they flew. It was soon clear that their second Hollywood stay would be longer than their first, which from November 1930 had lasted about four months. While they were still working on their first film in the fall of 1936, RKO took up their option of $70,000 for a second movie, and by December George and Ira also signed on for a third, with Sam Goldwyn.

Fred Astaire and Ginger Rogers were enjoying a run of great musicals for RKO. They started with *Flying Down to Rio* (music by Vincent Youmans) in 1933, which was followed by *The Gay Divorcee* (Cole Porter), *Roberta* (Jerome Kern), *Top Hat* (Irving Berlin), *Follow the Fleet* (Berlin), and *Swing Time* (Kern). When George saw *Swing Time* he oddly felt Kern's music and the lyrics, by Dorothy Fields, were not up to the current standard. Today, we can appreciate the enduring classics from that film: "The Way You Look Tonight," perhaps Kern's best-known song, as well as "Pick Yourself Up" and "A Fine Romance." The movie also included some of Fred's most memorable dancing, but George wasn't impressed (ironic, since in retrospect *Swing Time* is generally considered the best of the series).

George was excited to be working with Fred Astaire and Ginger Rogers again, even if it meant putting himself at the mercy of the Hollywood studio system. Ira and George had worked with the two of them on Broadway (with Fred in *Lady, Be Good!*, etc., and with Ginger in *Girl Crazy*) but not with the two of them together. George and Fred were almost exact contemporaries, less than eight months apart in age. The two had met twenty years before when they were both just beginning their incredible careers. In 1915, Fred was part of a vaudeville act with his sister, Adele. Fred met George when the young composer was plugging songs at Remick's on Tin Pan Alley. This was when George is said to have made his lighthearted prophecy about working with Fred one day, and they did with *Lady, Be Good!* in 1924 and with *Funny Face* in 1927. Fred and Adele continued to work together until Adele got married in 1932, and then Fred faced the serious decision of what to do with a career that was defined by his now retired sister, who had the greater star power of the pair. He decided to take a crack at Hollywood, and by divine providence

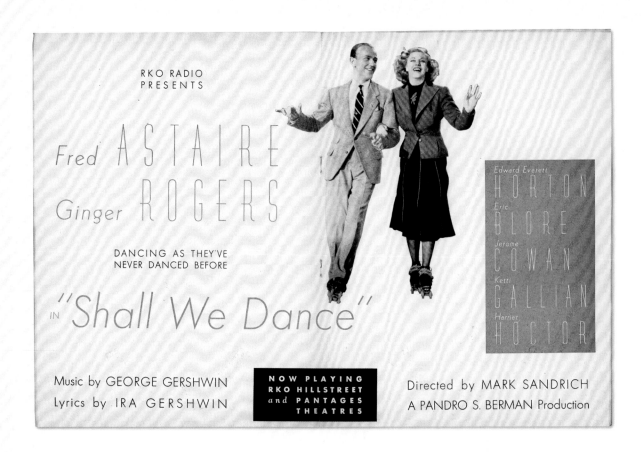

RKO RADIO
PRESENTS

Fred ASTAIRE
Ginger ROGERS

DANCING AS THEY'VE
NEVER DANCED BEFORE

IN "Shall We Dance"

Edward Everett
HORTON
Eric
BLORE
Jerome
COWAN
Ketti
GALLIAN
Harriet
HOCTOR

Music by GEORGE GERSHWIN
Lyrics by IRA GERSHWIN

NOW PLAYING
RKO HILLSTREET
and PANTAGES
THEATRES

Directed by MARK SANDRICH
A PANDRO S. BERMAN Production

and the casting decision of RKO Studios, Fred started working with Ginger Rogers.

Fred Astaire was an inspirational figure for George. They shared a genuine adoration for each other. George wrote one of the themes for *An American in Paris* with Fred in mind. It wasn't necessarily his intention that Fred dance the piece, but Fred was George's muse. He was an extraordinarily talented dancer and had the same impeccable rhythmic sense that George brought to his music. George would show Fred tricks on the piano and good-naturedly laugh at his "cornball" piano playing while Fred, in turn, would try to teach George some dance moves. George was a good, not great, dancer, but he knew enough, and

was bold enough, to offer advice to Fred. When the two men worked together on *Lady, Be Good!* in 1924, Fred was stuck for the ending of a particular dance routine. George jumped up onstage and showed him a "traveling" step. "Hey, Fred, what about this?" Fred used it in the show.

Now, years later, they were working in the movies together. *Shall We Dance* was the eventual title of their first project in Hollywood, but the earlier titles, *Stepping Toes* and *Watch Your Step,* also show how much prominence Fred and Ginger's dancing was given in the film. George crafted his music specifically for Fred—the rhythm of "Slap That Bass" from *Shall We Dance,* for example, is a perfect evocation of Fred's flying feet in musical form.

Trade advertisement for Shall We Dance.

"THEY CAN'T TAKE THAT AWAY FROM ME" was one of the earlier numbers written for *Shall We Dance*. There's some debate as to whether George started the song while he was in New York, but it was certainly finished when he and Ira were in Hollywood. Ira told me George played a melody for him, a phrase of three short notes followed by a long note at the beginning of the chorus. Ira contemplated the tune for a bit until he said to George, "If you can give me more notes preceding the long note, I have an idea." George gave Ira just two more magical notes and Ira came up with the lyric:

> *The way you wear your hat.*
> *The way you sip your tea . . .*

Perfect.

This is one of the relatively few instances in George and Ira's work where a lyrical idea precipitated a musical solution. Ira had felt that adding notes to that phrase would allow him to lend the words of the line more weight. The three short notes before the longer one were too constricting for him to work with. The phrases a lyricist might use in that tight space would be too light and inconsequential, because four syllables aren't enough to express a significant feeling or emotion, at least one we haven't heard before. ("I love you sooooo," etc.) Once again, Ira demonstrated his tremendous understanding of the indefinable touches that make a song work. It can be as simple as going from "Da da da dee" to "Da da da da da dee."

I first saw *Shall We Dance* when I was in my teens in Columbus, and I liked the film at once. The sounds and rhythms of that long-lost era were a tonic for my young soul. The overall sound of the score was deeply compelling and captured my fancy. My favorite song from the score was "They Can't Take That Away from Me." At the time of the Gershwin renaissance in 1973, the year George would have been seventy-five, I bought some of the Gershwin records and sheet music that were published then, along with books like *Gershwin Years in Song*. For the first time, I started singing the songs publicly. It was a remarkable experience of joy and catharsis. Many of Fred Astaire's early movie recordings were reissued around the same time. Hearing Astaire's recordings of the songs from *Shall We Dance*, with arrangements by Johnny Green, is what hooked me on the score, and especially this seminal song. Little did I dream

GEORGE WOULD SHOW FRED TRICKS ON THE PIANO WHILE FRED, IN TURN, WOULD TRY TO TEACH GEORGE SOME DANCE MOVES.

that in just a few short years I would become close friends with Johnny as well as Ira.

"They Can't Take That Away from Me" has been recorded hundreds of times, beautifully, by many people. And as much as I love Fred Astaire's first version of it, I like other performances, too. I like the versions by Peggy Lee; Cy Walter, who did it instrumentally; Mary Cleere Haran, who died in 2011; and Ella Fitzgerald. I performed the song many, many times with Rosemary Clooney, and often think of her now when I do it because we used to sing it together at the end of our concerts. We also first practiced it in her house, coincidentally where George and Ira wrote it, and I felt a sense of George's spirit in that space.

Because of its long and resonant history, I get a good response whenever I sing this song, as I hang on to the coattails of what it represents in the hearts and minds of the listener. There are fewer and fewer songs recognized solely from their introduction, and when they are, it's usually the most evocative love songs: "They Can't Take That Away from Me," "I've Got a Crush on You," "Love Is Here to Stay," "Embraceable You," and "Someone to Watch over Me"—songs that evoke the deepest emotional connection. Ira's lyric for "They Can't Take That Away from Me" is mature and sophisticated, and the allusions it makes are more personal than what he would have written when he was younger. Certainly people think of their own loved ones where they hear it.

This is one song that can lose its depth of emotion unless it's carefully handled. I like the song with a gentle swing, but when singers try to do it up-tempo, snapping their fingers and trying to be hip, they strip away the essence of what this song is about and it can quickly become vapid and bloodless. The most recent unfortunate case in point is the rendition by true Gershwin enthusiast Brian Wilson (whose iconic earlier work I adore), which will certainly be obscure by the time you read these words (at least it is in my house).

In my mind, the long tradition of misusing "They Can't Take That Away from Me" began with its first appearance. In *Shall We Dance*, Fred sang the song to Ginger in a scene set on a ferryboat to Hoboken. There's not much romance to be found on a commuter boat crossing the Hudson River, or at least I haven't experienced it. The song is a ballad, but it was given a very static presentation and it contains just one chorus of the opus, ending before you know it. George also wrote a beautiful extended orchestral ending that he pleaded with the producer to keep in the film. They cut it. Perhaps the fact that a big dance number was coming up in the next scene compelled the director to keep this one simple. It seems that no one saw the potential in the song, which is hard to fathom. (It wasn't the only song mistreated in that movie: "Beginner's Luck" was originally written with two choruses, both of which were filmed, but only one was used.) "They Can't Take That Away from Me" is reprised in the movie's final dance sequence, but is hampered by the intrusion of oddly contorted ballet moves that simultaneously fascinate and repel.

The RKO executive who produced the Astaire and Rogers films was Pandro S. Berman. George had a good working relationship with Berman, and Berman listened to George more than another producer might have, but George was still at the mercy of other people's opinions and how they decided to treat his songs. He had little say in the scoring or editing process, so the first time he saw the finished product was when he saw the movie in a preview. (Contrast this with the constant participation he was used to on Broadway.) Needless to say, George wasn't happy with the way his songs had been used, and he expressed his dissatisfaction about the situation in his letters written at the time.

On its release in the spring of 1937, *Shall We Dance* received a mixed critical reception. Some said the score was inferior to some of the Kern or Berlin efforts for Fred and Ginger. The film did poorly at the box office. "They Can't Take That Away from Me" and "Let's Call the Whole Thing Off" were hits, but they were modest, reminding us that only time determines what is classic and destined to join the Great American Songbook.

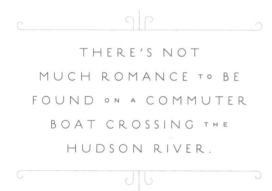

THERE'S NOT MUCH ROMANCE TO BE FOUND ON A COMMUTER BOAT CROSSING THE HUDSON RIVER.

George also wrote some instrumental pieces for the film, one of which—"Walking the Dog"—went on to have a life of its own. "Walking the Dog" was printed in 1960 under the title "Promenade." Once I was in Patelson's Music House, the now defunct store in Manhattan that was across the street from Carnegie Hall, and I heard someone request "Walking the Dog." The clerk was scratching his head because he couldn't find it anywhere. As I was walking out the door, I looked back and tipped them off: "It's called 'Promenade.'" Then I promenaded out of there. Ira had changed the name upon the work's publication, never expecting

that anyone in the sixties would recall that this instrumental gem had first appeared in a largely forgotten film from the thirties.

BEFORE THEY HAD EVEN FINISHED *Shall We Dance*, George and Ira set about working on *A Damsel in Distress*. Directed by George Stevens (of *Swing Time*), the film was an adaptation of a P. G. Wodehouse novel that had already seen life as a movie and a play. This was another Fred Astaire project, but now he was being partnered with the very young Joan Fontaine. Fred and Ginger had decided they needed to take a professional break and the script called for a British actress to play Lady Alyce, the posh love interest of the unsuitable American Jerry Halliday (Astaire). If the movie had used a stronger musical counterpart to Fred than Joan Fontaine, who was a beauty but no singer or dancer, it might have done better.

(The story was that the studio wanted to cast British singer-dancer Jessie Matthews, who was a huge star in the U.K., to play Lady Alyce. Jessie, known as "The Dancing Divinity," would have been a marvelous partner for Fred. I worked as accompanist with her in 1979 and she told me she had wanted to do the film, but her movie company refused to release her. Jessie was prone to fantastic inventions, so who knows if her casting was a real possibility. She regretted for the rest of her life that she never got the chance to dance with Fred Astaire, who, in his later years, only seemed to have the vaguest recollection of who she was.)

Despite the best efforts of Astaire and Fontaine and co-stars George Burns and Gracie Allen, *A Damsel in Distress* was not a success. One dance number, the Fun House sequence, won an

Oscar, but the movie lost money, the first of Fred's films to do so. (The Academy Award was won by Fred's longtime choreographer, Hermes Pan, in the Best Dance Direction category, which was only awarded three times, from 1935 to 1937. It then joined other retired categories, such as Best Engineering Effects, which survived only the first awards, in 1929.)

There were some good things about the movie: Burns and Allen, for one, and the song "Things Are Looking Up," which is one of my favorites, though it's not well known. More renowned are the standards, "Nice Work If You Can Get It" and "A Foggy Day (in London Town)." Ira noted that George started working on "A Foggy Day" at one o'clock one morning after he got home from a party. While thinking about a particular spot in the script, George quickly came up with a suitable

theme and a title, and the two men dashed off a complete refrain in one hour flat. The brothers then slept on it. When they still liked the song after they got up, they started on the verse, of which Ira was most proud.

> I was a stranger in the city.
> Out of town were the people I knew.
> I had that feeling of self-pity:
> What to do? What to do? What to do?
> The outlook was decidedly blue.
> But as I walked through the foggy streets alone,
> It turned out to be the luckiest day I've known.

Ira was proud that two Jewish boys from New York could channel their inner Irish.

GEORGE WOULD HAVE LIKED some time off after finishing movies back to back, but as soon as their work was done on *A Damsel in Distress*, the brothers had to start on *The Goldwyn Follies*. It was their last collaboration.

Through the spring of 1937, George kept up a busy athletic and social schedule—tennis with composer Arnold Schoenberg, who was teaching music at UCLA (a matchup immortalized in some home movies); roller rink parties with Ginger Rogers and Gloria Vanderbilt; and a dinner for Stravinsky given by Edward G. Robinson, with guests who only need to be introduced by their surnames: Chaplin, Fairbanks, Dietrich, Capra.

The first public inkling that something was wrong with George's health came when he gave

Sheet music cover for "A Foggy Day" from A Damsel in Distress.

a performance of the Concerto in F in February 1937 and made a mistake in a simple passage that normally gave him no trouble—none of them ever did up to that point. Oscar Levant was present in the audience and was taken aback by the error, which was so unlike George that it gave Levant an eerie feeling. George had been smelling strange odors like burning rubber and he began suffering headaches, dizziness, and nausea. He seemed listless and depressed.

Friends looked for clues as to the cause of his malaise. George, who had always loved new technologies, had taken to wearing a helmet-like electric gadget that was said to reverse baldness, so when he fell victim to crippling headaches, some people, including actress Lillian Gish, blamed the machine. Fellow Goldwyn tunesmith Harold Spina suspected that the culprit was the drafty cottage that George worked in on the movie studio lot.

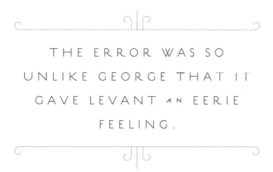

THE ERROR WAS SO UNLIKE GEORGE THAT IT GAVE LEVANT AN EERIE FEELING.

For a time, nobody thought George was seriously ill. Irving Berlin made the cruelest remark when learning of his illness: "There's nothing wrong with George that a song hit won't cure." It was a quip that later haunted Berlin. There were periods from February through June when George was perfectly fine, and he would get his energy and strength back. He'd think that everything was okay, but he'd be struck down again. It was confounding for a man who had always taken such good care of himself and was one of the few people who had a gym in their home. He jogged in the Hollywood Hills and prided himself on his physical prowess. Now, at a dinner party one night, George had to leave suddenly and sit outside on the curb with his head in his hands because he was in such pain.

Lee Gershwin was particularly unsympathetic because her personal code dictated that a person should never let on that anything was wrong. At one point as his illness was progressing, George faltered during a dinner at their home, dropping his fork and making a mess, and Lee with great frustration hissed, "Get him out of here!" She wasn't going to tolerate a scene at the dinner table. Ira held his tongue, knowing that when Lee got into a rage like that, there was nothing he could do to assuage it. Ira later said that he would never forget the look on George's face as he was gently led away from the table, a combination of sadness and humiliation.

In my naïveté, early in our relationship I asked Lee if she got along with George. The only response she could muster was, "I once gave George a box of chocolates and he said to me, 'You're a sweet woman.' Would someone who doesn't like you say, 'You're a sweet woman?'" People have talked about Lee's cruelty to George when he was sick. She was a person who couldn't stand weakness in people, especially herself. Lee didn't know that George was really sick; how could she? In hindsight, of course, she regretted her actions.

· · · · ·

GEORGE'S BEHAVIOR STARTED to become erratic, so much so that in one stunning incident a few days before he died, he tried to push his assistant Paul Mueller out of a moving car. During that period, when George was displaying more advanced symptoms and his headaches had become terrible and often crippling, Johnny Green, who superbly arranged the songs for the first commercial *Shall We Dance* recordings sung by Fred Astaire, came to the Gershwin house to play him the just-processed test pressings. Johnny was a Gershwin acolyte. He had only been a student when he'd attended the first performance of *Rhapsody in Blue* and was bitten hard by the Gershwin bug. He was also an accomplished songwriter ("Body and Soul") and was deeply admired by George. (He later went on to music-direct *An American in Paris,* his personal love letter to George.)

On hearing Fred singing Johnny's arrangements of the songs from *Shall We Dance*, George started crying because he was so thrilled by the presentation. Johnny had exercised great imagination in preparing the settings of Fred's performances. His own music was cathartic to him and George said, over and over, "Thank you, Johnny. Thank you." Green was grateful for George's appreciation of his work, but also confounded by this outburst and by his idol's condition.

In that same late period Oscar Levant brought his over new girlfriend (and future wife), June Gale, to meet George and they spent about an hour together. June said that it was apparent George was not well, and as he sat next to her he kept rubbing her leg, not in a way that June interpreted as sexual but more as the response of someone who was ill and wanted comfort. It was the only time she ever met him and it troubled her for the rest of her days.

At the earliest onset of his symptoms in February, George went to see a doctor but nothing was found. George felt worse and worse and in late June he finally went to a hospital for tests, including X-rays. But these tests were inconclusive, and believing there was nothing physically wrong with him, he refused to submit to a lumbar puncture that would have revealed the tumor growing in his brain. Thus the recurring diagnosis was that his problems were psychological.

But George's worsening headaches—they were now incapacitating—coupled with seizures belied the diagnosis. Yip Harburg's house was vacant and the declining George was taken there for some peace and quiet. By the time George lapsed into a coma on July 9, 1937, and his condition was finally diagnosed, it was too late to save him.

In those last terrible days, as Ira realized that his brother was fading away, he hurriedly had George give him power of attorney. (The always impeccable Gershwin signature is unrecognizable on that legal document, a poignant illustration of the artist's pathetic decline.) The last conversation George and Ira had was about work, discussing songs from *A Damsel in Distress* and Fred Astaire's singing of them. Despite the unbearable pain Ira was feeling, he was trying to focus on their shared joy, the work of music. George tried to say something about Fred, but his speech was garbled. Those were his last words.

George's coma was treated as a national crisis. After the brain tumor was finally diagnosed, the U.S. Navy sent two destroyers to Chesapeake Bay to locate one of the country's best neurosurgeons,

Dr. Walter Edward Dandy, who was vacationing on a yacht. But surgeons at Cedars of Lebanon in Hollywood decided they couldn't wait for Dandy to get to L.A., and they operated. Ira initially told people that the operation was a success and that George was going to be all right. But the tumor—a glioblastoma multiforme—was too advanced, and George died five hours after the operation, at 10:35 A.M. on July 11, 1937. He was thirty-eight.

People occasionally ask whether more modern medical techniques could have saved George. I have spoken with surgeons about this over the years and the answer is always the same: George wouldn't have been able to live any kind of normal existence even if he had survived the operation. He would have been diminished mentally to a catastrophic extent and the tumor would likely have re-formed. No one knows if anything could even have been done earlier, if there'd been a chance that he could have been saved back in February when he missed the musical passage while playing the Concerto in F.

In the eighties, I was hired to play a Christmas party for the casting director Terry Liebling, Marvin Hamlisch's sister and a beautiful soul, who worked on movies like *Apocalypse Now* and *The Postman Always Rings Twice.* I knew that the famous psychic Peter Hurkos was going to be there performing psychometry, which involves giving a reading about the energy in a physical object and picking up information encoded in the object about the person who has possessed the object, present or past. I took along a watch chain that was George's. (Of everyone at the party, only Terry knew whose chain it was.) Hurkos was a very theatrical guy, and as soon as I gave him the chain, he put his hands

to his head and said, "My head hurts, my head hurts, my head hurts!" He said the owner of the piece had died young, that doctors had operated on him in the wrong place, and he could have lived. Terry and I looked at each other, wide-eyed.

‖ RA WAS DEVASTATED BY HIS BROTHER'S DEATH. I think it's fair to say that he never got over it, even though he lived another forty-six years. During his ordeal he somehow brought himself to listen to some of the Johnny Green recordings of Fred Astaire singing the *Shall We Dance* songs he'd written with George. Listening to the excitement, the rhythm, the joy, in these songs gave him some comfort.

IT WAS A COUPLE
OF YEARS BEFORE IRA
REALLY CAME OUT OF HIS
DEPRESSION.

It was a couple of years before Ira really came out of his depression, but these songs were the first glimmer of light he had in those dark times. He said that he felt George was sending a message through the music to tell him to go on, and Ira was as far from being a believer of such things as you could get. Until the end of his life, whenever he heard "They Can't Take That Away from Me," Ira inevitably thought of George and that period of their lives together. It encompassed the joys, sorrows, ambitions, fulfillment, and loss that is inevitable and ever present.

"They Can't Take That Away from Me" was the only song George wrote that was nominated for an Academy Award. When the Oscars were presented in March 1938 at the Biltmore Hotel, everyone expected it to win. In neither the first nor the last Oscar upset, George and Ira lost to a song called "Sweet Leilani," written by Harry Owens, which Bing Crosby sang in the movie *Waikiki Wedding*. Harry Owens was a bandleader who had moved to Hawaii and specialized in island songs. He had written "Sweet Leilani" for his daughter, and Crosby had sung it in one of the most successful films of the year. Oscar Levant, among others, was shocked at the loss of the Oscar to what many thought was an inferior song. At that time he quipped, "I'd like to say something about Harry Owens, the composer of 'Sweet Leilani.' His music is dead, but he lives on forever."

In *Lyrics on Several Occasions*, Ira pointed out that his three Academy Award–nominated songs have two things in common. "They Can't Take That Away from Me," "Long Ago and Far Away," and "The Man That Got Away" all failed to win an Oscar; and the title of each song includes the word "Away." "So?" wrote Ira. "So— away with 'away'?"

I N 1938, JEROME KERN SENT some melodies to Ira in an attempt to engage him and get him working again, but it was only a temporary diversion. Ira's first major work after George's death was his collaboration with Moss Hart and Kurt Weill on the musical play *Lady in the Dark*. Moss Hart reached out to Ira at the beginning of 1940, work commenced, and the play reached Broadway, at the Alvin Theatre, in January 1941.

Lady in the Dark is a very interesting musical in its own right. The subject matter was certainly more weighty than that of the musicals Ira worked on in the twenties. Gertrude Lawrence played Liza Elliott, an editor at *Allure* magazine who undergoes psychoanalysis before she gets married. In the *Times*, Brooks Atkinson said Ira's was the work of a "thoroughbred." His lyrics were "uproariously witty" and "in impeccable taste." The show was a major success for Lawrence. It played on Broadway, went on tour, and came back to a larger theater in New York, running for more than 750 performances in total. Finally Lawrence reprised the role of Liza in a radio dramatization in 1947.

The play has proved difficult to revive successfully without Gertrude Lawrence in the years since. Celeste Holm starred in a British production in 1983. There was an Encores! production in 1994 and one in Philadelphia in 2001 with Andrea Marcovicci. Maria Friedman played Liza in a production at the National Theatre in London in 1997. Everyone liked her performance, but the *Daily Telegraph*'s critic said the revival was "an exercise in theatrical archeology." Psychoanalysis is no longer a mysterious thing—in 1941 it was much more obscure—and *Lady in the Dark* offers a simplistic view of this world. Today, the talk of the psyche and the brain that frames the songs feels fanciful and overdramatized, because it's practically a badge of honor to speak of one's transformations at the hands of a guru or therapist.

When I was working for Ira, there were a number of Americans interested in *Lady in the Dark*. Diana Ross was one, and the notion of her African-American point of view and star power was

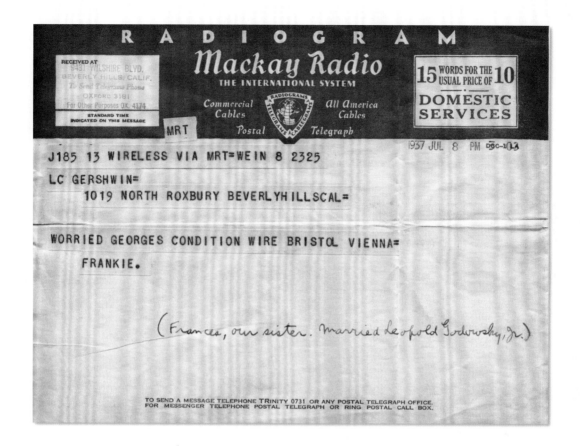

RADIOGRAM
Mackay Radio
THE INTERNATIONAL SYSTEM

15 WORDS FOR THE USUAL PRICE OF 10
DOMESTIC SERVICES

Commercial Cables All America Cables
Postal Telegraph

RECEIVED AT
9431 WILSHIRE BLVD.
BEVERLY HILLS, CALIF.
To Send Telegrams Phone
OXFORD 3181
For Other Purposes OX. 4174
STANDARD TIME
INDICATED ON THIS MESSAGE

MRT

1957 JUL 8 PM

J185 13 WIRELESS VIA MRT=WEIN 8 2325

LC GERSHWIN=

1019 NORTH ROXBURY BEVERLYHILLSCAL=

WORRIED GEORGES CONDITION WIRE BRISTOL VIENNA=

FRANKIE.

(Frances, our sister. Married Leopold Godowsky, Jr.)

TO SEND A MESSAGE TELEPHONE TRinity 0731 OR ANY POSTAL TELEGRAPH OFFICE.
FOR MESSENGER TELEPHONE POSTAL TELEGRAPH OR RING POSTAL CALL BOX.

compelling to Ira, who appreciated her immense talent. Perhaps a more on-the-nose approach was offered by Julie Andrews, who would have sung the score with crystalline magnificence and acted the part perfectly. Andrews had played Gertrude Lawrence in the 1968 biopic *Star!,* in which she sang "My Ship" from *Lady in the Dark*. Andrews once discussed *Lady* with me at the home of actor Roddy McDowall and wanted a way to make the story edgier for contemporary audiences, but eventually she dropped the idea.

In the late seventies, Ira's longtime agent, Irving Lazar, decided that his wife, Mary, needed a project and was suddenly deep in the throes of creating a package of star-studded names for a film production. It eventually petered out, and Mary never again attempted to produce anything after that. Irving was a larger-than-life character who had the most impressive client list in Hollywood and beyond, and I was not very fond of him. He was dismissive of anyone he did not deem significant, including me. When he came to visit Ira and Lee, I would answer the door, and he would sweep past me as though I wasn't there and instantly hurry to greet Ira or Lee.

One day Lee observed this lack of decorum and stopped Irving in his tracks by saying, "Irving, Michael is a very important part of this house and you must treat him with the same respect with which you treat us." She was using her imperious voice,

Radiogram from sister Frances to Ira at the time of George's illness.

and Irving knew she was serious. Properly chastened, he apologized and went about his business.

The next time he arrived at the house, I once again opened the door, only this time he briefly paused and said, "Nice to see you," before once again sweeping past. Lee, who was just entering the room, stopped Irving cold and said, "Did you greet Michael?" and Irving sputtered, "Yes, Lee," and turned to me and jabbered, "Didn't I just say 'nice to see you'?" "Yes, Irving," I replied, with amusement, and in those two words saved his position with Ira and Lee. He was extraordinarily relieved and did become genuinely nicer after that incident.

known, had an intense dislike of the ditty and insisted it be cut even though the remembering of the song was a key plot point. Ira was bemused: with almost a decade in Hollywood he was well accustomed to the ego-driven peccadillos of Tinseltown producers.

After *Lady in the Dark*, Ira worked with Weill twice again on Broadway and in Hollywood. A show with Arthur Schwartz came and went quickly in 1946. Then he teamed up with a former New York collaborator, Harry Warren, on songs for an MGM movie called *The Barkleys of Broadway,* which was released in 1949. Fred

IRA WAS BEMUSED: WITH ALMOST A DECADE IN HOLLYWOOD HE WAS WELL ACCUSTOMED TO THE EGO-DRIVEN PECCADILLOS OF TINSELTOWN PRODUCERS.

The most popular song from *Lady in the Dark* is "My Ship," which I have sung many times. There's also a delightful song called "One Life to Live," and another where Liza and Randy, her true love, sing "This Is New." Oddly, "This Is New" is about reincarnation and "One Life to Live" is its polar opposite. But since these songs were about dreams, and dreams often don't make sense, it's a woman's prerogative to change her confused mind.

Lady in the Dark was made into a movie in 1944, with a miscast Ginger Rogers starring as Liza. It was a success in its time, but it doesn't hold up today, especially with the excision of the climactic "My Ship," which is the song that unlocks the key to Liza's tortured past. According to Ira, producer Buddy DeSylva, for reasons now un-

Astaire was supposed to do the movie with Judy Garland, but she fell ill and was replaced by Ginger Rogers. (Harry recalled that one day while Garland and Astaire were previously working together on *Easter Parade*, Garland seemed stoned and grabbed the shy Astaire in the crotch. He was so shaken that he fled the set, and shooting was suspended for the day.) After ten years apart, Astaire and Rogers were reunited for what ended up being their last movie together. Oscar Levant was also in the film, which had a screenplay by the team of Betty Comden and Adolph Green, and a curiously tepid score by Harry and Ira. Many years later on one nostalgia-infused night I played songs from the score of *Barkleys* for Comden and Green, and they sat in stone-faced and silent disapproval with each rendering from the film. Forty years on, and they still hated the score.

The film needed a big dance number and someone had the idea of reprising "They Can't Take That Away from Me," which had been given such short shrift in *Shall We Dance*. This time it was properly presented as a lavish song-and-dance number. The orchestration was by Conrad Salinger, the dean of Hollywood arrangers at the time, whose work is still unsurpassed. Salinger inserted snippets of the Concerto in F as an homage to George, which he played for Ira to make sure he approved. The arrangement used in *The Barkleys of Broadway* became Ira's favorite version of the song, even though Harry Warren wasn't pleased that the song that got the most attention in the movie was the one he had nothing to do with. Harry later said about working for the studios: "Hollywood never disappoints one's low expectations," yet he also had to admit that this execution of the Gershwin number was magnificent. It is one of the many scores that were later jettisoned by MGM, so I had it painstakingly restored and recreated just so I could perform it with symphonies. It was well worth the effort.

Gertrude Lawrence and Victor Mature in Lady in the Dark *(1941).*

. . . . .

IN THE YEARS SINCE GEORGE GERSHWIN'S DEATH, New York and Los Angeles have retained their positions as the two entertainment capitals of the country. With all due respect to important cultural centers like Nashville, Chicago, and New Orleans, New York and L.A. are dominant, with Broadway in one, Hollywood in the other, and the television and the music businesses divided between them. The two cities are different from one another in the same ways they were seventy years ago. Everyone knows the stereotypes: the ultra-high-speed lifestyle of New York versus laid-back La La Land; "fuggedaboutit" versus "whatever, man"; intensity versus relaxation; the subway versus the freeway. (Nashville is now perhaps the most creative musical center of the country, yet it is fundamentally different from the two coastal cities.)

It might be said that the contrasting traits of the two cities were mirrored in the personalities of the Gershwin brothers. George and Ira: New York and L.A.; yin and yang. Although George took full advantage of L.A.'s fabled weather, walking six miles a day through the canyons, swimming, and playing tennis and golf, he felt more at ease amid the relentless hustle and noise of New York. Ira, who was not very physically active, responded to Los Angeles's slower pace with sedentary gusto, if such a thing is possible. George commented that his brother was able to relax in L.A., "and you know how Ira loves his relaxation."

When he arrived in California in 1936, Ira was happy. He loved the sunshine, the blue skies, and the lifestyle. He was planning to buy a place in L.A. for visits. Had George lived, Ira would

have gone where the work took him—most likely back to New York. But because George died, he no longer had any reason to go back east. He had his things sent out to California, including George's favorite piano, and there he stayed.

In 1940, Ira and Lee bought 1021 North Roxbury Drive, next door to the house where he and George had lived when they worked on those three movies during the last year of George's life. It was at this house, which he referred to as the Gershwin Plantation, that my own path crossed with Ira's, forty years after George's passing.

Ira had moved out of 1019 when George died because of the sadness connected with the place. When Ira and Lee were looking for a home, they heard that 1021 was for sale and, when they met the seller, she said that she wanted Ira to have the house. Apparently when George and Ira were living next door, the woman had been undergoing a long convalescence. Since her second-floor bedroom was just across the way from where George worked on his upstairs piano, she would lie in bed and listen to him playing and composing hour after hour, day after day. George's music had

Vincente Minnelli, Ira, Gene Kelly, and Arthur Freed on the set of An American in Paris *in 1950.*

extended her life, she said, and she wanted to repay the family by giving Ira a good price on the house. Frugal Ira was only too happy to accept.

My friend Rosemary Clooney lived at 1019 North Roxbury for almost fifty years until her death in 2002. Despite neighborhood efforts to save the house in homage to the Gershwins, 1019 was demolished by a developer in 2005. George and Ira had only rented the place for eight months, and by 2005 it was such a mess that it would have cost more to renovate than rebuild. It didn't help that the practice of historically landmarking a building in Beverly Hills is almost nonexistent.

Some of the Gershwin residences have survived and been commemorated. At 501 West 110th Street, a memorial announces that George and Ira lived in the building in 1924, "the year they [*sic*] wrote 'Rhapsody in Blue' . . . on an upright piano in the back room of a D line apartment." Along with a blue awning announcing the "Gershwin House," there's a small plaque on the building on 103rd Street in Manhattan put up by the block association that reads, "Gershwin Family Residence 1925–1931. George Gershwin—composer, and Ira Gershwin—lyricist created many memorable works here." There's a red plaque on the building at 33 Riverside Drive, but not at 72nd Street. The house where George was born on Snediker Avenue in Brooklyn was torn down in the late 1970s.

With my residence in Indiana, I spend a great deal of time there to tend to the Initiative for the Preservation of the Great American Songbook, but I also divide my time between houses in Los Angeles and New York, shuttling between the two places where George and Ira lived and worked. But if I had to choose only between those two coastal outposts, I'm with Ira—I prefer California to New York, which is shocking to some people. I see George's and Ira's ghosts in both places. My home in California is only a few blocks from the former hospital where George passed. It is now the Scientology headquarters, and I often wonder if anyone who works there is aware of the Gershwin connection. When I drive through Beverly Hills or walk around the Upper West Side, I try to imagine the Gershwins in their element. Even though so much has changed since their time, I feel a sense of the atmosphere in which they created their songs—especially in California, because of the time I spent there with Ira. I picture his drawers filled with artifacts saved from George's life, such as the little black book filled with his girlfriends' phone numbers or the pipe he smoked during his last year. I see Ira's library of books, and the oversize dictionary on a stand that once belonged to Cole Porter. The paintings by George, Ira, and others that so richly adorned the walls. These rich memories have often carried me through life when I'm feeling down.

George and Ira, with mother Rose, at 1019 North Roxbury Drive.

WHEN I FIRST MET IRA at 1021 North Roxbury, he rarely left the house. He stayed home with Lee, safely cocooned in his world of musical memories, until he eventually became bedbound. He never had a car. (When asked why, he had a quip at the ready: "Suppose somebody honks at me?") Ira had regrets about many things, feeling perhaps that he'd wasted time and could have done more, the classic duality of wishing he had accomplished more yet succumbing to the pull of seclusion and slumber. Most of all, he felt responsible in some way for George's death, a not uncommon reaction, especially for someone like Ira.

Ira never understood why a soul imbued with that kind of genius would be taken away before it had realized its potential. For him, George's death confirmed that there could be no God. He had been the first to identify George's talent. He had watched his brother bloom and was his chronicler. Where Ira was timid, George was strong, always facing life head-on and without fear. How could Ira possibly outlive George? Ira spent the rest of his life trying to cope, seeking some motivation for going on with his life after George's death.

EARLY ON THE MORNING of August 17, 1983, when I had been working for Ira for six years, Rosemary Clooney called to tell me there was an ambulance next door at Ira and Lee's house. That was not an infrequent occurrence, so I didn't go straight over. Rosemary called back twenty minutes later to say Ira had died. I went to the house right away. As I drove there I was in a daze, filled with sadness. We had become close over the years, to the point that he would tell me that he loved me, something he never would say so directly in a song. The emotions were all jumbled as I tried to make sense of what I knew had been coming for so long. What would Lee do now? How would she handle being without him? How would we continue? What was I going to do?

When I saw Lee, I cried and told her that I was sorry that we hadn't been getting along. She hugged me and told me that I should see Ira, so I went upstairs and saw him sitting peacefully in a chair, his head tilted to one side. The undertakers took an age to arrive, and a few more friends came to the house. While we were waiting, Lee asked me what Ira's favorite piece of music was. I said it was a theme from George's Concerto in F and she insisted I play it as Ira was carried down the stairs, still sitting in his chair. It was the last thing I wanted to do at that moment, but it was what she wanted, so I played the piece. (Later I was asked to play it at the memorial for Jack Lemmon.)

One of the people who came to pay his respects at the house was Fred Astaire, who was an old man himself by then. Fred's career had first become intimately entwined with the Gershwins more than sixty years before. Fred had trod the path to a grieving Gershwin house once before, decades earlier. It had only been when Fred came the day after George had died that Ira had first been able to show his true emotions—he broke down in tears. Fred must have been transported back to that terrible time, because when he showed up to offer his condolences to Lee, he somehow confusedly went to 1019—George and Ira's old house, where Ira had mourned George in 1937. Now, in 1983, one of Rosemary's kids was shocked to answer the door and see Fred Astaire standing there. They then had to gently tell Fred that Ira had lived next door. For the past forty-three years. ·

IRA AND MICHAEL ON
THE LYRICIST'S 85TH BIRTHDAY.

"I GOT RHYTHM"

— from *Girl Crazy*, 1930 —

VERSE

Days can be sunny,
With never a sigh;
Don't need what money
Can buy.

Birds in the tree sing
Their dayful of song.
Why shouldn't we sing
Along?

I'm chipper all the day,
Happy with my lot.
How do I get that way?
Look at what I've got:

REFRAIN

I got rhythm,
I got music,
I got my man—
Who could ask for anything more?

I got daisies
In green pastures,
I got my man—
Who could ask for anything more?

Old Man Trouble,
I don't mind him—
You won't find him
'Round my door.

I got starlight,
I got sweet dreams,
I got my man—
Who could ask for anything more—
Who could ask for anything more?

 · C H A P T E R 11 ·

GEORGE GERSHWIN'S
MUSICAL REPUTATION

N THEIR INTRODUCTION TO THE 1973 REISSUE of Ira Gershwin's *Lyrics on Several Occasions*, originally published in 1959, Betty Comden and Adolph Green, who penned the lyrics and screenplays for some of the most beloved musicals and Broadway shows of the mid-twentieth century, wrote that people will remember the name Gershwin as long as they remember anything about the twentieth century. But in this twenty-first century, if you ask Americans who George and Ira Gershwin are or were, my guess is that most won't know. A friend, a voice teacher, told me one of her students announced she was going to sing "Summertime," by Porgy and Bess. Funny but sad.

We have to accept the fact that millions of Americans have never heard of George Gershwin, let alone Ira. Cuts in arts funding and the almost complete disappearance of music teaching in schools will guarantee that such ignorance about our cultural heritage will only get worse. George's widespread anonymity is a sad fact that would have greatly disturbed the man himself. Lee Gershwin was known to have coveted the name Gershwin more than her prized diamonds, using it to get the best tables at restaurants. Today the odds of getting anywhere using that name with a maître d' are probably small.

Having said this, I believe George Gershwin is also more appreciated today than at any time since

George at the piano.

his death. How can this be so? I think his reputation in the music community is better than ever: no one questions George's place among American music's greats. This was not always the case. Even though Gershwin is no longer a household name, the influence of his legacy is mighty and it will ever be strong. Hearing a Gershwin song for the first time can still be a life-changing experience—I know because people tell me about it all the time at my concerts. It's very personal to them.

If they were able to check in after their demise, important figures in any field would find their reputations ebb and flow as times change and their legacies are dissected using different criteria. George would surely be pleased to find that his work is part of the classical repertoire. But at his death, he was better known as a great popular entertainer. *Time* magazine, which had featured George on its cover in 1925, mentioned in its obituary on July 19, 1937, that George had been able to attract eighteen thousand people to concerts at Lewisohn Stadium in Manhattan, and that he had heard the country sing his songs. His other achievements were refracted through the prism of his first discipline. The article read: "Serious musicians joined pluggers and crooners to mourn the 38-year-old composer who had made the world sing his songs and who never, even in his most pretentious work, disdained the antic, impertinent data he had picked up in Tin Pan Alley."

The tone is somewhat dismissive of George for anything other than his songwriting (and also perhaps of pluggers and crooners for being in a separate category from "serious musicians"). And in one sentence, where George was allowed the satisfaction of having America sing his songs, the

now-standards "Somebody Loves Me," "I Got Rhythm," "Embraceable You," and "Let's Call the Whole Thing Off" were described as "ephemeral." Ouch, and *wrong* is my first reaction, but did anyone know what was going to happen with the long-term recognition of these songs? Even Ira didn't, or should I say, especially Ira.

Much of the praise for George over the years has been dotted with these kinds of dismissals, some fainter than others. Now he is best known for the classical works and the song standards. The lightweight musical comedies from whence most of these songs came are historical curiosities for the most part.

In his lifetime, George's reputation was sullied by association. Jazz, one of the musical forms he incorporated into his work, is now a canonized art form, indisputably great and undeniably American. But the influence of jazz certainly had

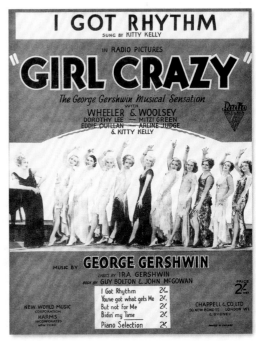

Cover for the British edition of sheet music for "I Got Rhythm" from the 1932 film version of Girl Crazy.

310

a deleterious effect on George's critical legacy for many years, and some critics and listeners dismissed him because of his association with it. In the twenties, jazz was new, brash, and thoroughly disreputable. It was as "dangerous" as rock 'n' roll was in the fifties. The fact that many of the greatest jazz artists were African-American added to the distrust of the white musical establishment. Jazz—free-thinking and improvisational,

Lady, Be Good!," written in 1924, became another jazz favorite in George's lifetime, and many of George's other songs underwent the same trajectory of interpretation and reinterpretation: "Fascinating Rhythm," "Stairway to Paradise," "Liza," and "'S Wonderful," to name a few.

But George's name is conspicuously absent, or underplayed, in many newer accounts of the origins of jazz. He is not mentioned in Ken

THE INFLUENCE OF JAZZ CERTAINLY HAD A DELETERIOUS EFFECT ON GEORGE'S CRITICAL LEGACY FOR MANY YEARS.

and played in smoky clubs—may seem to be the opposite of the buttoned-down classical music intoned in most cathedral-like concert halls, but part of Gershwin's genius was that he showed how readily one form could influence the other to the benefit of both.

These days I think George's legacy is suffering from the opposite problem—his name has been unfairly dissociated from the history of American jazz. Not only did George use jazz themes in his work, but many of his songs are naturally conducive to jazz interpretations.

George did live long enough to see "I Got Rhythm" become one of the most popular jazz instrumentals of its time. One writer (whose name I forget, thus ensuring I'll hear from him as soon as he reads these words) observed that the chord changes of that song have been the basis for literally hundreds of other jazz compositions. The thousands of improvised flights of fancy on those chords is a gargantuan legacy to ponder. "Oh,

Burns's PBS series at all, nor was any other songwriter. George seems to share an association with the "King of Jazz," Paul Whiteman, who is viewed as an interloper, more than with his contemporary Duke Ellington, who like George was as much a composer as performer, if not more so.

BACK IN 1924, WHEN HE WROTE the *Rhapsody*, George was too young and too busy to be thinking about his artistic legacy. But when it came to writing *Porgy and Bess*, George certainly had more of an eye on his place in history, and some blamed his self-conscious imitation of standard opera form for his overuse of recitative. After he became famous George jokingly said to Oscar Levant, "Let's start a correspondence for posterity," but that was only when he was certain that posterity would be interested. In 1924, he had no thoughts of mortality or immortality—*Rhapsody* wasn't even thoroughly finished when it premiered.

Numerous judges, most notably Leonard Bernstein, love to point out the deficiencies of the piece, especially the relative ineptness of its construction. Bernstein wrote an introduction to Charles Schwartz's jealous and faux-scholarly 1973 biography of Gershwin, ostensibly a laudatory piece, but he couldn't help taking a couple of shots at the *Rhapsody*, calling it "structurally weak" and "[a] model of structural inefficiency." I can't help but feel that Bernstein, like many great musicians who followed Gershwin, was jealous of the fact that this unusual piece of music had such an extraordinary impact on people, and it wasn't written by him. Yet Bernstein wrote

sody" rather than using a term that carried with it association with any musical conventions.

George became accustomed to the kind of jealousy later demonstrated by Bernstein and others, but he never totally got over it. George couldn't have known, of course, that Bernstein always especially wanted to write the Great American Opera but that feat had already been accomplished by his deceased rival. (Who among us, though, wouldn't happily "settle" for the exquisite *West Side Story* instead?)

In George's lifetime, many people had trouble coming to terms with the range of his talent, and some suggested that he didn't orchestrate his own

GERSHWIN WAS AWARE that HIS PIECE HAD SHORT-COMINGS, WHICH WAS WHY HE CALLED it a "RHAPSODY" RATHER THAN USING a TERM THAT CARRIED with it ASSOCIATION with ANY MUSICAL CONVENTIONS.

in his 1982 book, *Findings,* that George was one of America's "true, and authentic geniuses," so bearing in mind his mixture of praise and criticism, he clearly held George to an almost impossibly high standard.

It's true that some parts of the *Rhapsody* don't fit with other parts, but that doesn't mean it's hopelessly flawed. It would have been more deftly constructed had George written it later in his life, no doubt, or taken more time over it when he did write it, but it still has more form than it is given credit for. Gershwin was aware that his piece had shortcomings, which was why he called it a "rhap-

pieces; his friend William Daly must have done it. Richard Rodgers, who competed with George for preeminence on Broadway, went into therapy over his feelings of envy for George and was not able to acknowledge them until decades later, when the fruits of his therapy finally resulted in a late-life purging of those suppressed emotions. After years of therapy, Rodgers was able to confess his jealousy to George's kid sister, Frankie. It had been clinically painful even for the great Richard Rodgers to watch the meteoric ascent of Gershwin, culminating in the creation of an opera that was dazzling beyond comprehension.

Similarly, the talented composer Virgil Thomson's caustic reaction to *Porgy and Bess* has already been noted. The irony is that Thomson, if he is remembered at all, is known as much for his bitchy paragraph regarding *Porgy* as for his own music. Every time I read his comments, knowing what I do about critics who are also frustrated creators, it becomes clear that this quote must be put in context. Thomson was an intellectual, homosexual, short, unattractive man who lacked all of the advantages that were born to Gershwin. He also spoke with an impossibly high-pitched voice that was ridiculed behind his back, and his music was probably dismissed by many simply because of who he was, which must have filled him with fury. The fact that his all-black opera was not given an iota of the attention paid *Porgy* also must have made his blood boil, and that, combined with the "Who the hell does he think he is?" attitude regarding Gershwin's ability to suddenly tread on his territory, had to have affected him.

When we review George's musical legacy, we see evidence of this pernicious snobbery that existed in George's lifetime and still exists to an extent today. It centers around George's refusal to restrict himself to any clearly defined "box," a refusal that led to the rampant category confusion critics faced after they saw *Porgy and Bess* and that attached the perceived stigma of Tin Pan Alley to any discussion of his other music. What makes a writer of pop songs think he can tackle an opera? How can someone who writes music for movies expect his piano concerto to be taken seriously? Who the hell does this guy think he is?

Many composers have had a difficult time when they tried their hand at something different, and not everything George wrote was brilliant. The Norwegian composer Edvard Grieg is best known as a miniaturist with his *Lyric Pieces* and his music for Ibsen's play *Peer Gynt*. Grieg's Piano Concerto is his masterpiece, but he also wrote a symphony as a young man and then inscribed "Never to be performed" on the score and tried to suppress it. (The symphony was recorded and is available on iTunes—so much for honoring the artist's intentions.)

Victor Herbert, famous for his operettas, met similar resistance to his category crossing when he tried his hand at American grand opera with the Native American–themed *Natoma,* staged in 1911. The best thing the *New York Times* could say about the opening night in Philadelphia was that the opera house looked nice. But Herbert expected such retribution from the critics for his sin of previously writing popular operettas. On the opening night of *Natoma* he gathered the cast afterward and read them a series of scathing reviews, only to announce at their conclusion that they were the opening night reviews for the first production of *Carmen.*

GEORGE WAS MINDFUL of his lack of formal musical education and pained by the lack of acceptance he was accorded in some quarters. As a result, he was constantly working to improve his musicology and formal compositional technique. When he took on a new project, he learned as much as he could, took no shortcuts, and didn't ask for any concessions. He wanted his Concerto in F to be taken as seriously as any composed by one of the greats—Mozart, Brahms, Schumann, or Beethoven. While

Edward Weston
1936

Dear Mr Gershwin:
with your leaving audience
from

to

yours
Arnold Schoenberg
November 26, 1936

George had tremendous confidence in his own ability, it was undermined by concern about how others saw him.

There's a story that has been oft repeated, but it perfectly captures George's desire to further his musical education. When he met Maurice Ravel, he asked if the composer would give him lessons; Ravel turned him down, saying he was better off being a first-rate Gershwin than a second-rate Ravel. There's another one about George asking Igor Stravinsky for help. Stravinsky supposedly asked George how much money he made and when George told him, the great Russian maestro supposedly said, "It's me who should be taking lessons from you!"

Of the several teachers George did see, the most important was Joseph Schillinger, who worked with him from 1932 to 1936. Schillinger taught composition using a system of mathematical calculations that seemed to be at odds with George's instinctive channeling of music. Ira said he found "strange graphs" George made of his work with Schillinger, with headings like "Rhythmic Groups Resulting from the Inference of Several Synchronized Periodicities." Still, Ira insisted that the palpable influence of Schillinger was solely evident in only one single section of *Porgy and Bess*, and that was the Fugue. Ira felt that Schillinger taught people to use his system as a means of coming up with musical ideas when they couldn't find them out of inspiration. George certainly didn't need help in that area.

As George augmented his talent with diligent study, he won over many of the established composers he met, among them his Beverly Hills tennis partner Arnold Schoenberg, as well as Alban Berg, Stravinsky, and Ravel, who was a generation older than George. They met in 1928; Ravel saw George and Ira's musical *Funny Face*, and he went to parties and concerts with George, including a trip to Harlem to see Duke Ellington's band. Ravel's G Major Concerto, first performed in 1932, clearly shows the influence of George's *Rhapsody in Blue* and the Concerto in F, and his jazz-tinged works. It was Berg with whom George was most fascinated because of Berg's reciprocal interest in his music. After playing dozens of his songs for Berg, who was a nontraditional modernist, he could no longer contain himself. "Why are you so interested in my simple songs when you write such complex music?" he asked. Berg replied, "My dear Mr. Gershwin, music is music."

Perhaps the most secure part of George Gershwin's legacy is the impact he had on other composers. Whenever I listen to *Porgy and Bess*, it always strikes me that Leonard Bernstein wouldn't have been who he was without it, nor would Stephen Sondheim. Every composer who came after Gershwin was deeply influenced by what he created.

And what George created was such a small sample of his potential. Had he lived longer, he would have written more classical works and broadened and deepened his musical legacy. He is judged as a classical composer on the strength of one piano piece that defies classification, one opera, one concerto, and some smaller pieces that in many cases are ephemera. And let's not forget that *Porgy and Bess* was his first opera; the Concerto in F his first concerto. In a world that loves to put people in neatly defined boxes, George defied categorization. He was sui generis and therefore by definition was incomparable.

(OPPOSITE) *Inscription and musical quotation on photo from Arthur Schoenberg to George. Photo taken by Edward Weston.*

Today, George's place at the top of the American music heap is rarely questioned. In 2007, the Library of Congress instituted a prize for contributions to popular music called the Gershwin Prize for Popular Song (named for both George and Ira). The first recipient was Paul Simon; Stevie Wonder was presented with the award in 2009; Paul McCartney in 2010; and Burt Bacharach and Hal David were the winners for 2012. As a member of the advisory committee, I think the same thing whenever a recipient is selected: "They may be great, but they're still not as good as George."

I'M DELIGHTED TO BE PRESENTING A RECORDING of "I Got Rhythm" here because I've never made one, and I only added the song to my performing repertoire fairly recently. Some songs are so overdone, and their myriad interpretations accumulate so much baggage, that they challenge a music maker to dare to find something new about them without violating their provenance. Earlier in my career, I most often performed solo, accompanying myself at the piano, and this is not an easy song to perform that way, because it takes a lot of focus to simultaneously do both well, and the presentation is somewhat static if you're not by nature a jazz improviser, and fundamentally I am not.

The small groups I sometimes play with now allow me to do the song greater justice. If someone requests it when it's just me and my piano (and they do; it's a big fan favorite), I'll do it, but it's hard work for me to find the freshness in such an interpretation. Being who I am, I always insist on finding the sense of discovery in any song I play,

and perhaps the challenge of "I Got Rhythm" has been blown out of proportion by my own musical code of ethics. In fact, I'd rather listen to the song than perform it like that in front of an audience.

This is the song I played Ira the first time we met. I sat down at his piano and played it in the style of Rachmaninoff, Bach, and Beethoven. That was fun! Ira hadn't known that I could play at all and he was delighted. George wrote most of *Porgy and Bess* on that piano, so it was a special thrill to play on it. It was also nerve-wracking, because Ira casually dropped that fact right before my hands struck the keys for the first time, and they suddenly felt as if they had turned to mush.

I can't remember when I first heard "I Got Rhythm." It was probably on a television variety show, something like *Sing Along with Mitch,* Mitch Miller's show that ran on NBC from 1961 to 1966, or *The Lawrence Welk Show,* which was on ABC between 1955 and 1971. These were music-based programs largely composed of performances of pieces from the Great American Songbook. *The Bell Telephone Hour,* which was on NBC through most of the sixties, had Gershwin specials. There was one in 1959, in which Ira briefly and nervously appeared with singers Ella Fitzgerald and Vic Damone, with André Previn at the piano. Previn was also in a Bell "Portrait" of Gershwin that aired in 1966. Network television has abandoned programming like this, meaning that people who are unfamiliar with George are less likely to run into him. It's another reason his popularity is less widespread.

Some of the TV specials were wonderful. I fondly remember a ninety-minute spectacular in 1972 called "'S Wonderful, 'S Marvelous, 'S Gershwin" that featured Fred Astaire at the top of the bill. A cast recording of the show was released and while the arrangements weren't particularly idiomatic, it still carried the joy of its subject, especially as espoused by host Jack Lemmon. In 1975, Steve Lawrence and Eydie Gorme made a George tribute, called *Our Love Is Here to Stay,* that guest-starred Gene Kelly. So I was lucky enough to be familiar with many Gershwin songs when I was younger.

HEARING THE COMPOSER PLAY THOSE SONGS WAS EQUIVALENT TO RIDING A ROCKET TO THE MOON.

There were also the Gershwin-related musical films that played on the television late show that my parents were kind enough to let me stay up and watch, movies like *Shall We Dance, Rhapsody in Blue,* and *An American in Paris.* The movies were filler, played at uncivilized and, for the network, unprofitable, times of night.

Around the seventy-fifth anniversary of George's birth a double LP, *Gershwin by Gershwin,* consisting of radio broadcasts and some of George's piano rolls, was released. This album marked the first release of two 1934 radio shows featuring George and an appearance on the *Rudy Vallee Show* (or, as it was known for its sponsor, *The Fleischmann Hour* for Fleischmann's yeast), which yielded two versions of "I Got Rhythm" with George at the piano. Hearing the composer play those songs was equivalent to riding a rocket to the moon as far as I was concerned. I couldn't believe that I was hearing Gershwin himself, and I played those discs until the grooves turned gray from wear. What sheer joy and unbridled electricity he manufactured, and how often, I wonder, has the word "electricity" been used in the description of his playing?

"I Got Rhythm" was composed in 1930 for the Broadway musical *Girl Crazy,* which starred Ethel Merman and Ginger Rogers. The score of *Girl Crazy* yielded several hits, including "Embraceable You," "Bidin' My Time," and "But Not for Me." George proved over and over that he got rhythm. He knew how to put complexity in popular songs, both rhythmically and harmonically, but he never did it for the sake of showing off: they just came out that way. The songs would really "turn on" dancers or anyone with a certain level of musical sophistication, yet even those who didn't possess these qualities could feel the exuberance and power of his youthful fire.

One of the consequences of George's early death was that he never got to hear the big band arrangements of the forties or the swing sounds of the fifties and didn't get to hear the myriad versions of "I Got Rhythm" recorded over the past seventy years. "I Got Rhythm" is endlessly adaptable because of the tension within the song's structure. The beat of the song is a quick and steady *one-two-three-four,* while the melody is "I got rhythm / I got music" with a spare beat before each phrase. It's not easy to explain without the music, and perhaps dangerous to do so, but no one interpreting the song today ever sings it exactly that way anymore, the way Gershwin wrote it. The beat continues on—*one-two-three-four;*

one-two-three-four—but around that structure the song is a dynamic entity that has been changed and revised by singers through the years.

It was that rhythmic tension that made the song such a hit on its debut. Kay Swift, George's paramour and a superior musical mind, would take anyone to task who violated the original structure of his creation, and she was right. She loved to demonstrate how it lost something without that tension, but like a child growing up and leaving home, it later gained different life experiences and different trappings of identity by which it was defined.

Just as George toyed with the music, Ira was endlessly creative with the lyrics, making up words and phrases to fit his frequently complex rhyming schemes. He could also get ungrammatical when necessary, as he did on this occasion. "I got" is punchier than "I've" and fits perfectly with the music. "I" allows for the equal separation of each word in the phrase and fits the staccato notes far better than "I've." "I've got rhythm" is much too formal. Also, if the singer had to enunciate "I've," the words would meld into each other, the spacing would be lost, and the impact would be muted. Of course, partisans of grammatically correct phraseology have ever thus thwarted Ira from the start and have corrected the words, to his eternal consternation. One time I found a pad of stationery emblazoned with the phrase "I've Got Rhythm." When I showed it to Ira, he snatched it and marked out the "'ve" of "I've" and wrote: "corrected by the lyricist, Ira Gershwin."

Another part of George and Ira's legacy was their ability to make stars out of performers like Ethel Merman, who got her first big break singing "I Got Rhythm" in *Girl Crazy*. The Gershwin

songs are challenging, but in the right hands they can be transformative, for the audience and the performer alike. There are many performers whose reputations have been advanced or even created because they were able to take on George and Ira's material and fly alongside it. Fred Astaire is another; so is Sinatra, and Ella Fitzgerald.

When *Girl Crazy* was being put together, nineteen-year-old Ginger Rogers was cast, and the producers started looking for the second lead, a strong, hot female singer who could handle, among other songs, "I Got Rhythm." Then the producer, Vinton Freedley, saw a young woman called Ethel Merman, who had a voice that boomed out like a siren, singing at the Brooklyn Paramount theater.

Ethel Zimmerman was born in Queens, New York, and worked as a stenographer while hoping to be discovered as a singer. She was given a contract by Warner Brothers, shortened her name, and was singing in nightclubs and theaters until the studio found a suitable film role for her. But Freedley got to her first. Although she was three years older than Rogers, Merman had less experience and was less well known when she was called in to audition for George Gershwin at his Riverside Drive apartment. Lee Gershwin's sister, Emily Paley, vividly remembered how shy Ethel Merman was, and how awed she was by the swanky penthouse, with its sweeping view and George's large art collection.

George played Ethel the songs her character would sing in the show: "Sam and Delilah," "Boy! What Love Has Done to Me!" and "I Got Rhythm." Ethel might have been impressed by her company and her surroundings, but she was hardly intimidated. When she sang "I Got Rhythm," George was in turn impressed with her. He loved the way she sang—she had the belting delivery that was needed on Broadway in the days long before microphones were widely used. (Mics didn't come into general use until the sixties.) It was clear her voice would carry effortlessly over the footlights and up into the last row of the balcony. (Irving Berlin later said, "You'd better never write a bad song for Ethel because if you do, you'll hear it!") She also had a musicality and a swagger that perfectly matched the jazzy excitement of the song.

When she finished singing, George said something along the lines of: "Miss Merman, if there's anything you don't like about these songs, I'd be happy to change them." And Ethel, taken aback by the idea that the great George Gershwin might

Queens and never tried to change her manner of speech or obscure her humble background. Perhaps one could compare her to Bette Midler, but Merman had an inimitable and unfailing clarion voice and confined obscenities exclusively to her offstage exploits. She was very smart, very funny, and spoke her mind. She was also crass and somewhat vulgar and not worldly, so it was unlikely she'd be appealing to someone as circumspect and decorous as Ira, who may have been the least vulgar person who ever lived.

Perhaps Ira was prudish outwardly, but he certainly knew the score when it came to an understanding of character and human nature. There's a story about Ethel's Manhattan apartment, which

ETHEL ANSWERED PROUDLY, "IT'S AN ORIGINAL." TO HER, THAT WAS THE PINNACLE.

rewrite a song to suit her, said, "They'll do very nicely." She got the part.

In her later years, Ethel Merman would tell the story of how George Gershwin offered to rewrite his songs according to her preference when they'd only just met. I once asked Ira, "Would George have really changed the songs?" Ira smiled and said, "He was just being polite," adding that if Ethel had asked for a B flat in the sixth bar rather than a B, George might have considered it.

Ira, unlike George, never liked Ethel Merman's singing. He thought it was too brash, too "in your face," as one might say nowadays. Most people thought Ethel Merman was charming in that she remained the same street-savvy girl from

she bought after she'd had some success. A friend who was touring the new place asked, "Ethel, what's that painting? It's beautiful." Ethel answered proudly, "It's an original." To her, that was the pinnacle. Merman used to say odd things about Ira that made me wonder if there had been some sort of friction between them, even insinuating that Ira was gay. Ira certainly never found anything about Ethel carnally attractive, and she might have misinterpreted his lack of interest. But I find it unlikely that he ever would have had any cross words with Ethel—Ira was so afraid of conflict.

Ira's opinion about Ethel as a performer was very much in the minority. On opening night, October 14, 1930, she stopped the show cold with her singing, and the audience demanded many encores. Ira couldn't stand it, though he was delighted at the reception of "I Got Rhythm." The next day, when George called to offer his congratulations, Ethel said, "For what?" George said, "Haven't you seen the papers?" She said she hadn't, as she was so inexperienced concerning the ways of Broadway that she was unaware reviews even existed, so George told her, "Get them. The reviews are out. You're a star." The *New York Times* said her singing style was "peculiar" but that she performed "to the vast delight last evening of the people who go places and watch things being done," whatever that means.

(Another interesting note on the original performers of *Girl Crazy* was the extraordinary array of talent in the orchestra pit. George conducted the band, which had been put together as a swing

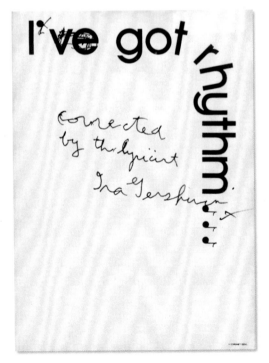

outfit, which was highly unusual for Broadway at the time, since this was at least five years before swing became really popular. Many of the band members had worked with bandleader Ben Pollack and went on to be stars—Benny Goodman, Gene Krupa, Jack Teagarden, Glenn Miller, Red Nichols. The trumpeter Red Nichols and his ensemble made the first recording of "I Got Rhythm," in 1930, and it was a hit. The following year, Ethel Waters also had a hit with it, as did Louis Armstrong in 1932.)

ETHEL MERMAN, WHO WASN'T a recording star, didn't record "I Got Rhythm" until 1947, and she did then with a more forties pop orchestration, quite unlike what she sang on Broadway. A newsreel from 1932 captures her performing part of the song wonderfully, and she sings the whole song in a 1937 Gershwin memorial radio broadcast. There's also a 1931 newsreel of George playing "I Got Rhythm," on piano of course, at the opening of the Manhattan Theatre.

"I Got Rhythm" and Gershwin are forever associated with Ethel Merman, because she introduced the song on Broadway and George was instrumental in making her a star. More than forty years later, Merman appeared in the 1972 Gershwin television special "'S Wonderful . . ." Whenever she performed "I Got Rhythm," she always did the choreography from the original show. She made a little pointing gesture with her fingers and alternated it between her left hand and her right, flipping one, then the other in time to the music as if she were throwing roses to the audience. It is believed that it was Hollywood producer and vocal arranger Roger Edens who came up with these hand moves.

Ira's lyric correction on a piece of stationery.

Even though Ethel didn't ask George to change the song at her audition, she didn't sing it exactly as George wrote it. (Edens was behind this as well.) Ethel held one note for six bars while the orchestra continued with the melody. This held note became a trademark for her, and other singers would copy it, perhaps unaware that it's not in the original score. Even if George didn't write it that way, he admitted to loving Ethel's version, feeling that it enhanced the excitement of the song.

Ira, on the other hand, would cringe when he heard that interminable note. I once decided to have a little fun with him. I took a recording of Ethel Merman singing "I Got Rhythm" and duplicated her six-bar "held note" phrase several times onto a tape recording so she seemed to be sustaining it for more than a minute—"*Who could ask for anything more-ahhhhhh . . .*" Ira listened to it and his eyes got wider and wider and he finally said, "Okay, I give up. I surrender. I surrender."

"I Got Rhythm" became so popular that Gershwin composed a piece called the *I Got Rhythm Variations,* which he debuted on his 1934 concert tour. It has never become as well known as some of his other concert works, but the extraordinary success of the song is made evident by the fact that, a scant four years after it was composed, the creator turned it into a work that was performed by orchestras in concert halls alongside his classical pieces, such as the Concerto in F. It's interesting to note that *I Got Rhythm Variations* starts with a solo clarinet, just as did *Rhapsody in Blue.* Ben Kanter, a pop clarinetist who auditioned for Gershwin, played the clarinet glissando from the *Rhapsody* and was immediately hired for the job.

Paul Whiteman recorded the *I Got Rhythm Variations* in the mid-fifties with Buddy Weed as the piano soloist, and he added a modern swing sensibility, reflecting the changing sounds of jazz, with the rhythm section cannily altering the instrumentation. He completely changed the feel of the piece, but I think it is fantastic and would have intrigued the always forward-looking composer.

AN ARTISTIC LEGACY TAKES DIFFERENT FORMS. Just as an artist's reputation could be measured in ticket sales in his lifetime, the most easily measured piece of George's legacy is the income that flows to his estate from the copyrights on his music, particularly on *Rhapsody in Blue.* George made a lot of money from the piece in his lifetime, and it has been a steady source of income for his family ever since, particularly since it was licensed by the George Gershwin estate to United Airlines shortly after Ira's death in 1983 to use in its commercials. When Ira was previously asked to license the *Rhapsody* for a television commercial, he said, "Over my dead body," and they ultimately obliged. The airline still uses the piece and has described *Rhapsody in Blue* as its "signature music."

Many artists have an extremely keen interest in copyright law. When a song or a book is protected by copyright, the artist (or estate) has to give permission for another party to exploit the work, and that permission usually comes with a price tag. If a work is out of copyright, it's in the public domain and it becomes fair game. The law is particularly complicated when it comes to works that were written in the twenties, such as *Rhapsody in Blue.* A copyright law from 1909 allowed for twenty-eight years of protection plus another twenty-eight (later forty-seven) if the copyright was renewed. Another act in 1976 (which became law in 1978) mandated that anything created after that date was protected for the life of the author plus fifty years. Works already under copyright were protected for seventy-five years from the date of creation, meaning that *Rhapsody in Blue* would enter the public domain in 1999. However, in 1998 that term was extended to ninety-five years and the new material to life of author plus seventy years. Are you following me? Neither am I. And neither is Congress, which needs to create uniform copyright laws to conform with other properties and the rest of the world. But that's another book entirely.

Copyright laws obviously have dramatic implications for the estate of any successful composer. Overnight, a revenue stream can disappear. George's solo work is now all unprotected in Europe. In this country, some of George's earlier songs, like "Swanee," are already in the public domain and the rest of his output will follow in due course, including *Rhapsody in Blue* in 2019.

A COMPOSER'S LEGACY IS ALSO JUDGED by the status of his compositions. How often are they played? How much have they influenced other musicians? How is the composer's musical reputation? When it comes to very established pieces, the world is often compelled to create "definitive" versions that supposedly represent the composer's true intentions. In George's case, as we have seen, this tendency has most frequently been applied to *Porgy and Bess*.

Ira always considered *Rhapsody in Blue* to be sacrosanct. It was suggested to him many times that he write lyrics for it, but he insisted that the piece shouldn't be tampered with. Even when he was told that by writing a lyric for the *Rhapsody* he could extend the life of the copyright, he still couldn't bring himself to do it. Ira well understood the monetary implications of his inaction, but to him, the piece belonged in the concert hall and to change it would be to demean and trivialize it. Fred Astaire did come up with a lyric—"Play me that *Rhapsody in Blue*, written by Gershwin, played by Paul Whiteman . . ."—but Fred was joking.

Of course, *Rhapsody in Blue* is "that United Airlines tune" for many people, but it has a power and a resonance that transcend time and its role in an advertisement. And as much as Ira would have hated the trivialization of the music for a commercial, even he would have had to admit that it hasn't seemed to have harmed the work one whit. It's a dynamic piece of music that musicians and listeners still find relevant. To say that it was an anomaly, something that was "ahead of its time," reduces it to some kind of semi-freakish party trick that George Gershwin pulled out of his hat as if by accident. That was part of the old-school establishment thinking that once surrounded the work, to the consternation of its creator.

When the piece debuted in 1924, people were skeptical about its long-term survival. The *Rhapsody* was created quickly at a time when George was working on a number of other projects. He did not scratch away in a garret for ten years before emerging disheveled and malnourished, masterpiece in hand. At just twenty-five years of age, he had not yet paid his dues to classical music in any real way. All of these circumstances probably encouraged critics to take the piece less seriously. And despite the

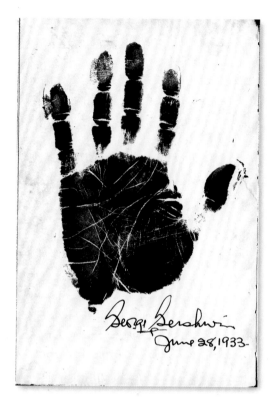 

fact that George was commissioned to write his Concerto in F for the New York Symphony Orchestra by Walter Damrosch and had his works performed at Carnegie Hall, Gershwin was somewhat denigrated by the major symphony orchestras. When he appeared and played his own music, the concerts were wildly successful, but an orchestra was unlikely to play Gershwin unless he was in the house. It wasn't until the sixties that Gershwin became a staple in the concert hall.

Just as Ira and George essentially created the careers of many artists such as Ethel Merman, certain performers helped cement aspects of the Gershwin legacy. In the forties and fifties, Oscar Levant, the most famous concert pianist of his time, championed the integration of Gershwin into the standard orchestral repertoire by insisting on performing the works with all of the great symphony orchestras of the age. Levant had become a celebrity via his appearances on a radio show called *Information Please*, and once he was engaged for concerts, he requested the Gershwin repertoire, which was otherwise rarely performed in those days. The success of his concerts opened the floodgates for others to follow suit.

Levant recorded all of George's piano works, including the *Three Preludes,* published in 1927. The great violinist Jascha Heifetz transcribed the preludes for violin and piano in the forties, and those are now in the repertoire of numerous violinists, or at least ones who are able to handle the difficult idiomatic combination of jazz and

George's signed palm prints.

fiendish virtuosity. One critic called the Heifetz transcriptions "Porgy in Moscow." This legitimization of Gershwin in the world of classical music is a relatively recent phenomenon.

THERE ARE TWO KINDS OF GENIUSES. There are those who become great through sheer effort, mastering their craft through practice, hard work, and years of repetition, and then there are the "naturals," people like Gershwin, who was a genius from the get-go. At the same time, George was extremely driven and self-directed. He felt a compelling need to do what he was doing, and he worked hard throughout his career to make his music better. Most people cut corners, even geniuses. Not George. Even though he channeled music, plucking it out of the air as if it were traveling through the atmosphere on a frequency only he had access to, he also worked extremely hard. Even when a good tune or idea came quickly to him, he would sometimes put it aside if it didn't feel 100 percent right and save the melody for future use.

Ira was the other kind of genius, one who worked his way up to his success. George would come home from a party at 1 A.M. and say to Ira, "Do you want to do some work?" Then he'd sit down and tap out a melody. Ira would roll up his sleeves and spend the rest of the night trying to find a lyric for it.

Painstaking labor is one of the reasons Stephen Sondheim is considered such a genius—he doesn't take shortcuts when he writes a score. He still uses perfect rhymes in his lyrics even though many today say conventional rhyming is outmoded; if that is so, then why is it that his music sounds so fresh and contemporary? I believe Sondheim's legacy will be secure for the same reason that George's is, because of the continued relevance of his art through the years. As new audiences discover Gershwin, it works the same magic and has the same effect that it had on their great-grandparents eight decades earlier.

There are other great composers and songwriters whose legacies deserve to be as secure as George's. They all possessed a remarkable facility for creating great works that endured. Like George, Richard Rodgers was able to make it look easy. One time Rodgers was listening to a younger composer play a new song he'd written and my friend Gordon Hunt heard Rodgers say, "I can pee better tunes than that." Rodgers and his lyricist, Lorenz Hart, were very productive: *The Girl Friend*, *Peggy-Ann*, *A Connecticut Yankee,* and *Ever Green* were among their output from 1926–1931 alone. Cole Porter was prolific but he wasn't facile musically, in that he had brilliant ideas but had difficulty realizing them on paper. He could write lyrics quickly but he had to work very hard at the music. Porter's efforts produced songs such as "Begin the Beguine," songs that are unique in the canon, but it wasn't easy for him to get there. In some ways Porter was a natural, but he had to sweat his way to greatness. His manuscripts sometimes look laborious, but he kept working and driving until he got it right. For Rodgers, though, it was easy, like falling off a log.

Many of these Rodgers and Hart songs stand up as well today as do George and Ira's. Off the top of my head I can think of quite a few: "My Funny Valentine," "With a Song in My Heart," "My Heart Stood Still," "Blue Moon," "You Took Advantage of Me," "It Never Entered My Mind," "The Lady Is a Tramp," "Where or When?," "Manhattan," "Mountain Greenery," "Bewitched, Bothered and Bewildered," "Isn't It Romantic," "There's a Small Hotel," "Falling in Love with Love," "My Romance," "Glad to Be Unhappy," "Lover" . . . and I could go on. These songs are imbued with a kind of unique insouciance that unmistakably brands them as brilliant and delicious, yet so different from Gershwin.

Rodgers and Hart wrote hundreds of songs together. Lorenz Hart was an alcoholic and quite unreliable. According to Rodgers, Hart could write only when the two of them were in a room to-

are only three lyric writers who can rightly use polysyllabic words in modern songs. Irving Berlin, Buddy DeSylva and Ira Gershwin are the three." It was a characteristically generous gesture from the tormented master.

Johnny Mercer is undoubtedly equal to Rodgers and Hart and the Gershwins. Mercer was the most versatile of all—he could write any kind of song, and did. He could write about the countryside and the South and the simpler values in life, songs about the human condition, songs of irony, songs with extremely sophisticated lyrics. His

AN ORCHESTRA WAS UNLIKELY TO PLAY GERSHWIN UNLESS HE WAS IN THE HOUSE.

gether. Rodgers needed to pin his collaborator down to get him to focus, but when he was able to bear down, he came up with lyrics that were among the best of the best. Rodgers would come up with the melody first—when he worked with Oscar Hammerstein after Lorenz Hart died in 1943, it was often the case that the lyrics came first.

Lorenz Hart was well schooled in the classical poets and German greats like Schopenhauer and Schiller, and he had a tremendous sadness about him that imbued his work—a sense of longing that was unusual for pop songs of the time. Ira prized a laudatory letter he received from Lorenz Hart in 1925. Furthermore, in print, in a 1927 book called *Jazz Music: What It Is and How to Understand It,* by Isaac Goldberg, one of a popular series of tiny (three-by-four-inch) titles, Hart was quoted as saying, "My belief is that there

reputation in lyric history has grown incrementally over the last several decades, and the shadow that his giant body of work casts is mighty.

Johnny grew up in Savannah, Georgia (born in 1909), and was raised among the music of that locale: blues and gospel and hillbilly music. He listened to a lot of vaudeville and jazz—songs like "Hard-Hearted Hannah (the Vamp of Savannah)," Ager, Bates, Bigelow, and Yellen's 1924 standard— and to Gilbert and Sullivan. Though he had heard some Rodgers and Hart songs, he didn't pay much attention to them. When Mercer moved to New York in 1930, he was exposed to the Gershwins, Cole Porter, and Richard Rodgers, and his tastes changed. He developed an appreciation for the sophisticated lyrics of Lorenz Hart, whose references to urban life had meant nothing to Johnny when he was down south. This amalgamation of different places and types of music is what enabled Mercer to become so versatile. He could write jazz and blues, he could write for theater and film, and he could rhyme brilliantly, too.

Johnny's last major work was *Good Companions*, a musical he wrote with André Previn that was produced in London in 1974. In the title song, he mentions "sitting duck and sticky wicket, this whole life's a game of cricket." It's the rare American who can refer to the game of cricket without making a fool of himself. Johnny could do anything, though he felt his least successful work was for the stage.

Mercer always said that George and Ira's contemporary Yip Harburg was his guru. Harburg had an ability to inject humor and wit into just a couple of lines, like "I'd become passionate / If there's some cash in it." He wrote "Lydia the Tattooed Lady," a very funny song, for Groucho Marx. Sustaining humor in a song is difficult. You can come up with a good joke, but where do you go from there? Harburg had a rare ability to follow the joke through to the end.

THE PATH BY WHICH MUSIC is brought into the world can be long and twisting, even when it is walked by geniuses such as these. A melody has to be written and lyrics penned that complement the tune. The song has to tell a story, or describe a mood or a feeling, or evoke a character. A song must go through gestation, childhood, and adolescence before it ever reaches an artist or, ultimately, the public. Then, it faces the next battleground—will people connect to it? If they do, a song might become a significant thing in their lives, an illumination, a resonance, something that in a small way makes the world a better place. We can feel a special gratitude to someone for that hard work and inspiration.

Ultimately, the best argument for George's legacy is simply to listen to his music. It still transports audiences. In a world full of choices, these songs continue to have a very special place in the hearts and minds of many people. And this in spite of the fact that most of them were created for specific moments in musicals that are rarely staged anymore. There's something distinctive about George's music, a special resonance. You hear it in *Rhapsody in Blue*. You hear it in "I Got Rhythm."

In 1935, Richard Rodgers wrote a congratulatory letter to George after the opening of *Porgy and Bess* that was in his own words "not easy to write." It seemed so easy for George, and many people couldn't find it in themselves to be happy for him. This was not the universal reaction. Kay Swift fell in love with George, among other reasons, because she saw true genius in thirty-two bars in spite of the fact that her classical music professors had filled her with loathing for Tin Pan Alley pabulum. Marvin Hamlisch's mother once appeared on the *Today* show for a Mother's Day feature on the moms of famous people. The interviewer jokingly asked Mrs. Hamlisch, "Who's your favorite composer?" Mrs. Hamlisch, a very tough Viennese lady, said, "First, Gershwin. Then, Hamlisch." To beat out a mother's love for her own son—now there's a reputation. But who knows what Rose Gershwin would have said in answer to the same question. Shortly before her death in 1948, she confided to a friend, "I wish that I had never had children." ·

(OPPOSITE) *An Alajalov illustration of George painting himself at the piano, from* George Gershwin's Song-book, *published in 1932.*

"LOVE IS HERE TO STAY"

from *The Goldwyn Follies*, 1938

VERSE

The more I read the papers,
The less I comprehend
The world and all its capers
And how it all will end.
Nothing seems to be lasting,
But that isn't our affair;
We've got something permanent—
I mean, in the way we care.

REFRAIN

It's very clear
Our love is here to stay;
Not for a year,
But ever and a day.

The radio and the telephone
And the movies that we know
May just be passing fancies—
And in time may go.

But oh, my dear,
Our love is here to stay.
Together we're
Going a long, long way.

In time the Rockies may crumble,
Gibraltar may tumble
(They're only made of clay),
But—our love is here to stay.

CHAPTER 12

WHAT MIGHT HAVE BEEN . . .

N 1978, ON WHAT WOULD HAVE BEEN GEORGE Gershwin's eightieth birthday, *Washington Post* critic Richard L. Coe wrote a piece positing that George was alive and was being feted with a gala concert celebrating his many achievements of the last six decades. Coe even speculated on what such a concert might include, and named several imaginary works that might have been created through the ensuing decades had George lived. Ira told me he enjoyed the article and the fantasy of having George present. He felt that Coe had skillfully captured the flavor of what might have been, but the melancholy that accompanied his feelings for his brother was never far away. The cherished memories he had of George were

clouded by the cruel circumstances of his death. Sure, they shared music and laughter and love, but there could have been—*should* have been—so much more of all of it. Ira was never far away from depression when he delved too deeply into the ever-present weight of George's absence.

With George, it's impossible not to ask, "What if?" What if he had lived just another ten years, to forty-eight? And what if he'd lived as long as Ira, who died at eighty-six? Or Fred Astaire, who was the same age as George, and lived to eighty-eight, or Irving Berlin, who died at the age of 101? This speculation is irresistible because George died just as I believe he was about to come back with fresh vigor after a couple of relatively

Lee, Oscar Levant, Ira, and Arthur Freed at a screening of An American in Paris *at the MGM Studio in 1950.*

fallow years following the completion of *Porgy and Bess*. He was living in Hollywood, a place he liked to live but hated to work. George was writing excellent, mature songs, but he had ideas and plans that would have expanded his already broad horizons and taken him into new realms of music. I can't imagine he would have failed.

The events of his last year were devoid of the endless heady propulsion of the previous years, ones that were filled with excitement, success, and a worldwide community of idolaters. The fans were still there, but in his cocooned Hollywood existence he was usually isolated from the adulation that buoyed his ego in New York and made him happy. Then he was gone. A switch had been hit and everything numbingly ceased in mid-motion. It just so happened that George was in a relatively lean period. I am convinced he would have bounced back, stronger and more vital than ever.

We're left tantalized, dreadfully.

Gershwin knew what he had achieved with *Porgy and Bess*. He maintained it would one day become accepted and recognized and, indeed, it has been. He didn't know that his Concerto in F and *Rhapsody in Blue* would be regularly performed in concert halls around the world. Ira told me that it was a source of regret for him that George died before he knew he had been awarded Italy's highest musical honor from the Academy of St. Cecilia in Rome. Ira was delighted that a country with such a great musical tradition was recognizing George in a way that had eluded him in his own country in his lifetime. Ira always forcefully maintained that his brother would have continued to change the face of music and would have become as iconic as Beethoven or Bach. As self-effacing as he was about himself, when speaking of his brother, Ira became energized and animated. He was still defending his brother's place in music, and seeing to it that everyone knew the truth.

What George achieved was a fraction of what he could have achieved, and Ira was haunted by the "what if?" especially because Ira saw glimpses of what George was planning, and he hoped and fully expected for things to continue on as they always had. How could it ever be anything different? George was special, privileged, and at the height of his powers.

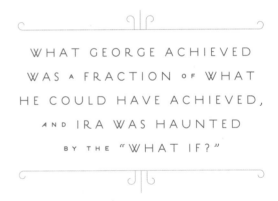

WHAT GEORGE ACHIEVED WAS A FRACTION OF WHAT HE COULD HAVE ACHIEVED, AND IRA WAS HAUNTED BY THE "WHAT IF?"

We do know that at the time of his death, George had already conceived the whole of a string quartet, sadly, none of which survives. Had he lived even six months longer, we would probably have the whole piece to add to his repertoire. George played fragments of the quartet on the piano for Harold Arlen, among others; upon learning of George's death, after offering condolences, Arlen asked Ira if George had notated the string quartet and was told he hadn't.

Contained in George's little tune notebook that he later carried in his jacket are several exquisitely notated bars of music in his hand, and no one knows what they are. They could have been a theme for his quartet, an idea for his planned symphony, or a phrase for a song. Or anything else that struck him in the moment.

Dating from his formative years, there exists one quarter of another quartet, the viola part, but it is a work written when he was a youngster, probably as a composition exercise. It is not to be dismissed merely as an early effort, for his beautiful lullaby for string quartet was also created as an early exercise and is a marvelous, fully formed piece. The maddening thing is that it is only the viola part.

It's amazing how these things turn up. About twenty years ago, an autograph dealer bought several items from the estate of Irene Gallagher, who was secretary to George's onetime publisher, Max Dreyfus. Among the items he purchased was a viola part for a string piece that George had written, obviously a string quartet. It was an ink manuscript in George's hand, with pencil notations of fingering by the string player, so it had been played. The piece is untitled; the manuscript just says "Viola" in the upper right-hand corner, also in George's hand, and it bears no other writing. The autograph dealer who owns it is asking big money for it, and I suppose that is why it is still in his possession. He claims that the entire piece could be reconstructed from the one part and I say, get real. There is only so much you can tell from a single part of a work, even when it's a quartet. Who knows if the viola ever has any of the melody at any point, or if one of its lines is a harmony to some other melody? It's impossible to tell.

We so yearn for there to be more of George's work out there. When something does turn up, it can create overheated expectations. Another Gershwin song appeared in the late eighties, something called "A Voice of Love." Ira wrote a song called "The Voice of Love" with Robert Russell Bennett and Maurice Nitke for the 1924 musical *The Firebrand*. But in 1916, the same year that George's first published song, "When You Want 'Em, You Can't Get 'Em . . ." (with lyrics by Murray Roth), was written, he also wrote something called "A Voice of Love," also with Roth. It was an undocumented and unknown work until it turned up in the hands of a man who thought he had hit the lottery and would retire on this gem. Problem is that it's a copyist's copy that isn't in George's own hand, and I was only shown a copy of just the first page as a teaser. The whole song would have cost me something like $100,000. It's not a particularly interesting song; it's young, early Gershwin; and the manuscript isn't worth $100,000 because it's not in George's hand nor is it of great musical interest, but the owner refused to share it with anyone unless they paid him a great deal of money. Well, wherever it is now, it's truly no great loss, and I say this as a self-confessed completist.

People often offer me Gershwin artifacts, for which I am very grateful, though they sometimes turn out not to be as represented. Over the years I've been shown various manuscripts, pianos, paintings, and more, all linked in one way or another to Gershwin and all fake. Most of the time people are well meaning but other times not.

Composers have paid George the compliment of writing musical tributes to him in period shows and movies to evoke a Gershwinesque sound. Steven Spielberg produced a TV series called *Amazing*

Stories that ran from 1985 to 1987; it included an episode that contained some fictional Gershwin songs performed to superb effect. It was one of the last episodes of the series, a charming piece called "Gershwin's Trunk." It's a story about two rival songwriters, Jo-Jo Gillespie (played by Bob Balaban) and Jerry Lane (played by John McCook), who are working on competing musicals. Gillespie is desperate for a Broadway hit, but he's suffering from writer's block. At the advice of his housekeeper, he goes to see a psychic called Sister Teresa (played by Lainie Kazan), who conjures up the spirit of George Gershwin to write songs for him.

rivers to us / but I discovered you." Another song, called "Ticklish Toes," was inspired by "Fidgety Feet" from *Oh, Kay!* "Fidgety Feet" went, "I've got fidgety feet, fidgety feet, fidgety feet!" and *Amazing Stories'* version went, "Ticklish toes, ticklish toes / That's how it moves / See how it goes."

The episode was scripted by Paul Bartel, a marvelously eccentric filmmaker who's since passed away. Of course, by 1987 Ira had died, too, but I think he would have been delighted by the show. I have a copy of both series of *Amazing Stories* on VHS, but for some reason only the first season has been released on DVD, and not this

OVER THE YEARS I'VE BEEN SHOWN VARIOUS MANUSCRIPTS, PIANOS, PAINTINGS, AND MORE, ALL LINKED IN ONE WAY OR ANOTHER TO GERSHWIN AND ALL FAKE.

Both Jo-Jo's and Jerry's shows are opening on the same night, so Jo-Jo decides to postpone his opening by one day because he knows that his score is going to be superior—after all, it's by George Gershwin. But when Jo-Jo goes to see Jerry's show, the performers burst into the same song that Jo-Jo's show is meant to open with. It turns out that Jerry was seeing the same psychic as Jo-Jo because they shared the same housekeeper.

The imitation Gershwin songs written by John Meyer for the show were very funny. One written with Clay Boland, Jr. was a takeoff of "They All Laughed": "Balboa thought it was terrific / When he discovered the Pacific / Columbus sailed the ocean blue. / Both Clark and Lewis gave

episode. Recently I reminisced with Spielberg about the show, and he chuckled with delight at the remembrance of the whole wacky premise. Any show that features Lainie Kazan as George Gershwin is an instant camp classic. Yet the whole idea was yet one more riff on "what might have been" in connection with Gershwin.

. . . . .

ACCORDING TO IRA, WRITING IN *Lyrics on Several Occasions*, "Love Is Here to Stay" is the last song George Gershwin wrote. Ira said that he and George worked for six weeks on the score for the movie *The Goldwyn Follies* and had completed

George and Ira's siblings, Arthur and Frances, unveiling a plaque in George's honor at his birthplace, in 1963.

five songs. (Ira wrote that he and Vernon Duke filled in some of the missing verses later on.) The five songs were "I Love to Rhyme," "Love Walked In," "I Was Doing Alright," "Just Another Rhumba," and "Love Is Here to Stay." In his book, Ira placed the lyric as the last in the section that he titled "The Element of Time." It's the perfect spot. The last verse is:

> *In time the Rockies may crumble,*
> *Gibraltar may tumble*
> *(They're only made of clay),*
> *But—our love is here to stay.*

THAT LAST LINE WAS NOT INTENTIONALLY written as the last line in the lifelong collaboration of George and Ira. It's just the last line of a song for a movie that had a plot requirement. But circumstances decreed that it was the last line in their last song and, as such, it serves to stand as an eloquent memorial to the brothers and their life and work together.

We can't make too much of the fact that this was George's last song. The brothers were working on a number of things at the same time, and this happened to be the last one that had both their attention before George suddenly slipped into a

coma. Even though he had taken a leave of absence from Goldwyn Studios on July 1, George continued to work on the score when he felt able, and the diversion did him good. George made a sketch of the song in his tune notebook, but he died before he'd completely notated it, and Ira was still working on the lyric. The loyal Oscar Levant remembered the finished melody and transcribed it.

Other songs were in the process of being completed by them—"Love Walked In," for example—and it was only in retrospect that Ira recalled which was in fact the last. There was no intention that this be his final musical statement, though Ira used the means of completing the lyric after George died to pour out his pent-up feelings of devastation.

The songs George wrote at the end of his life for the movies (*Shall We Dance*, *A Damsel in Distress*, and *The Goldwyn Follies*) are very sophisticated harmonically and reflect his musical growth. Despite that, many people in Hollywood at the time seemed turned off by them, and I can't figure out why. The conditions that George and Ira worked under in Hollywood hadn't changed much since their first visit and still weren't the most conducive for the making of great art. Sam Goldwyn, who made the *Follies*, was musically illiterate but insisted on sitting in judgment on the composers and songwriters he employed. So George would have to road-test his songs for Goldwyn and his henchmen, who would sit quietly until Goldwyn said, "I like it," and then they'd all applaud, like trained seals.

George complained. "You know, I've spent my life studying and working in music, to have to audition for Sam Goldwyn . . ." He was doing it, as I'm sure he reminded himself frequently, for the money. In a letter to his mother on June 10, 1937,

Goldwyn Follies *film poster.*

George wrote that he'd had enough of Hollywood and couldn't wait until he could come back east to New York and maybe go to Europe. He could be moving on to the next phase in his musical life. Except that he only had a month to live.

"Love Is Here to Stay" was created because the producers needed a couple of ballads—slow love songs—for the movie. The first was "Love Walked In," which was mostly completed before George died. And then there was "Love Is Here to Stay."

The premise for the song was the permanence of love in the face of the general dissolution that surrounds us. In one of his early drafts for the lyrics, Ira wrote about the flowers and the trees changing and dying, themes that didn't end up in the final version. After finishing the familiar chorus, he wrote the music and the lyric for the verse and Vernon Duke notated it. Although Ira was not a composer, out of necessity he came up with music for the verse, and it worked for his purposes.

Later, Vernon Duke claimed authorship of the verse and part of the overall music, and Ira defended himself, saying in his self-effacing way that the music for the verse was so undistinguished, wasn't it obvious that he wrote it? If Duke had had something to do with the music, I am sure Ira would have happily given him credit. It was his nature.

It's hard to set aside the fact that this was George and Ira's swan song, but "Love Is Here to Stay" is still distinguished enough to be considered one of their greatest works. Melodically it's a beautiful song. One of the things that is so delightful is that it has a foxtrot or dance feel to it. Because of the variation of the rhythm of the first phrase, it starts out metronomically in a drawn-out "Ya-da-da-daaah," and then it moves on, quickly, to "Our love is here to stay," and on those words there is a rhythmic movement that makes the section irresistibly danceable. It is a great way to continue the melody, starting out with the long-flowing "It's very clear . . .," then rapidly to "Our love is here to stay."

That two-stage progression is characteristic of George. He inserted a rhythmic idea into a ballad to propel it forward with a lot of energy, and then he continued the idea until he reached the bridge. The melody in the bridge is contiguous in that musically one phrase ties into the next. When we hear, "The radio and the telephone and the movies that we know," the music is perfectly complementary.

The melody in the bridge is long and flowing, and then, when we get back to the repetition of the first eight bars, it picks up the first strain again. It's an even more delightful contrast after the long lines of the bridge. The end of the song then repeats the bridge music, giving it a sense of tying everything up, returning to the original lyrical idea. It's unusual for bridge music to recur toward the end of a song: "In time the Rockies may crumble, Gibraltar may tumble . . ." It's a mirror of the lyrical idea in the bridge, but takes it one step further. The lyrics reinforce the music; the music reinforces the lyric: it's an artistic whole, a complete little work of art.

"Love Is Here to Stay" is the mature George Gershwin, and it indicates the direction he was seemingly headed: sophisticated and accomplished, inventive and refined. But the song was horribly mistreated in the movie, almost thrown away, with part of it obliterated by dialogue. It was originally sung by Kenny Baker, whose delivery was bloodless compared to the way he rapturously sang "Love Walked In" in the same film.

THE GERSHWINS AND ME

For audiences, "Love Is Here to Stay" was largely overshadowed by "Love Walked In," which was a simpler, more populist song musically and lyrically, and a much bigger hit at the time.

I have a couple of radio transcriptions of broadcasts from 1938 in which "Love Is Here to Stay" is played. In one show, called *Chevrolet Musical Moments,* the song is performed by Victor Arden, George's friend and former Broadway pit pianist, with his orchestra. It is a gorgeous, majestic orchestral performance of the song in an easy, sunny, and flowing tempo. When I heard it, I thought, "Wow, that was one of the few times people heard this song when it was new." Otherwise, they only had the extremely attenuated movie version.

The song was also recorded in 1938 by Larry Clinton and his orchestra with Bea Wain. When the Goldwyn Studios issued a radio promo of *The Goldwyn Follies,* they played this commercial recording of the song rather than the studio performance of it. There was another recording in 1938 by Red Norvo and his orchestra with Mildred Bailey, and both it and the Wain versions were modestly received. Yet otherwise, no one seemed to know about or pay any attention to this stellar creation.

The song was mostly ignored until Gene Kelly sang it in the movie *An American in Paris,* and it quickly took its rightful place in the Gershwin pantheon. Ira had insistently suggested it for the film, which was a compendium of Gershwin songs both well known and obscure. The project had begun with a query to use only George's 1928 piece *An American in Paris* for a movie, and Ira gave permission as long as it was used in the context of other of his works. The movie makes wonderful use of George's tone

poem, with beautifully colored backdrops providing a perfect accompaniment. According to George's biographer Howard Pollack, the estate received $300,000, and Ira $50,000, for the use of their songs in the movie.

The star of the film, Gene Kelly, together with director Vincente Minnelli and musical supervisor Saul Chaplin, visited with Ira and played through songs that they might use in the movie. These were musical people that Ira trusted, and he suggested "Tra La La," because they were looking for a simple song that could be reworked into a plot situation. Then after Ira's cajoling, Kelly decided on "Love Is Here to Stay" because it was a great Gershwin ballad that was at that stage relatively unknown. It was one reason Ira was very proud of the movie *An American in Paris*—it "gave" that song back to world.

The song has changed in interpretation since then and has been sung any number of ways. It was always a ballad, but Kenny Baker sang it with something of a dance tempo, almost a foxtrot. Gene Kelly performed it as a languid ballad with a very romantic Conrad Salinger orchestration— a Hollywood sound that had become much lusher than when the song was written. With each succeeding decade, ballads have been sung slower and slower, but the ones from the thirties weren't always written that way and have more nuance to them. For me, there are certain songs that live best in the tempo intended by the composer, and this song is one that is better served at the slower pace Gershwin specified.

Gershwin was deceased by the time his song was first used in *The Goldwyn Follies,* and I question whether he would have liked hearing it at

(OPPOSITE) *The leave of absence between Ira and George and Samuel Goldwyn, drawn up when George became ill.*

5.   During the term of the leave of absence
herein provided you shall not and shall not
have the right to render services of any kind
for yourself or for any person, firm or corporation other than ourselves without first
obtaining our written consent.

       If the foregoing is in accordance with your
understanding of our agreement, kindly indicate your
approval and acceptance thereof in the space herein provided.

              Very truly yours,

              SAMUEL GOLDWYN INC., LTD.?

              BY:_____

APPROVED AND ACCEPTED:

George Gershwin
      (George Gershwin)

Ira Gershwin
      (Ira Gershwin)

                                        July 1st, 1937

Messrs. George and Ira Gershwin,
c/o Samuel Goldwyn Inc., Ltd.,
7210 Santa Monica Boulevard,
Los Angeles, California.

Dear Messrs. Gershwin:

       Because of illness Mr. George Gershwin is now
temporarily unable to render services pursuant to your contract with us dated December 3, 1936.   You are willing to
cooperate with us so that during a period of two weeks
which, it is estimated, is the length of time before Mr.
Gershwin will be fully recovered, we shall be relieved of
any obligation to compensate you and you shall be relieved
of any obligation to render services for us.

       Accordingly, this letter will confirm the
following agreement between us:

   1.   We hereby grant you a leave of absence for a
period of two weeks commencing as of June 28, 1937.

   2.   Your employment under your contract with us
dated December 3, 1936 shall be and it is hereby
suspended both as to services and compensation for
the two week period of the leave of absence hereinabove referred to.

   3.   The term of your employment with us and the
time within which you are to deliver the musical
material and lyrics to us is hereby extended for a
period equivalent to the duration of the leave of
absence hereinabove referred to.   Accordingly, said
leave of absence shall not affect your obligation
to render services to us for a net period of Sixteen
(16) weeks as set forth in Paragraph 22 of your contract with us, dated December 3, 1936, and we shall
not be relieved of our obligation as set forth in
Paragraph 21 of said contract to compensate you for
a net minimum of sixteen (16) weeks.

   4.   Nothing contained in this agreement shall be
deemed to affect any right of suspension, extension,
or termination which we may have in the event of the
occurence of any of the contingencies set forth in
sub-divisions (a), (b), or (c) of Paragraph 15 of our
contract with you, except that we shall have no
right of suspension, extension, or termination for
any period during the duration of the leave of absence
herein provided that any of said contingencies occur.

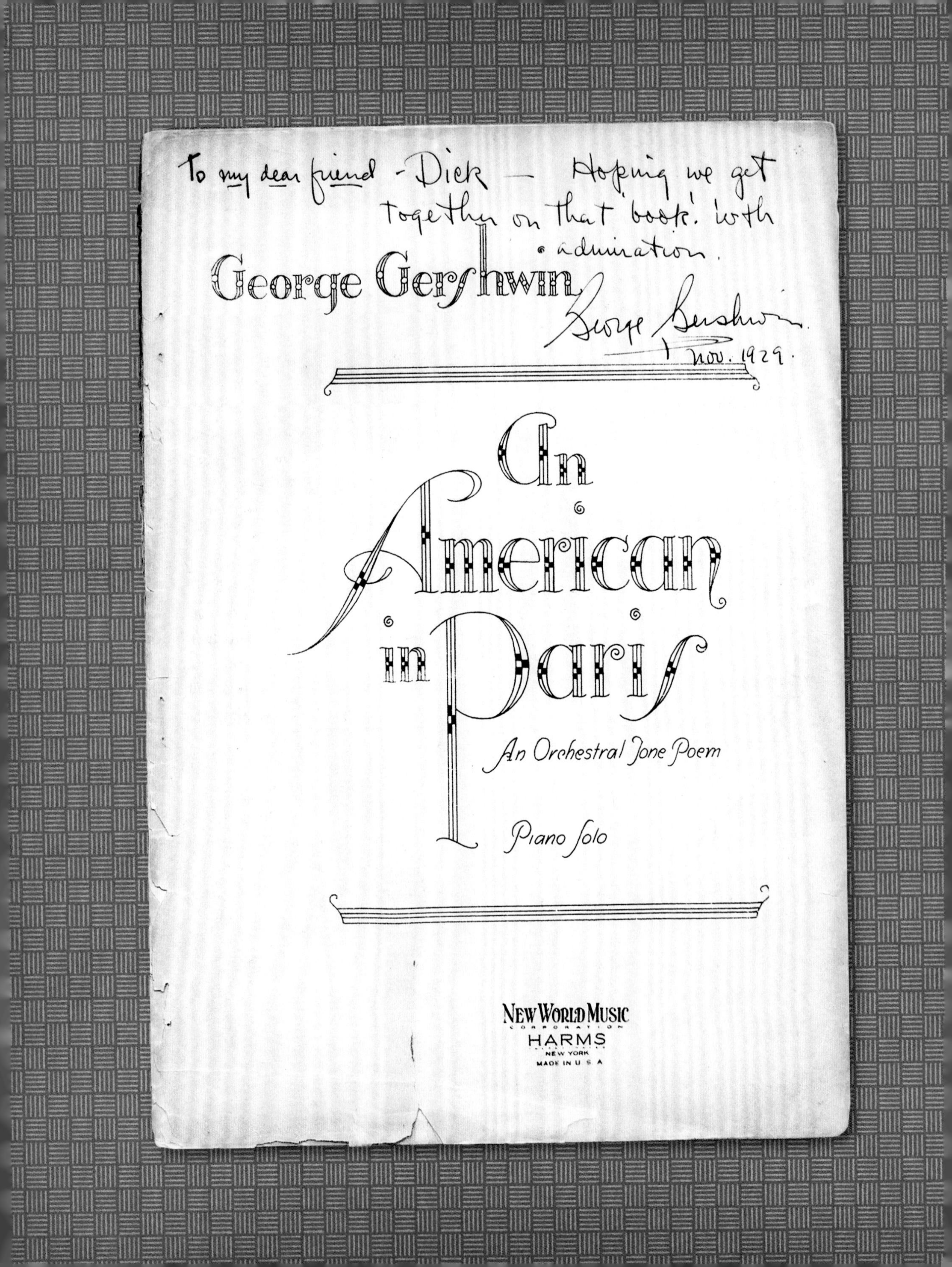

To my dear friend - Dick — Hoping we get
together on that book. With
admiration.

George Gershwin,
George Gershwin.
nov. 1929.

An American in Paris

An Orchestral Tone Poem

Piano Solo

NEW WORLD MUSIC
CORPORATION
HARMS
NEW YORK
MADE IN U S A

that foxtrot tempo chosen for the film. Ira didn't. When a singer performs it too up-tempo, it might ruin the song for me, because there's a certain connection to the heart that is missing. You can lose the poignancy of the lyric as well. Ira had become accustomed to slower renditions of it from later times, certainly preferring the Gene Kelly tempo to the Kenny Baker clip. There's a happy medium between too fast and too slow, and it is often difficult to find.

As I've noted before, Nelson Riddle used a bluesy riff throughout the song for his version with Ella Fitzgerald and while I revere his work, in this case it sacrificed the beautiful original Gershwin harmonies, and I miss them. Where Riddle added blues riffs, others have taken away. Beneath the first three notes of "Love Is Here to Stay"—"It's very clear"—George wrote beautiful chords that

words cannot do justice to. But in most arrangements, the singer sings the melody, and the chords are omitted. Whenever I play it for myself, I revel in those special opening chords.

The CD accompanying this book will mark the fifth time I have recorded this particular song, so it seems like I'm glutting the market with interpretations of "Love Is Here to Stay." The first time, for my debut album, released in 1985, I did it with a rhythm section. The second time was 1998, and that was sung with solo piano. There was a live version released on a compilation, and then I performed it in 2001 with the Israel Philharmonic in a full symphony version, arranged movingly by Alan Broadbent. Each interpretation is unique in feel and tempo, which is determined by the accompaniment and the way I feel in the moment of creation. It's never quite the same, and that is what makes a song live on. It feels like it's being freshly created as it's performed. While I might not like a particularly different imagining of a standard, it is one of the things that keep it alive, for better or for worse.

GEORGE HAD PLENTY OF PLANS when he died. In addition to wanting to write a symphony, he was also actively engaged on another opera. He mentioned his desire to revisit the form to DuBose Heyward, and he was involved with Oklahoma-born playwright Lynn Riggs on *The Lights of Lamy*—Lamy is a train depot in New Mexico on what was the Atchison, Topeka and Santa Fe Railroad line. Gershwin and Riggs, who was part Cherokee, were planning to explore themes of the American West. These were historical and cultural events that

(OPPOSITE) *Signed copy of the sheet music for* An American in Paris, *for Dick Simon, of Simon & Schuster.*
(ABOVE) *"Love Is Here to Stay" sheet music cover from* An American in Paris, *1951.*

were as significant as the African-American ex-perience George had written about in *Porgy*.

Riggs had already written *Green Grow the Lilacs,* which had a modest run on Broadway in 1931. What is much better known than the play is the musical that was based on it: *Oklahoma!* (It's another great "what if?" of history. What if Riggs had worked with Gershwin on their col-laboration? Would *Oklahoma!* ever have hap-pened? Might George have written it?)

Of course George would have written for the theater again, because the theater was itself ever evolving, offering him so many possibilities. In many ways it was his first love. Ira would have been able to stay in Hollywood, and happily become slothful. With the increasing sophistication of movies, George might have become more inter-ested in Hollywood and he knew songwriters could make a lot of money there, but the lack of creative control would always have been a problem. Films were for commerce over art and Broadway was more balanced and daring on the creative side. The musical films of the forties did not keep pace with the Broadway musicals. *Oklahoma!* and *Carousel* had much more substantial books than the musical films of that era, which remained vehicles for big production numbers. Very few musical films of the forties hold up plot-wise. *Singin' in the Rain* and *The Band Wagon* are hailed as extraordinary musicals, but they have endured because of their superior screenplays, crafted in the fifties by Broadway veterans, Betty Comden and Adolph Green. Conversely, the musical arrangements used in films were far more sophisticated than their Broadway counterparts, perhaps compensating for the lack of significant plots.

George liked to write songs in a dramatic theatrical context, but he was also interested in ballet, symphonies, and opera. I believe that if there were a substantial theatrical property, an interesting book, he would have written for it and further erased the lines between opera and musical theater. He might have written a piece that was more linked to opera but would have been done on Broadway, or maybe he would have combined ballet and other elements, as Rodgers and Ham-merstein did in *Oklahoma!* Let's face it, whatever it is that we can imagine Gershwin creating, he would have us outdone from the get-go. It would be like trying to keep pace with a greyhound.

I'VE ALREADY NOTED THAT I BELIEVE George was born at the perfect time for the maximization of his range of talents, or what might today be called his skill set. Today it's a sad fact that young people who are interested in the type of music that I like will have a harder time making that music their career. The same would even have been true for George Gershwin if he had been born in 1988 rather than 1898.

The main reason is that the art of playing the piano is disappearing. Remember that George was already able to play when his family bought a piano, because he had learned at a friend's house. It's doubtful that families in an equivalent socioeconomic group today would be saving up to buy a piano. The world is so fundamentally different that it makes it all the more significant that his work survives, as the point of view of the musical world from which most young people spring is so foreign to the basics of the world in which Gershwin and his contemporaries once

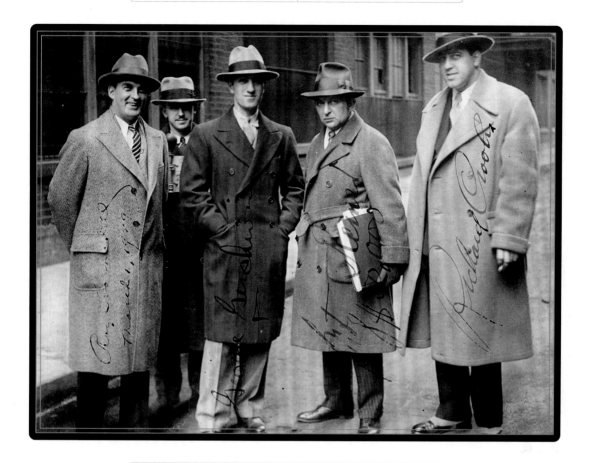

(LEFT TO RIGHT) *Roy Hornikel, manager of the Cincinnati Symphony; James Rosenberg, who played the taxi horns; George; Fritz Reiner, conductor; and Richard Crooks, tenor, Cincinnati, 1929, gathered for a concert featuring* An American in Paris.

created. We need to maintain the connection with the past, its culture and people that this music brings so vividly to life.

Just as many of the jobs George had in the music industry no longer exist, the path I took in my career would be very difficult to navigate today. Piano bars were an important part of cultural life for many years. My father, who was a traveling salesman, knew the piano bars in every city and loved to listen to an accomplished pianist play as well as raise his voice in song. Now there are very few piano bars, nor are pianos set up in hotel lobbies or in department stores. Nordstrom once employed live pianists in Los Angeles and in most of its stores but has replaced many of them with piped-in hits (or misses). This is a great cultural deprivation. People who aspired to be pianists could find work playing popular songs in piano bars, hotel lobbies, or department stores until they could get a job doing something more "serious" with their art. Now that opportunity has been denied them. Nor was playing music considered lowly or less than, regardless of whether it was in a hotel lobby or arcade, because you had to have talent to do it.

From my own experience having a nightclub in New York, I know how exceedingly difficult it is to find talented pianists and singers. The number of people who are educated in playing the piano is rapidly shrinking, and if students are studying the instrument at all, they're studying classical piano or other forms of musical expression. There are very few people who can sit down and play popular songs. Also, many people don't see the difference between a live pianist and canned music unless they experience a real performance and realize that it's a more powerful sensation.

I'm often asked, "How do I get into this business?" and I have to answer that it's very hard. I played five hours a night in piano bars for years to hone all the fundamentals I needed as an entertainer. I sharpened my musical skills and learned how to relate to people, how to put a list of songs together that had a dramatic arc, and what to say between songs. The only way to learn these things is by appearing in front of an audience. And that venue—the piano bar—and the opportunities it offers are disappearing. So creative brainstorming is required for an aspiring musician to find a place where he can be heard. Yes, there are more challenges, but I cling to the belief that the emotional resonance and quality of good music will survive and find an audience if one is strong and clear enough to follow his intuition and serve the muse.

This is not, of course, the only instance of cultural deprivation. It used to be (and not so long ago) that culture was measured in terms of artists like Leonard Bernstein hand in hand with pop and other kinds of music. There was a great variety of music and culture available in a collective mass way, an experience shared by millions. It was watching the New York Philharmonic and the Boston Pops on television, it was watching *The Bell Telephone Hour,* which featured everything from children's choirs to the Bolshoi Ballet to Arthur Rubinstein. Such treasures are a rarity on television today.

THERE ARE VERY FEW PEOPLE WHO CAN SIT DOWN AND PLAY POPULAR SONGS.

Am I saying that contemporary music lacks quality? Not necessarily, and I know it's treading on shaky ground to pass judgment on any kind of art. It just seems to me that we have a responsibility to preserve and refresh the classic music for new generations by going back to the essence of what made it great and not having to add trappings of electronic wallpaper and droning pop beats to make music appeal to young generations. One of course needn't be sacrificed for the other, yet that is what appears to be happening.

Without wishing to sound melodramatic, I believe our country is falling apart culturally, in case you haven't noticed. Actually, it *has* fallen apart, in that we have lost the foundation of a basic education in musical history. There is no music education in most schools. When I was in school we were given music appreciation classes and exposed to many different types of music. We were taught about symphonies, opera, jazz; about Aaron Copland and Verdi and Louis Armstrong. Now there's no money for musical instruments or teachers. The shortsightedness of this is appalling. There are still heroic teachers and organizations that are working to keep the music alive and save it for all of us, but it has to start in the home and with parents who understand what the music will do for their offspring. The irony is that with Web resources, there is more potential than ever to reach people.

This country will end up with a dangerous lack of cultural balance. I truly believe (in the words of the English playwright William Congreve) that music does have charms to soothe the savage breast. Not offering an education in music is like feeding children a diet of only protein and no carbohydrates, or all sugar—that child is going to have an imbalance in his body. Arts spending is always viewed as the least important and the most expendable, but the result is this cultural drift. Obviously, these consequences are terrible.

As a nation, we can't sit still. We're not terribly interested in anything with depth, but we are fascinated by more and more of the surface. *American Idol* and shows like it have given people permission to judge, to hate, to mock, to humiliate, to denigrate deficiencies in other people in the most vocal way. It's not about *music;* it's about turning kids into commercial performers. It's not teaching them how to interpret a lyric or the essence of what the music is about; it's telling them that a high note at the end of the song will cause people to stand up and scream. What about all the kids who like other kinds of music like classical, jazz, and musical theater? Their role models (not Idols) are nowhere to be seen.

Meanwhile, record companies are dead in the water, and their business model has collapsed. A friend of mine who works for a major company put together a three-CD Benny Goodman centennial compilation, but the company decided it wasn't going to issue the set because it didn't think it was going to sell enough copies. This is Benny Goodman! Such a compilation should be issued whether it sells fifty thousand copies or five hundred. It should be out there.

Great music executives like Goddard Lieberson, the president of Columbia Records for fifteen years starting in 1956, and from 1973 to '75, believed it was their duty to issue a certain number of classical and jazz recordings, even though they knew they weren't going to sell. And they amortized that with their pop releases. The priority was to make the full spectrum of music available. I have an ambition to make a lot of recordings of obscure songs and put them in the iTunes store so they're available for people. To me it's about the preservation of music. And while I'm happy to have recordings that still sell, like my *Sinatra Project,* I'm more interested now in making recordings of songs I think need to be preserved.

The Sinatra Project was a great way to garner attention from an audience that wouldn't necessarily know of my work and to build a bridge. These days the key is to get noticed for what you are doing. You have to have a hook or an idea;

you have to have some kind of concept that will pique the public interest.

In my field, it's also about marketing, because the audience at large doesn't know the songs of Burton Lane or even Irving Berlin the way previous generations did. So it has to be something that grabs people's attention. Noël Coward wrote a play called *Nude with Violin* that came to Broadway in 1957, and he knew exactly what he was doing with the salacious title. The hoax novel *Naked Came the Stranger* (1969) proved this point. It was an erotic novel written purposefully badly by a committee of twenty-four journalists in an attempt to show that people would buy any book with the promise of enough sex in it. And they succeeded—the book was a bestseller.

And yet, and yet . . . in the midst of these signs of the inexorable decline of our civilization, there is still hope. Years ago, a record executive told me that his three-year-old son loved to listen to *West Side Story*. The kid responded to it viscerally. He didn't like *Barney*; he liked *West Side Story*. I was the same way as a kid. People underestimate the ability of children to respond to very sophisticated music. They feel it, even if they don't understand it. There are always going to be kids like him and like me and like many of the people interested in something that is not mainstream but deeply and personally affecting.

For the people out there who want other kinds of music, this new technology that I have sometimes bemoaned is a godsend. The Internet offers access to music that was undreamt of twenty years ago. Someone might hear a couple bars of a song sung by Billie Holiday in a TV commercial and she can look her up online and discover her

for herself—read about her life and buy her recordings. Of course some individuals then go on to illegally download her music or have someone clone a CD for them, but that's another issue.

I am constantly astounded by what I can find on the Internet. A fellow named Lou Carter, who was on the Perry Como show in the fifties—he was known as Louie the Cabbie—wrote and sang silly nonsense songs. After having a conversation about him with Tyne Daly, I went online and discovered that he had died long ago, but there were existing recordings of him shared by a fan who wanted to see his work perpetuated. At dinner recently, the film actress Arlene Dahl was talking about how, when she started her career on Broadway in 1946, she was dating a bandleader named Joe Ricardel. I said, "Oh, he wrote a hit song in 1940 called 'The Wise Old Owl.'" She said, "That's right! He also wrote 'The Frim Fram Sauce,' which Nat Cole sang." After she left, I looked him up online and discovered that he had been living in Palm Beach until he died in 2002, and learned more about another life in the music arena. Every life, every story, adds up and contributes to the rich history we all share. It's remarkable—you can get answers to anything you're curious about in ten seconds, and get even more confused faster than that. Especially if you go to Wikipedia, which once claimed that I had married actress Kim Cattrall. Now, perhaps my memory isn't what it used to be, but I think I would remember that.

The Internet is where a lot of musicians now make their careers. There are artists who have made recordings they've sold on the Internet, with "success" being measured as five thousand or ten thousand downloads. Some are thrilled if they sell five hundred copies of something. The days of selling a million records are over unless you're a rare phenomenon like Lady Gaga, or can arrange to die in your prime. Every six months, I read about the further demise of recordings, and since the royalties for downloads from iTunes are a tenth of what they are for a CD, the income for the classic songwriters' catalogues has dropped significantly the last few years, especially for the likes of Gershwin, Berlin, and Rodgers.

I HAVE AN AMBITION TO MAKE A LOT OF RECORDINGS OF OBSCURE SONGS.

Everyone involved in music—the artists, composers, agents, record companies, publishers, promoters, and concert venues—is struggling to adapt to the new paradigm. The consumer has won out in some respects, because the ways music is offered to them are simpler and more varied and often cheaper than they ever have been. But the choices in new music are certainly constrained.

I'm sure that George would have been thrilled by what new technology could have offered him. His lifetime spanned the eras of silent movies and electronic music and he was always very forward-looking. The Hammond organ, a precursor of the synthesizer, was invented by engineer Laurens Hammond, with the first commercially available version, the Model A, going on sale in June 1935.

George received one of the first instruments and placed it upstairs in their Beverly Hills home. (Speaking of marketing, Hammond made a point of saying that George had bought the very first Hammond Model A off the production line.)

I once asked Ira if there was one moment of George playing the piano he could have preserved, what would it have been? He immediately mentioned the Hammond organ and said George played for him for at least forty-five minutes one day, just improvising one tune after another using the different sounds and colors that organ could produce. Ira said it was transporting to listen to as George performed ever-greater feats of extemporization. "That is what I would love to be able to hear again," Ira said. And George, who once made his living playing piano rolls, was excited by advances like this, and he would have continued to explore the new avenues technology opened up to composers had he lived.

Late in life, Ira wasn't resentful of the way music had passed him by. He might say of a song, "I don't like that, but that's what people are listening to now." He wasn't like Yip Harburg, who'd bitterly complain, "They're killing us. They've destroyed our music." The state of contemporary music didn't make Ira angry. Anger was not something that came readily to Ira at all, although he did tell me about one occasion when he did get riled—he had to testify before the California Senate Fact-Finding Committee on Un-American Activities in 1948, and at the end of his testimony Senator So-and-So said, "By the way, Mr. Gershwin, I have to tell you that your brother George was one of my favorite songwriters of all time." And Ira said, "When he said that, I

thought, *What about me, you son of a bitch?*" Other times, somebody would ask Ira for an autograph and he would say, "Oh, you really want George's autograph" and then give them one of George's canceled checks. On these occasions, it was done without rancor.

Ira carefully and lovingly watched over George's legacy. He educated himself in the laws on copyrights and renewals. Issues appeared that never would have occurred to him. In 1938, a year after George's death, the Library of Congress asked Ira for some mementos of George's, and Ira sent them some things. He had also given away some of George's manuscripts as souvenirs but he quickly realized he shouldn't have done that. A manu-

script seemed unimportant to Ira at the time because they were always present, and new ones were always generated. Who knew that one day a single page of music in the hand of George Gershwin would bring a tremendous price? So Ira began to understand the significance of the artifacts left behind by George. His responsibility was to keep everything together and in shape, and he did a good job of that. Lee dutifully continued Ira's work and ensured that the Library of Congress would always be beneficiaries of Ira's financial legacy. She understood the importance of keeping it alive. Ira never could have imagined giving money to the government after so many dreaded years of paying taxes, but that is exactly what happened.

Ira and Lee viewing a painting by George, New York, 1968.

Presented with the same circumstances, a lesser person might have spent his life exploiting his famous name, becoming a professional Gershwin. Some relatives of iconic celebrities have done that and even changed their names to their famous counterparts, when it was not their given last name. Ira continued to work after his brother died; he just didn't work as hard as he would have if George had been around to push him. He would try to accept two job offers at the same time so he could turn them both down, saying he was committed to the other. This is another facet of the tragedy of George's early passing—we have been denied more of Ira's lyrics for music that George didn't compose. If George had lived, Ira would have remained more alive too in the creative sense.

Among others, Ira worked on *Lady in the Dark* (1941); the war propaganda film *The North Star* (1943); the early Gene Kelly classic *Cover Girl* (1944); an antiquated stage operetta, *The Firebrand of Florence* (1945); the movies *Where Do We Go from Here* (1945) and *The Barkleys of Broadway* (1949); the ill-fated Broadway revival of *Of Thee I Sing* (1952); his final MGM effort, *Give a Girl a Break* (1953); and *A Star Is Born* (1954). Ira felt throughout this period that he was still growing as a lyricist, but he was permanently scarred by George's passing and he was never as motivated again. The thrill, the excitement, was gone. There was nobody who ever excited him musically as much as George had. George was the only true genius, he said. No one could do it like him.

In the years after *A Star Is Born* through the period when I knew him, Ira retreated from public life. People were interested in meeting him, even if they were fascinated more by George, but

Ira became less and less inclined to indulge them. Sometime in the mid-sixties, Ira received a letter from a music fair that was putting on a production of *Girl Crazy*. The organizers asked Ira if he would come and make an appearance as an added attraction. Ira replied, "I'm afraid the only thing I'd be would be an addled attraction."

He was interviewed once by French television and was so ill at ease that he wouldn't allow the channel to televise the piece because he came off as inarticulate, something that he normally was not. There are some audio interviews with Ira that survive and some people who have heard them say, "He sounds so out of breath; he doesn't sound well." He became so nervous when he did an interview that he imploded. Ira would happily and wistfully talk to people privately about George, but after a while he couldn't do anything more in public. George's ghost was always present some-

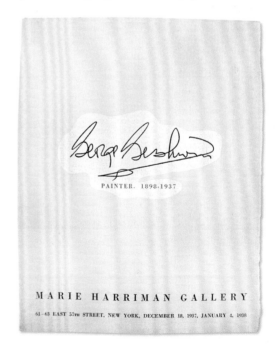

Program from a posthumous exhibit of George's paintings, 1937–1938.

where in the room. You felt him and expected him to show up at any minute.

Ira passed away in 1983. George had died in California almost a half-century before, but Ira lived in Los Angeles all that time. Perhaps he couldn't have returned to New York, because there was no point doing so without George. It's not worth dwelling on—what happened happened—but the magnitude of George's brilliance and the attendant scale of his tragedy force us to yearn for a different ending. It's personal, his passing, an offense to humanity and to fairness.

What George Gershwin accomplished in his short life was a fusing of different types of music to create what became the musical voice of America. Of all those who dreamed and tried, for George it seemed predestined, with joy and a sense of purpose that was at times confounding. If there is an American soundtrack, Gershwin

ment ever sent abroad." When the New York Philharmonic played its historic concert in Pyongyang, North Korea, in 2008, the two main works it presented were Dvorak's *New World Symphony* and George's *An American in Paris.*

George's reason for being on this earth was the music that insistently came through him. As it poured out of him he seemed as surprised by it as anyone, but he knew it would keep coming even if he didn't always know how or why. Until one day his body let him down. If only we could have shared a few more decades' worth of his ebullient genius. George was a comet lighting up the sky, his trail tracked and measured by his brother. His brilliance was utterly and magnificently ascendant.

As all things must come to an end, it is comforting to know that somewhere there will always be a beginning for someone else. They will hear Gershwin for the first time and will feel the lure

IF THERE IS ᴀɴ AMERICAN SOUNDTRACK, GERSHWIN OWNS A GOOD PORTION ᴏꜰ ɪᴛ, WITH WORDS ʙʏ IRA.

owns a good portion of it, with words by Ira. Their tunes still hummed and heard are typical Gershwin, that familiar sound of New York that is both fresh and vibrant.

George's influence was not only musical but cultural—he helped shape what people thought of when they thought of America. In 1956 Truman Capote reported that a production of *Porgy and Bess* the U.S. government had financed on a four-year tour around the world was described in many places as "the 'best ambassador' the State Depart-

of his siren songs and embark on a path of realization that will make them feel just a little more alive, more fully awake. They will have that heightened sense of purpose and share in the endless and unceasing flow of creation. So as the song finishes, the tune starts again and yet again, while the lyrics spread Ira's simple truth about the Rockies tumbling and Gibraltar crumbling. Not to worry, they say, because we'll always have Gershwin.

FOR EVER AND A DAY.

GEORGE AND IRA IN 1928.

GERSHWIN® and GEORGE
GERSHWIN® are registered trademarks of
Gershwin Enterprises
IRA GERSHWIN™ is a trademark of
Gershwin Enterprises
PORGY AND BESS® is a registered
trademark of Porgy and Bess Enterprises
All Rights Reserved

C D

Produced by Andy Brattain and
Michael Feinstein

Co-produced by Alex Sterling

Recorded, edited, and mixed by
Andy Brattain and Alex Sterling,
www.alexsterling.net.

Mastered by Alan Silverman,
Arfmastering, www.arfmastering.com.

Recorded Feb. 22–23, 2012,
Hirsch Studio, NYC.

Vocals: Michael Feinstein

Piano: Cyrus Chestnut

Special thanks: Terrence Flannery, Starleigh
Goltry, Andrew Leff, Kathleen Battle, and
Jim Morey.

"Strike Up the Band!" by George Gershwin
and Ira Gershwin
WB Music Corp. (ASCAP)

"The Man I Love," by George Gershwin and
Ira Gershwin
WB Music Corp. (ASCAP)

"'S Wonderful," by George Gershwin and
Ira Gershwin
WB Music Corp. (ASCAP)

"I've Got a Crush on You," by George
Gershwin and Ira Gershwin
WB Music Corp. (ASCAP)

"They All Laughed," by George Gershwin
and Ira Gershwin
George Gershwin Music (ASCAP) and Ira
Gershwin Music (ASCAP)
All rights administered by WB Music Corp.

"Someone to Watch over Me," by George
Gershwin and Ira Gershwin
WB Music Corp. (ASCAP)

"Embraceable You," by George Gershwin
and Ira Gershwin
WB Music Corp. (ASCAP)

"Who Cares? (So Long As You Care for Me),"
by George Gershwin and Ira Gershwin
WB Music Corp. (ASCAP)

"I Got Plenty O' Nuttin'," by George
Gershwin, Ira Gershwin, and DuBose
Heyward
DuBose and Dorothy Heyward Memorial
Fund Pub. (ASCAP), Ira Gershwin Music
(ASCAP), and George Gershwin Music
(ASCAP)
All rights administered by WB Music Corp.

"They Can't Take That Away from Me,"
by George Gershwin and Ira Gershwin
George Gershwin Music (ASCAP) and Ira
Gershwin Music (ASCAP)
All rights administered by WB Music Corp.

"I Got Rhythm," by George Gershwin and
Ira Gershwin
WB Music Corp. (ASCAP)

"Love Is Here to Stay," by George Gershwin
and Ira Gershwin
George Gershwin Music (ASCAP)
and Ira Gershwin Music (ASCAP)
All rights administered by WB Music Corp.

PRINTED LYRICS

"The Real American Folk Song (Is a Rag),"
music and lyrics by George Gershwin
and Ira Gershwin
© 1959 (Renewed) Chappell & Co., Inc.
Used by Permission of Alfred Music
Publishing Co., Inc.
All Rights Reserved

"Fascinating Rhythm," music and lyrics by
George Gershwin and Ira Gershwin
© 1924 (Renewed) WB Music Corp.
Used by Permission of Alfred Music
Publishing Co., Inc.
All Rights Reserved

"Hang On to Me," music and lyrics by
George Gershwin and Ira Gershwin
© 1924 (Renewed) WB Music Corp.
Used by Permission of Alfred Music
Publishing Co., Inc.
All Rights Reserved

"The Half of It, Dearie Blues," music and
lyrics by George Gershwin and Ira Gershwin
© 1924 (Renewed) WB Music Corp.
Used by Permission of Alfred Music
Publishing Co., Inc.
All Rights Reserved

"Love Is Sweeping the Country," music and
lyrics by George Gershwin and Ira Gershwin
© 1931 (Renewed) WB Music Corp.
Used by Permission of Alfred Music
Publishing Co., Inc.
All Rights Reserved

"Isn't It a Pity," music and lyrics by George
Gershwin and Ira Gershwin
© 1932 (Renewed) WB Music Corp.
Used by Permission of Alfred Music
Publishing Co., Inc.
All Rights Reserved

"Fidgety Feet," music and lyrics by George
Gershwin and Ira Gershwin
© 1926 (Renewed) WB Music Corp.
Used by Permission of Alfred Music
Publishing Co., Inc.
All Rights Reserved

"Aren't You Kind of Glad We Did?" music
and lyrics by George Gershwin and Ira
Gershwin
© 1946 (Renewed) George Gershwin Music
and Ira Gershwin Music
All Rights Administered by WB Music Corp.
All Rights Reserved

"Of Thee I Sing," music and lyrics by
George Gershwin and Ira Gershwin
© 1931 (Renewed) WB Music Corp.
Used by Permission of Alfred Music
Publishing Co., Inc.
All Rights Reserved

"Mine," music and lyrics by
George Gershwin and Ira Gershwin
© 1932 (Renewed) WB Music Corp.
Used by Permission of Alfred Music
Publishing Co., Inc.
All Rights Reserved

"It Ain't Necessarily So," (from *Porgy
and Bess*) words and music by George
Gershwin, DuBose and Dorothy Heyward,
and Ira Gershwin
© 1935 (Renewed) George Gershwin
Music, Ira Gershwin Music, and DuBose

and Dorothy Heyward Memorial Fund
All Rights Administered by WB Music Corp.
Used by Permission of Alfred Music
Publishing Co., Inc.
All Rights Reserved

"A Foggy Day (in London Town)," music and
lyrics by George Gershwin and Ira Gershwin
© 1937 (Renewed) George Gershwin Music
and Ira Gershwin Music
All Rights Administered by WB Music Corp.
All Rights Reserved

"Strike Up the Band!" music and lyrics by
George Gershwin and Ira Gershwin
© 1927 (Renewed) WB Music Corp.
Used by Permission of Alfred Music
Publishing Co., Inc.
All Rights Reserved

"The Man I Love," music and lyrics by
George Gershwin and Ira Gershwin
© 1924 (Renewed) WB Music Corp.
Used by Permission of Alfred Music
Publishing Co., Inc.
All Rights Reserved

"'S Wonderful," music and lyrics by George
Gershwin and Ira Gershwin
© 1927 (Renewed) WB Music Corp.
Used by Permission of Alfred Music
Publishing Co., Inc.
All Rights Reserved

"I've Got a Crush on You," music and lyrics
by George Gershwin and Ira Gershwin
© 1930 (Renewed) WB Music Corp.
Used by Permission of Alfred Music
Publishing Co., Inc.
All Rights Reserved

"They All Laughed," music and lyrics by
George Gershwin and Ira Gershwin
© 1936 (Renewed) George Gershwin Music
and Ira Gershwin Music
All Rights Administered by WB Music Corp.
Used by Permission of Alfred Music
Publishing Co., Inc.
All Rights Reserved

"Someone to Watch over Me," music and
lyrics by George Gershwin and Ira Gershwin
© 1926 (Renewed) WB Music Corp.
Used by Permission of Alfred Music
Publishing Co., Inc.
All Rights Reserved

"Embraceable You," music and lyrics by
George Gershwin and Ira Gershwin
© 1930 (Renewed) WB Music Corp.
Used by Permission of Alfred Music
Publishing Co., Inc.
All Rights Reserved

"Who Cares? (So Long As You Care for
Me)," music and lyrics by George Gershwin
and Ira Gershwin
© 1931 (Renewed) WB Music Corp.
Used by Permission of Alfred Music
Publishing Co., Inc.
All Rights Reserved

"I Got Plenty O' Nuttin,'" (from *Porgy and
Bess*) words and music by George Gershwin,
DuBose and Dorothy Heyward, and Ira
Gershwin
© 1935 (Renewed) George Gershwin
Music, Ira Gershwin Music, and DuBose
and Dorothy Heyward Memorial Fund
All Rights Administered by WB Music Corp.
Used by Permission of Alfred Music
Publishing Co., Inc.
All Rights Reserved

"They Can't Take That Away from Me,"
music and lyrics by George Gershwin and
Ira Gershwin
© 1936 (Renewed) George Gershwin Music
and Ira Gershwin Music
All Rights Administered by WB Music Corp.
Used by Permission of Alfred Music
Publishing Co., Inc.
All Rights Reserved

"I Got Rhythm," music and lyrics by George
Gershwin and Ira Gershwin
© 1930 (Renewed) WB Music Corp.
Used by Permission of Alfred Music
Publishing Co., Inc.
All Rights Reserved

"Love Is Here to Stay," music and lyrics by
George Gershwin and Ira Gershwin
© 1938 (Renewed) George Gershwin Music
and Ira Gershwin Music
All Rights Administered by WB Music Corp.
Used by Permission of Alfred Music
Publishing Co., Inc.
All Rights Reserved

IMAGES

The George Gershwin Family and the Ira
and Leonore Gershwin Trust: p. 11, p. 12,
p. 13, p. 21, p. 22 (top left and bottom
row), p. 23 (top left and bottom left), p.
28, p. 33, p. 43, p. 47, p. 49, p. 51, p. 55,
p. 64, p. 70, pp. 72–73, p. 93, p. 98
(left), p. 99 (right), p. 103, p. 112, p.
117, p. 123, p. 132 (left), p. 135, p. 138,
p. 152 (left), p. 154, p. 155, p. 161, p.
164 (bottom left and right), p. 166, p.
172 (left and top right), p. 173 (left and
bottom right), p. 176, p. 177, p. 186 (top
left and right), p. 189, p. 192, p. 195, p.
198, p. 204, p. 213, p. 238, p. 240, p.
243, p. 247, p. 257, p. 263, p. 264, p.
265, p. 268, p. 283, p. 289, p. 303, p.
304, p. 305, p. 309

Courtesy of the author: p. 7, p. 15, pp.
17–19, p. 23 (bottom right), p. 26, p. 27,
p. 52, p. 58, pp. 66–67, p. 69, pp. 76–77,
p. 81, p. 83, p. 84, p. 85, p. 88, p. 89, p.
91, p. 97, p. 98 (right), p. 100, p. 107, p.
113, p. 118, p. 121, p. 125, p. 132
(right), p. 137, p. 147, p. 149, p. 158, p.
162, p. 164 (top left), p. 172 (bottom
right), p. 173 (top right), p. 174, p. 179,
p. 180, p. 183, p. 186 (bottom left), p.
199, p. 201, p. 210, pp. 218–219, p. 226,
p. 229, p. 239, p. 248, p. 250, p. 253, p.
254, p. 255, p. 260, p. 269, p. 274, p.
277, p. 281, p. 284, p. 287, p. 292, p.
296, p. 307, p. 310, p. 320, p. 323, p.
327, p. 337, p. 338, p. 339, p. 341, p.
346, p. 349

George and Ira Gershwin Collection,
Music Division, Library of Congress: p.
22 (top right), p. 23 (top middle and top
right), pp. 24–25, p. 31, p. 32, p. 34, p.
36, pp. 38–39, p. 57, pp. 60–61, p. 63, p.
65, p. 87, p. 99 (left), p. 102, p. 104, pp.
108–109, p. 111, p. 124, p. 127, pp.
130–131, p. 141, p. 142, p. 145, p. 151,
p. 152 (top right and bottom right), p.
167, p. 175, p. 225, p. 231, p. 232, p.
278, p. 301, p. 314, p. 329, p. 333, p.
334, p. 347

Irving Caesar Papers in the ASCAP
Foundation Collection at the Library of
Congress, Music Division: pp. 170–171

Motion Picture, Broadcasting and
Recorded Sound Division, Library of
Congress: p. 86, p. 148, p. 197

By permission of the estate of Roddy
McDowall: p. 115

THERE ARE MANY WHO HELPED TO MAKE this book a reality and for them I give fervent thanks. Through the years I have been lucky to meet and know many friends and coworkers of the Gershwin ménage. To all of them I owe a part of this book, especially Ed Jablonski, Lawrence D. Stewart, Robert Kimball, Alfred Simon, and Howard Pollack, all friends and important chroniclers of the Gershwin legend. Ian Jackman is a tireless and talented man who shaped so much of this book, and I shall always be grateful to him.

Mike and Jean Strunsky are two of the finest people I know and their help and friendship are treasured. The Ira and Leonore Gershwin Trusts were paramount in making this book possible, especially Michael Owen and L. J. Strunsky. Thanks to the entire George Gershwin Estate and Family, especially: Marc George Gershwin, Adam Gershwin, and Todd Gershwin. The Library of Congress Music Division graciously provided full access to the George and Ira Gershwin collection at the library, and I adore the entire staff. Thank you to Sue Vita, chief of the Music Division; Ray White; Mark Horowitz; photo researcher Amy Pastan; and Betty Auman, among others.

Luckily for me, Jon Karp and Simon & Schuster are continuing their long tradition of publishing Gershwin books, and I am honored to be part of their family. My special appreciation to Rachel Bergmann, Nick Greene, Sybil Pincus, Elisa Rivlin, Julia Prosser, and Elina Vaysbeyn. Charlie Melcher and Melcher Media are the best at what they do, and the handsome design of our book is a testament to that. Thanks especially to Lauren Nathan, Nadia Bennet, Gabriella Paiella, Kurt Andrews, Duncan Bock, Bonnie Eldon, and Lia Ronnen. Thanks also to Paul Kepple and Ralph Geroni of Headcase Design.

Thanks to my literary agent, Linda Chester. To my wonderful friends at Morey Management: Jim Morey, Trudi Morey, Andrew Leff, Kyle Whitney. And to my personal staff: Starleigh Goltry, Andy Brattain, Patricia Vigueras, Martha Alvarez, Lexie Kessman, John Vannucci. Thanks also to Doug Cook Associates and Kent Powers.

For permissions I'd like to thank James Grupenhoff, Alfred Music Publishing, and Warner Chappell Music. For tireless public relations: Miller Wright Associates, Miller Wright, and Dan Fortune.

For the recording: Alex Sterling, Alan Silverman, Arfmastering, Concord Records, Hirsch Studios, and Cyrus Chestnut for his dazzling musicianship.

For special help and friendship: Maya Angelou, Kathleen Battle, Ken Bloom, Angie Dickinson, Amber Edwards, Josh Getlin, John Meyer, Liza Minnelli, Judy and Jerry Sheindlin.

And especially for my parents, Mazie and Ed Feinstein, and always for Terrence Flannery.

Produced by

MELCHER
MEDIA

124 West 13th Street
New York, NY 10011
www.melcher.com

Publisher: Charles Melcher
Associate Publisher: Bonnie Eldon
Editor in Chief: Duncan Bock
Editor: Lauren Nathan
Associate Editor: Nadia K. Bennet
Production Director: Kurt Andrews
Editorial Intern: Gabriella Paiella